MERCY

MERCY

HUMANITY IN WAR

CATHAL J. NOLAN

OXFORD
UNIVERSITY PRESS

OXFORD
UNIVERSITY PRESS

Oxford University Press is a department of the University of Oxford. It furthers
the University's objective of excellence in research, scholarship, and education
by publishing worldwide. Oxford is a registered trade mark of Oxford University
Press in the UK and certain other countries.

Published in the United States of America by Oxford University Press
198 Madison Avenue, New York, NY 10016, United States of America.

© Cathal J. Nolan 2023

Library of Congress Control Number: 2022941565

ISBN 978–0–19–007728–0

DOI: 10.1093/oso/9780190077280.001.0001

1 3 5 7 9 8 6 4 2

Printed by Sheridan Books, Inc., United States of America

To all who encounter suffering in war
and choose mercy over cruelty

CONTENTS

Introduction   1

PART I: CULTURE
1. *Stories*   11
2. *Heroes*   29
3. *Killers*   42

PART II: COMBAT
4. *Pity*   61
5. *Grace*   79
6. *Dissent*   100
7. *Truces*   120

PART III: PROTECTED
8. *Medics*   143
9. *Prisoners*   165
10. *Civilians*   186

PART IV: TECHNOLOGY
11. *Steel*   213
12. *Stealth*   229

13. *Wings* 244
14. *Conclusions* 262

Author's Note 267
Notes 273
Index 307

INTRODUCTION

The quality of mercy is not strained. . . . It is twice blessed. It blesseth him that gives and him that takes.
> —William Shakespeare, *The Merchant of Venice*, Act IV, Scene I

This is not a book about war. It is about mercy and humanity. It is about what the Welsh poet Wilfred Owen penned before he was killed in November 1918, in the last week of the Great War. He wrote that his verses were not about the war "nor anything about glory, honour, might, majesty, dominion, or power." Owen called his subject "the pity of war."[1] We see it in an unexpected flash of recognition of shared humanity. Mercy happens in a microsecond, wrapped inside a surprise moment of mortal danger. It restrains baser instinct and reminds us about higher things. This book shows that mercy limits cruelty in ways laws and honor codes seldom do, because mercy is the highest personal and moral quality any of us achieves. It is above all other virtues, even justice and courage.[2] It is superior to bravery, especially in a soldier. It is the greatest gift we give to those we meet in civilian life who are suffering and whom it is in our power to aid or harm. Greater still when offered to the defenseless in war. It defines evermore, above all in soldiers' self-awareness, those who offer quarter or deny it to people who are exposed and vulnerable to the exercise of will and power. It is never about one person. Mercy is the grace that happens between those who have a fleeting superiority of physical power and those who cannot save or protect themselves. It is greater than a gift to the helpless and the innocent, for as Shakespeare wrote, it elevates the merciful, too.

Whoever goes to war, there war is. Right in front of them, marked by ugliness and moral starkness but also insistent calls to conscience. War is a confusion of reason, restraint, and calculated violence. It can be anarchic, annihilating customs, rules, and laws. It always challenges hope for mercy and sometimes obliterates it. War presents the most extreme moral environment we encounter: it is humanity at its most exposed and inhumane but sometimes also its most remarkably merciful. This book explores how, inside the essential barbarism of war, some still act with astonishing grace toward their enemy. What is resonant here are these wrenching narratives. The power of their stories cries out for recognition and appreciation of their generous spirit. Why some did what they did may transcend our ability to understand. Nonetheless, it demands our attention.

This book does not seek out the rarified few who are morally exceptional. It does not try to elevate anyone to secular sainthood, a status that is unattainable and hence less interesting to all the rest of us who tread on moral dilemmas with feet of clay. Models of altruism more often shame us than inspire our emulation, because imitation is too hard. Instead, this account depicts ordinary people caught up in an extraordinary swirl of savagery, who did not see themselves as saints or heroes at the time yet showed rare courage and moral restraint. They reacted in a moment of deep crisis with grace and compassion, with empathy for shared humanity with an enemy or the innocent. The goal is to recognize anyone who refused immoral or illegal orders, even at grave personal risk. Who would not pull the trigger to kill a hapless enemy. Who bound wounds, assisted the other side's medics, protected prisoners, shielded civilians. This book presents stories of those who in the midst of violent depravity saw a way back to shared humanity. Who resisted conformity and summoned mercy, if only in a gesture of kindness to a suffering or dying enemy that had no larger consequence. Uninterested in saints, it looks to map a more modest, achievable, and relatable lesson taken from the annals of humanity in war. It begins an accountancy of that mysterious, elegant, and deeply compelling virtue we call mercy.

The misery that greets humanity in each new war is orders of magnitude beyond the suffering of all but the most arduous of impoverished lives. For the most part, anguish is inflicted and is suffered by ordinary men and women. The focus of this account is therefore everyday soldiers, sailors, pilots, nurses, and medics who retained a humane perspective inside the moral fog of war. It takes no regard of nation or uniform. It disdains the false moral claims of commonplace nationalism and related military chauvinism. It gathers tales of any person in any uniform who showed mercy while all around them was extreme violence, and often a promise of state absolution should they commit willful war crimes. It is about those who did an uncommon thing at high risk to their own lives. It searches for clues about why they acted as they did, asking if they had innate integrity while others nearby acted so differently. Was their virtue individual, or did honor codes and officer accountability help stay the hand of cruelty? Is the ideal of mercy in war respected mainly in the breach? Is it all mostly myth: Saladin the Merciful; chivalry as a warrior ideal in the medieval West; ideas of the Just War that rode alongside crusade and jihad; aristocratic notions of the honor of elites and officers; *bushidō* in 20th-century Japan, fabricated by the Meiji state to bind its new model army to itself and the nation?

Traditional military history framed a secular hagiography of warriors in stained-glass windows, calling for us to stare upward and admire them. Like cathedral images of dead saints of the old religions, the effect, if not the intention, is to distort memory into legend, deflect examination of harder facts, and substitute triumph for truth. We celebrate flawed generals like Caesar or Arminius, Henry V or Tokugawa Ieyasu, Michel Ney or Robert E. Lee, Georgy Zhukov or Võ Nguyên Giáp. Such grand heroes too often provide a façade for lies to manipulate the young and public opinion. They disguise political and cultural myth-making and, too often, terrible crimes. Mercy is a truer mark of heroic character in war. It appears in almost every war. We see it in compassionate soldiers serving in nearly every army, even the most vile. We see it in Germans and French facing off across a pockmarked no-man's-land, not shooting at enemy work parties or mortaring latrines or attacking during breakfast. Also in a Medal of Honor winner who killed hundreds of Germans in 1918, yet turned his gun on his own company to save a helpless German boy solider whom they intended to murder.

Mercy animated a young lieutenant wearing Nazi Germany's *feldgrau* in the Hürtgen Forest in 1944, who died while trying to rescue a wounded American lying beyond the hearing of his own medics. An older Ukrainian tanker chose not to pull the trigger on his counterpart scrambling to flee a damaged Russian tank in 2015, then posted on Facebook a call to his enemy's mother pleading for her son to leave the war. We find mercy in medics who move from under cover to reach the wounded; nurses who brave front lines or work themselves to physical and moral exhaustion in burn or gas wards; doctors who surrender to stay behind with the wounded; surgeons who operate on enemy prisoners first, before less urgent cases on their own side; soldiers who tenderly care for a dying man who tried to kill them the day or an hour before. We find it in officers who allow ambulances to come and go or who supply food and medicine to cut off medical units from the other side.

Mercy is found in war on land, at sea, and even in the air. We see it in a light cruiser skipper in the *Kaiserliche Marine* (Imperial Navy) in 1914 who fought with exceptional moral restraint. He did so even as naval warfare grew close to total, as the old rules collapsed into merciless orders and sometimes also depravity. We recognize it in a group of U-boats that tried to save hundreds of survivors from a torpedoed passenger liner mistaken for a troopship. In an Italian submarine captain who twice towed lifeboats to safety and brought women and children inside his boat, to the disdain of his German allies and open scorn from the top Nazi admiral. We locate it in a *Luftwaffe* fighter pilot who would not shoot down a badly damaged American bomber returning from ruining a city in his homeland, instead escorting it to safe passage over the North Sea. And in a Japanese pilot who pulled away from a passenger plane, against his orders, after seeing a woman's face inside. Civilians also confront profound moral choices: what to do with straggler enemies left behind as a hated invader finally pulls out, or with shipwrecked sailors who wash ashore, or bomber crews who bail out and land near their town, or abject refugees streaming in from far away? War is more than soldiering. It is engagement with the true nature of humanity.

This book looks at lonely acts of mercy and conscience that stopped illegal killing and cruelty by one's own side, and at odd-couple enemies who together worked out humane arrangements across active front lines. It considers compassion for surrendered soldiers and sailors and air crew. It recounts truces agreed in order to bury the dead or recover wounded or pause fighting for a cultural holiday, providing a few hours of minimal relief from shelling or machine guns or snipers. War at sea is so different from ground combat when it comes to possibilities for compassionate restraint that it warrants separate consideration. So too do expanded realms of modern war in and from the air and cyberspace. Are there fresh opportunities for conscience in these arenas, or do new modes of fighting take mercilessness to lower depths than we saw with older technologies of killing and destruction? What does it mean that we deploy lethal drones and amoral AI and robotic killers? Can conscience and mercy survive advancing military technology?

Like all historians, my daily practice is to observe the affairs of humanity in the remote, far-off country of the past. I have listened to soldiers talk about their personal wars, their physical wounds and aching moral injuries, and sometimes their crimes. Some were asked or ordered to do terrible things and witnessed humanity at its most debased. Many struggled years later with guilt and shame over what they did or failed to do, and became better people. A few found their best selves while at war, discovering qualities of unstrained mercy that allowed them to react with compassion even for their enemy, and always to the innocent. These are their stories. Tales of mercy that illustrate how ordinary men and women behaved with moral grace while inside the most extreme circumstances, far beyond the experience of most of us. I try to let them speak for themselves, in quiet voices otherwise lost inside the dehumanizing cacophony of the calamity that is war.

To understand and appreciate the quality of their acts of mercy, I have also shown the merciless ferocity of modern war, weaving stories of extraordinary virtue through harsher realities that are its more common fabric. Implicit in each tale and moral dilemma is the question "What would I have done?" If answered honestly, it will illuminate the human condition. But that means admitting that those of us fortunate never to have been tested by war do not truly know what we might have been capable of doing under its radical ethical and psychological challenges. Would we have grown more selfishly malicious or more merciful? Maybe we would have come back to our prewar homes and lives and families with our decency intact, or we might be burdened evermore by a weight of grievous "moral harm." We might have obeyed illegal orders, going along to get along. Or would we have dissented, as these brave and merciful people did? The essence of genuine heroism is to choose and act rightly. These everyday heroes discovered in themselves qualities of mercy and humane courage that astonish. Because they were not secular saints but ordinary people, they are models for us all. For if such graceful humanity can thrive even amidst war, we may hope for a gentling rain of mercy to fall on us in peace as well.

THIS BOOK IS ORGANIZED INTO FOUR parts. Each is built around a theme about how mercy connects us and conveys humanity under the intense circumstances of war. Part I sets the necessary cultural context. It explains how war stories, whether false or true, official or privately told, shape perceptions of the previous war in order to ready the public to wage the next one. It looks across cultures, locating patterns of myth-making from Western states to "martyr" stories that animate suicide bombers in the Middle East. It notes how all sides use stories about heroes and the best killers to justify war as virtuous on our part, pernicious and hateful by our enemy of the moment or the future. It advocates for considering a different kind of hero story, about ordinary men and women who expressed high moral valor and sacrificed to bring mercy to the helpless and vulnerable.

Part II deals with mercy in combat, stretching over decades and many wars and armies. It finds mercy in the trenches of the Great War, wandering the bitter woods along the Rhine, or walking the eastern bloodlands. It considers humane local truces that did not end all combat but paused war for a short while. It recalls moral courage under fire and the spark of recognition of shared humanity that pauses terror, making way for mercy. It considers varied forms of moral protest, from refusal to shoot to military strikes to mass desertion, and actually changing sides and uniforms. It lingers over the profound pity of war, grace to an enemy, and dissent amidst ruin.

Part III deals with classically and legally protected classes of people: medics, prisoners, and civilians. It explores the degree to which they were extended more or less mercy than promised. It ranges beyond armies to civilian volunteers who went off to wars not their own, to provide succor to the wounded at risk to their own life, limbs, and mental health. Part IV asks what the effects of advancing technology are on prospects for mercy. It explains how much more difficult, yet not impossible, it is to offer quarter at sea or in the air than on land. It recounts stories of valorous captains who insisted on fighting by old-fashioned rules while wanton actions occurred all around. It highlights German U-boat and Italian sub skippers who tried to save people floundering in the water, at enormous risk of being sunk themselves. It contrasts their mercy with a celebrated U.S. Navy captain who waged murderous submarine war against Japanese merchant mariners, and other Americans and Japanese who found mercy for a foe but also life-time moral injury. It recalls dogfighting in fragile little aircraft that permitted acts of grace but also boyish grandstanding. It contemplates total air war over Germany and across the Pacific, later above Vietnam, and drones circling Kandahar. It asks how much mercy will remain in future missile wars? We want precision-targeting, but a different reality too often happens on the ground. The conclusion argues for more attention to the role of mercy, not just for mercy's sake but because acting compassionately will actually help you win at war.

PART I

CULTURE

CHAPTER 1

STORIES

This great evil, where's it come from? How'd it steal into the world? Who's doing this? Who's killing us, robbing us of life and light? Is this darkness in you, too?

—James Jones, *The Thin Red Line* (1962)

After invading and annexing Crimea in 2014, then nibbling at Ukraine's outer provinces in a smoldering "small war" in Donbas for eight years, Vladimir Putin launched a full-scale invasion on February 24, 2022, widening the first war of territorial aggression in Europe since September 1939. Succumbing to the allure of battle, the short war delusion,[1] the Russian Army struggled to envelop Kyiv and Kharkiv with armored pincers. It advanced along too many axes, while also crawling along the southern coast, taking Mariupol but falling short of Odessa. Ukrainians waged hit-and-run ambushes, attritting poorly protected columns while readying their cities to become 21st-century Stalingrads. As the Russian Army stalled, it shifted from shambolic attack on Ukrainian military defenses to a merciless assault on civilians in towns and cities. Noncombatant status did not grant immunity from missiles, rockets, and shells. Mercy was spare on the other side as well, as war corroded compassion. Lieutenant Tetiana Mykolaiyivana Chornovol, onetime journalist and politician, commanded an antitank missile unit east of Kyiv four weeks into the war. "I shoot at armor," she said. Asked what she thought about young Russians inside the tanks she set on fire, she shrugged: "If they climb inside, it's their fault."[2] At the same time, a deeper humanity saw volunteer medics and doctors and aid pour in, while millions of refugees fled from the fighting and were welcomed into a dozen neighboring countries. As always, behavior in war ranged over the full moral spectrum, from cruelty to mercy.

A month into an escalating war, actor Arnold Schwarzenegger recorded a message warning Russian soldiers not to obey immoral "superior orders"[3] and thereby suffer "moral injury,"[4] as his father did while fighting for the Nazis on the Eastern Front in World War II. Gustav Schwarzenegger was a committed Wehrmacht soldier and a true believer in the Nazi cause. He was wounded during the siege of Leningrad, not just physically but spiritually as well. His experience of war inflicted lifelong moral injuries, which his son witnessed and now referenced in his message to Russian soldiers. "When my father . . . left Leningrad," he told them, "he was broken physically and mentally. He lived the rest of his life in pain . . . from a broken back, pain from the shrapnel that always reminded him of those terrible years and pain from the guilt that he felt. . . . I don't want you to be broken like my father."[5] Schwarzenegger did not make any reference to modern rejection of the legal defense of following "superior orders." He did not point to laws of war that are supposed to govern every soldier's behavior. He appealed to their humanity. He invoked their longing to come out of combat with an intact sense of decency. He asked them to be mindful of mercy not just to spare Ukrainians but in order to preserve themselves.

———

WAR STORIES TELL US HOW TO respond at the time or even decades later. They range from state propaganda and nationalist literature to heroic myths masquerading as memories, and personal tales told by veterans about their uncommon combat experiences that in the end can all seem the same. This book focuses on stories drawn from diaries and memoirs, interviews and reminiscences by ordinary people whose humanity was tested in war. They are decidedly unofficial and often confound the official line. Most are not enshrined in national monuments or mythology or annals of public records. They form a subset of stories about the behavior of ordinary men and women in the most extraordinary circumstances in which they ever found themselves. They are about private acts of profound mercy and conscience, even when no one was looking. These stories do not reflect on grand gestures or heroic fighting or avowed masterful and "genius" generals turning the hinges of history. They are concerned with what takes place behind the thunder of the guns, in war's odd corners where humanity is quietly reasserted amidst the inhumane. They reveal uncommon moral valor by those from whom we might have expected it least, confusing customary and nationalist storylines about who is virtuous and who is not.

Rupert Brooke was an irrepressible romantic who volunteered to fight as soon as he heard that war broke out in August 1914. Without ever seeing a German or a gun, he quickly published five sonnets under the title *Nineteen Fourteen*, a celebration of the classical belief in war he had imbibed in school. The country was in heroic mode, having had only a foretaste at Mons of the mass slaughter to come along the Somme and at Passchendaele. So he wrote skillful paeans to a cold marble ideal, greeting with glad heart a war that left all dullness behind. He rejoiced that its outbreak had banished a soulless peace, gifting him and an overcast generation the chance for sunlit glory of a glittering, pristine death: "God be thanked Who has matched us with His hour, and caught our youth, and wakened us from sleeping!"[6] Ernst Jünger wrote much the same. But at least he waited until 1920, after taking multiple wounds and killing a lot of Brooke's countrymen during four years of war: "Grown up in an age of security, we shared a yearning for danger, for the experience of the extraordinary. We were enraptured by war."[7]

In his signature, elite schoolboy manner, Brooke grafted fashionable sentimentality onto the classical ideal of perfect youth meeting with a flawless death: "Blow out, you bugles, over the rich Dead! There's none of these so lonely and poor of old but, dying, has made us rarer gifts than gold. These laid the world away; poured out the red sweet wine of youth."[8] He seemed willfully unaware, wholly missing the point that anonymous industrial carnage had obliterated all refined taste and manners and good character in war. Lewdly, he placed graceful lyricism into service to unabashed nationalist ardor, which endears him still to more effete English readers over a century later: "If I should die, think only this of me: that there's some corner of a foreign field that is for ever England."[9] He retained his combat virginity into 1915 but failed to emerge from the war with grandeur or his life. He died from blood poisoning from an insect bite while en route to the Dardanelles, failing to join the Allied assault on Gallipoli that ended in a spectacular bloodbath. By then his war sonnets were widely popular. They were enshrined in the culture by his quick death, despite his distance from any brush with energetic heroism.

Others were wiser, grimmer, more honest, with real experience. Wilfred Owen was 25 years old in 1918 and just coming into his poetry, writing in between barrages in sodden trenches in the last months of his violently aborted life. He refused to compose verses about the "old lie." His subject was "the pity of war."[10] Brooke's naïve, schoolboy enthusiasms about war were displaced by Owen's tragic, experienced observations. Together they framed the calamity of the Great War of their generation. Weary tragedy echoed in others who suffered alongside Owen, or across from him on the far side of no-man's-land. Siegfried Sassoon, highly decorated and twice wounded, arrived at righteous anger that drove him to open dissent and protest against the war in 1916.[11] Robert Graves fell into cold, cynical detachment, leading him to write a bitterly ironic memoir 10 years later and thence to lifetime exile.[12] Across the Narrow Sea, older volunteer Henri Barbusse's grim novel *Le feu* gave the French nation a taste of real war at Verdun, of *la guerre d'usure,* "the war of wearing down."[13] Men described themselves as *viande à canon* (cannon meat). It was war as attritional grinding, not *la gloire* as supposedly experienced under Louis XIV and Napoleon, two authors of the old lie. It all resounded 20 years later during a greater catastrophe and far more destructive war, fought by most of the same nations and empires to finish disputes left unresolved by dead heroes or the shells, by wartime stories and postwar treaties.

Most of the war poets who heard the thunder of guns firsthand tried to pull us all down into the mud and blood with them to stop us reverting to literary and poetic heroism, to make us look at vivid horrors of industrial warfare. They refused to pretend that their war was manly and glorious, or morally worthy of its truly astonishing costs in lives and limbs and sound minds. Some thought with H. G. Wells that their war was so uniquely horrible it would be the one to finally end all war, or at least end the gallant squint that produced endless war hero literature everywhere.[14] Yet the old lie repeated: battle is glorious, war should be welcomed, and no death is as worthy as that of the pure young man who sacrifices for his people. All that pity in the poetry of the war, yet the pious lie returned over and again in pitiless propaganda. It killed tens of millions over the first half of the 20th century, many millions more in the second half. In varied languages and religious and national traditions it is killing around the world even today. For the poets, artists, and novelists did not speak for everyone in the trenches or behind the lines. Most men did not find any poetry or higher art in the filth and stench, in the slit latrines and foul rear area brothels, or carrying coal sacks on stretchers that were filled by shovel with disconnected body bits of a dead childhood pal. They stood beside poets and artists whose impressions filter and shape our perceptions yet blot out the voices of the silent millions who were illiterate or inarticulate or died too soon. Plain soldiers found their own meaning, or none at all.

And yet, the vast majority of those conscripted to fight each other did not desert or mutiny, not until the very end in most cases. They endured in places they could not leave, stood a post on their turn, went on patrols in no-man's-land. They griped and grumbled but were proud afterward of their military service and of their nation's proclaimed cause. Their families endured with them as soldiers in every uniform received and delivered attacks, dug trenches, learned to live in dugouts until ordered out and "over the top." They went on leave but most came back. They adjusted to terrible food and smells, to trench rats and lice. And they grew more skilled at killing. They were committed to the cause of their nation, in each nation, giving silent consent to the war by fighting it. Most were not pallid victims of distant lies. All were trained to be active killers, and many embraced the role. Not all sank into solitude or despair or paralyzing trauma. Most coped in ways that are hard for us to understand. The key veteran's account of the *Weltkrieg* in Germany was not, as is usually taught, Erich Maria Remarque's heartfelt pacifist outcry *Im Westen nichts Neues* (*All Quiet on the Western Front*). It was highly decorated, many times wounded Ernst Jünger's prowar *In*

Stahlgewittern (*Storm of Steel*). Remarque discovered shared humanity with his enemy across no-man's-land, writing with deep loathing for war. But his work was better received outside postwar Germany than within. Not so Jünger's earlier, more vigorous book, which documented his achievements as a soldier, arguing manfully for a synthesis and celebration of male toughness and industrial war.

Remarque found a worldwide audience in multiple translations and a 1931 motion picture. But his antiwar novel was banned then burned inside Germany when the Nazis came to power two years later. Jünger's prowar work appeared in English in 1929, the same year as Remarque's novel and Ernest Hemingway's *A Farewell to Arms*.[15] Admirers who read Jünger included the leader of the Nazi Party and many World War I veterans. Wounded seven times, he was one of a handful of infantry company leaders awarded the *Pour le Mérite*, the highest medal for valor in the *Kaiserheer*.[16] Jünger openly embraced war and fighting, celebrating the *Weltkrieg* as a transcendental experience for young men of his generation. He embodied the warrior-writer in ways that combat virgin Brooke merely fantasized and the habitual war voyeur Hemingway might only envy from his rear area ambulance post with the Italian Army or sitting on a barstool in Milan or Madrid. Jünger celebrated killing like a hunter recalls taking down a stag. Remarque's characters grew ever more morose and morally inert and injured. Hemingway's self-referential protagonist barely engaged, shooting an unarmed deserter who was finished off by another driver. He was not hurt by directed fire but "blown up while we were eating cheese."[17] Jünger came close to death several times. Hemingway was hit by a stray frag as he gave chocolate and cigarettes to the troops.[18] Hard truths of war were in the trenches, not at the bar.

Fake battle scenes serve merely literary purposes in Hemingway, while less comfortable, far more disturbing real-world truths slither beneath Jünger's calm narration of personal combat experience. He led trench raids, endured days of falling shells, picked up pieces of soldiers and trench mates blown apart or buried alive. He killed many times, in different ways, over four years in the trenches. He had turned away from privileged youth to locate himself in war. He agreed more with Heraclites that "war is the father of us all" than with William Wordsworth that "the child is father of the man." He believed the *Weltkrieg* made his generation both hard and different. He spent the war years not in quiet contemplation of "intimations of mortality" all around but with daily, screaming butchery by shot and shell and leaf bayonet. He spoke about killing as the essence of all war, its key act, the parted crimson curtain of violent stagecraft. He wrote with poetic savagery about his own willingness to kill with no hesitation or regret. And yet, one incident with the drapes closed and no one looking to judge him must make us ask if even this iron man was as brittle toward humanity as he claimed. In a moment of mercy, he declined to kill a helpless man. He chose not to pull the trigger. He did not remain the cruel warrior, the man with "iron in his soul" that was smelted to steel by Father War.[19]

Even Jünger found some place for mercy in the trenches, although he confessed long afterward that he did not understand his motive for sparing a wounded enemy. One day in no-man's-land, a foreboding place deep inside the *Inferno* that neither Brooke nor Hemingway ever reached or knew, "a bloody scene with no witnesses was about to happen." Jünger came upon a wounded man: "I set the mouth of [my] pistol at the man's temple. He was too frightened to move. With my other fist I grabbed hold of his tunic, feeling medals and badges of rank." It was an officer, which meant there was all the more reason to kill him, as Jünger had so many before. But then a flash of recognition of shared humanity: "With a plaintive sound, he reached into his pocket, not to pull out a weapon but a photograph which he held up to me. I saw him on it, surrounded by numerous family all standing on a terrace. It was a plea from another world." A world where mercy mattered and murder was forbidden. The gesture reached into Jünger's calcified decency. "Later, I thought it was blind chance that I let him go and plunged onward." And yet, "that one man of all, often appeared in my dreams."[20] It was as close as he ever came to admitting that his adored war left him with a tarnished conscience and moral harm.

Stories about mercy and cruelty in war mirror ourselves, our societies, and all humanity. That is why all war stories matter. As the Việtnam War veteran novelist Tim O'Brien put it, "Not bloody stories necessarily. Happy stories, too, and even a few peace stories."[21] We absorb heroic stories about expert killers and commanders well enough. But mostly neglected are tales about merciful virtue, not just toward one's own wounded or suffering civilians whom our troops treat kindly but toward the enemy as well. And more shockingly, mercy by that same enemy for the vulnerable and hapless on our side. Because key questions about mercy in war should not be belabored, I have not compiled sociological lists of qualities or conditions that might lead to decent conduct or to its opposite. Artificial constructs will not help us resolve the human element of mystery that surrounds these signature acts of mercy. Jünger never understood his own compassion, leaving a man alive whom he more likely would have killed or ordered killed if he had not been alone and touched to see the man before him not as a uniform but a life and father with his family, inside a worn leather frame. Enigma remains, no matter the formal structures we erect or worked-over definitions. In the end, these stories stand before us on their own, just as solitary men and women stood alone in great moral angst and the key crises of their lives.

IT IS TELLING THAT WE FIND mercy in the oddest places and also in quite surprising uniforms. Cruelty also. This is true even setting aside self-deception or propaganda lies and official concealment that forms a "wilderness of mirrors" that curves and bends the truth almost past recognition.[22] The most important question is whether moments of mercy are only isolated acts of private conscience. Does decency mainly exist independently of cultural and social frameworks, carried off to war by individuals alone and thus not replicable by training and enforcing rules or honor codes? We must also counter nationalists, and far too many historians, who avoid stories about genuinely honorable enemy who show mercy to our soldiers. Such tales lie outside the traditional heroic narrative that claims exclusive decency. Odd tales about how an enemy showed uncommon sympathy and compassion shade our perception away from starker blacks and whites into moral grays. That is welcome, as a far truer picture of the complex nature of humanity in war. We should embrace stories that muddy our cliché assessments of the enemy, make us query the higher morality we want to believe adheres solely to our cause. Maybe facing grayer moral facts can teach us something richer about humanity, helping us reach out for a little of the pity of war amidst all the pious cant and hypocrisy.

Stories that allow only combat heroics reflect society's fears and hopes but also block understanding of war's deeper complexities. War is more than breaking machines and bodies, even by armies of virtue on the march to liberation. It overwhelms with stress, sears minds and memories over the years or decades left to survivors. If we won last time, the old stories assure us that we have the moral and martial qualities to win when we fight again. If we lost, we are taught by parables of war that leaders learned from the defeat and surely will know how to win next time. And so people lend their children to the fight against old foes whom they themselves had fought when young or against a new enemy of the current hour and crisis. Some place hope in an advanced weapons system that only we will deploy, in some "revolution in military affairs" promised by our most brilliant scientists and keenest engineers. Or old fallbacks are trotted out to shore up doubt: we will win because we are an exceptional race or culture or civilization. Our soldiers and generals are inherently superior, our plans more clever. The triumph of our driving will or national spirit has reshaped the playing table where the "iron dice of destiny" are rolling, tilting it in favor of our victory. Rest assured, the steel die of our next campaign will come up six time and again.[23]

Friedrich Schiller was hardly original in the themes of his 1799 trilogy on the mercenary general Albrecht von Wallenstein.[24] Like so many writers before him and who came after him, Schiller celebrated war as heroic and sublime, praising the transcendental soldier who embraces tragedy and "dies a glorious death for his Fatherland."[25] We might forgive him for writing that nonsense without knowing about the total world wars of the 20th century, except that he wrote it about the more catastrophic Thirty Years' War, the most lethal conflict in European history. It killed 15 to 25 percent of the total population of his German homeland, achieving a mortality rate that exceeded by three or four times each of the world wars 300 years later.[26] Moreover, he wrote maddeningly heroic plays and verse in refined personal comfort, averting his gaze and pen from the bloody wreckage of the Napoleonic Wars burning just over the horizon outside his study window.

He was not alone among artists. Probably more in history have served as pimps to glory and power, as Voltaire did to Friedrich II and Louis XV, than let out a wail of moral protest at all the obscene carnage done in vanity's name.

Leo Tolstoy started out as a naïve nationalist and enthusiast for war before he descended into diseased trenches in the Crimea. There, he saw war up close and ugly as a young tsarist officer and began a lifelong journey into dissent, religious conversion, and pacifism. Along the way from young jingoist to fierce rejectionist, he gave the world a far more jarring and realistic war literature, stripped of artifice and delusion, replete with images that should repel easy military romanticism.[27] Yet, Tolstoy's greatest work could not survive the larger culture's insistence on war heroes. Russians and foreigners have turned *War and Peace* into a heroic epic for television and movie screens, ignoring the bitterly antiwar moral thesis lying at its core. The farther from the disaster of Napoleon, the surer our return to military romanticism. On and on heroes marched over pages in kingdom after nation after empire, from Henry Fielding to Alfred Lord Tennyson and Rupert Brooke, Stephen Crane and Ernest Hemingway to Mikhail Sholokhov and Vladimir Popov. War was glorious and unquestioned, not protested. Mercy was forgotten along the way, until the 20th century deemed it just in the way of harder nationalisms that clashed in merciless fighting.

THE VOCABULARY THAT BEST HELPS US understand the merciful in war is limited. Words like "decency," "restraint," "compassion" may seem insufficient to the task. And yet, together they frame at least some hope for a culture of civilized behavior. They allow us to engage even with those who otherwise appall us, who show cruelty on some days but mercy and magnanimity on others. They provide context to men like Captain William Clark, who served in the U.S. Cavalry during the Great Plains Wars. He fought against the Oglala and Cheyenne nations but grew keenly interested in their cultures and histories and even learned their sign language. He helped avoid hostilities at times and was broadly sympathetic to the plight of vanquished Sioux warriors. He also herded defeated men, women, and children onto scrub reservations, and he was complicit in the murder of their great war leader, T̃hašúŋke Witkó (Chief Crazy Horse).[28] Likewise, these words give insight into General Henning von Tresckow, chief of staff of German 2nd Army in Belarus and eastern Poland in 1943–1944. He approved murder and child abduction, slave labor and collective retaliations on the rapid march to Nazi midnight. Yet, he refused to sanction all-out genocide and, earlier than many others, plotted against Adolf Hitler as the degrader of morality and German civilization.[29] How do we judge such men and soldiers? Were their decisions at all ameliorated by times and circumstances rife with assumptions of racial and cultural superiority? Should we demand mercy and moral accountability across all times? These are hard questions, cutting to core humanity. The answers are not at all easy to reach.

It is often said that truth is the first casualty in war.[30] If so, decency is the second. War is one of the defining activities of human history: we are the animal who makes war. I hear the objection that we are not beasts, that we are capable of mercy and reasoned action under any circumstances. All the religions say so. The modern law of war assumes it. Yet, it is we who make war, while beasts do not. And we do it over and over. Not across a few years or decades or even centuries but for millennia. Clerics issue edicts that invoke the better angels of our nature, yet we all and always proclaim that the gods are on *our* side when we divide into war camps. We dehumanize and caricature the enemy to persuade our reluctant and frightened armed teenagers to kill his scared and heavily armed teenagers, even as we proclaim allegiance to universal injunctions to act mercifully. We deny Shakespeare's moral admission: "There is no king, be his cause never so spotless, if it come to the arbitrement of swords, can try it out with all unspotted soldiers."[31] We ask far more of soldiers than we ask of civilians, forgetting that our leaders as well as ourselves are also dalmatianed by war. In peacetime, we write idealistic laws to constrain the darker impulses released in war. Then war comes and we quickly seek out every loophole and lawyerly evasion as pressures of fighting bend us back toward accepting crime. When short wars go long, we demand that our armed forces do whatever is needed to win, leaving morality aside until after their dirty job is done and our victory is secured. We like to believe that we will behave properly even inside the harshest of all arenas of moral choice and endeavor, that we will act when at war with a measure of compassion and mercy, not just malice. We fail nearly every time. At least we try again the next time. Then again, and again.

War still is as it was: the brute climax of political struggle, an extension of ongoing ethnic or national or territorial or ideological or religious or economic conflict into imposed resolutions by *force majeure*. It is a gory theater where clustered interests and visceral hatreds contend, where heroes walk and armies clash to exact and to pay the butcher's bill for vanities of elites and nations. All for a policy that will be indifferently remembered, if at all, by future generations. For centuries, war meant hand-to-hand fighting in brutal conflicts today barely recalled by some obscure statue or named street. Whatever the claimed morality of a *casus belli*, no matter how pure some knight's or samurai's or Janissary's resolve, what combat meant before the industrialization of modern war was looking your enemy in the face as you killed or brutally maimed him, his blood spurting all over your armor, his screams loud in your ears, his viscera falling onto your boots. Then the lines grew apart as science and industry allowed anonymous killing from ever greater distances. Armies became vast beginning in the 17th century, until they numbered millions, then tens of millions slogging it out over many years of battling in trenches and in forests and in decimated cities. Even at sea, the number of men dying on and under the water grew immense as war after war brimmed contested oceans with death, leaving behind and below the rusting hulks of 10,000 ships.

War darkened the skies as well. Aircraft went up, anti-aircraft fire followed, and pilots and crew came tumbling down along with burning machines, cratering green countrysides with strewn fields of burning alloys and mangled flesh. Or air crews stayed cocooned inside their finely calibrated killing machines, so high above some target city that the bombsights reduced it to a green and ghoulish abstraction. Not a collage of neighborhoods and families at work and play, of art and culture and huddling humanity that took over a thousand years to build. All gone in an hour or a day, or an atomic minute. Targeting technologies today promise precision but still seduce fire controllers holding a joystick over 500 miles away. The physical and psychological gap to the targeted grid point entices people to give the shoot order, to fire a shell or missile that plunges into what an imaging console insists is a gathering terrorist group but is actually a wedding party. A tragic targeting error. We'll learn and do better next time. Then it happens over and again.[32]

Mercy taboos wear down as war erases social hesitations that in peace govern how we judge the ethics of killing. Fighting abrades the legal ideal of moral and physical restraint. Compassion departs in cultural and legal wisps blown away by the howl of war. This is a cardinal truth. We must not be distracted by abstract debate over whether one weapon is less moral or humane than another one. Do we ban gunpowder, as popes tried to do in the 13th century? Or poison bullets, as outlawed by the Holy Roman Empire and France? Dum-dum bullets developed by the British in India were banned in 1899. After World War I, poison gases and corrosive chemical agents were prohibited for use but not manufacture. Spike pits as old as hunting and war were used in the Pacific theater by the Japanese in World War II, and again in Vietnam. In 1979 they were forbidden in a Conventional Weapons Protocol. Biological toxins that were outlawed in 1972 were used in Iraq and Syria after that, as were nerve and chemical weapons. Plastic fragments, land mines, and cluster bombs were subjects of more recent weapons bans, while a ban on dropping heavy ordnance on cities is currently being considered. Yet, all methods were used by Russian forces to wreck cities in Chechnya, then in Syria and Ukraine. Does the means used to kill the enemy and break his things matter? Is that where mercy lies? For each new rule we write, we compose new evasions and more complex and stealthier or more brutal weapons.

The battlefield is an arena where life-and-death decisions are made under extraordinary conditions of extreme stress and threat. It is not a philosophy seminar room or a courthouse, detached in time and place, where the ethics or laws of hard cases are argued. When one's life is in danger there is little or no time to consider the rights and wrongs or moral meaning of real-time actions taken, of immediate orders given and carried out. War is a poison chalice wherein chance, panic, spite, and malice mix. It forces choices that must be lived with afterward by damaged survivors. It dethrones reason, perverts emotion and judgment. It is difficult for normally decent people to resist what their state or society commits them to defend. War is awesomely powerful, so overwhelming and tidal in its psychological intensity that it is exceptionally difficult for most caught up in it to report, let alone dare to try to stop, war crimes by their own side that they may witness. War can traumatize the brain with PTSD, but also one's conscience with moral harm.[33] After returning from war, some are so regretful at what they did or failed to do, either not stopping or not reporting crimes they witnessed, that they kill themselves. That is what happened to a respected U.S. Army officer after deployments in Iraq and Afghanistan. His graduate school instructor told me that he took his own life at least in part because he could not get past "seeing someone pull the trigger when he shouldn't have."[34]

Others do astonishingly humane things while at war. Despite intense savagery all around, some courageous souls walk a veiled path through the Valley of the Shadow of Death. They reject the defense by Shakespeare's soldiers in *Henry V*, contemplating a hard morrow of killing the night before Agincourt in 1415: "We know enough if we know we are the king's subjects. If his cause be wrong, our obedience to the king wipes the crime of it out of us."[35] They disdain that old evasion of *respondeat superior,* or "superior orders," first rejected by an international tribunal in 1474 but not finally set aside until the Nuremberg trials after World War II.[36] In obedience to a higher natural law and moral duty, they will not obey leaders of superior rank but inferior conscience. They refuse to pull the trigger. Some go further, bearing witness. A remarkable few turn weapons against their own side to stop merciless crimes. These are the stories we need to add to the lexicon of memory.

WAR AT THE LEVEL OF STRATEGIC management is about high-stakes policy, choices, and gambles. About recruitment and training of immense armies, navies, and air forces. About grand stratagems and complex operations supported by new taxes, long-distance logistics, economic mobilization, and national debt. It deals with command and control, with selecting war-winning methods and choosing sequential objectives. Almost none of that takes place at the level of the experience of war by those who actually fight. A war might be just or just necessary. It may start in tragic error or in deception, in farce or in lies. It might be rooted in elite arrogance or in cultural ignorance. To most who fight, none of that matters much after the first shots are exchanged and first blood is spilled. Old struggles or fresh quarrels about hard national interests may guide decisions in distant capitals where wars begin. But for the average soldier a chill realization sets in that the cause does not really matter, only that I must kill or horribly maim men on the other side of some no-man's-land, or I will be killed or wounded myself. Quickly and inevitably, fighting turns primal, reducing to frantic small-group combat where the enemy may be no more than a flash of different-colored uniform in your gunsight. Then night falls, adrenal rush abates, bodies are counted, and a quiet private voice whispers in the dark, *You have killed.* Later, you find out that you are newly thought of as a war hero. Do you kill again?

Even good soldiers who kill lawfully in combat carry home the dread weight of homicide on their minds, or agonize because they don't.[37] Strains of combat inexorably, even inevitably, erode mercy toward an enemy who is doing us grievous harm. The longer a war lasts, the more this is so. Acts of humane sensibility may occur at any time in any army, in any war. Nevertheless, mercy is more difficult to locate the longer a war goes on, the more hardened it makes those who fight it, the farther it carries them from civilian lives and experiences and expectations. There might even be a rough equation between how long soldiers expect to fight and how mercifully they treat the enemy, almost with a defined start, middle, and end to the legal exemption from prohibitions against killing. That may be why the approaching end of a long war more closely resembles the naïve morality that was present at the start, before all the mutual carnage in the middle. Soldiers' outraged perceptions of themselves and of the enemy appear to mellow as they anticipate actually returning to civilian life, where killing is again prohibited.

All sides say that their soldiers fight in a righteous cause. Few admit that some also commit shocking crimes. A common dulling of self-righteousness occurs after every new war starts. This is felt much more profoundly by soldiers because they are forced to face intense moral dilemmas for which civilian life has not prepared them. First they may realize that they are really fighting for a lie, or at best for a partial truth. They see that their side is not uniquely virtuous or always rightly motivated or restrained.

Next they grasp that if the cause is not fully just after all, they must question orders they are given and the means provided to maim and kill the enemy. They are ashamed of what happens to civilians, who always get in the way when combat swirls around them. It happens every time we send our too innocent youths to tramp and trundle through other people's lives and countries, armored in false histories of all our previous "good wars." It happened to bewildered millions in stalled armies in World War I, uncomprehending American youths fighting in Vietnam or Afghanistan, and Russian conscripts told that they were liberating Ukraine in 2022, who instead met intense hate and fierce resistance. We safeguard soldiers behind metaphors of justice, shroud them in propaganda of our unquestioned right. It is a wonder that some still do the right thing, despite the rest of us.

Most soldiers are young, and all start as combat virgins. Many think that war is going to be an adventure akin to those they read about in stories or saw in sanitized hero movies. They may dip into shallow cultural memes about idealized knights or samurai, see all that in themselves as they preen before a mirror in a first uniform, then try to behave like their heroes in the old stories. As the war drags on they see more horror, more callous and cruel acts by both sides. Many move farther from restraint than they thought possible about themselves, as they adapt to what everyone around them says are harsh necessities of the fight. They grow callouses over youthful moral sensitivity. They don iron emotional armor to get through frightful days and fearful nights. Or the whole process reverses: a youth starts out callow and cruel but mellows with experience until they are a more careful veteran, with sympathy for an enemy with whom they shared too much suffering. Then we ask them to become civilians again, to resume normal lives and relationships. Families take back hobbled veterans they no longer understand; couples can spend postwar decades together in shared solitude.

Over the course of the past 250 years, millions returned from war without an arm or leg or part of their stomach or lower jaw, or peered at the world from a partly melted face. Millions more, who do not count in the official rolls of war dead, died years or decades prematurely from old war wounds. The lucky mourn unrecoverable youth and their lost innocence. The unlucky fall into trauma and numbness, ruined. It is why so many combat narratives illustrate a pattern of idealism that arcs into a logic of disillusionment, as the recruit turns into a veteran witness to the hard reality of war, then indifferent to the cause and the enemy. We see this in outline in the American Civil War novel by Stephen Crane, *The Red Badge of Courage.*[38] It is more explicit in the World War I autobiographical novel by the *Weltkrieg* veteran Remarque, *All Quiet on the Western Front.*[39] It underlies the 1987 feature film *Full Metal Jacket.* It is far more powerfully captured in the Afghanistan War documentary *Restrepo* (2010), filmed at an outpost in the Korengal Valley that U.S. troops later abandoned as untenable, as they did all of Afghanistan in 2021 after 20 years of failed plans and policy.

Decency seems to be an individual rather than a cultural quality, self-justifying and self-motivating. To judge by later confessions, most veterans know this. Many will worry years after their war ends, often for the rest of their lives, whether they behaved rightly back then or not. A craving to think of oneself as essentially decent will inform profound feelings of remorse and guilt decades later. This is not a psychiatric or psychological disorder. It is a form of moral harm or injury or dissonance. It is what Schwarzenegger warned Russian troops about as they moved into Ukraine to wreck it for no reason beyond the vanity of an isolated dictator, a resentful great power elite in long decline, and misplaced nationalist romanticism about the special historical virtue of a failed empire. The idea of moral injury in war is ancient, although wide use of the modern term dates to Jonathan Shay's seminal study *Achilles in Vietnam.*[40] He linked the idea to various stages of the 10-year voyage home of Ulysses, a deeply morally wounded veteran of the Trojan War.

Moral harm has symptoms that overlap with elements of clinical definitions of PTSD, but others that differ.[41] It starts in acts known to be wrong at the time or in witnessing war crimes or cruelties by others that grate on one's cherished prewar beliefs and values. Karl Marlantes confessed to this effect of the Việtnam War honestly and eloquently in his memorial essay *What It Is Like to Go to War.* Douglas Pryor gave us a profoundly confessional medical article about moral injury, while William Broyles challenged convenient assumptions in his provocative article "Why Men Love War."[42] One of the chilling questions soldiers face is not knowing who will suffer from it. Who develops moral harm, and who does not? Who has a sense of its peril for themselves before pulling the trigger?

Even more confusing to routine narratives of our righteous wars are stories retelling acts of humanity toward us by the enemy. They intrude into a storyline that says the enemy's soldiers are morally inferior to ours, making it harder to appropriate empathy solely to our people and narrow cause. It is why all wartime propaganda is black-and-white and too much military history is written from a starkly nationalist point of view. This avoids honest accountability, while pandering to a market assumption that honor belongs to us while dishonor blots the enemy. Too often missing is an honest accountancy of mercy, which knows no exclusive faith or nation or uniform. Foul policy flows downward from criminal regimes and out from vicious ideologies, but foul deeds spread wherever any war reaches. The merciful thus may appear in odd uniforms that will abide in history as symbols of true evil, while cruel killers may be wearing ours. It is hard for us to admit this about our soldiers and ourselves. It may be the single hardest thing. It is true, nonetheless.

The longer we let our best killers loose with permission to kill, the more likely it is that they won't always kill the right people. Meanwhile, we learn later that some among those serving terrible leaders or criminal regimes were individually capable of grace and even serene humanity. This is a deep paradox: the history of war demonstrates that atrocities are universals and that decency too does not stop at national or cultural borders. Some among a despised and hated enemy act with kindness toward those who are helpless: lying wounded on the field, or naked and vulnerable as prisoners of war, or civilians. As wartime passions cool we often discover that our declared *casus belli* was not the real one, or find out that our air force or fleets carried out indiscriminate targeting that we had eagerly approved then but have come to regret. To complete the moral accountancy we need to hear another, different kind of tale than customary ones told on all sides about combat bravery and unique sacrifice by the best warriors. We need to hear mercy stories.

CHAPTER 2

HEROES

Now Grendel and I are called together, and I have come.
—Beowulf, hero of the Geats, in Old English epic poem *Beowulf*,
8th century CE

War heroes abound in all cultures, dating at least to Babylonian and Akkadian tablet tales of the great warrior king Gilgamesh and to tomb cults in Iron Age Greece in the eighth century BCE.[1] Writers crafted world literature around tales of war heroes that are still read centuries after their cultures died. War may be presented in such classic works as warping and wrenching, its heroes as tragically flawed characters. Yet we watch the play, yearning for more tales of war and woe. Major characters who strut the stage of war call us to worship their fearful and darkly stormy gods as well. For warriors are imitators of the gods, and war is divine. Bend down low to Horus or Mars, kneel before Ishtar or Wodan or Chiyou, venerate wrathful Kumara or the great, bright god Sarutahiko holding his ruby spear. Sing the Ambrosian Hymn to honor the victory of our warrior king, ultimate agent of the gods' purposes on Earth.[2] Honor all who serve with sword and shield, blood and bone. War is a godly invention, its heroes crystal prisms of virtue and grace. It doesn't matter that the old deities are dead in the modern world. We have new, secular gods to worship: the state and nation. Fight on for the *patrie*, the Fatherland, honor and *la gloire*. And let every soldier return from the wars as a hero to his village.

————————

THE WARRIOR IS UPHELD AS ULTIMATE exemplar of heroic idealism, seamlessly virtuous even in childhood, destined for greatness.[3] He may be damaged morally and psychologically. He might be cruel and pitiless. Nonetheless, he remains the paradigm instrument of cultural propaganda. Homer's damaged hero Ulysses calls to us to watch him do great deeds of war.[4] Achilles, Ajax, Agamemnon, and Hector, also flawed heroes of the Trojan War, are full of rage. They are relentless: merciless and remorseless, yet memorable.[5] Plutarch gave us an apologia for Alexander of Macedonia, paired with an onslaught on the tyrant but war hero Julius Caesar.[6] Virgil opened the epic *Aeneid* with a promise to Romans, by far the most successful martial people of the ancient world: "Of wars and a man I sing."[7] Legions of panegyric poems venerated King of the Franks and Holy Roman Emperor Charlemagne (Carlos Magnus), upheld as the supreme exemplar of a Christian war hero and a sovereign lord.[8] Or Richard the Lionheart or Louis IX, saint king of France; or Salah ad-Din, founder of the Ayyubid dynasty. The 13th-century German epic song *Nibelunglied* celebrated those who fought to the death inside the thick Black Forest, refusing calls to submit.[9] Luo Guanzhong's classic *Romance of the Three Kingdoms* tracked hero General Guan Yu through the end of the Han dynasty.[10] Every hero finds a publicist, someone to record and frame great acts for the public even when they include murder: Thomas Mallory's *Le Morte d'Arthur*, Shakespeare's *Henry V* and *Titus Andronicus*, Leo Tolstoy's heroically ambiguous *War and Peace*, alleluias to Napoleon and to other heroic and so-called genius generals that echo down the centuries.[11]

Modern sensibility prefers heroes who start out as ordinary yet become extraordinary. Alvin York was a blacksmith, one of 11 children raised in poverty by hardscrabble Tennessee farmers. He looked every bit the robust combat hero in 1918, when he received the Medal of Honor for killing a dozen Germans in a one-man assault on a machine gun outpost.[12] Sergeant York seemed to embody the American Expeditionary Force (AEF) in

France, seen back home as a righteous army of simple, unassuming men. With war clouds gathering once again in 1941, his story was turned into the top-earning Hollywood movie: the humble everyman was played by legendary screen actor Gary Cooper.[13] But Alvin York was a model hero from an earlier war, and each new war demands fresh heroes. He was thus displaced by Audie Murphy, a thin and modest man more suited to a war that engaged the entire nation in ways World War I had not. John Wayne would scale Mount Suribachi on Iwo Jima in a feature film made in 1949,[14] but Audie Murphy lived the role of real war hero. His autobiography, *To Hell and Back*, became a bestseller that was made into a movie wherein he played himself.[15] He was then tagged for a classic role in *Red Badge of Courage* (1951), which premiered as the Korean War broke out. Into the first years of the next war (there is always a next war), this time in Indochina, Murphy obliged the public's craving for champions, playing the archetypical American: a self-effacing man transformed into an eternal minuteman to fight against tyranny in a war he did not start, his martial and moral virtues securing justice and liberty for all.[16]

Lingering social divisions over Vietnam precluded that war's ethically blemished heroes succeeding those of World War II: the latter dominated movies and popular culture for 50 years. Then a brief moment of unity following the 9/11 attacks called for heroes who were not tainted by Vietnam. That is why Navy Seal Chris Kyle, the top sniper of the war in Iraq, ascended to celebrity hero. He did not obliterate an unseen enemy from a B-29 or with napalm or a cruise missile or artillery. He picked off individual targets with a scoped rifle, a method better suited to counterinsurgency wars that seemed at first cleaner than Vietnam or even World War II. His claimed sniper kill total was unparalleled, his skill set perfectly fitted to on-the-ground images preferred to combat conducted at distance from the air. Sniping resized wars in which a list of *homo sacer*[17] (outlaw) names was printed on a deck of ID cards given to troops in Iraq, while a second list of al-Qaeda leaders was kept by President George W. Bush in the Oval Office. How markedly different from lists of German cities kept by Air Chief Marshal Arthur Harris at the head of Royal Air Force (RAF) Bomber Command, or Japanese cities destroyed by the U.S. Army Air Forces (USAAF) under General Curtis

LeMay, or carpet-bombing overmatched targets that were hand-picked by President Lyndon B. Johnson on table maps of North Vietnam.

It was easy to show dramatic clips of cruise missile launches on nightly news but impossible to make a drone into a celebrity. And each war demands its heroes. Kyle's sniping prowess minimized air strikes that sometimes obliterated the wrong target, or caused "collateral damage" even when they hit the right one. A war hero thus emerged who found resonance with the public in a bestselling autobiography. In its title, *American Sniper: The Most Lethal Sniper in U.S. Military History*, he brazenly celebrated not just expertise but his all-time lead in kills.[18] The screen version, directed by Clint Eastwood, was more morally nuanced in ways nationalist audiences and jingoistic TV pundits missed as they embraced Kyle as an all-American hero.[19] His kill total was a source of derivative pride for many in the audience, as his name became celebrated in patriotic homes across the country. Hailed as a man of faith and humble heroic virtue, he was a merciless killer.

Chris Kyle was not a subtle man: "When God confronts me with my sins, I do not believe any of the kills I had during the war will be among them. Everyone I shot was evil. I had good cause on every shot. They all deserved to die."[20] He had a crusader cross inked on his trigger forearm: "I had it put in in red, for blood. I hated the damn savages I'd been fighting. I always will."[21] He was unable to comprehend the irony of his prose or the savagery of his own actions. For Kyle, a counterinsurgency campaign should be waged without garlands or mercy, denying the enemy's humanity while himself sinking to the same perceived level of barbarity. "You know how Ramadi was won?" he asked about the 2006 battle for that city. "We went in and killed all the bad people we could find." Every slaying was a deserved execution of an evil man (and some women, whom he also shot). "I like war," he boasted more than he confessed. Yet, he didn't understand much about war beyond tactics. "We killed the bad guys and brought the leaders to the peace table. That is how the world works."[22] Actually, that is seldom how the world works or how that war ended. Nor is it how war and peace usually connect, finding grayer terms negotiated to somehow wind a path back out of the scalding tar pit.

"I don't shoot people with Korans. I'd like to, but I don't," he wrote.[23]
He could not understand that as basic a tactic as searching all houses, in an
honor culture with strict codes of male-female interaction, might be viewed
as defilement. So he could not see how it might be perceived as calling for a
violent response to recover family honor. No adjustment could be made to
the war he was actually in. Many targets were legitimate. But he never saw
the other ones, or the shared humanity of those destined to die at the end
of his scope. He simply pulled the trigger and moved on. Unlike many veterans of Iraq, he voiced no bitterness or sense of betrayal by those who had
sent him out to kill in a war of dubious causation. He expressed sentimental
nationalism and conventional religious chauvinism. He had the moral self-
awareness of a teenage video-gamer who thinks killing is inconsequential
beyond the fun of the shot and competition with other gamers. Contrast
his savage swagger with a female Red Army sniper after she killed her first
German invader: "I fired. Then I immediately regretted what I had done,
and I started to cry."[24] Her reaction was not weakness. It revealed her humanity. Kyle was guided only by an oversimplified honor code with little
honor, that did not admit shared humanity or consider real-world nuance
and mercy. There is a huge difference between experiencing war and understanding war. Kyle was the war's top killer but really did not know or understand war at all. He was shot dead in 2013 by a fellow Iraq veteran whom he
took to a gun range in Texas as a form of PTSD stress alleviation.

What about on the steep valley sides and teeming cities on the other
side of Chris Kyle's wars, the ones which snipers like him actually proved
incapable of winning in the end? Children were told to admire a different
kind of war hero from a distinctive and much older culture. Disdaining the
standard Western terminology of "suicide bomber" for the clearly euphe-
mistic but also internally and culturally ennobling "sacred explosion," dead
al-Qaeda were renowned and celebrated not solely for being war heroes but
as religious martyrs. Recruiting into soi-disant martyr units soared, drawing
on Islamic legends incorporating local tales that for centuries had morally
and psychologically skewed children in wilder parts of the Greater Middle
East. They were not basically dissimilar to war hero tales told near everywhere else or Kyle's embrace of a crusader myth and identity learned from

films and story books. One analyst explained it this way: "Osama bin Laden reawakened the mythic past, allowing potential recruits to imagine themselves wielding swords and riding stallions to glorious death."[25] As usual, it was mostly lies that called for denial of mercy for the enemy or one's own misled and abused children.

In immiserated, penniless, but ethnically homogeneous Gaza, families of children lured or coerced into suicide bombings keened private sorrows over their *Istishhadiyin* (child martyrs). The dead left behind videos, mainly showing deluded and confused children reading prepared texts. Then they were fêted in what to outsiders were macabre scenes of street dancing and tossed candies.[26] We must understand what is similar in the embrace of Chris Kyle and these death cult exhibitions that seem so alien. All sides heading into and coming out of war proclaim heroes real and imagined and teach war stories, both true and false, to their rising generation. We must accept this if we are to understand the power of stories about the best hero-killers, told by all sides, that obscure deeper truths to co-opt and deceive youth to fight in the next war. We need to hear and appreciate a different kind of hero story: tales about risking life and limb, full of courage, honor, and integrity but not killing.

Understanding war more fully means facing a more complex moral reality. We usually acknowledge that bravery exists on each side in every war. Less often will we admit that we are also likely to find examples of dishonor and crime on both sides. We say that honor belongs only to us, as does everyone we fight. In the brilliant satire *Catch-22*, Joseph Heller makes the point with sardonic wit: "What is a country? A country is a piece of land surrounded on all sides by boundaries, usually unnatural. Englishmen are dying for England, Americans are dying for America, Germans are dying for Germany, Russians are dying for Russia. There are now fifty or sixty countries fighting in this war. Surely so many countries can't all be worth dying for."[27] Because we want to appropriate claims to goodness entirely to our side we are puzzled by uncommon and uplifting behavior by some on the other side. This was especially true over the course of the 20th century, when *everyone* embraced the truly pernicious concept that "enemy civilians" might be justly targeted by heavy bombing campaigns or starvation blockades. To compensate for such brutal policies every war had to serve holy purposes, even as mercy was stripped from the bomb bays of opposing air forces before each mission flown over Warsaw or Dresden, Shanghai or Yokohama.

We are even more shocked to learn that the enemy does the very same: thinks of their cause as the only legitimate one and ours as damnable. We share more with that enemy in both directions than we are comfortable confessing, as seeking a different kind of hero story demonstrates. Beyond one-sided tales that narrowly celebrate our superiority at killing or sheer physical courage, we must seek stories about higher morality and merciful sensibilities. True tales about men and women who showed high moral courage regardless of their uniform are more uplifting and valuable than warmed-over lies or propaganda, which also fill too many histories. We need stories about those who placed themselves at grave risk to stop murders. We should praise *anyone* who intervened to stop rape or murder or atrocities, wearing whatever uniform chance or citizenship had put them in. We should honor those who disobeyed immoral "superior orders," who rejected conformity despite threats of retaliation. Yet, it is more often true that those courageous few are scorned and threatened by their own. Military authorities and governments find it too hard and too troublesome to recognize moral heroes in their own ranks during wartime. How can this be?

Because if intervention to stop an atrocity was necessary then somebody else who was fighting for us was complicit in it. More often, therefore, war stories about moral heroics by our own people are actively suppressed. We do not hear any praise from our top leaders about those who try to stop unwarranted killing, because to openly recognize their ethical valor will complicate the political or historical narrative that underwrites wider claims that justify the war. That is why the moral heroes who tried to stop the massacres at Mỹ Lai in 1968 did not receive any formal recognition of their righteousness for 30 years after fellow Americans in uniform had murdered an estimated 504 Vietnamese civilians, mostly women, babies, and toddlers. Helicopter pilot Hugh Thompson, his crew chief Glenn Andreotta, and gunner Lawrence Colburn landed their chopper between homicidal soldiers and Vietnamese civilians on March 16, 1968. Thompson actually warned the American infantry on the ground that if they tried to kill any more civilians he would open fire on them: "I figured, at that point, that was the only way the madness, or whatever you want to call it, could be stopped."[28]

In 1998 the U.S. Army awarded all three men the Soldier's Medal (one posthumously), citing them for "heroism not involving actual conflict with an enemy." It was a reluctant award, given long after the harsh truth of Mỹ Lai was repressed by U.S. government officials, including a president and his national security adviser. The medals came only after 30 silent years when these men's heroism went unacknowledged and their loyalty and personal reputations were sullied. They had some defenders in the press but others pilloried them. Their careers were blocked as some fellow officers called them traitors. They received death threats and dead animals were dumped at their doorsteps at night because they did the right thing that day in 1968, the only proper thing. Their moral valor thereby caused a problem for the whole U.S. war effort. Their merciful intervention transformed cliché images of the "enemy," some of whom were clearly victims. It exposed the way that the war in Vietnam was being fought as profoundly flawed. Yet, these genuine heroes of mercy were treated like criminals by some of their military peers and by elements of the public, while some actual war criminals were protected by government and fêted by society.

A shamed country took three decades to praise them, the same year they went back to Mỹ Lai to be honored by forgiving victims. Thompson was profoundly humbled by astonishing humanity he discovered among survivors he had saved: "One of the ladies that we had helped out that day came up to me and asked, 'Why didn't the people who committed these acts come back with you?' And I was just devastated. And then she finished her sentence: she said, 'So we could forgive them.' I'm not man enough to do that. I'm sorry. I wish I was, but I won't lie to anybody. I'm not that much of a man."[29] When he returned home, more death threats awaited.[30] He had testified at the trial that convicted Lieutenant William Calley in 1971 for his part in the massacres at Mỹ Lai, where babies were held close by their mothers in futile protection against *rat-at-tat* guns. Thousands demonstrated at so-called Calley rallies. Gallup reported that nearly 80 percent disapproved of his court-martial, though some likely did so wanting his superiors charged as well.[31] Calley was not pardoned but he was paroled years early. Overall, there was wide support for the convicted perpetrator yet slander, denunciation, and death threats against three men who stopped the murders.

Little has changed: the politics of war still overwhelm mercy for the helpless and block punishment of war criminals who wore revered national uniforms. In 2019 President Donald Trump pardoned a convicted soldier who spent five years in prison for murdering an Iraqi prisoner. To acclaim from his supporters, he pardoned three more soldiers accused of war crimes. He did so even as the United States and its NATO and European Union partners were accusing Syrian forces of extreme brutality and indiscriminate murders and other crimes against civilians.[32] Three years later, the pardons made it harder to credibly talk to non-Western audiences about international war crimes charges for Russians for what they did in Ukraine.

Much the same happens across eras and cultures. Sinhalese waged a religious-ethnic civil war in Sri Lanka, utilizing extreme suppression tactics against rebel Tamil. In 1983 Tamil murders of 13 Buddhist Sinhalese soldiers sparked a pogrom in which 3,000 Hindu Tamil were butchered. Guerrilla attacks began. In 1987 the first suicide bombing was carried out by the Tamil "Black Tigers." Massacres followed on either side in the 1990s, with the conflict moving past guerrilla fighting to siege warfare, naval blockade, air and artillery bombardment, and mass civilian casualties. In 2000, Staff Sergeant Sunil Ratnayake slit the throats of eight Tamil civilians, including three children, and then dumped their bodies into a nearby sewer. The facts were confirmed at his trial in 2015. Five years later, during local and global media distraction caused by the COVID pandemic, the president of Sri Lanka slipped a pardon for this war criminal past the medical panic.[33] In 2021, documentation of massacres and mass rapes by Ethiopian and Eritrean forces in a new war in Tigray led to morally compromised UN resolutions and to incoherence from Western outsiders.[34] Expectation of high-minded internationalism did not sustain responsible statecraft or even a small measure of accountability. In a pandemic panic, and given massive economic contraction, law gave way to chauvinism and bullying militarism behind the excuse of COVID lockdowns.

It is hard to admit that cruelty and mercy alike cut across the moral no-man's-land that separates us from the enemy. Doing so means accepting that there are likely some soldiers recruited in our hometowns and neighborhoods who are capable of atrocity. Yet, even a cursory reading of the history of war confirms that cruelty and transgression are indifferent to nationality or culture or any cherished uniform. Americans were deeply shocked to relearn this basic truth from their TV news in 1969. They should not have been. Still pictures showing dead babies from Mỹ Lai, covered up by investigators 18 months before, suddenly interrupted more anonymous, and therefore seemingly also more acceptable, images of U.S. carpet bombing of North Vietnam that was killing civilians on a far more massive scale than the infantry ever could.[35] General Curtis LeMay opined that the principle of carpet bombing was basic: "Kill people, and when you've killed enough they stop fighting."[36] In 1969 almost no one yet understood or regretted that Allied air forces *targeted* civilians in Germany and Japan in World War II, as opposed to causing collateral damage while trying to hit military targets. They watched on TV as a far greater tonnage fell on Indochina before and after Mỹ Lai. It was not in the country's interest to tarnish images of the "good war" against fascism where Americans had freed far-off nations, as they surely did, with ugly facts about desolation of designated "enemy cities." Keep the wars separate. Let every bombardier return as a hero to his hometown.

Most Americans who belatedly heard about Mỹ Lai in 1969 had already forgotten, or never learned about, older massacres of women and children committed closer to home by the U.S. Cavalry at lonely places like Sand Creek and Washita.[37] They more likely learned about how the Five Nations were forced onto the "Trail of Tears" by President Andrew Jackson, who ordered Chickasaw, Cherokee, Choctaw, Creek, and Seminole forcibly relocated to the Oklahoma Territory in what amounted to a death march. Fewer know even today about the awkward complication of Black slaves who were taken on that forced march by their First Nations owners and kept in bondage for several decades more.[38] Hardly anyone in 1969 recalled diseased concentration camps used to suppress Filipino resistance to American "liberation" in 1904, and other tactics used in the Pacific that originated in the American Civil War and Great Plains Wars. Or knew of massacres of Jolo Moro in a truly savage campaign of oppression disguised as a war of emancipation of their local slaves.[39] Schoolboy antics of Teddy Roosevelt in Cuba are in all the textbooks. Hardly anyone reads how, as one historian wrote, in the Philippines U.S. Army Colonel Frederick Funston ordered "prisoners shot, houses burned, and personally took part in the looting of churches."[40]

While no Vietnam War atrocity was more widely reported or is as roundly and deservedly condemned today as that perpetrated by U.S. soldiers at Mỹ Lai, the Army of South Vietnam (ARVN), the Việt Cong,[41] and the Army of North Vietnam (PAVN) all committed massacres in a savage war that ushered in multiple atrocities. Việt Cong considered heroes on the communist side made a practice of disemboweling or burying alive village chiefs who had refused to cooperate. A South Vietnamese journalist wrote 50 years later, "I make no excuses for . . . Mỹ Lai" but complained that the atrocity was seemingly invoked alone whenever the war was discussed. She asked, "Why not the mass graves of civilians in Huế during the Tết Offensive of 1968?" when communist troops took over the old imperial capital.[42] It was a bitter account by an exile deeply committed to a lost cause. For in truth, the mass murders in Huế, which exceeded by 10 times the victims at Mỹ Lai, were reported at the time and in most accounts of the Tết Offensive written since then.[43] None of that means we should submit to the facile assertion that all sides are equally guilty in war or shrug *à la guerre, comme à la guerre* (when at war, as at war). But we do need to accept that all wars are so ripe with red temptation that we should not be surprised what some killer heroes do in our name and uniforms. What may surprise is how often we encounter unreported mercy.

SAMUEL JOHNSON OBSERVED IN 1755 THAT "patriotism is the last refuge of a scoundrel."[44] Nearly 300 years later it still is. On site at the USS *Arizona*, President Trump said that he did not know what happened at Pearl Harbor until he visited the memorial. But he promised, "Our heroes will never be forgotten. Our youth will be taught to love America."[45] His presidential committee to rewrite the national history curriculum downplayed slavery and eliminated mention of mistreatment of Native Americans.[46] Such war cant by civilian leaders is nearly universal, though seldom as starkly rife with hypocrisy.[47] In states that control media and censor curricula, chauvinist myth-making and cultural-military indoctrination is standard. War stories about near superhuman heroes are piled atop lurid tales of enemy crimes in an earlier war, or warnings about the next one. They always teach that the enemy is so evil he wants to annihilate us, although we are innocent and righteous. We are devoid of malice, while their soldiers can seem to children to be evil incarnate. Like the devil, they always "have the best tunes."[48]

Beyond governments and nationalists who warp children with militant hatred because it is useful in politics, fear and definition of the historic enemy slips into childhood in bedtime stories and over family dinner tables and in school and places of worship.[49] Ethnic or religious or national heroes and enemies are named. Hatred is taught by parents and preachers, imams, rabbis, and schoolteachers, troubadours and nationalist historians. All uphold iconic heroes to admire and emulate, regardless of what they did or how merciless and brutal they were. Hate is taught also by poets who let their verses get in the way of their humanity. It is scrupulously handed down through the culture in tales of ancient atrocities by historic enemies. Even young children quickly learn who the tribal or racial or religious enemy is, know the astonishing evil of which they are capable, and may make innocent vows into their pillow to take up arms when it is their turn to fight. That is how I was taught to hate as a child, by family and the blinders of one-sided war hero stories.

I was born in Ireland but grew up 4,000 miles away in Western Canada. I was far removed from "The Troubles" of that island but could not quite escape them. I went to school with Ukrainians and Germans and French, Cree and Blackfoot. We were all taught bad history that uncritically avowed that all things British were higher. At home, I heard much darker things about that ancient enemy of the Irish. Centuries removed from Oliver Cromwell's conquest, I listened to lurid stories about babies tossed high to be caught on pikes and about terrible slaughters at Drogheda and Wexford.[50] The siege of Drogheda by a Parliamentary army lasted a week, ending in the execution of its Royalist garrison and a slaughter of uncertain numbers of Irish civilians. In my house, we heard in hushed tones about the Irish rebels but no one cared about the Royalists. I was baptized into confessional quarrels not my own: sacramental suffering of the Plantation of Ulster, land clearances, Penal Laws, hedgerow schools, the "Great Hunger" of the potato famine that drove so many into exile. My mother could make the "Croke Park massacre" of 1920 sound like the worst atrocity of the century. She never explained how it was provoked by "Bloody Sunday" killings by Michael Collins and his men carrying out what today would be called urban guerrilla or even terrorism. Or that he then fought for the Irish Free State when my family were all pro-IRA. His anti-British exploits were legend in my home while his civil war stance was not discussed. Nor was I asked to weep for 400 peaceful demonstrators killed around the well at Amritsar the year before, with another 1,000 wounded.[51] That was someone else's cause.

Instead, I marveled at martyr's poetry by Pádraig Pearce and at the purity of the Easter Rising. I memorized William Butler Yeats' *The Rose Tree* and his more ambivalent *Easter 1916.* I was excited to know that at age six my father waited outside Kilmainham Gaol to hear the firing squads carry out the first fateful executions. I did not learn until many years later that my father was waiting because my grandfather was a jailor for the British doing his job that grim day inside Kilmainham and throughout the War of Independence. I did not know that he favored the Free State side in the Irish Civil War. I was taught to thrill only to heroism by irreconcilable IRA men like Tom Barry and Dan Breen, whose unforgiving memoirs I read and re-read all those miles and several decades away.[52] Before I reached my first teen years I learned to hate all British soldiers. I cheered reported deaths of young lads from London or Liverpool who were trying to keep the sides apart in Belfast or Derry in the early 1970s. It took me almost to my 20s to reject and shake off all that taught hate and tribalism. Who were your heroes as a child? Who were *you* taught to hate? Maybe it was Germans or Russians, Japanese or Chinese or Viêt. Perhaps it was Hindus or Muslims or Arabs or Jews, or Americans. Have you recovered yet?

CHAPTER 3

KILLERS

It is forbidden to kill. Therefore all murderers are punished unless they kill
in large numbers and to the sound of trumpets.

—Voltaire, *Candide, ou l'Optimisme* (1759)

To everything there is a season: a time to mourn, a time to hate, a time of
war, and a time to kill.[1] In every culture, the best killers are upheld to inspire
emulation by novice fighters and admiration by civilians. War propaganda
works best if the great hero is also a foremost killer. The most acclaimed war
heroes were thus also the best killers in classical epics from ancient Greece
to Pharaonic Egypt, medieval India to Ming China and pre-Meiji Japan.
They dominated Persian and Roman histories, inspired the first Muslim
fighters as well as the Crusades. They appeared as warrior saints in medieval
tapestries and stained glass, slaying all enemies, heretics, and dragons. In
medieval Spain, for both Christians and Muslims the highest praise was re-
served for knights who could behead an enemy with a single sword stroke.[2]
A similarly idealized skill among samurai in premodern Japan encouraged
beheading by sword-wielding officers from the First Sino-Japanese War in
1895 through World War II. Today, killer-heroes populate sprawling fantasy novels, globally marketed television series and feature films, and mass
participant online games.

A reputation for killing prowess serves as a feared model to be imitated by ordinary soldiers. For civilians, it becomes vicarious virtue for those who John Milton said only stand and wait, on the will of war as much as the gods.[3] Hero stories about great killers raise morale, or the willingness to fight, in every prideful culture and each flagging nation. Their stories preempt the experience of the vast majority of ordinary soldiers who encounter war mostly as persistent dullness, punctuated by occasional flashes of horror and mortal terror. In all times and cultures, killing promiscuously is exalted. It then elevates a whole people's sense of martial prowess, engaging tribal or national or religious or other identity loyalty. In 20th-century wars this often meant sports reporting–style bragging about fighter pilot score cards, sniper kill totals, tank buster counts, and submarine captain sinkings and tonnages. When it is all over we commemorate those slain in war but we celebrate the slayers.

POLITICIANS WHO START WARS, AND OFFICERS who lead young men and women into combat, should recognize that not all soldiers are going to shoot only designated people. Some will be seduced by the electric violence and ethically anarchic act of killing. They may lose self-control, morally compromise themselves and their unit while undermining military reputation and the political mission. In 1993 Canadians were shocked by posed photographs showing the torture and murder of a Somali teenager by members of their elite and admired Airborne Regiment serving as peacekeepers and protectors of food convoys in a famine relief effort under United Nations auspices.[4] Documents were altered and a cover-up effected by senior command, until a public inquiry finally led to charges against nine paratroopers. Sharp criticism of senior officers led to severe cuts to the overall military budget and disbanding of the Airborne Regiment. The country remained largely ignorant of earlier war crimes by Canadian troops that took place during World War II and the Korean War. With regard to Afghanistan, reaction to the earlier Somalia scandal was upheld as an insulating boast that Canadians had resolved the problem, and now behaved better than other Western forces..[5] In any case, one will find similar examples of suppression of war crimes reporting in any armed force that is around long enough to have a history. British war correspondent and military historian Max Hastings makes this point succinctly and well, cautioning that we must continually "remind ourselves that the unique selling point of soldiers, even if tarted up in fancy dress uniforms and bearskins, is that they are trained killers."[6]

MANFRED VON RICHTHOFEN, THE "RED BARON" who flew a daringly all-red Fokker triplane, was the leading "air ace" on any side in the 1914–1918 world war. A former cavalry officer, he was the subject of intense publicity before he was killed at age 26, in April 1918. With 80 confirmed "kills," he was "ace-of-aces," top of the league table in long shoot-down contests recorded in daily tallies in the morning newspapers and keenly followed by millions. It should be noted that "kill" referred to bringing down a machine, not the man flying it. But that was just another way of hiding harsher truths. René Fonck led Allied aces with 75 kills for France, while Canadian flyer Billy Bishop was the top Commonwealth ace with 72. Late to the game, Eddie Rickenbacker led American aces with 26 kills. They were all skilled flyers and aerial combatants but they were not all moral heroes. When Richthofen shot down a plane behind his own lines he went by car to recover bits of it, sometimes picking around a dead flyer. He mounted these trophies like stag or boar heads in his quarters. Even so, a century after his death his killing talent is still recalled in movies and video games and on enthusiast web sites. The sports response to air war happened again during World War II, a total war that saw off hundreds of thousands of air crew and over a million civilians crushed or burned by falling bombs.[7] None of that dissuaded editors or eager publics from thrilling to competitive sports tables once again published in their hometown newspapers. *Luftwaffe* ace Erich Hartmann was credited with downing 345 Red Army Air Force (VVS) planes and another seven American aircraft. Like other German ace numbers, his were inflated by older, ill-equipped, and substandard Soviet aircraft met early in the war. On the other side, Soviet air aces were led by Alexander Ivanovich Pokryshkin, who scored 65 Axis planes and was thrice awarded the top citation of "Hero of the Soviet Union."

Germans tracked U-boat captains like Günther Prien of *U-47*, hero of a Scapa Flow night attack on October 14, 1939, that sank the battleship HMS *Royal Oak* while at anchor. That was a major warship and a target worthy of celebration. But they also cheered U-boat aces waging the tonnage war against merchant ships and flocked to see Josef Goebbels' propaganda movies like *U-Boote westwärts!* (1941). They did so while the U-boat fleet lost three of every four submariners who went on war patrols. Postwar U-boat movies were similarly heroic, downplaying Nazism among submariners, never mentioning that mass starvation was the goal U-boats were built to achieve. From the early revisionism of *U-47: Kapitänleutnant Prien* (1958) to *Das Boot* (1981), tonnage aces and crews were portrayed as ordinary men waging an honorable war, or even as secretly anti-Nazi.[8] In a different ocean, American submarine captains pursued a ruthless interdiction campaign around Japan. As detailed below, while some U.S. Navy captains wanted to refuse orders they saw as immoral, others capriciously murdered civilian fishermen or merchant mariners floundering in the water. Exploits of the most ruthless skipper were celebrated while his war crimes and atrocities were hidden or approved.

In 1920, Ernst Jünger beguiled Germans with a near mystical approval of the *Weltkrieg* laced through his war memoir. He was oft wounded but manfully proud of his killing record and warrior ethos, in ways that helped clear the way for a second world war.[9] A generation later, Waffen-SS special forces colonel Otto Skorzeny was greatly admired by Germans, including Hitler. He carried out spectacular special operations, notably rescuing Benito Mussolini from captivity atop a cable car system in the Alps.[10] After the war he escaped from an internment camp, fleeing to Spain and thence to Egypt. He helped other war criminals evade justice and recruited Waffen-SS and Wehrmacht officers to train the Egyptian Army.[11] It then used poison gas in a four-year campaign in Yemen starting in 1963.[12] None of that prevented Skorzeny being fêted in Ireland or living the good life in Madrid for many years afterward. Similarly, Kurt Student was a fighter ace in World War I. In Hitler's war, he commanded elite *Fallschirmjäger* (paratroopers), notably in the invasion of Crete. He was tried and convicted in 1947 of murder of Allied prisoners there, although his reprisal massacres of civilians remained uncharged. Student was released years early, in 1948. He was an exceptional killer who lived out his last 30 years as an admired war hero, and not just in Germany.

On the other side of the Eastern Front, Vasily Zaitsev and Red Army snipers were raised to epic hero status in the Soviet press. Praised for their superior kill totals, they were renowned even decades later in novels and films, including outside Russia.[13] In 2022 a female Russian sniper with 40 kills in Donbas since 2014 was captured after being wounded and abandoned, according to Ukrainian military intelligence. Irina Starikova had used the alias "Bagira" (or "Bagheera"), taken from the black panther in Rudyard Kipling's *The Jungle Book* (1894). That same month, a Ukrainian sniper called "Charcoal" was hailed as the latest "Lady Death," knowingly echoing the famous moniker of the Red Army sniper Lyudmila Pavlichenko, officially credited with 309 kills during World War II. She had fought mainly in Odesa and Sevastopol before being wounded in the face, then was sent abroad to raise support for the Soviet war effort in Allied countries. She briefly met FDR and was celebrated in song by Woodie Guthrie.[14] "Charcoal" trained with Ukrainian marines in 2017 and fought pro-Russian rebels in Donbas, opposite from "Bagira." She left the military in January 2022, but a month later returned to kill more Russians. From behind a mask, she told a British reporter, "We must take them all out. . . . These people are not human beings. Even the fascists were not as vile as these orcs," she added, using a term for mythical, utterly wicked minions of destruction portrayed in *Lord of the Rings*.[15]

———

THE MỸ LAI MASSACRE WAS NOT an isolated event in Vietnam. Over a seven-month span in 1967 a string of atrocities were carried out by a sub-unit of the U.S. Army's renowned 101st Airborne Division, known to most Americans today from its role in the D-Day invasion of World War II, not for war crimes in Vietnam.[16] An elite, all-volunteer, 45-man "Tiger Force" drawn from the 101st, or "Screaming Eagles," tortured prisoners with electric shocks from field telephones, raped and murdered a 13-year-old girl, mutilated enemy dead, killed unarmed civilians and then planted weapons on the bodies. A U.S. Army investigation that lasted four years concluded that 18 soldiers had committed crimes from rape to murder to torture and gross dereliction of military duty. Yet, not one perpetrator was charged or prosecuted. Three were permitted to remain on active duty. Six were encouraged to resign but were allowed to do so before the criminal probe ended, thereby avoiding prosecution and attendant bad publicity for the U.S. Army or the war effort.[17] This episode was one of over 200 formal war crimes investigations carried out, almost all in secret. Names, careers, and the overall reputation of the military were protected, while victims were denied justice or compensation. Only a few of these atrocities became well known at the time: Mỹ Lai, a murderous raid on the hamlet Thang Phong, and a massacre of civilians at Son Thang that is sometimes referred to as the "Marines' Mỹ Lai."[18]

Illicit killings were carried out again and covered up by Western forces in Iraq and Afghanistan. On a smaller scale, but of a kind with Vietnam-era atrocities, was the "Kill Team" scandal wherein a small group of U.S. soldiers hunted down Afghan civilians, then posed for photographs with their bodies as if they were big game trophies bagged in Maine or Colorado. The photos were published in Germany by *Spiegel*, compelling U.S. Army leaders to admit the killings and issue a formal apology.[19] Like the few war crimes the public learned about contemporaneously in Vietnam, those that got past the censors and cover-ups, "Kill Team" murders were only the tip of a buried pyramid of atrocities in the Afghanistan War. A key factor in both Vietnam and the Greater Middle East wars was lack of command accountability. Investigations were most often buried with the dead, mainly to avoid repercussions at the command level and any public shaming of coalition forces. It is a common pattern in all war, even with otherwise law-abiding and respectable armies, to protect illegal killing by one's own side while trumpeting any war crimes by the enemy. Sometimes the latter are invented from whole cloth, as the Russian Army and propaganda apparatus did in Ukraine well before actual war crimes by some Ukrainian troops took place.

ON A TENEBROUS NIGHT IN AFGHANISTAN in 2004, a U.S. Army officer sat on a ridge staring north. He was talking casually to a NCO who had arrived from Fallujah after the opening battle of the Iraq War, just when the descent of that city into infamy began as U.S. and coalition forces crushed resistance both out of sight and outside the rule of law.[20] The normal banter of soldiers gave way to worry. The officer recalled years later that the NCO "began to confess war crimes to me." Along with several others, he "had shot innocent people and planted weapons to cover it up. They captured and drugged teenaged boys [and] crucified [them] to the hoods of their Humvees to deter attacks." They spreadeagled the boys with ropes and other bindings. It was not lethal crucifixion but it was cruel and criminal all the same. A platoon leader had lined up 40 Iraqis and threatened to murder them all. Then his general arrived in haste and asked, "What the hell is going on?" The general was there because someone from the 82nd Airborne Division called in a report. But no one was ever investigated or held accountable. Russians pulling back from Kyiv's outskirts in 2022 similarly used children to shield their tanks from attack. ISIS routinely used civilians, including children, as human shields in Iraq and Syria, as did Somali fighters in Mogadishu in 1993.[21]

That officer told me years later that the confession "came blurting out in the dark, giving me enough space to halt him and claim that the confession was from an unknown soldier." He told the NCO, "I would have to report any further admissions as I was legally obligated to do. The only person who could not report them was the chaplain, whom I promptly called to assist." The officer met the deeply troubled NCO a few years later, just "as he was out-processing the Army for mental-health issues, all of which I would bet my life originated with the immoral actions he witnessed, and partook of, in Fallujah." His overall conclusion from this episode and others that he witnessed, while serving in one of the more law-bound armies of modern times, was that horrors and crimes are "Buried. Ignored. Unrecorded." And worse, they must be "borne by otherwise good men in silence."[22] He did not say it when I conversed with him but it was obvious that he, too, fell into that category. He carried a silent burden that weighed on him. He had returned to peace in New Hampshire, where he started a family. But even so he lived still, and likely evermore, inside a shroud of war.

The behavior this U.S. Army major described was almost certainly "moral harm" or "moral injury," the result of witnessing or participating in dread acts in war that is increasingly recognized in medical literature.[23] Officers and soldiers below senior command levels best understand the problems and importance of moral harm in the conduct of war. The same officer confided, "The effects of moral injury on soldiers, otherwise fine with the casual brutality of battle, are pronounced in our veterans today. There is appreciation of this in wider military circles but little discussion in [an active] military that is more comfortable returning to battle seeking contests."[24] Senior officers are aware of the strategic value of reputation and go far to keep reports of soldier misconduct out of the public eye. At a political level and in training, they express appreciation of the need for advanced military ethics, if only as a matter of good political and public relations. However, when tasked to grapple with this fraught problem in the field they are often less than sure how to proceed. Arguments about the bad strategic effects of poor tactics leading to merciless acts are too often swept aside. There is a real seductive simplicity, and career advantage, to winning battles even if each firefight stands alone, unconnected to a larger war-winning strategy. And that assumes tactical and operational success is actually tied to a coherent strategy, which is far less often the case than most outsiders or even soldiers realize. Local combat, taking and losing lives, and attendant destruction thus fails again and again to achieve strategic ends. This is especially true in modern fights against asymmetric enemies who will not play the game by conventional tactical rules. Who instead hunker down to endure what suffering they must, inflict whatever damage they can, and ultimately outlast a militarily superior but strategically and politically inept enemy force. Left behind on both sides are all those physically and morally harmed, their grieving families, and damaged or even broken societies.[25]

Returning repeatedly to fight in Afghanistan over more than a decade, a U.S. Army major witnessed operations that gave no serious thought to how the war was being fought, or to its inept cruelty: "We were led by a group . . . who wanted nothing more than to fly around in helicopters and . . . kill whatever was there." He was morally and tactically disgusted: "There was no pretense to honor. There was no strategy. It was pointless."[26] Few superiors considered how bad ethics in the conduct of war fighting might undercut a strategy of winning over the Afghan population.

They just did not see that the ways they were winning engagements and running up the score of dead Taliban fighters would lose the war in the end, in spite of overwhelming material superiority. It was the Vietnam fallacy of winning by body count all over again, without regard for moral, political, and cultural effects that undermined the whole military project. Decent people who thought the war could bring betterment to Afghanistan felt trapped. They did not want to kill indiscriminately, with total disregard for how a war for hearts and minds could actually be won, or lost. They were confined by force structures and operations practices put in place by theorists and senior leaders steeped in an all-out battle-seeking culture that had developed over decades. They were inhibited and frustrated by immoral and counterproductive actions of bad actors among the Afghan allies they fought alongside, as detailed below. They also had to deal with bad actors who wore the same uniform they did.[27]

The major lost a man at least indirectly because of dereliction by his superiors, who then covered it up and even came after him with charges to suppress his testimony. He pursued the matter courageously, at permanent cost to his career and extensive cost to his mental health. He was "trying to do the right thing" by his men out on patrol, but served under a set of senior officers "willing to turn a blind eye" to negligence and incompetence leading to needless casualties. They even ignored and covered up rape by a U.S. brigadier general who was "in charge of all logistics. . . . There was no one at the helm."[28] One day the officer's unit began to run out of Counter-IED gear, after repeated requests to his HQ for resupply. He ordered a patrol to gather spare equipment from base. En route it struck an IED. It "would have been harmless if we had had the equipment we were going to get." A 19-year-old Ranger was trapped in the burning vehicle. "Our efforts to retrieve him floundered as grenades and missiles began to cook off in the extreme heat until eventually, he fell silent." Holding to the code of not leaving behind any fallen comrade, he "set up security around the burning vehicle and waited for the flames to die down." The Taliban unit that set the IED trap, "seeing what was happening, out of decency or self-preservation I cannot say, left us alone."[29] It was a scene of horror seldom put on the internet, let alone on a cable news TV screen. Blue dot censors.

A teenager was immolated, one of many on both sides. His commanding officer recalled a decade later, "I can still remember the smell of burning flesh." He kept himself under control, but "the horrified guys around me cracked. Many wept openly. Many stared in abject horror." But someone had to retrieve the body before the Taliban changed their mind and reopened fire. "Only telling those horrified young men that [he] was one of us, that no one but those who loved him should recover him, got a few of us into the vehicle to recover his remains." They waited for a helicopter to take away what was left of him, the first leg of a journey back to his family. Back at base camp, a caring officer could no longer hold it in: "I got five minutes alone after that patrol to cry my eyes out, put my helmet on and head back out onto another mandated patrol through the same fields laden with IEDs."[30] There was trauma in his words.

The commanders who left his field unit without enough proper protective gear "lied about everything. They falsified everything, including the death report to [the young Ranger's] family." His angry conclusion: "Atrocity, hubris, and pointless killing went on because it was deemed less desirable to relieve the commanders engaged in this misconduct. [That was] too embarrassing."[31] It took the officer years to recover enough to be able to tell that story without breaking down as he retraumatized over it. Most men who were there that day still cannot speak of it. It led the officer to a career decision to move into military justice reform, especially as he and others who reported command negligence were investigated in direct retaliation. The same endemic, structural command failure was also reported by an official Fort Hood abuse investigation.[32] It happened in other Western militaries in Afghanistan as well. It is not just about military law or the pity of war, retold in new forms but around the same old themes. If command evasions are allowed we may expect less mercy and yet more crime by unbound killers in all future wars that will be undertaken in our name.

IRAQ DESCENDED INTO DARKNESS UNDER SADDAM Hussein, one of many authors of the old lie. He initiated four wars and was also a mass killer of his own people, including with poison gas. It was thus always going to be a long road back to approximate normality. Then Americans and others came with "shock and awe" bombing and another generation was lost to insurgency and murder and rage amidst the ruins. Before the F-18s and Apaches and Abrams tanks arrived, Brigadier General Salah was a brigade commander in the Iraqi Republican Guards. He had been a killer for Saddam in the Iran-Iraq War and the invasion of Kuwait, thus a top public enemy for U.S. smart bomb targeters in 2003. Actually, Salah was more decent than his appearance on the coalition target list suggested. A favorite tactic while carrying out orders from Saddam was to use his reputation for ruthless punishment to tell would-be rebels what would result if they continued disobedience. Then he offered an alternative to defuse tensions. It helped keep Iraq whole even as no-fly zones and sanctions and Saddam all remained in place. In a war-torn and impoverished country where trust came at a premium and all senior leaders planted spies in other commands, family was the only safe bet as inner circle, to let him get away with shading his orders from Saddam. Thus, his main subordinates in the brigade were sons, brothers, cousins, uncles, and a few friends.

During the "shock and awe" U.S. bombing that launched yet another Iraq war in 2003, Salah's barracks were among the first targets U.S. forces struck, killing more than a dozen of his family members. One officer who met him soon after recalled, "He was crushed and turned his back on everything."[33] As Iraq fell into chaos Salah did nothing, sunk in despair in his home. Another Iraqi general urgently asking for his help personally drew him out by telling Salah that his country was desperate in its need for decent men and that, as a decent man, it was his duty to serve.[34] It took a while for the point to settle as Salah recovered from the loss of his extended family. Then one day he put on his old uniform and went to watch the coalition make war. A U.S. Army officer recalled the day: "He showed up at HQ and was stone silent when he saw us working with Iraqi staff." He watched Americans and Iraqis go off to battle together and how they coordinated to provide water for parched policemen in the desert sun. "He watched how we treated Iraqi civilians, how we gave candy to children!"[35] Salah came back day after day to observe the work. "He watched us risk our own lives to save theirs, and the opposite. . . . He witnessed my profound sorrow at losing my Iraqi friend [name redacted], father of six, and 24 of his subordinates in a desert ambush."[36] Still, Salah said nothing.

But he took it all in, other men's personal losses piled on top of his own. Others who lost family found new family of a sort, in barracks life and in armed comradeship and their shared sacrifices. One day he pulled the young American officer aside and said in perfect English that "had we been anything less than decent, he would have spotted it." Then it all spilled out: "He shared the story of how we murdered his family as I stared on in shocked, horrified silence. He spared no details. His anger and sorrow were tangible." The officer still does not understand why Salah talked, confiding that he had forgiven "all of us who wore the uniform of those who murdered his family on false pretense." He said he would "help us build a better country because we were . . . good and honorable." It was extraordinary generosity of spirit and reconciliation by a man who spent his life at war and paid a high price for doing so. The American thought that he had never seen a more profound example of forgiveness. But more than that, his experience with Salah that followed persuaded him that ethics were incredibly important to winning counterinsurgency war. That what mattered was to seek out and deliberately empower decent leaders among local allies.[37]

It shows there may be another way to fight counterinsurgencies without dropping into the moral gutter with insurgents who respect few limits in their tactics or targeting practices. A U.S. officer had a varied experience working with Iraqi police leaders, one of whom took a much different approach than Saddam's old supporters. Lieutenant General Hussein Jassim Al-Awadi was "one of the bravest, and . . . most honorable men I have ever met." His post-2003 stewardship of the Iraqi National Police, pulling them back from endemic corruption and aimless murders under Saddam, established trust and correctness that was highly effective in doing police work essential first to winning the war then to securing the peace. "He started by firing every division, brigade, and battalion commander, created an Internal Affairs section to investigate all [their] replacements, then fired half the commanders again." Al-Awadi, said the officer, brought in ethics advisers from foreign police and militaries, and Italian Carabinieri to train his force beyond what anyone in Iraq had ever seen or the minister of the interior desired. Only then did he allow his police out to conduct operations. "Led by good men, honorable men who were expected to do honorable things, the result was incredible."[38]

National Police were the only ones to stand in Basra throughout an insurgent uprising. There followed similar successes in Baquba, Anbar, Mosul, and Baghdad. "In a year, we went from civil war to virtual peace. . . . People were absolutely desperate for 'decency.' Little old ladies who we had been instructed to treat with great reverence but to never initiate communication with, waltzed right up, pulled our sleeves and directed us to [insurgents] in hiding." What changed was the moral perception by the population of who the National Police were. "It was easy because we were decent. Iraqis [were] shorn of it, desperately craved it when they saw it . . . from Americans or Iraqi, Sunni or Shi'a, they did not care. They saw that we were good and acted accordingly." The National Police trained and restructured by Al-Awadi was one of only two security forces to survive the ISIS onslaught in Iraq a decade later, as other units ran. In the judgment of one U.S. officer who saw it all firsthand, it was mainly because "being decent was all that mattered there."[39]

IN COMBAT IN AFGHANISTAN, MOST COALITION soldiers did the right thing. Some were physically heroic in ways that are traditionally recognized by medals of valor and in the warrior narrative: to aid fellow soldiers they exposed themselves to Taliban fire or charged uphill into a blazing enemy position and somehow did not die. No one bothered to record thousands of quieter acts of moral bravery and deep compassion. Unlike physical courage, moral valor was less well recognized or rewarded. Combat command, after action reports, front-line journalism, phone uploads to social media, all tended to fit a warrior narrative favored by higher commands and watching publics. Breaking through from time to time, especially as support for the "forever wars" ebbed and the public and more journalists turned against the wars, were acts of special barbarity that fit a much different political narrative: morally corrupt soldiers were waging a brutal imperialist and strategically bankrupt war. We may dispute that analysis, which was as wide of the mark as its mirror image of a war noble in intention and pure in execution.

Barbarity in war commands headlines but not kindness. There were few press reports of U.S. Army soldiers treating badly injured Afghan children or dealing with illness in some village, although it happened frequently. On the other side, in principle the Taliban banned anyone from cooperating with coalition forces, even when their child was wounded or deathly ill. Despite such warnings from the Taliban, when a child was badly hurt by indirect fire from either side, or by a land mine or booby trap, parents invariably took that child to the nearest U.S. or coalition combat aid outpost. They knew that Americans and other coalition medical personnel would spare no expense to help. Taliban commanders were usually brutal in enforcing their writ of noncooperation with the enemy, unless they had struck some local deal that favored them. In this one area, however, they allowed villagers to contact the Americans and go to the aid stations to receive medical help for a hurt child. They did not actually carry out standing deterrent threats to retaliate against any family seeking coalition treatment. They let the matter pass.[40] There were many truly merciless fighters among the Taliban, some made that way by the war or their ideology or a lack of mercy on the other side. But not every Taliban commander was indecent.

Senior U.S. officers served two-year stints in Afghanistan. That limited tenure produced urgent pressure to differentiate among the most ambitious, competing for career promotions. This created a strong incentive to demonstrate one's warrior credentials by leading troops into combat, whether or not that served any strategic goal. One army officer I interviewed two years after he returned from nearly 20 years at war in Iraq and Afghanistan conceded that there were many senior officers who were "thoughtful, cautious, intelligent, and honorable." Too often, however, there "were those who had us walking around minefields in Afghanistan, conducting pointless attacks on villages and then returning them [the same as the battle for hills in Vietnam], and who were wedded to the idea of battle seeking when it was demonstrably counterproductive."[41] Two active-duty attack helicopter pilots on academic leave in 2010 similarly lamented a culture and warrior-first mentality that led to counterproductive combat surges by each new replacement brigade commander. They hoped that limited success might be achieved but thought that would take perhaps 30 more years of engagement. NATO was out of Afghanistan in 10. A fourth officer who served in U.S. Army military intelligence recalled to me much the same.[42]

Seduced up the same valley to kill Taliban as one's predecessor had, or scouring the desert for Iraqi guerrillas, new arrivals to what seemed to be forever wars succumbed to the allure of battle of an entrenched culture that emphasized destruction of enemy forces. They thought their only job was to fight all-out, that seeking and killing the enemy was a war-winning strategy, even the only one. Some yearned for action out of vanity: a career-enabling combat badge. After scorching helo raids or bloody ground missions, in the wake of rolling death up mountain valleys and into arid towns, unbridled violence pushed fresh recruits into Taliban or Iraqi militias. Misapplied coalition firepower and collateral damage destroyed hope, elevating local resistance to foreigners. It was a constantly unfolding attritional waste, and a shared tragedy. One veteran who saw it happen out on patrols and then as a staff officer in brigade-level HQs in both places concluded, "We may have won the battle at Fallujah in Iraq or Marja in Afghanistan, but those victories did absolutely nothing to bring our enemies to heel." What worked better was "sitting down with tea during the Sunni Awakening." It was also much more effective to enter an Afghan village to talk than to fight. His patrols often met "an honorable mullah who was clearly Taliban," who stood in sharp contrast to a "corrupt district commander on our side." It made questions "about why we were fighting the mullah and his guys inevitable."[43]

Within special forces in particular, a cultural canyon divided those who prized correction of transgressions from an officer corps that cared most about reputations of commanders. This was not just true of Americans. In 2021 Britain settled 417 compensation claims for cruel and inhumane treatment, arbitrary detention and assault by British soldiers in Iraq, and another 13 in Afghanistan.[44] A year later, a BBC report learned that Special Air Services (SAS) "repeatedly killed detainees and unarmed men in suspicious circumstances" in Helmand province, and that the head of SAS at the time did not report the incidents to murder inquiries by the Royal Military Police. A single SAS commando may have murdered 54 Afghans inside one year. The murders were covered over with drop weapons, as successive SAS squads competed to exceed each other's kill counts.[45] In 2020

Australia formally apologized to Afghanistan after the Australian Defence Force (ADF) reported that 13 special forces soldiers had murdered 39 civilians or prisoners there. Some were active murderers, others accessories or just witnesses. More gave dishonest and dishonorable testimony under oath. An additional 19 ADF Special Air Service men faced prosecution for murder. SAS patrol commanders had been treated as "demigods" who required soldiers to shoot prisoners to achieve their first kill for the unit, a process they called "blooding" their troops. Weapons and radios that suggested links to the Taliban were planted on bodies, which were rearranged to make it seem as if they died in combat. Some killings were video-recorded, others photographed. Among the accused was one of Australia's most decorated soldiers, alleged to have ordered murders and threatened death against his own men.[46]

ADF General Angus Campbell attributed the breakdown of law, discipline, and basic decency and mercy to a "warrior culture" in the SAS that led to a "blood lust." He decried competition killings, describing the murders as "possibly the most disgraceful episode in Australia's military history." A spokesman for the Afghan government said the report left his people with "a sense of despair . . . and anger that foreign forces can so easily get away with cold-blooded murder." He knew the facts allowed the Taliban to blame foreigners for the suffering of Afghan civilians "even though Taliban fighters are responsible for the deaths of over 100,000 civilians in the past decade."[47] Lack of mercy in the field led to political erosion, thence to total military collapse in 2021. Taliban were more numerous by then, and better armed and disciplined. More experienced at fighting, and far more capable of contesting for primacy in any renewed civil war than they had been 20 years before, when first swept out of the cities and up the vales. Lack of mercy helped lose a war that more merciful warriors might have wrangled to a compromise instead, in a negotiated settlement that might have come many years before the final collapse in 2021. Leaving mercy out of the basic concepts of counterinsurgency war undermined the whole project in Afghanistan, until it collapsed.

PART II

COMBAT

CHAPTER 4

PITY

My subject is war and the pity of war. The poetry is in the pity.

—Wilfred Owen, *Poems* (1920)

Europe's empires were smug before the Great War began in the late summer of 1914. Elites were convinced of the inevitability of progress, confident that their civilization was superior to all others and that science and enlightened rationalism would be victorious over barbarism. Europeans did not yet know that by mid-century, if not before, the "heart of darkness" would beat all along the Rhine, Danube, Volga, and Thames, more than it ever did down the Congo. In Joseph Conrad's *Heart of Darkness* (1899), Kurtz's moral injury and cry of "The horror, the horror!" predicted what was coming inside Europe.[1] Before the darkness fell, the most urgent table talk was of Robert Scott gone missing in the Antarctic, wonders of automobiles and flight, and the tragic loss of many hundreds on *Titanic* in 1912. It seemed impossible that so many could be lost at sea in just a few hours.

Two years later that many and more were lost in an hour or a day, every day, across 1,500 days of the Great War that began in August 1914. Ten million or more were dead by the end, with killing and dying and maiming right up to the last minute of the last hour of the last day on November 11, 1918. Not really stopping even then, as empires came apart, dynasties collapsed, and social orders broke down into chaos born of military defeat. It had all begun so grandly, with confident armies making sweeping advances during the first weeks, committing to all-out offensives that all failed, one after another. Then every army stopped. By November, impassible hedgerows of barbed wire marked the borders of hundreds of miles of shallow trenches. No army could pass the tangled wire or stay and hold on the other side if it ever did. By December, all Allied counterattacks were spent. Germans were exhausted too, but they were dug in on high ground and always on other peoples' lands. All was stalemate.

THE GRAND DELUSION THAT IT WOULD be storybook persisted as war broke out. The public everywhere, along with ordinary soldiers and nearly all the generals, believed that older tactics would still work. Some expected bold cavalry charges, ignoring that the glory days of decisive action by horse soldiers were long since past.[2] British only vaguely remembered their catastrophe in Crimea 60 years earlier, when an inept and futile charge of their light cavalry ended in abject slaughter, achieving little beyond infamy in verse: "Into the valley of Death rode the six hundred . . . Theirs not to make reply, theirs not to reason why, theirs but to do and die."[3] In the dense topography of Western Europe the armies went into a mass infantry war with outdated cavalry forces deployed in the manner of their great-great-grandfathers, as scouts and screens. The BEF was a small imperial army of 80,000 men at first deployment. It was more suited to the small Zulu Wars or the Boer Wars or other imperial policing than to an all-out fight with Imperial Germany, which fielded over 2,000,000 men. Yet the horse soldiers trotted ahead of the slogging infantry, oblivious.

Cavalry in each army carried modern weapons such as rifled carbines but they also wielded lances and sabers. Germans sported high plumes in crested helmets and brightly polished cuirasses, or breastplates, as did French cavalry farther down the front. At Mons on August 22, 1914, BEF dragoon scouts ran into a screen of cuirassiers riding in front of dense columns of advancing *Kaiserheer* infantry and horse-towed artillery. There followed an archaic argument of mounted men who behaved as if at war in 1814, not 1914. It was perhaps the last beau geste of chivalry, the honor code of the horse-borne warrior class. The dragoons advanced assuming they would make inexorable progress. The horsemen were under strict orders not to take prisoners because that would slow the advance. But they were told not to kill any Germans who surrendered because that would be ungentlemanly. They were ordered to search and strip prisoners of weapons, then just let them go.[4] It was a posture akin to catch-and-release in trout fishing more than to war, as it was in the past and would be yet again. It all changed the next day when infantry armies clashed bloodily at Mons, as did mass infantry all down the frontiers of France, in Serbia, Galicia, and East Prussia.

Yet, war must have its romance when so many inexperienced and unhardened romantics find themselves in it for the first time. Two weeks into the fighting, as the BEF's forced retirement in the face of *Kaiserheer* strength turned into a desperate retreat, an odd funeral for two British dead took place in the middle of a pell-mell battle. Germans dug a single shallow grave, placed the dead inside and covered them, making a small burial mound. Then cuirassiers formed a close honor guard alongside the grave, opposite disarmed British prisoners who stood lining the other side. Germans stood rigidly at attention, their officers with drawn and extended swords. A command was barked. Three rifle volleys *cracked!* in salute to their respected, departed enemies.[5] It was as if boys on either side had been only playing at war and someone got hurt by accident. Then they played at a funeral, showing a solemnity about the loss of individual enemy lives that would soon disappear on all sides. Ernst Jünger would write in 1920: "[T]rench fighting is the bloodiest, wildest, most brutal. . . . There's no mercy there, no going back."[6] But at first, kinder exchanges also took place on the Eastern Front in the first autumn of war, before the long winter of attrition and mass death and military frustration arrived for everyone.

Concert violinist Fritz Kreisler recalled a ceasefire between his Austrian Habsburg regiment and Russians that took place in early September 1914, after weeks of marching and missing any contact. When they finally met off the march, both sides halted and dug in. Seeing each other as individuals across an untilled field humanized everyone, encouraging unexpected gestures of restraint and oddball humor. Cautious friendliness followed, bonding opposing soldiers. All were at least minimally trained and ready to kill but now they briefly found the whole idea absurd. Contempt for the enemy was encouraged by all wartime governments. Humor pierced that. After enduring artillery fire and expecting infantry and Cossack attacks, Kreisler's regiment settled into its shallow trenches 500 yards from the Russians. That was almost within hailing distance. With the aid of field glasses, each side made out faces on the other side until they came to recognize individual features. They stayed put for four days, interacting only at a distance with shouts and waves. Then open fraternization began: "Russians would laughingly call over to us and the Austrians would answer. The salient feature of these three days . . . was the extraordinary lack of hatred."[7]

That would change as the war went long and total, as combat and weariness made veterans hardened to humanity. But for now a little local ceasefire broke out among reluctant civilians in uniform on both sides, provoked by comic antics of a particularly persistent Russian. "We knew nearly every member of the opposing trench, the favorite of my men being a giant red-bearded Russian whose constant pastime consisted in jumping like a jack-in-the-box." He would pop up and down in the Russian trench, "crying over to us as he did so. He was frequently shot at, but never hit." Perhaps that is why the big Russian grew bolder, "showing himself longer and longer until finally he jumped out of the trench altogether, shouting to us wildly and waving his cap."[8] What could Redbeard want, out from behind any cover, risking his life for a joke? Was he mad? No officers controlled either side's next reaction to this odd behavior.

A nimble Austrian jumped and waved back, as if accepting a dare from a bolder boy across a schoolground. All firing stopped as everyone looked on, "laughing like boys at play." Redbeard drew a step closer, "and our man boldly advanced too." Russians urged on their man. He made a sudden, large leap forward then stood still. The Austrian also jumped forward, then each man repeated the move: "And so, step-by-step, they approached until they nearly touched each other." Neither had taken his rifle, and every man in either trench held fire, watching the curious exhibition between the lines. "We thought that they were going to indulge in a fist fight," Kreisler recalled, "all of us being sorry for our champion, for he was a small and insignificant-looking man." The bigger man held out a package of tobacco. The Austrian reached into his pocket and with an air of quiet triumph "produced a long Austrian cigar."[9] The simple humor of it all precluded precautions against a possible *ruse de guerre*. Almost without thinking, behavior reverted to civilian patterns as the humanity and individuality of a singular man and moment displaced rote and implanted violent responses at the sight of an exposed enemy. Humanity trumped the war, for a short time.

Kreisler recalled, "We were surprised to find ourselves out of the shelter of our trenches and fully exposed to the Russians, who in turn leaned out of their own trenches and showed their heads in full. This unofficial truce lasted about twenty minutes." Whether or not it mattered or could change anything about their situation or the war, which told them to kill each other no matter what they thought, it was a welcome respite at the least, and perhaps a little more. Fighting resumed "with all its earnest fierceness, but from this moment on a certain camaraderie was established." Between episodes of firing "an unofficial truce would frequently be called for the purpose of removing the wounded." Whenever "stretcher-bearers were busy, no shot would be fired on either side."[10]

One must pause to fully appreciate how truly odd that was, though also a frequent occurrence. Two groups of heavily armed men tried to kill and maim each other and sometimes succeeded. Then they all held fire while the wounded were collected from the no-man's-land that lay between them. Then they again tried to kill and wound men on the other side. Two deeply conflicted impulses competed for the same territory across a moral no-man's-land as well as the physical barrier that lay between: self-preservation and compassion. The first was brought on by the onset of war and hard orders to pick up a rifle, march toward the enemy, and defend the Fatherland. The second lingered from old habits and more natural, merciful instincts. Then everyone waited to see how long a return to normal decency lasted as the shells started to fly once more.

OPPOSING INFANTRY BY THE MILLIONS FOUGHT all-out from August to November 1914. Men and horses died in unprecedented numbers across

Belgium and in evergreen forests astride the river frontiers marking off France from Germany. More died along the Meuse, at the Marne, across the Aisne and the Somme. More on the Eastern Front. More fell into first snow in the high mountains of Serbia and Galicia. More to come across the Ottoman provinces, in Italy and Africa, at sea and under it and in the air. And so the war plans all came apart. And so began descent into old barbarisms known in the ancient world and new barbarisms invented in the 20th century. Elaborate pauses, military burials, chivalric practices, and comic antics did not survive for long. Not in a total war where salutes and swords and honor volleys were put aside as casualties exceeded 1,000,000 in just the first five months. Not when endless artillery barrages churned dead and living men alike inside stewpot craters. Where a man who fell to enemy fire in no-man's-land on a trench raid was left there unburied, to be fed on by fearless corpse rats, his rot adding to the persistent stench of front-line putrefaction.

War was a lot louder. Marvelous new machines roared with internal combustion, belched high-explosive ordnance, clanked and crashed and blew apart. At the fronts, there was a near permanent shellfire that drove some barking mad as death fell with parabolic screeching from the sky. Perhaps screaming, shrieking terror shells were the model for J. R. R. Tolkien's wailing Ringwraiths, who also drove men to mad panic: he served on the Somme in 1916. Tens of millions of cased explosives hurtled up in parabolas from unseen miles away, sometimes over days and nights or even weeks. They preceded each offensive that went nowhere, yet left hordes of dead behind. Killing was mostly by shelling but there was machine gun fire mad as a box of frogs, fighting hand-to-hand with rail spikes, trench knives, spades and fists, grenades and flamethrowers. There was poison gas released from pipes and canisters, later sent flying overhead by bomb and shell. War was waged against animals, too: men shot horses, clubbed corpse rats made fearless by too much easy food, burned fat lice inside their crummy uniforms. The only silence was that of muted men, their words stolen away by trauma. Others split the darkness with screams, trapped inside night terrors.

Instead of knightly gestures, soon stretcher-bearers were fired on by all sides. Maybe from a sudden rage or in reprisal because somebody heard a rumor about the enemy shooting at *our* medics. Spiraling decline into indecency was quick and extensive. Rumors and propaganda made things worse. Germans accused British of using expanding or "dum-dum" bullets, invented in India in the 19th century but banned in the 1899 Hague Convention, and of gouging out eyes of wounded Germans. British troops resented the standard *Kaiserheer* sawtooth knife which stayed in service into 1917 and was indeed a nasty weapon.[11] Little local atrocities multiplied on all sides, on all the fronts. Men were morally as well as physically fatigued by the time the first trenches appeared a month before Christmas. British troops had endured a fifth or sixth or tenth week of marching and fighting that ended with yet another bloodbath at First Ypres. French, Germans, Russians, and Austrians were all exhausted by the time winter arrived. Barbed wire was uncrossable. It grew in long hedgerows for hundreds of miles.

Waiting ahead by 1916: flamethrowers and lethal gas; tanks and terror bombing and shelling of cities; food blockades at sea; death on the wing and under water. And harder governments everywhere responding to demands to justify initial bloodletting by promising total war that would spill even more. Newspaper casualty listings appalled every warring society and each waiting family, whether their son's name was on the fresh list or not. Still, conscripts were called up who looked younger every year. Still, women went out to work herds and farmland to feed all the armies. Some also went to factory floors to make bullets and bombs and hundreds of millions of shells, poison gas, and high explosives used to kill each others' husbands, brothers, and sons: 700,000 worked in German factories, 950,000 in Britain, more in France and Italy and Russia. They were known as *munitionettes* in France. In Britain, the unkind quipped they looked like "canary girls," after overexposure to nitric acid in the TNT they handled turned skin a bright yellow. They made so many tens of millions of steel shells to thud down on both sides of no-man's-land that duds buried in French soil today will take seven more centuries to rust away and threaten the living no more. Over a century after the artillery fired in anger, curious children playing with unexploded shells turned over by a plough or exposed by rain still lose a hand or life.

Survivors are recorded as "war casualties" and paid a pension in euros that is based on the 1914 soldier rate.

Trenches were in essence long, connected fortifications. They were new to the practice of siege warfare mainly in terms of their exceptional length, depth of defense, size of armies, and extent of national and imperial commitment needed to hold them. Or to try to break through, in repeated efforts to re-create attackable flanks. They were not uniform. They bent and crinkled, zigged and zagged up hills and along ridges, through forests and across flat plains. They avoided towns but built natural barriers such as small rivers and canals into defense-in-depth systems wherever possible. They even went down inside large, interconnected caverns where barbed wire divided perpetually dark little no-man's-lands, forcing men to fight among blind snakes and sudden bats and a multitude of crawling troglofauna. Fighting from trenches presented opportunities for different moral behaviors than was possible in the opening battles of encounter or in later massive offensives. Boredom from daily inaction on long sections of front meant that both sides indulged a growing lassitude about the war, its causes and commitments, their physical nearness to the enemy and his supposed irredeemable aggression and wickedness. Trench living was so hard it induced a "live and let live" attitude when higher-ranking or just attack-enthusiastic officers were not around to order shelling or sniping, night patrols and prisoner raids. That led to odd episodes of observation and contact, as well as to daily practices of indifference to active fighting in "quiet sectors" and long stretches of front in the south of France, where warring sides were a mile or so apart, unlike the 80 to 100 yards of no-man's-land in Flanders.

IT WAS A COMMON PRACTICE IN some sectors to exchange artillery poundings that pleased rear-area HQs but were purposely ritualized in time and duration: everybody knew when and how long to take cover. Suspending artillery fire, the greatest killer in industrial war, or tacit agreement to overshoot opened up other actions that rose closer to fraternization. These ranged from shouted greetings and distant nighttime conversations to suspending patrols and all shooting, to bartering goods or encouraging desertion. In "active sectors" where topography pushed the frontline trenches closer, similar practices developed during months-long respites between the major battles, only to break down when a new attack order launched men back into active hostility and mad minutes of shooting and killing. Large raids and smaller patrols again went over-the-top. The shells fell in "walking" steel curtains and exploding sheets of mayhem. As the war overall settled into grinding attrition, whether or not mercy reached out often came down not to any preconceived culture or formal legal code but to individual encounters. Did *this* wounded man live or did an enemy with advantage finish him off in the heat of combat or maybe after, in cold blood? It became a roulette spin of chance meetings in battle, with casino odds favoring killing but sometimes stopping short when someone decided not to pull the trigger or chose not to plunge a steel bayonet into an exposed gut.

BEF Private Percy Clare chose mercy. Others in his regiment did not. Making an advance across no-man's-land, he moved under cover of a creeping barrage that left behind fields of saucer craters that French troops called *marmites*, or "cooking pots." Clare's unit overran a section of German first-line trench one day. "I found two stricken Huns very badly wounded from our shellfire." From their resemblance to each other and age difference he judged them to be father and son. They lay together with hands clasped tight. "Deep compassion for them took possession of me." Orders to dragoons at Mons to catch-and-release prisoners unharmed were long since buried in the Flanders mud. Clare's commanding officer instead warned his regiment the night before the attack was made that they must "show no mercy" to any Germans they met on the other side.

Yet, Clare lingered. He hoped that the stretcher-bearers would come to save this badly wounded duo. "One or two of our fellows passing by raised their bayonets as if to thrust them through, when their cries were truly piteous. Plenty of men could be found who never bayonetted any but wounded Germans, and I stood for a few moments restraining any who in the lust of killing, and having in mind our C.O.'s lecture, might thrust them through." Clare did not trust his countrymen: one or more of them might commit murder in the moral blindness of combat, or because they were trained and conditioned to obey a superior's orders. He wanted mercy for the two wounded Germans but he knew that it was unlikely: "Poor fellows, they were doomed. I had to go forward." He learned later that a soldier in the second or "mop-up" attack wave just behind his had stopped to stab the pair with his bayonet, "not even troubling to see that he had really put an end to their miseries."[12]

SOLDIERS KNEW THAT THEIR WAR WAS not at all like adventure tales from Charlotte Yonge's *Book of Golden Deeds*, a widely read Victorian anthology.[13] Nor like Stephen Crane's *Red Badge of Courage*, or a 1903 anthology written to lure boys to war, *Deeds of Daring by the American Soldier*.[14] They sneered at what the governments said about vital sacrifice, in propaganda that reads today as if it was written in a central place then translated into the babel of languages of the belligerents. For the majority, those nameless ones recorded in official histories only as part of drear casualty statistics that none of us can really comprehend, the war was not about heroic or tragic poses struck in verse or painted in pastels or trapped in bitter prose of a postwar memoir. They knew better as soon as they got their first taste of combat. They may not have thought things out in a poet's refined words. Yet, most men realized quickly that they were not inside a tale from gloried war stories they had read at school. The sourness is especially striking in accounts by French soldiers, including *guerre imaginaire* (imaginary war) novelist Émile Driant, who was killed at Verdun.[15] It saturates notebooks kept by a barrel maker from Languedoc, Corporal Louis Barthas. He fought from August 1914 to the very end in November 1918. But already by 1915 he concluded that the war was class martyrdom, a national nightmare, and a kind of death slavery for ordinary men.[16]

A battered but determined *Armée Française* stood behind the wire to defend most of the length of 440 miles of trenches that held back the Germans on the Western Front. More hundreds of miles of trenches stalemated the Alpine, Southern, and Eastern Fronts, as Germans built ultimate defeat into the deep structure of their war plan and operations. It is a wonder that it took four years for it all to fall apart. The reason was that the Allies did not yet know how to win.[17] Behind the complex lines in the west were 25,000 more miles of supply and communications trenches, a defense-in-depth on each side of a sinuous and deadly no-man's-land. Barthas spent most of the war in the trenches. In 1915 and 1916 he was also in three of the goriest fights of the whole war: Champagne, Verdun, and the Somme. Afterward, he turned his notebooks into a memoir that equals any personal record from any war, although it was not published until a quarter-century after he died in 1952.[18] In unvarnished prose, his notebooks document evolution of sentiment among the *poilus*, the "hairy ones" who bore the brunt of sacrifice and suffering for France, as they arced into apathy and anger.[19]

Like others, Barthas started out full of naïve élan and a sense of justified vengeance for his violated nation. Then he progressed to bitter anger toward senior officers. Next, he moved to frank unwillingness to make what the *poilus* saw as senseless offensives or trench raids and stupid local attacks. France's army had grown distant from its officer corps by 1916.[20] Troops resented officers who repeatedly conducted bloody yet inept offensives, "nibbling" at enemy lines, forcing the *poilus* to endure chronic attrition.[21] Much the same was happening on the other side, more so if the Germans holding out over there were Saxons or Bavarians rather than stiffer Prussians. This shared sulkiness led to frequent fraternization and ultimately to military strikes in the Tsarist Army and parts of the Habsburg Army early in 1917, in some divisions of the *Armée Française* that April, and to a hidden military strike by German armies in 1918.[22] More and more, Barthas' daily encounters with Germans after 1916 reflected a complex mix of lethal skill on either side of the barbed wire, pragmatic lethargy about any attacks, and humane refusal to kill enemies against whom he held no personal grudge.

Scrupulous restraint was self-interested but also inspired by a rising sense of the stupidity and senselessness of the whole war. The shift in mood was tempered as well by growing anger toward rear-area "château generals" and civilians who kept the war going to no just end that Barthas could discern. His epiphany came in September 1915, while exploring a communications trench in his role as a frontline scout. Turning the corner between a zig and a zag he was surprised to stumble upon a sitting, wounded German "who gave me a terrified look. '*Kamerad, Kamerad*,' he stammered. . . . I gave him a couple of sips of peppermint schnapps, which comforted him both physically and mentally, because I think he was expecting a bayonet thrust instead of a helping hand." Stretcher-bearers said they would carry the wounded German to the rear only after all French wounded had been taken away. Before night fell, they kept their word. Days later, other men in Barthas' unit decided they had enough: they refused to attack when ordered. They all stayed quietly in their dugouts, as did the Germans opposite.[23] Undeclared, little local ceasefires like this were becoming commonplace for certain elements of the contending millions who grappled in the trenches.

Germans shared the quiet across from the French in ways that, except for the "Christmas Truce" of 1914, was more rare with the British or late-arriving Americans. Barthas recounts how he would make noise to alert Germans opposite where a French work party was. "They never fired a shot. This was reciprocal; we rarely fired at each other's work details."[24] Other acts of mutual restraint were forced by conditions soldiers did not control. For example, in late 1915 a heavy rain flooded the Neuville sector. That forced men on both sides of no-man's-land out of their trenches, to climb onto the parapets so as not to drown. Again, no one fired. Barthas' working-class and socialist politics clearly influenced his conclusions about what happened next and why. "Our common sufferings . . . melted the hatreds, nurtured sympathy between strangers and adversaries. . . . Frenchmen and Germans looked at each other, and saw that they were all men, no different from one another." Perhaps. But sharing wet misery and just not wanting to start a firefight while exposed on the parapet must have played a large part. "Hands reached out and grasped; we shared tobacco, a canteen of *jus* [trench coffee] or *pinard* [red wine]." His political sensibilities seem better fitted to another incident when a large German stood up to denounce the war then "smashed his rifle on a tree stump." Men broke into song, not *Stille Nacht* as they sang during the Christmas Truce of 1914 but the anthem of solidarity and brotherhood of the working man, the *Internationale*: "No more deluded by reaction, on tyrants only we'll make war. Soldiers too will take strike action, they'll break ranks and fight no more!"

Officers took a far dimmer view of rising fraternization at the front lines. Barthas believed that French guns were ordered to fire indiscriminately on any frontline assemblies. Probably not, but warnings were made that the penalty for leaving trenches without proper authorization was death. Then his regiment was disbanded and his division was sent to the rear to rest, refit, and reorganize.[25] In the Champagne sector in mid-1916, with battles at Verdun and the Somme also raging down the Western Front, Barthas recorded a rising incidence of open disobedience to officers who never led troops in any attack and did not appreciate them. "It was long ago that they had lost the esteem of their men. Now they had earned their scorn."[26] If the officers did not fight, why should the *poilus*? One night he was called to hasten up to the parapet. A lookout pointed to a German who was crouched just yards away. Barthas watched him in the mirror of a trench periscope. He was a tunneler who inadvertently broke through too close to the French parapet. He was rigid with fear. Barthas refused to hurl a grenade at the hapless man, writing that he would not betray his socialist principles by ever again shooting at a German "unless in legitimate self-defense." An honest as well as a merciful man, he quietly asked his notebook if his motivation might be less exalted than he wanted to believe: "Was it in our interest to break the neighborly relations which existed between our two adjoining outposts?"[27]

That is the kind of pragmatic, situational consideration that makes it impossible to say with any confidence that a moment of moderation or apparent mercy arose from moral idealism. It may instead have come from hardheaded reciprocity and self-interest. Barthas recognized this duality in all the little undeclared truces: "Some will consider this sublime, others will call it criminal. It depends on whether you place the ideal of Humanity above or below the ideal of Patriotism." He mused: "By whose pen will the next generation, struck with stupor, disconcerted by this universal sanguinary madness, learn about these acts of fraternity, which were like a protest, a revolt against the mortal fate which set, face to face, men who had no reason to hate each other?"[28] By his pen, although not for another 60 years. Not until after France and Germany and the whole world had suffered through an even worse war and graver barbarisms than poison gas and troglodyte dugouts. A century later and no one has done what he fervently wished for in the mud, writing in his notebook how he hoped one day a statue would go up near the Arras battlefield to recall brotherly feelings among men compelled to kill each other there, against their will.[29]

AMERICAN WAR HERO STORIES APPEARED IN newspapers as soon as the doughboys arrived in France, quickly spreading as well into the new medium of motion pictures. National press competed with local papers in relaying hero stories, including a vulgar publicity race to identify the first doughboy to shoot a German in France.[30] Most were about the usual derring-do editors and readers loved, during the brief yet also bloody foray of Americans on the Western Front. One story still defines warrior virtue for the U.S. Marine Corps. Diminutive 1st Sergeant Daniel Daly, a two-time Medal of Honor winner for prior actions in China and Haiti,[31] led an attack at Belleau Wood while shouting out, "Come on you sons-o'-bitches! Do you want to live forever?" He was awarded the Navy Cross for capturing a machine gun with only his pistol and grenades. He put out a fire at an ammo dump, then evacuated wounded men while under fire. Gunnery Sergeant Fred Stockham was posthumously awarded the Medal of Honor for giving his gas mask to a wounded man whose own mask was shot apart. While choking, the 37-year-old helped other gassed and wounded doughboys before he collapsed from inhaled poison, dying a hard death over the next several days.[32] There was rare physical and moral courage in his final choices and acts.

Most stories focused on American killing prowess and claims to coolness under fire.[33] Many were tall tales, the doughboy and his rifle in France replacing Paul Bunyan and his axe in the Red River country. Others were documented by eyewitness accounts. Alvin York would eventually emerge from the war as the archetypical American hero but he might have been challenged by John Lewis Barkley. An unusually proficient killer, Barkley was awarded the Medal of Honor for an isolated action on October 7, 1918, a month before the war ended. He was alone in a forward observation post overlooking the German line, which by then was not an unbroken set of deep trenches but an ad hoc defensive position thrown up by a beaten and rapidly retreating enemy. Barkley repaired a damaged machine gun and mounted it unsteadily in a broken-down French tank. Firing through a tear in the turret of the disabled tank, he beat off an attack by several hundred Germans, "killing and wounding a large number of the enemy." He remained alone in the Renault FT providing cover, peppered by return rifle and machine gun fire and by "potato masher" grenades tossed from nearby in fragmentary showers. He broke apart a second German infantry attack after a 77mm cannon firing from just a few hundred yards away hit the drive wheel of his disabled *Char Renault*.[34] He told no one what he did but others watched and reported it. General John Pershing pinned the Medal of Honor on him after the Armistice, overseas with occupation forces in the Rhineland. It was one of six medals Barkley received for valor, including from several Allied nations.

Serving in "Rock of the Marne"[35] or American Third Division, Barkley was a highly capable soldier who enjoyed fighting and often bragged about his prowess at killing. He knew how to inflict terrible damage on his enemy, moving out in hand-to-hand combat where the goal was to kill efficiently and quickly, or more usually, in his assigned roles in close reconnaissance and sniping. He wrote unabashedly after the war: "We shot a German in the head always if we could."[36] Roughhewn in speech and style, his 1930 memoir is closest in its vitalist spirit to Jünger's work. It is not at all like Graves' lingering sneer at war and its many lies,[37] or Remarque's moral and cultural lamentation disguised as a novel.[38] Barkley offered no apology for killing hundreds of men. In fact, the dust jacket of his memoir proudly proclaimed that he was one of those "who fight and like it."[39] He could suspend all empathy in order to kill, as a sniper must to survive or to fulfill an assigned mission. He went much further. Like an infantry imitator of Richthofen, he collected souvenirs from the bodies of Germans he killed, usually bits of uniform. He was also capable of mercy, as when he refused to kill a hapless enemy then turned his gun on his own squad to stop them from committing murder. That act of moral valor did not win him any medal. Perhaps it should have.

Late in the war, Barkley knew from prisoner interrogations that the Germans he would face in an attack across no-man's-land were from the 1920 class of call-ups. Mere boys, in other words. He had reason to be full of hate for them. He lost his battalion commander to a sniper a few days earlier and lost his best buddy hours before, on "the worst day I ever spent at the front." A dozen men from his unit were then killed during an attack that started with shelling and ended in hand-to-hand combat and slaughter. Instead of hatred, he wrote magnanimously that the Germans opposite him that day were "first-class fighting men, young and fresh and full of confidence." He was inflating their mettle to enhance his own. In fact, they were scared kids with little training, the last sacrifices hurled into battle by a flailing empire close to its last day. They died by buckets as the attack went in as planned, against a well-sited position hidden inside a small copse, across a road that ran past a quarry cut into the base of a steep hill. An all-out fight developed in the quarry that engaged about 50 men on each side. It was an utterly savage affair, sudden and extremely violent, with Lugers and Mausers going up against Colts, Springfields, and close-quarter shotguns. In just minutes, Barkley's unit suffered a dozen casualties but left 50 Germans dead or dying, many from gaping shotgun wounds. He recalled: "When the smoke from the firing cleared away, we saw what a mess the quarry was in. The floor was covered with the bodies of the dead and wounded. The walls and our clothes were spattered with blood and brains."[40]

Americans carried out their own dead and wounded then, as if clearing out an abattoir, they dragged out dead Germans and threw them carelessly in a shallow ditch beside the road. As they set up a quarry defense against potential counterattack, with scouts in the woods and atop the hill, Barkley noticed something odd: "I saw what looked to me like a boot sticking out of a crevice between two big rocks back in a dark corner. I held my forty-five in one hand, grabbed the boot with the other, and yanked." Surely it was a moment to finish off the last enemy in the quarry? "A man came out, clutching at the rock with both hands. He kept yelling, '*Nein!…Nein!…Nicht!…Nicht!*'" Barkley rolled the German onto his back then "jabbed him in the belly with my pistol. He had a Luger in his belt and I took that." Barkley did not kill him, but he was not gentle: "I had to kick him in the side to make him understand that I wanted him to get up. He was holding his arm over his face, and he was so weak from fright he could hardly get onto his feet." When the man took his arm down Barkley saw that "he was just a kid, towheaded and with baby-blue eyes. He was built more like a girl than a man. He began to cry like a baby." Now other doughboys crowded around the boy prisoner. "One of them growled, 'kill the yellow son-of-a-bitch!' He didn't mean it for any joke. I whirled around and faced the gang, my forty-five in one hand, the Luger in the other. I brought them both to a level. Most of the faces in the crowd were just curious. But some of them looked mighty mean." The threat to the boy from men not yet cooled off from the fight was mortal. Barkley would not have it: "I said, 'Cut that stuff.' "[41]

A sergeant approached with a cocked pistol in his hand and ordered Barkley to put up his gun. "But something told me that the little German wouldn't live very long if that sergeant got his hands on him. I shifted the forty-five. It was lined directly on the sergeant. . . . 'I'm through talking. Back up—all of you!' Instead of that they crowded closer." Fortunately for Barkley, two of his pals arrived: Jesse James and William Floyd, both Native Americans. They shoved through the armed crowd from the back, then stood with Barkley facing the sergeant with cold murder in his eye until he backed down. James did it for unstated reasons, Floyd only to help out Barkley. He "was for me, against the gang. But his sympathies were all with them about the proper way to treat a prisoner." It was not over for the German boy crying inside a bloodstained quarry.

Barkley noted two guns Floyd had tucked inside his belt, as they decided the boy's fate. "All the time I was arguing with him, he kept . . . eyes on the prisoner's face. . . . The kid wasn't crying any longer. He was too scared." Barkley made a sudden decision, in a flutter of mercy: "I'd made up my mind that I'd shoot Floyd before I'd let him have his way with my prisoner." Floyd finally gave in, seeing the look in Barkley's eye and knowing him as a killer. Still, he stayed alongside with one eye always on the scared boy wearing field gray. After dark, Barkley heard a detail of German prisoners being marched along the quarry road. He took the boy outside and handed him off, returning all his confiscated trinkets as he did. He concludes the tale the way most real war stories end, which is why many people prefer military fantasy: "I got word that his body had been found thrown in a creek near the town. It was murder."[42]

Out of 50 Germans in the quarry, in a small fight that did not decide the day let alone the war, only one survived. A conscript boy was saved from murder because in a moral flash Barkley saw through his grief and combat exhaustion to terrified, trembling humanity. As soon as he did, he whirled and stopped war-hardened men on his own side from completing what they had started in the woods. A man shifted from killer to lifesaver in a moment, seeing in a crying, childish face not an enemy waiting in ambush behind a rock but a boy, too scared to come out. Crowded and threatened in a high-noon stand-off with his own side, he faced down a bullying herd of armed men who wanted to shoot the child prisoner in cold blood. It is notable that he was one and they were many, at least to start. One man moved to self-endangerment by pity for a stranger, an enemy prisoner. Many more ready to commit cold murder. His comments on his squad's views about prisoners suggests that they had murdered before. We know someone did so again soon after, killing the boy Barkley had managed to save for a few hours. What remains is the core humanity of the moment, a minute of grace in a rock quarry spattered in gore and brains from a firefight just barely over. What we must ponder is a singular act of mercy, looking past grief and rage while encased in a hard amber of hatred during the last month of the last year of a world war that killed 10 million.

GRACE

I couldn't shoot him. He was defenseless. . . . What would you have done?
—Norbert Gubbels, General Infantry, Ardennes Woods (1944)

Dense woods and low rolling hills of Germany's borderlands hosted war many times over two millennia.[1] Full of ill intention or just looking for revenge for invasions that had started out the other way, Germans pushed through the forests against ranks of skilled Roman legionaries who barred their wild descent onto the northern plain of Gaul. There was chronic war but no repeat of the victory by the tribes of Germania in the Teutoburger Wald in 9 CE.[2] They fought again in hardscrabble bands to hold onto leafy Marches all through the many unnamed small wars of the Middle Ages. And again during the Thirty Years' War of the 17th century, when the confessions burned people and burned out the land, until popes and preachers and theological disputes were displaced by more cynical kings and secular precepts of Machiavelli and Richelieu. Germans fought huge armies of Louis XIV and Louis XV under forefather forests in the 18th century, and against both Napoleons in the one that followed. They smashed the remnants of the *Armée du Rhin* at nearby Sedan in 1870, humiliating France, toppling one emperor even as they uplifted another, thereby uniting Germans by force of arms under one Reich as they had not been united in 1,000 years.[3]

German armies won at Sedan once again in the opening frontier battles of August 1914, before the *Kaiserheer* suffered a decisive defeat by the French at First Marne that September. As they lost the first *Weltkrieg* four years later, they retreated back under forest cover. That's when John Lewis Barkley and his fellow Americans joined Allied armies breaking out of trenches to surge east. Only the Rhine and Armistice stopped them crossing into Germany, for its broken armies could not have. Twenty years later the Germans were back, riding panzers and half-tracks through the dark woods in a gambler's thrust that stunned France and drove the British back to their home island.[4] Then the mad plan all came apart. By mid-1944, Germany's cities were mostly rubble and its armies beaten and retreating on every front. By autumn they had returned to the Ardennes forest, where they fought the Allies through that winter. Steel shrapnel and tree burst splinters again ripped into young Americans as they did in 1918, when armies from across the Atlantic first fought across these rolling hills and under the tall fir trees. Dead from centuries of ancient wars nursed forest saplings not yet grown to mighty trees and conversed bone-to-bone with the new arrivals. Yet again, serried woodlands straddling the Rhine gazed in silent witness at carnage, brutality, savagery, and wanton murder. But also on rare moments of mercy more profound and inexplicable than all the killing.

───────────

TWENTY-FIVE YEARS AFTER WORLD WAR I American troops again steamed across the North Atlantic, headed for war with Germany. Once again, the fight had been already underway for years: the enormous Red Army of the Soviet Union was massed in the main fighting arena on the Eastern Front of the Nazi empire. The war against fascism had shifted from defense to all-out offense on all land fronts, at sea and in the air. This time, Americans arrived in enough numbers and in time to help turn the tide of war in North Africa, then in Italy and across Western Europe. This time, they did not come as an underequipped "beggar army," as was said of them by their allies in World War I. Their corps were fitted out with every imaginable weapon and with vast quantities to follow, with still more supplied to their allies and yet more building up a huge reserve. They fought the same German enemy along-side old allies and some new ones: Free French, British, Commonwealth, Belgians, Dutch, Norwegians, Poles, and a few Italians. Americans and Germans sent the sons of men of Barkley's generation to fight each other in North Africa in 1942, Sicily and Italy in 1943, in the thick *bocage* in Normandy in mid-1944, then racing over the broad plain of northern France. They fought deep into the Low Countries and partway back again. Then everyone was stopped at the edge of bitterly defended forests abutting the Rhine, where the armies had last met in 1918 and their fathers and uncles had killed each other wantonly and willingly. Although some did it reluctantly and regretfully, wounding their souls.

Western armies were disciplined as they broke from entangling *bocage* and enclosed pastures of Normandy in the summer of 1944, smashed the *Westheer* at Falaise, then advanced across northern France. Allied armies invaded France a second time that August, leaving from Italy and Corsica to land on the Côte d'Azur. Germans staggered backward, running rather than retreating to the Rhine and the forest border. But the Western Allies outran their logistics and fuel supplies, pushing against a firming resist-ance. Then they tried to go too far too fast, failing to thrust over a narrow front across the great river barrier. Germans blocked British paras from crossing at Arnhem in the Netherlands; knotted down Canadians among the canals, broken dikes, and polders; held up Americans at the tree line.[5] A broad advance sputtered to a halt farther south as well, abutting woody borders of a Nazi empire that now flailed and clawed against its military de-feat and coming political collapse. A much reduced but still partially effec-tive and dangerous *Westheer* resisted French and American armies heading into Alsace-Lorraine,[6] tired British and Canadian armies struggling across the Scheldt estuary,[7] and a poorly led American army in the *Hürtgenwald* (Hürtgen Forest).[8]

In the woodland hills of the *Hürtgenwald* the U.S. Army was channeled by rolling topography and narrow roads to batter itself bloody against fixed positions, suffering one of its worst defeats in World War II.[9] There was also a less well-known debacle farther south at Metz, where General George Patton ordered a straight-on assault against strong fortifications. He led U.S. Third Army into heavy casualties to almost no gain over two bloody months of hard fighting. It was hidden at the time by Patton's bluster and fawning press officers and press corps, and afterward by his too admiring biographers.[10] He had never outgrown a farcically archaic view of war, then sacrificed too many men to it as he pursued not just the enemy in Sicily and France but also his vaulting vanity.[11] Germans seemed just as fanatic falling back to the Rhine as Japanese during the Allied island-hopping approach to Japan. They did not quit fighting in 1944, as widely predicted. The war was *not* going to be over by Christmas, as most soldiers hoped and some planners promised. It might drag on for another year, over a bloody slog all the way to Berlin. On October 18, 1944, General Dwight D. Eisenhower cabled his lieutenants: "The enemy has continued to reinforce his forces in the West. Present indications are that he intends to make the strongest possible stand on the West Wall in the hope of preventing the war spreading to German soil." He sent seven armies to advance to wood and river frontiers on a broad front, in three phases: into the *Hürtgenwald*, the Argonne, and finally the Ardennes.[12] It was a fateful decision.

By November the *Westheer* was dug in along 400 miles of riverine and forested borderlands. Over months of fighting it resisted Allied efforts to quickly break Hitler's partly fortified *Westwall*, which Americans called the "Siegfried Line." Starting on September 19, Americans made a tragically inept offensive thrust into the *Hürtgenwald* and Eiffel Mountains. Lieutenant General Courtney Hodges, in command of U.S. First Army, explained his ill-conceived, unforgiving tactics: "Too many . . . battalions and regiments of ours have tried to flank and skirt and never meet the enemy straight on. [It is] safer, sounder, and in the end, quicker to keep smashing ahead."[13] Brutally unimaginative attacks went up the steep sides of nude ridge tops, thence down along narrow roads, winding under tall firs in interlocked woody ravines.[14] Five U.S. divisions were mauled trying to cross 14 miles of hilly woodlands, suffering 33,000 casualties on the Hürtgen's treed slopes while inflicting 28,000 casualties on their dug-in enemy. The *New York Times* cautioned its worried readers: "Here in the dark alleys of Huertgen Forest our infantry, fighting at bayonet point, is making slight progress. It is a bitter, inch-by-inch battle reminiscent of the Argonne or Belleau Wood in World War I."[15] It was evocative of what the Red Army had faced as it plunged into the winter forests of Finland in 1939 and was initially rebuffed. Nothing of value was secured by pushing into dense, bloody, impenetrable woods. On the German side, a rare late war tactical victory was achieved by clever economy of force and a sensible and effective defensive posture. Still, it could not stave off losing. It was too late for that. All that remained for German troops was to delay the fatal end until some other tomorrow. And die in hordes on the final miles.

A SINGULAR ACT OF MERCY BY a German officer toward a wounded G.I. (General Infantry) played out deep inside the *Hürtgenwald*. It so impressed U.S. Army veterans who were in the fight that they went back a half-century later to dedicate a memorial honoring a former enemy's magnanimity. It stands today tucked inside the entrance of the *Kriegsgräbertätte* (Military Cemetery), the main burial ground for German dead from the fighting in the Hürtgen. The initiative for the memorial came from Major General (Ret.) John Ruggles, who was a lieutenant colonel in the 22nd Infantry Regiment in November 1944. He quietly organized fellow veterans of the fight to honor *Leutnant* Friedrich Lengfeld, just 23 years old when he was killed trying to lend medical aid to a stranded and badly wounded American. The ceremony was overshadowed by presidential and other official commemorations taking place in Normandy and the Ardennes in 1994. The memorial received no press coverage: there is no story about the ceremony in the digital archives of the *New York Times* or other major U.S. newspapers. It was not reported anywhere until Ruggles was persuaded to talk about the trip to his local newspaper in Arizona in 1995.[16] He was a veteran of a horrific, lost forest battle in a war of liberation against Nazi tyranny. Yet, he and his fellow veterans paid for and dedicated a secluded memorial to a German soldier from 50 years before, to honor an act of mercy that in peacetime would have been expected and unremarkable. A normal offer of mercy became an atypical act of humanity because it was carried out by an enemy in the midst of combat. And because it cost that young enemy his life.

What happened under the snowbound pines on a winter day five decades earlier stirred old men to once again cross the ocean, returning to a place of their most horrific memories from youth. They went to meet former enemies, to shake hands that once held rifles and shot at them from the other side of a narrow road. Men who threw grenades in hand-to-hand combat under bitter pines, sniped from farm sheds, machine-gunned them as they advanced over a whitened field. They went to reconcile with enemies they, too, once sought to maim and kill, calling in mortars and artillery strikes or directing machine gun or tank fire into the trees. What happened was ordinary and even expected of any decent person in peacetime but became humanely exceptional in the context of combat. That is often the case in war, that hardened realm of odd behavior where a routine outreach of pity or kindness seems reckless. Where lending first aid to a hurt man in a different uniform requires real courage. Where the everyday charitable act of helping an injured man takes on special meaning as others hesitate. When men look up at their lieutenant in bafflement as he orders a rescue party to aid an enemy calling weakly in mortal pain, saying that he will personally lead them out from under cover into the open in an active combat zone. When the story is about courage leading to compassion, not killing.

It was just after first light on November 12, 1944, another day following another hard night of brutal slogging inside the Hürtgen. Standing in snow, in windfall and uneven shavings and branches from loud tree bursts, cold and tired, alert to the next attack sure to be made by the Americans, Lengfeld looked past the trees toward the enemy's lines. He was in command of a greatly reduced rifle company, part of the Fusilier Battalion of the Wehrmacht's 275th Infantry Division. His unit had taken severe casualties fighting the U.S. 22nd Infantry the day before. During the night, after close and bloody combat with the Americans, 2nd Company recaptured a forester's house it had lost a few hours earlier. As dawn broke, Lengfeld's men heard a badly wounded American left over from the night fight crying out in pain, asking over and over for help. They could barely see him in the gray light as he lay inside a nearby German minefield. He had been left behind as his unit pulled back under fire from Lengfeld's position. There were choices: let this enemy die or help him along with a sniper's bullet; call out to Americans and chance giving away a hidden position; go out to see what could be done for him. No one knew what to do. Someone was going to have to make a decision or no one would.

A witness to Lengfeld's last morning of war and life, to a final act of compassion, was communications runner Hubert Gees. Fifty years later he remembered the wounded American moaning and crying weakly for help. He recalled that the dying man had been left lying in the middle of the minefield called *Wilde Sau* [Wild Boar] in the little no-man's-land between the German defenders and briefly withdrawn Americans. Lengfeld sent Gees running to the company's forward machine gun position to deliver an order that "in no case should it shoot if American medical aid men should come to rescue the severely wounded soldier."[17] Then Gees and his lieutenant and all the other Germans waited, for hours. No American medics came across the open space near the road to help the wounded G.I., who continued to moan and implore for aid. Lengfeld judged that no American medics were close enough to hear their man's waning pleas or to lend him comfort. He pondered as cries from the minefield grew weaker over four hours of what everyone listening knew must be appalling agony. Decades later, Gees recalled the baleful scene and fading cries for help of a wounded enemy, repeated again and again.[18] Now, in full, bright, midmorning light, Lengfeld ordered up an ad hoc rescue team, decked in lively red cross vests. The men held up white flags mounted on rifles or on pine branches and set off to aid an anguished American they had pushed down the road toward death hours earlier. A little mercy mission crept into the open. Lengfeld led the way, moved by his sympathy and a nobility that cost him his life. For as he worked past tank mines to reach the moaning man he made a fatal misstep.

Gees told the story tersely, many years later: "Lengfeld went on top of [led] the rescue squad on our side of the road. The road itself was secured with antitank mines whose positions were relatively easy to locate." The lieutenant moved ahead of the small clutch of men holding aloft the white flags. Just when he crossed to the other side of the road approaching the G.I. an exploding antipersonnel mine "threw him to the ground." The explosion mortally injured Lengfeld but it did not kill him; the inanimate in war lacks that rare quality of mercy that only the animate may muster. It was now his turn to endure drawn-out agony from puncture wounds to his gut and big tears in his feet and legs; he would not die for eight hours. The rescue squad forgot about recovering the American as they hastily carried their lieutenant back to their own lines. "In a great hurry, he was taken back to our command post to be given first aid." The wounds were bad, Gees recalled. "Two holes in his back . . . the size of a coin suggested severe internal injuries. Young Lengfeld moaned, in great pain." Gees had seen battle wounds before. He knew his commanding officer needed more medical help than they could provide in the front line, so they carried him to the closest medic station. "Led by a lightly wounded NCO, he was brought back to casualty station *Lukasmühle*." The medics tried to stabilize him, then he was moved again. "He died [at] the main casualty station at Froitzheim." Whether the wounded American they left behind among the land mines lived is unknown.[19] It seems unlikely.

The singular story of Lengfeld's final choice under the snow-laden trees made him an enemy his foes could not forget. Within hours of hand-to-hand combat contesting a small forester's hut, he and his men risked their lives to help an enemy they had tried to kill just the night before. No law of war required that they step out from under cover to bring aid and comfort to a dying American, exposing themselves in the bright daylight. They did it anyway, following the example of tender valor provided by their young leader. His act of mercy and grace so impressed his former enemies they again crossed the Atlantic 50 years later to gather in silence to honor him. That is even more notable because, decades after the U.S. Army's bloody defeat in the dark woods, it had not commemorated its own soldiers lost in the *Hürtgenwald*. As if shame of that military debacle fell upon troops led into it by bad plans and worse generals. Unlike soldiers lost in famous victories in Normandy and at "The Bulge," there was no large tribute paid that year to troops lost in the defeat in the *Hürtgenwald*.[20] There was, however, a memorial erected there by American veterans, honoring a German.

Hubert Gees was taken prisoner about 10 days later, one of only seven men of 2nd Company of the Fusilier Battalion to survive. He spoke through tears at the dedication ceremony in 1994, standing in his white hair and twilight of his life amidst Americans he had faced in battle, now also arrived at the dusk of their lives. A small plaque dedicated by his reconciled enemy to his *Kompaniefuhrer* reads in English and German:

No man hath greater love than he who
layeth down his life for his enemy.

In Memory
of
LIEUTENANT FRIEDRICH LENGFELD
2ND CO., FUES. BN., 275TH INF. DIV.

Here in Huertgen Forest on November 12, 1944,
Lt. Lengfeld, a German officer, gave his life
while trying to save the life of an American
soldier lying severely wounded in the "Wilde
Sau" minefield and appealing for medical aid.

Placed at this site on October 7, 1994.
The Twenty-Second United States
Infantry Society—World War II

"Deeds Not Words"[21]

A monument erected by Americans to honor a German soldier is even more remarkable when one considers how few memorials to Wehrmacht troops who fought for Hitler stand on German soil. It was hard to argue for new war hero statues after 1945; most older statues were torn down instead. This one stands in quiet nobility, as uncommon in its presence as the merciful warrior it remembers.

FIGHTING IN THE *HÜRTGENWALD* WAS AT close quarters, as dictated by a few narrow valley roads and deeply dug-in German positions. U.S. infantry encountered impressive enemy strongpoints in the dense woods, including tanks buried up to their turrets in logs and dirt and pre-sited rifle and machine gun fire from behind downed trees. G.I.s had minimal ability to counter the dug-in panzers: tank and air support was limited by bad weather or difficult terrain and heavy tree cover.[22] One soldier explained at the time: "You can't get all of the dead because you can't find them, and they stay there to remind the guys advancing as to what might hit them. You can't get protection. You can't see. You can't get fields of fire. The trees are slashed like a scythe by artillery. Everything is tangled. You can scarcely walk."[23] The 1st Division had already suffered heavy casualties well before its 16th Infantry Regiment moved forward on November 16, attacking toward the heavily defended village of Hamich. It was four days after Lengfeld stepped on a mine and died slow and hard at a Wehrmacht forward aid station.

The advance was met by stunning defensive artillery fire, heavy mortars and large tanks firing from inside the trees, and by intense infantry automatic and rifle fire. There was mortal terror that day, and immense moral and physical courage. Metal shrapnel flew at the attackers, joined by thick splinters from tree bursts plummeting onto exposed and slogging infantry. The advance stopped after 500 yards, then Germans left their fortified positions to counterattack. They came to within five yards from the rear of one stalled-out infantry company, to be repelled by a shower of hand grenades. Lieutenant John Beach remembered: "Two surviving Germans immediately jumped up with their hands in the air. We disarmed them and sent them to the rear." Running toward a hidden machine gun position his company killed one German, wounded a second, then accepted a few surrenders. Nothing morally special in that: fight, kill, honor honest surrenders according to the established rules of war.[24]

Suddenly his exposed men and position came under withering artillery fire that reduced their numbers to 14 out of 56 who had attacked. There was no respite. Beach lost four more men killed and others wounded by machine gun fire. Then he was nearly killed while performing an act of courage that he described matter-of-factly, not seeming to recognize his own moral heroism. Someone in front of him waved a white flag, followed by several German medics running out from cover, "turning over the green-clad bodies to determine who survived, dragging the living out of the firing area." Beach recalled relaxing his trigger finger along the slack of his "tommy gun" while thinking: "I was no medic but there were some of my men out there, too." He made a decision to take a chance with his own life. "I laid down my submachine gun, stood up empty-handed and walked quickly but carefully toward the spot where several motionless olive-drab figures lay."[25] Suddenly, he heard the German machine gun open up and "saw flashes of fire from beneath and alongside the white flag, and felt sharp stabs of pain in both legs. I felt paralyzed."[26] Was it a cruel deception, a ruse de guerre under false cover of a white flag asking for a ceasefire to care for the wounded? It might have been a flash decision driven by nervous fear of one man with his finger hovering near the MG-42 trigger or a crueler man who deliberately chose to fire. That night, Germans policing the clearing discovered Beach. They took a blanket from the pack of a dead man, improvised a stretcher, and carried him to one of their triage centers. Such is the oddity of war, where one encounters lethal malice and surprising mercy from an enemy inside the same few square yards.

ELEMENTS OF THE U.S. 9TH INFANTRY Division pressed an attack over the edge of the forest. It was a disaster. A German officer reported: "The enemy attacked five or six times. The regularity was amazing, the more so since each attack was repulsed mostly with great losses." Americans requested a one-day ceasefire to recover their wounded and bury the dead. It was granted. Then they repeated the blunt attack "the next day, at the usual time."[27] By mid-November fighting in the *Hürtgenwald* was so intense the dead were left uncollected in the snow. Many immobile wounded could not be reached or recovered. Dozens lay inside German-held woodland unaided for days, unreachable by their medics. U.S. Army Medical Lieutenant Felix Lauter knew they would die from suppurating wounds or pneumonia induced by the bitter cold if he did not get to them. Major Albert Berndt tried to arrange a truce but was told by his German counterpart: "We have no contact with some of our own units and cannot guarantee that your stretcher-bearers and ambulances will not be fired on."[28] That did not matter to Lauter or to Lieutenant Floyd Johnson, who volunteered to drive his ambulance over to the German line to see if it would draw fire.

Aidman Bill Bryant volunteered to ride along. Johnson conferred with the German captain, who agreed to a small arms truce to allow the Americans to recover wounded. He repeated that he did not control the nearby artillery and thus could not promise that the medics would not be shelled. The ambulance drove across regardless, surprising distant gunners but also alerting them with unexpected vehicle movement between the established front lines. It was snowing as they headed over but cleared just as they arrived, making them certain targets. Sure enough, the big guns fired from distant positions, shells exploding near Johnson's clearly marked ambulance. Lauter told a combat reporter only a few days later: "We were under direct observation [and] we came under a rain of German shells and mortar fire." Yet, seven more ambulances made the dash, shells falling all around but not bothered by small arms.

As soon as they arrived at the German line a hurried search for wounded men began. Lauter told the reporter that litter squads had to negotiate "a steep and muddy slope uphill for 250 yards." He wasn't sure what would happen next. "I was kind of nervous and suspected maybe the Germans might change their minds and hold the lot of us [prisoners]." He talked to an implacable lieutenant in field gray who asked about the U.S. election a week before. Lauter informed him that Franklin D. Roosevelt had won, at which the German spat and boasted that if Hitler "ever grabbed [FDR] he would string him up." Lauter laughed, saying if the two leaders ever met it was going to be "the other way around." Most of the Germans knew they were losing the war. Terror of the *Ostfront* stayed with them even while they fought a pitched battle against Americans. A sergeant asked Lauter if it was true that all POWs captured in the west were being transshipped to Siberia and Red Army control. He denied it, as the *Leutnant* joked about visiting him soon. The eight ambulances by then had loaded 54 recovered wounded. German infantry held its fire as they departed, although distant guns again tried to take them out. All eight made it back.[29]

AFTER 1949, INFATUATION BY NATO THEORISTS with panzers and German "mission tactics" (*Auftragstaktik*) obscured the fact that there was a real stumbling quality to German operations that still mostly goes unremarked.[30] In 1918, the final year of Germany's first lost *Weltkrieg*, General Erich von Ludendorff tried to drive a wedge between superior Allied armies, without any true strategic objective.[31] Asked to sum up the essence of vaunted German tactics, Ludendorff snarked: "We punch a hole and see what develops."[32] By late 1944 another superior coalition of Germany's own making, provoked into existence and to war by serial Nazi aggression, was closing a steel ring around the deflated *Vaterland*. Hitler decided to revisit 1918, hearkening to his old commander. Instead of digging in to defend along fortified borders to raise costs to advancing Western Allies, as Eisenhower had predicted to his subordinates, Hitler ordered an offensive.

Hitler and the German high command would push a panzer attack westward in an effort to drive a wedge between the Allied armies by reaching the sea at Antwerp. Just like Ludendorff did, Hitler thus hastened ultimate defeat by altering the timetable of the Allied advance while wearing out the last German reserves, to no good purpose. He would punch a hole into Belgium to force what? Something. Anything. It was an armored thrust that had no chance of operational success and no strategic goal at all. In an added nod to cheap sentiment, the operational order cited a 19th-century patriotic anthem meant to rally Germans to defend the homeland, dubbed *Wacht am Rhein* (Watch on the Rhine), or in plainer prose, *Die Ardennenoffensive* (Ardennes Offensive). This was the German way of war: focus on tactics and operations without regard for the strategic context or the likelihood that exaggerated ambition met with objective material power. This time, as also happened in 1918, all they would achieve was a salient jutting into the Allied line. Americans finishing the fight inside the *Hürtgenwald* thus faced another bloodbath in the dark woods of the Ardennes. They called it the "Battle of the Bulge."[33]

The respite from immediate downfall that German victory in the *Hürtgenwald* permitted was squandered by Hitler almost at once. Yet again, now for the last time, he rolled the steel dice of war. Americans were badly bogged down in the Hürtgen woods but Soviet and Western armies had advanced on multiple other fronts, right up to Nazi Germany's frontiers. Everyone knew the final push was coming sooner rather than later. Hitler chose to attack instead of defend. He would thrust in the west with the Wehrmacht's last operational reserves, which lacked enough fuel even to reach initial target points. The panzers were told to find whatever they needed to keep going by capturing American fuel depots. Such logistical madness befit a regime and a military that was always unprepared for the kind of war it started. But this was almost mindless desperation. Even so, on December 16, 1944, a depleted Wehrmacht stabbed into surprised Americans adjacent to the Hürtgen, resting inside the abysmal Ardennes. The countryside was already brilliant white. Landing shells hurtled up a dark loam of corrupted treefall to make neat, round, black holes in the snow. In places, soil scattered atop the white mixed with blood and body parts in red-and-black blotches where the mortars landed.

IN 1944 NORBERT GUBBELS WAS A scared replacement just arrived in France from Osmond, Nebraska. He quit school after the eighth grade to help work the family farm. Unlike many boys, when he heard that Japan had attacked Pearl Harbor and Germany declared war on his country four days later he did not want to run off to war, to seek his own "red badge of courage." He did not volunteer. Age 16 in 1941, he was frightened when he thought about leaving home and family behind, scared to think that he might die in the war. He was drafted shortly after his 18th birthday. "I went in the closet and cried all by myself," he recalled 70 years later. "I didn't want anyone to see me."[34] Exiting basic training, he shipped out in September 1944, heading to Liverpool on the troopship USS *Wakefield.* He passed through several staging camps in France as higher-ups hurried him and other replacements to badly depleted 4th Infantry Division, then taking awful losses in the *Hürtgenwald.* Gubbels was afraid of everything, all the time. The first bodies he saw were Germans stacked beside a road. The sight shook him. As did seeing tiny living enemy in the distance, hearing rifle shots seemingly all around him, and the low *thrum! thrum!* of artillery.[35]

His first job was loading frozen American bodies in the back of two-and-a-half-ton trucks parked inside a conifer wood, already shattered and splintered by the far-off guns. Deliberate tree burst shelling by German artillery had caused terrible wounds in the dead men he carried, the like of which he had never imagined.[36] Many of the dead were no older than he, slaughtered by infantry fire or by more distant artillery raining in from both sides. "What could you think? That could be you," he said years later.[37] Other men carried bodies rigid from cold out from under the high snow pines. He helped lift them up and onto tailgates of the "deuce-and-a-half" trucks.[38] A third team stacked them in rows along the truck beds. Gubbels had seen pallid dead men in funeral parlors back home but this was the first time he saw the inner works of a man's body, secret places and things only surgeons and butchers know. He was a normal man, even unusually sensitive: the ugly sights made him physically ill. Conventionally religious, he prayed silently all the while he shifted the bodies. The next day he saw his first combat.

His unit attacked a fixed hilltop position. Screaming wounded lay on the slope all around Gubbels even before panzers hove into view, machine-gunning and firing their main guns into crawling men, running over and squashing others. He fired a bazooka but the round *clanged!* off thick side armor. He got away as the huge beast ignored him, turning its big gun against another threat. He fired his rifle into German machine gun posts and at small groups of enemy infantry, killing or wounding men as he was trained to do but which his gentle nature rebuked him for, there and then. A few Germans with scared faces managed to surrender, their hands held high. He saw others try to give up who were shot down as they called out, asking mercy from armed men wearing a different uniform. That's how Gubbels lost his innocence at war, and about war.[39]

Nine days before the Wehrmacht launched its last offensive in the west his battered unit was sent a few miles into Luxembourg to rest and recover, minus nearly half its original complement.[40] On December 16, the first day of the Ardennes Offensive, Gubbels was part of a four-man improvised scout team told to walk point for a column of five Shermans heading right toward the advancing Germans. He was told to scale a road bank and report movement. The other three scouts were killed one by one. His sergeant was shot in the head as he inched upward to peer over a roadside berm. Gubbels looked all about in fear and confusion: "There must have been thousands of Germans there. You didn't know which way to go. There was gunfire everywhere." By nightfall he was alone, the last of the scouts left alive. All five Shermans were gone, too. It is a shocking thing to see a tank destroyed, a huge armored vehicle so much bigger and more powerful than you. It provokes feelings of smallness and naked vulnerability. The loss of his companions also left him terrified, and permanently traumatized. Alone in the dark woods, sacred nearly witless, he stumbled in crusty snow through dimly lit trees. Tumbling out of the darkness, he saw a stone manor ahead at the edge of the crossroads village of Lauterborn, deep in the bowl of a small valley with short hills and enemies all around.

On one side of the large manor was a clearing littered with dozens of dead in dull gray. In front were four bodies that looked like dead Americans. Gubbels learned later that they were English-speaking German infiltrators, summarily shot when captured while wearing U.S. Army uniforms. They were part of Operation *Greif*, a special forces gambit led by Otto Skorzeny and outfitted with captured Allied uniforms and vehicles. It failed in its main goal of securing bridges over the Meuse to permit a rapid panzer thrust but caused some confusion behind American lines. Like the overall German operation, it had no achievable objective. Inside the manor house was an antitank platoon of 17 men, along with a few stragglers like him who arrived from other shattered units. The platoon was completely cut off, stuck in place behind the leading edge of the German attack. There was no chance of quick reinforcement and it was bitterly cold. Men hunkered down as they watched for German movement through broken windows of the big stone house they all called "the castle." They looked for a flash from one of the hilltops that must be followed by shouts of "Incoming!" They tried to spot any quick, gray movements by a repositioning enemy readying to launch a sudden assault. They waited out the still before the storm.

A large stone building made an obvious target for snipers and mortars. Even so, the platoon could not believe its luck: the manor had hot running water and central heating, huge bathrooms and big bedrooms, and its larders were stocked with fine foods and wines. It even had a tall Christmas tree. Château de Lauterborn was built in the time of Napoleon, mimicking the glories of a triumphant French Empire. In June 1944, it was hastily abandoned by its owner, who left behind several handsome portraits of himself. The collaborator René Deltgen was the most famous actor in Luxembourg, an irony completely lost on him. He starred in several wartime propaganda films made by Joseph Goebbels, including *Mein Leben für Irland* (My Life for Ireland) in 1941 and *Anschlag auf Baku* (Attack on Baku) in 1942.[41] That was the same year the *Ostheer* failed to reach the oil fields at Baku. The same year Hitler fatally split his southern offensive, diverting 6th Army and two Romanian armies to Stalingrad while sending a weakened main thrust into failure in the Caucuses. Deltgen thrived under the Nazi invaders until the Western Allies landed in France, when he left his château and ran. He never understood that, as Joseph Conrad put it about another invader: "They were conquerors and for that you want only brute force—nothing to boast of, when you have it, since your strength is just an accident arising from the weakness of others."[42] Deltgen did not see that the Nazis were the true "heart of darkness." He was imprisoned briefly after the war, before resuming his acting career.

In December 1944, less guileful men lay dead or were about to die on the snow carpeted gardens of his half-ruined estate. They were blanketed by a pretty two-day snow: the manor and grounds looked like a Christmas card, a gentle illusion that hid the horror lying beneath. It would be revealed in time, once the first warmth of spring uncovered mounds of stinking, deliquescing human flesh. From third floor windows German infantry were seen repositioning on low, surrounding hills. The watching Americans wondered why they did not attack. Maybe they were waiting for panzers to arrive to knock the old manor down so that an infantry assault would not be necessary. Perhaps they hoped that the defenders would flee, without forcing them to attack a stone position. Maybe they were also sick of the war or no longer believed in an absurd offensive where their tanks and half-tracks did not have enough fuel to reach their final objectives. Whether one hoped for tanks to arrive or feared the moment when they did, they were not here yet. In the brooding wait that was endured by men on both sides, something extraordinary took place. Like everything else Gubbels experienced in his brief but frantic time spent at war, it marked and changed him for the rest of his life. A very ordinary and always frightened young soldier was about to be tested in ways he never imagined. The experience elevated him from the everyday to the exceptional, revealing a moral valor that he briefly matched to high physical courage. It also changed others waiting with him behind the cold stones, revealing some as callow and others as brave.

It did not happen all at once, as so many things seem to in war. It started when a window lookout warned that he saw movement in the space in front of the manor where dead Germans lay strewn in tumbled white heaps, along with four dead pretenders in American uniforms. Gubbels looked into the long courtyard and saw an arm held up about 150 yards away, waving weakly yet persistently. He then heard distinctive cries of pain. Shots rang out as someone in the manor fired at what was surely a wounded German. Why not? He was a living enemy. Or was he? Was so badly wounded a man really an enemy anymore, lying there slowly dying in the snow? Others shouted to stop shooting. Gubbels remembered: "I couldn't shoot him. He was defenseless." An argument broke out as Sergeant Charles Sweet said they should bring the man inside, to give him whatever relief they could.[43] Gubbels recalled: "Some of them wanted to shoot him. I said let's go on and help him. He might have been my enemy, but that was before." Others held out for shooting, saying it was the high road to mercy. Meaning it or not.

The platoon's lieutenant was 25-year-old Morgan Welch. He thought the plan was too risky. He had landed at Utah Beach on D-Day, seen more than his share of death and horror, and made hard command decisions over the six months since then. He said many decades later about the wounded German: "I didn't think he'd last that long." About the men who wanted to go out, he said: "Their lives were my responsibility. I didn't see much point in exposing them to fire. We could see the German soldiers out there on the high ground. I said 'They'll pick you off, too.' " Sweet insisted on leading a recovery mission, nonetheless. Welch relented. Sweet asked who would help him carry the wounded German back to the castle. Gubbels and two other men volunteered.[44] With a bit of bedsheet tied to a rifle, Gubbels carried a slung blanket as a makeshift stretcher as four men stepped outside the château door.

Standing upright in clear, sunlit view of snipers on the hilltops, the rescue team spread out and moved gingerly across open space. They had to step over or around clods of flesh and clumps of dead, mangled and tossed recklessly about by now quiet mortar barrages. After 150 yards in which no sniper rifle *cracked!* or mortar fell, they reached the arm. The man attached to it could not speak. He was severely wounded, kept alive likely by the sharp night cold that had slowed his bleeding. He did not expect mercy: he feebly reached for his fallen rifle. They tossed it aside, along with other weapons found nearby and a Lugar taken from inside his greatcoat. They checked him for booby traps, then carefully lifted him onto the blanket. All the way back, a much slower journey, they met an eerie silence instead of sniper fire or mortars, whose crews surely knew the range and could see the four Americans now all pressed together. Within a few seconds of carrying the wounded man over the threshold and inside the main door of the manor loud shooting started up again, going in both directions. Whether or not it was a kind of salute showing respect between enemies, it confirmed that the Germans chose to hold their fire until the rescue party was safe.

Welch examined the German as they pulled off his wet, heavy, frozen greatcoat and sticky, blood-soaked uniform. They found a Wehrmacht ID, photos of his girl, and small Russian coins in his pockets. Corporal Heinrich Schroder had probably seen action on the dreaded *Ostfront* against the Red Army. He was also a Catholic like Gubbels, to judge by his rosary beads and prayer cards. He had frostbite, a chest wound that pushed bone and bits of lung out his back, two broken legs, one gangrenous where he was missing the foot. He was going to die, faster now that his body was warming up. They gave him water and brandy, bandaged his wounds as best they could with strips of torn bedsheet, jabbed him with two vials of precious morphine they might need themselves, then sat and listened to his moans. The groaning lasted for a day and a night and drove some men stir crazy. Again, a hard few argued that he should be killed: shot or knifed or maybe his throat cut the way they all were trained. Two men pointed rifles at the prone German but Gubbels yelled at them not to shoot, pleading not for the man's life but against his murder. Others agreed. Some still argued the other way, that he had tried to kill them a few hundred yards away and barely two days ago. Mercy or murder rested in the balance. Gubbels recalls his lieutenant saying: "Men, we're going to care for him throughout the night but Gubbels, since you care so much, if he's alive in the morning you're going to kill him."[45] Would he have done it for mercy's sake? He never faced the awful question. He prayed over the dying man far into the night then fell asleep beside him. When he awoke, Corporal Schroder was dead.

As the rest of the platoon and stragglers came in and saw the corpse they said nothing, except for a few who made a point of thanking Gubbels. Some wanted to throw the body out the upper-story window but it was instead agreed to lay him beside a dead American in a small woodshed. Gubbels nearly joined the pair, as later that day a mortar hit the outside stone window frame where he sat watch, knocking him senseless. He recovered, so that on the fourth day he joined the platoon in escape from the village. They had to move fast: the radio said panzers had crossed the Sauer River and would soon reach the collaborator's château. They must make a run for American lines a few miles distant, down a narrow road. Welch loaded his wounded into one half-track. Gubbels got in the other. All went well until the driver swerved to avoid a tree felled across the road, which put the half-track on top of a landmine. He was knocked out, again. With everyone scattered he was alone in the pine woods, again. He heard German voices in the darkness as he stumbled and staggered in deep, off-trail snow and through an icy creek. He reached a road where he avoided a small caravan of refugees. He saw a sluggish truck with a stenciled white star pass and caught it up from behind. He climbed over the tailgate, falling asleep in an odd load of kitchen supplies. He was not discovered until the heavy truck rumbled into a Third Army command post many miles beyond where his broken division was still fighting.

Gubbels came under fire a last time when an isolated sniper shot a soldier standing near him. He took cover as armed protectors from Third Army burned down the building with the German still inside. He wobbled and vomited, falling down as he watched and smelled the crackling blaze. He lay unconscious, for a third time. Perhaps it was the result of his earlier head injuries, or maybe it was trauma resulting from fatigue and fear. It might have been moral nausea over watching a man burn alive. Or all three things. He was carried unconscious to a field hospital, where he was diagnosed as suffering "combat fatigue" and relieved of combat duty.[46] Sent to the quiet south of France, he pulled kitchen work in a POW camp near Marseilles. He let Axis prisoners take extra bits of fruit and bread they were not allowed, and was treated kindly in return. He came to believe that Germans he met were not Nazis but "godly men" like him, as in the last war. Maybe he was right. Though clearly some on either side were not at all like him. Discharged in 1945, he returned to the family farm in Nebraska and resumed civilian life.

He was ever after stalked by memories that shadowed him from the haunted woods of the Ardennes. He had nightmares that grew more frequent and intense, lasting to the last days of his life in 2014. Over seven decades, he never forgot the mortally wounded German for whom he risked his life to offer a morsel of final comfort. When queried why he did what he did, Gubbels asked in quiet humility: "What would you have done?"[47]

CHAPTER 6

DISSENT

Before I can live with other folks I've got to live with myself. The one thing
that doesn't abide by majority rule is a person's conscience.

—Harper Lee, *To Kill a Mockingbird* (1960)

Today, it is not uncommon to dissent from history or from the nationalist
policies that lie behind past and possibly future wars. The most morally
valiant among us do it at the time. As a serving officer, Siegfried Sassoon
published his vehement dissent from Britain's war, which he supported
in 1914 but had turned against by 1916, in "A Soldier's Declaration."[1]
Pockets of resistance to regime exterminationist policies existed within the
Wehrmacht and in small civilian groups. Bishop Galen of Münster protested
Nazi euthanasia practices and denounced the Gestapo. There were a
number of individuals of conscience who did what they could to stop atrocities in China, France, Poland, and Lithuania. The student-children of the
White Rose anti-Nazi society lost their lives after they posted intellectual
dissent from Nazism in leaflets and graffiti that shocked insulated Germans
but provoked the Gestapo. Several diplomats defied their governments to
aid Jews. Some paid with their lives for their conscience and mercy. Public
opposition to U.S. engagement in the Vietnam War was minimal at first. But

it grew into a mass movement, spilling from pulpits and newsrooms into the streets, contributing something to turning the tide from war to peace talks; or at least, extraction talks. The post-9/11 Iraq War provoked extensive dissension, although that was less true of the Afghanistan War before it lost focus and lengthened to 20 years.

A committee of soldiers' mothers protested military secrecy during the Soviet occupation of Afghanistan. They played a major role in ending that war by turning grief into effective dissent.[2] After the 2014 invasion of Donbas and Crimea, mothers' groups exposed the official lie of "little green men" recruited locally.[3] They showed that Vladimir Putin sent in Russian troops, including their sons, some of whom came home with orders to be buried only in secret. Their mothers were arrested, censored, and silenced. In 2022 a Union of Committees of Soldiers' Mothers of Russia mobilized against Putin's second invasion of Ukraine. They were joined in street protests by many younger dissenters who rejected aggression aimed at re-creation of a reactionary, mystical Russian Empire.[4] Over 15,000 were arrested during the first month, under a new law against saying the word "war" rather than using the official term "special military operation." Marina Ovsyannikova, a producer at Channel 1, the main state-run propaganda TV station, expressed personal shame over her 10 years spent helping to "zombify" Russians, then interrupted a live TV news show with an antiwar protest.[5] Some Russian special police officers of the *Rosgvardia* refused to fight, arguing that the order to go to Ukraine was illegal. Conscripts deserted for reasons ranging from self-preservation to conscientious objection. Putin's response to all such dissenters was to denounce them as "scum and traitors" and threaten that Russia would spit them out "like a gnat." It got worse when demoralized battalion tactical groups were pulled back from the initial, and failed, Kyiv axis of attack then sent to re-enter combat in Donbas. More troops deserted en route or simply refused to go.[6]

Putin understood that the Russian public might recoil from his war in Ukraine if they could see real outcomes for armed Russian teenagers caused by his runaway militarization of foreign policy. Wars of defense are one thing but wars of naked aggression, or for social or political reform of someone else's county by armed force, are quite another. The horror of combat is a good reason to actually show the public how ugly real war is. Instead, censorship prevails. In most Western countries there is blue dot or digital blurring of print and TV news programs, usually with trigger warnings about how terrible are the images that are then not shown at all. It was a marked feature of the Middle East wars after 9/11 and in Ukraine. Across the West, only sanitized images appeared on TV while raw footage was left to apps like Telegram. It was far worse in Russia, from the start of war with Ukraine in 2014. It was total in 2022, as journalists were arrested or forced into exile and some were killed in Ukraine by Russian Army snipers. All independent news outlets were shut down as a digital iron curtain sought to cut off Russians from the truth about their war while the truth itself was criminalized.

CIVILIANS AS WELL AS SOLDIERS CAN face a deep moral choice when confronted by wartime atrocities, the most extreme circumstance anyone ever encounters in a war. Leading examples of dissenters from Nazism include Oscar Schindler, a Nazi Party member and bon vivant businessman who saved hundreds of Jews by protecting workers from deportation to SS (*Schutzstaffel*) death camps.[7] In 1937 another businessman, John Rabe, used his Nazi Party card and Swastika armband to get past drunken soldiers at roadblocks set up by the *Rikugun* (Imperial Japanese Army). He was able to establish rescue and safety zones for Chinese civilians being butchered openly in the streets and houses of Nanjing. He physically pulled Japanese soldiers off Chinese women they were raping, surely risking his life. He was later expelled from China by Japan, losing everything. He was interviewed by the Gestapo and fell under permanent suspicion, only with the consolation of having saved thousands. He also brought out a 1,200-page diary critical to the truth.[8] An American missionary, Minnie Vautrin, and her Chinese assistant, nurse Tsen Shui-fang, saved perhaps 10,000 in Nanjing by setting up a makeshift refugee camp at Ginling College.[9] Half a world away, an Iranian diplomat and a Swedish diplomat, working wholly independently, saved many thousands of Jews from death.

Abdol Hossein Sardari was in Paris when fascist police, Milice and Gestapo, came for the Jews. When the Germans invaded in 1940 most diplomats went south to Vichy. He stayed in Paris. In August 1941, an Anglo-Soviet force occupied Iran, deposing the old emperor and installing his son, Mohammed Reza Pahlavi. With Iran forced into the anti-Axis alliance its ambassador was recalled, along with Sardari, a member of the Qajar royal family. He refused to leave, staying to assist Iranian Jews. He sent a protest to Berlin in July 1942, asking to exempt them from deportations, cleverly arguing in upside-down Nazi logic that they were Iranians and therefore Aryans, who happened to be Jews by religion. He did not wait for a decision: he issued hundreds of family passports that did not declare any religion. Once all Iranians were protected he issued passports to French Jews. Adolf Eichmann personally intervened to stop him but not before 2,000 Jews were protected by papers.[10] The postwar government in Tehran repaid Sardari's dissent by accusing him of overreaching his diplomatic authority, which he had. It brought formal charges that effectively ended his career and then pushed him into permanent exile.[11] Thirty years later, the anti-Semitic regime that came to power in 1979 stripped Sardari of his diplomatic pension. He died in exile two years after that, destitute.

Swedish diplomat Raoul Wallenberg acted with similar courage. He intervened beyond his brief to save many thousands from death marches or execution in Budapest, even as Eichmann emptied the last ghetto before the Red Army arrived. Roving murder squads of Hungarian fascists from Arrow Cross, along with German SS under Eichmann, soaked flagstones with the blood of innocents. But not as many as they wanted. Wallenberg paid for his compassion and conscience with his freedom and his life. He was illegally arrested by Soviet occupation authorities in January 1945, and thereafter disappeared into the GULAG.[12] It was not until December 2000 that Russian state prosecutors finally admitted he was held in a Soviet prison for three years before he died (or was executed, which they would not admit).[13] The Yad Vashem memorial in Jerusalem recalls Wallenberg and Schindler as "Righteous Among the Nations." China today honors John Rabe.[14]

Wehrmacht Major Karl Plagge's actions are less well known, although he also chanced torture and death by protecting hunted Jews from the SS.

A trained engineer, Plagge joined the Nazi Party early on, as did many, but was appalled by how deeply sincere and murderous was Nazi race hate and ideology. During the war he was assigned to command HKP Unit 562, a military vehicle repair camp located in occupied Vilna. That was the locale of extensive collaboration with *Einsatzgruppen* and other SS in rounding up and murdering Lithuanian Jews. Plagge did not hesitate to dissent. He drafted as many Jews as he could into his repair unit, issuing work certificates and even forging papers for already arrested men. He brazenly told SS commanders who objected that all the Jews were skilled mechanics: they could not be spared from supporting the German war effort by repairing its tanks and trucks. He was able to save whole families, arguing that if men were surrounded by wives and children they would work much harder for Nazi Germany.

Plagge did not always succeed. Having removed 100 Jews from a train heading from Estonia in September 1943 to a death camp, he was called away. In his absence, they were reloaded and the train resumed its death ride. It is remarkable that Plagge was able to carry out his evasion schemes even into 1944, as the Red Army approached Vilna. Knowing the SS would come to kill all the Jews before they could be liberated, he told his workers: "You will be escorted during this evacuation by the SS which, as you know, is an organization devoted to the protection of refugees. Thus, there's nothing to worry about." Knowing what he meant, most packed what food they had and ran to nearby *melinas* (hiding places). Yad Vashem named Plagge "Righteous Among the Nations" in 2004. It estimates that 150 to 200 people he protected survived.[15]

OTHER DISSENTERS HAD LESS SPECTACULAR POSITIONS or records but should be commended nevertheless. One class of dissenters not usually identified as such were military deserters. Many ran from war for a mixture of reasons ranging from survival to opposition, with personal welfare paramount in most cases. In 2022 Russian soldiers dissented from invading Ukraine by deserting, some also sabotaging military vehicles as they left.[16] As during World War II, they were subject to arrest and even summary execution if caught. Ukraine's Minister of Defense Oleksii Reznikov expressed his sympathy for young Russians ordered to kill, offering mercy in the form of amnesty but also several million rubles if they stopped fighting.[17] As in many prior wars, some were so desperate to escape combat they self-mutilated. Others hid in the forests and swamps around Kyiv and Kharkiv. Or they drove tanks or trucks off-road, bogging down in seasonal swamps of the *Rasputitsa*, the season of mud that the Russian Army knew from its history but oddly ignored by attacking in February. In liberated Mykolaiv, one of the first towns overrun but retaken by Ukrainian troops after heavy fighting, Russian dead lay strewn in the streets and down inside basements as the thaw began. The mayor pleaded: "We're not beasts, are we?" He appealed for local residents to find and bury dead enemy they called "orcs," a term from popular culture that came into common use by Ukrainians to symbolize inhuman wickedness of the invading enemy.[18]

When the Russian Army withdrew from the environs of Kyiv a few weeks later it left hundreds of executed Ukrainians lying in the streets. There were signs of torture and degradation reminiscent of another invasion of Ukraine, by Germans. Except that over the last months of ground fighting by German forces in World War II the outcome was truly catastrophic. In just the month of January 1945, Wehrmacht dead exceeded 450,000. Each of the next three months averaged 280,000 military dead, for a total exceeding 1,000,000 in the last four months of the war.[19] Desertion rates rose abruptly with the war clearly lost and the regime distilled to its rabid and murderous essence, regarding even its own soldiers. Wehrmacht and Waffen-SS firing squads shot tens of thousands of ordinary soldiers caught while trying to desert. Military police and the Gestapo did more killing. Soldiers were hanged from lampposts by roving bands of Nazi Party thugs, including wounded men who had been properly discharged earlier in the war. An aborted state collapsed into ruin and crude nihilism as the revolution devoured its children, executing men it once coddled in the Hitler Youth.[20]

Surely after the war, with full revelation of the regime's crimes, the reputation and social acceptance of deserters would be revised from disloyal dissenters and traitors to victims of tyranny and anti-Nazi moral heroes. Instead, conscientious dissenters and deserters faced public and private contempt over many decades and were denied social recognition or military benefits they were owed. An older generation had to die off first, replaced in key cultural roles by their children and grandchildren. Public rehabilitation started only in the 1970s with their reclassification as "forgotten victims" of Nazism. Recognition slowly took hold that military courts had overseen gross miscarriages of justice. Initially unpopular deserter monuments were erected, a reversal of centuries of only nationalist myths and monuments and burying soldiers under granite lies.[21] The statues were deserved: dissenters in the German military had displayed acute moral consciousness, from some senior officers to *Landser* who refused to obey orders to kill civilians or prisoners.[22]

Much the same happened to young Austrians drafted by the Wehrmacht after the *Anschluss* of 1938, as conscription extended to all eligible males reclassified as German citizens.[23] That is how Richard Wadani ended up wearing the uniform of someone else's army. He was born in Prague but lived with his mother in Vienna when the *Anschluss* was carried out and stormtroopers marched in. As he left to fight for Nazi Germany, an unwilling conscript, his mother pressed him to try to desert. When interviewed in 2014 at age 92, he told a BBC reporter: "She was simple, but clever. She said: 'This regime must go,' and she supported me when we spoke about me deserting from the army. She gave me a white cloth, for safety, when I surrendered. I had it with me for years."[24] On the frightful *Ostfront* he drove a supply truck. He knew that he stood a good chance of being shot should he try to leave. He tried anyway, as did 20,000 fellow Austrians, of whom 1,500 are known to have been executed during the war for the military crime of desertion.

Was he terrified of the advancing Red Army and traumatized into fleeing? The danger he faced from partisans as a rear-area driver was not nothing, but it was minimal compared to that of *frontsoldaten*. Wadani fled Hitler's army not out of fear for his life but in moral revulsion at the death program he witnessed firsthand. He acknowledged decades later: "I was always behind the lines. I wasn't directly endangered by the front but I saw a lot of things that people [at] the front didn't necessarily see: genocide, mass murder, terrible situations." He refused to be complicit: "I couldn't keep on being part of it."[25] Instead, he tried to desert, to cross over to the Red Army one night. He failed. He tried again after he was redeployed to northern France in 1944. He crawled low under barbed wire and through a small grove, moving past German pickets and snipers to reach the British line. We may trust Wadani's claim that he fled from war crimes rather than from war, for he immediately volunteered to fight against the regime that drafted him: he joined an all-Czech unit fighting the Nazis under the auspices of the British Army. He did not desert the war just to avoid it. He turned his coat from *feldgrau* to khaki out of moral conviction. He knew what the Nazis were doing and chose not to pull the trigger in their cause. Then he pulled it against them. He chose to fight against what he saw rather than go along to survive, doing his bit to stop terrible war crimes to which he bore witness.

In 2014 Wadani attended the unveiling of a deserters' memorial in Vienna right across from the Federal Chancellery, in a place of political prominence and belated national honor. Austrian deserters had been pardoned only five years earlier, after decades of controversy and broad opposition. Even when resistance to the Nazis was their main motivation, the process of rehabilitation of war dissenters was never easy. Veterans' groups and many older voters in both Germany and Austria voiced anger at the challenge to their carefully cultivated postwar myth of a "clean Wehrmacht," which they said had fought to a heroic downfall for the Fatherland but not for Hitler and Nazism. They could not accept that it was proper for men like Wadani to shun the Wehrmacht, to desert it. Let alone that he fought against it because of objections to war crimes by a Nazified military in which he had been compelled to serve. Wadani's alternative war implied something too much about the choices made by the vast majority of Wehrmacht soldiers, and by the families that supported them during the war. It could not be plausibly claimed that all veterans had fought honorably in rightful service to their nation. Nor that all blame for the worst crimes fell solely on the Nazi regime and its private army, Himmler's Waffen-SS.[26] Set aside naïve and unwilling teenagers such as Karl-Heinz Rosch, whose story is told below. Leave out of the calculation others who were forced to wear field gray and fight for Hitler's cause and regime but were ambivalent about it, as well as scared.

The larger lesson is how hard it is to gain social and political recognition for moral dissent from most of a wartime generation.

The valor of those who risked their lives out of genuine dissent from a murderous and genocidal regime was a core challenge to all those millions who went along instead. That generation had to die off in Austria and Germany before the truth of the complicity of many was accepted, by honoring those who had refused to abet war crimes. To deny moral status to conscientious deserters was a position that could no longer stand after those shamed by their moral example were mostly gone. Even so, it took decades of political education and replacement generations of Germans and Austrians to accept that in some cases desertion was an act of righteous resistance. Given how obviously indecent was the entire Nazi cause, that long journey out of night confirms how truly hard it is for anyone, in any army, to stand up in moral protest or resistance and for their society to accept that their dissent was the higher patriotism. We may say from afar that we admire people of conscience who stand facing the majority and say "No!" But it is far more often true that their own societies condemn departure from social consensus and then shame dissenters from unjust wars waged for immoral causes.

REAL WAR ABIDES EVEN AS TECHNOLOGY on the battlefield changes. One thing about technology at least remains the same: it is morally neutral. Any new technology may be put to criminal uses or serve merciful purposes. It comes down to the values of leaders and the societies that make that technology available to soldiers, sailors, aircrew, and in targeting decision rooms. Technology is not governed by any ethical code. It does not respond to the laws of war. But it answers the quiet voice of conscience that echoes in an otherwise gaping moral silence in barracks and warships, among pilots, with ground crew servicing autonomous drones. A cheap and simple cell phone, for example, can be used to call down artillery strikes indiscriminately onto far-off target coordinates. Or it can cancel a planned drone strike when it is realized the attack will do untold collateral damage to innocents. Mobile phones were used in wars in Iraq and Syria, texting precise positions from forward observers or front-line soldiers to artillery, asking to take out a specific bunker or outpost. They were also used by insurgents to set off IEDs, one of which killed my former student outside Baghdad. They recorded murders by armed men in Africa, massacring ethnic enemies then sitting down to play video games amidst warm corpses and the still dying. Mobile phones can be used to document such acts of genocide, providing photographic evidence for war crimes trials. Or they may bring more assassins and rapists to join in the killings. It has all happened already.[27]

A cell phone was also used in an imaginative way that, until a Ukrainian farmer-soldier tried it, no strategist or war game planner or combat trainer anticipated. It happened in 2015 as a volunteer in a scratch, ragtag, ill-equipped Ukrainian Army fought Russians and secessionists in Donbas. The Russian Federation annexed Crimea in early 2014, then supported secessionists in eastern Ukraine with captured weapons from Crimea. And with volunteers, technical and intelligence information, and weapons and special forces from Russia itself. The trigger for a larger war was a military drive into the Donbas region starting on August 22, 2014. Skirmishing with rebels was already underway when a long "humanitarian convoy" crossed the border from Russia. It was actually a military thrust by disguised Russian troops who wore crisp green uniforms, absent identifying insignia. Putin denied an attack was taking place, even as unclaimed Russian nationals dubbed "military specialists" crossed the border to support rebels he backed and supplied.

A ceasefire in September broke down when fighting resumed in January 2015. Ukraine scrambled to send its small army, territorial volunteers, and a few older tanks east. They went into the Donbas to fight the rebels and stall Putin's territorial aggression. At stake was a newborn, democratic revolution inside Ukraine that deposed a Russian proxy president, posing a cultural and political threat to Putin's rule in Russia itself. Each side revived past war stories as what was old became new again. Propaganda soaked in unrequited hatreds recalled epithets from Soviet history and World War II, as "fascists" were again said to be fighting "communists." Putin and the rebels tore pages from the Soviet playbook to rewrite history, denying that the 1930s famine in Ukraine was deliberate Stalinist policy.[28] In Moscow, the natural heirs to tormentors of Winston Smith crowed: "Who controls the past controls the future. Who controls the present controls the past."[29] A grubby little war killed 13,000 over eight years. Then in February 2022, it was relaunched as hinge-turning, all-out aggression by Putin's regime and Russia's main forces.

In 2015, 50-year-old Ukrainian reservist Alexei Chaban was sitting in an older-model tank facing a concealed Russian crew in a Soviet-era T64-BV.[30] Most fair-minded people would think that facing the 125mm main gun of a huge Russian battle tank was proof that an invasion was underway. Such was not the case. Moscow continued its denial that it had sent troops, let alone battle tanks, into Donbas. To deploy Orwell again: "It was a bright cold day in [January], and the clocks were striking thirteen."[31] Chaban was a farmer who had served in Ukraine's reserves for nearly 30 years. He volunteered to defend Donetsk and Luhansk regions as a first lieutenant with the Ukrainian Army's too ambitiously named 17th Tank Brigade. His rank and unit designation made it sound like he belonged to a real army. He did not. "We don't have an army," a veteran Ukrainian border officer bluntly told a *New York Times* reporter visiting wounded volunteers at a makeshift, forward aid station. "These boys were sent [east] on buses, with rifles and just 30 bullets each. No body armor, nothing." They faced an enemy with far more firepower and other backing by Putin's more potent military. It was an unfair fight. "They were shooting at us like they were on a firing range," said a lightly wounded reservist. Another wounded youth grumbled that "there were no good flak jackets, weapons or equipment ... [and] it was difficult to get medicine."[32]

The terrible conditions, and taking casualties, angered soldiers as they lost ground and men in Donbas. But not Chaban, who resolved a moral dilemma commonly encountered in combat with uncommon compassion and native imagination. But first he was initiated into war's horrors, starting with a sharp skirmish in which his tank blew apart a rebel truck loaded with munitions. He mused about the event over his smartphone, posting melancholy meditations to his Facebook page that night. Soon thereafter, he came upon a Ukrainian soldier crushed by a rebel tank. The man was alive and in awful agony. "I don't know how to communicate these feelings," Chaban posted. "I'm even afraid to communicate these feelings and what I've seen to the civilian world. The scene I encountered screamed with horror."[33] He did not know it yet but he would find a way that no one before him had ever tried. It started with the next firefight, in which his tank engaged and disabled the Russian T-64. As a Russian officer and two crew clambered out of the stalled tank, as they scrambled down the chassis before running away, Chaban knew he could kill them easily. He chose not to pull the trigger. He did not shoot. He let them run.

Letting three enemy live is not the truly remarkable thing that Chaban did while at war in Donbas in an old and overmatched tank. Although it *was* extraordinary to exhibit life-saving mercy to his enemies when his side was losing badly to a much better armed aggressor, and he was still upset about the crushed man. When he investigated their broken tank he found that the scared officer had left his cell phone inside. It had a Russian SIM card with a list of Voronezh phone numbers. His crew salvaged the abandoned T-64, repairing it and adding it to the order of battle of the now mighty 17th Tank Brigade of the Ukrainian Army fighting in the Donbas. Experts later traced the serial number of the T-64 to Crimea. It was left behind after the annexation, then handed to the rebels to avoid any political complications for Moscow. But an officer's captured phone and his personal numbers proved it was crewed by Russians. Combing through the hastily forgotten phone, Chaban found and posted a photo of the unidentified Russian officer to his own Facebook page, along with Voronezh numbers he located on the SIM card.

Then Chaban appended a letter that he wrote to the Russian's mother, which he asked users outside the war zone to deliver to her. He wrote that he had spared her son's life: "When they got out of their disabled vehicle, we just had to push a button in our tank and all that would have been left of them would have been a memory of our sinful world." He told her, with simple eloquence: "We didn't kill them. We let them go." He said that Ukrainians were not the fascist murderers that Russian propaganda said they all were. The charge hearkened to unrequited hatreds dating to the famine of the 1930s and ethnic divisions and civil war between partisans and collaborators in the 1940s. They were not all heirs, Chaban wrote, to the legacy of anti-Soviet collaboration with Nazi Germany that saw thousands of Ukrainians join the Waffen-SS or right-wing militia to fight against the returning Red Army deep into 1945.[34] Some of his fellow soldiers actually were heirs to World War II fascism, though not Chaban. Nor did he make the obvious political point that it was Putin's regime that supported White Supremacist and neo-Nazi groups, recruiting fascist mercenaries to fight against him. They included the Russian Imperial Movement[35] and Wagner PMC, an outfit named for the internet call sign of its Nazi-admiring founder.[36] Wagner would also fight as a Russian proxy in wars in Syria in 2018, in Libya in 2020, and once again in Ukraine in 2022.

Chaban wrote: "Tell your son that making a living by depriving other people of their lives is not good. May he return home and find other work. May he live peacefully and not take sins on his soul."[37] The story of his letter whirled around the internet. Reuters learned of it and contacted him over Facebook. Chaban called far-off Berlin, speaking out of the war zone over a poor connection, confirming that he sent the letter. In print form, his tale was retold in a hundred newspapers in dozens of countries. He was not a sophisticated man. He was shocked to learn from the reporter that his letter and plea to an enemy's mother had found a global audience. When told how large, he blushed electronically over the bad connection to Germany: "I guess it's a big number, but I'm no expert in these things. I wasn't trying to do anything special. I'm just an average guy." Russian journalists denied the story was true, as did a woman in Voronezh who answered one of the three posted numbers the reporter called. She was either a FSB stand-in or was well briefed. She denied she knew the Russian officer in the photo, adding in a pitch-perfect voice: "Of course, Russians aren't fighting in Ukraine. I can't even imagine how two brotherly nations could fight each other." Chaban was told that the Russians were calling him a liar but he shrugged off the charge.[38] Seven years later, millions of Ukrainians used their mobile phones to reach inside Russia and bypass an iron curtain of state censorship, pleading with ordinary Russians, in many cases their own close relatives, to help stop an unprovoked war of imperial and regime aggression.

Although he volunteered in his country's hour of need, Chaban did not want to fight anyone. He was not consumed by hatred or a need to avenge a death or display honor or find his manhood. He just wanted to go home to his farm. His thoughts dwelled more on ploughs and the spring planting that awaited around the corner of another dreary fight on the steppe, less on vengeance for violation of the border or some other abstraction. He seemed puzzled to be asked why he showed mercy to his enemy. When asked why he let three men live yet declined to take them prisoner, he explained that it came down to a binary choice. Because the fight was ongoing his crew had to stay locked inside their tank. That meant they had to kill the three beaten and fleeing Russians or let them run away. "We could have shot them or let them go. We couldn't have taken them prisoner. It wasn't realistic." Was his decision rooted in ethics or his faith? "I can't say that at that moment I was thinking about God. But you can't kill unarmed people." He admitted that he might have chosen differently had he lost anyone from his unit and felt rising hatred. But he did not: the crushed man was from another outfit.

"I don't regret it," Chaban told the reporter in Berlin, a city at last at peace after two massive wars fought partly over the same fields and provinces where Ukrainians now fought Russians. His little war in the Donbas waged with outdated tanks and tactics might look to outsiders to be a parody of that war, filled with immense armor battles between the Red Army and Wehrmacht. It was the same in that occasions of murder or mercy still presented. "Why should we have killed them? I don't think those three will fight anymore."[39] His conclusion was not supported by evidence, nor his logic taught in Officer Candidate School or laid down in tactics lessons or principles of war primers. There were other T-64s waiting to be crewed on the other side of the war in 2015, or perhaps years later when a full-scale invasion came in 2022. The same running enemy trio might ride back into battle against him and his men on some future day. Next time, he might not get off the first antitank round or make the first disabling hit. His enemy might not show the same restraint in reverse. Logically, Chaban probably should have pulled the trigger and eliminated this future threat in a heated moment when he had knocked out a powerful tank. Instead, he sat back in his older tank defending a precarious cause, his palm hovering over a firing button but never hitting it. He allowed three enemy to live and possibly to fight him again on some not too distant day. His choice of mercy was not a militarily sound choice. Nonetheless, it was a decent thing to do.

————————

SEVERAL U.S. ARMY MAJORS I INTERVIEWED witnessed a desire by senior officers rotating into the war in Afghanistan to create active fights.[40] If you send in brigade commanders trained in a culture of battle seeking, who have only two years to prove their combat leadership in an up-or-out system, they will seek battle even if that is the wrong tactic. So push into Taliban areas to kill them and suffer casualties, while driving civilians caught in the middle over to the enemy. Hand the hard-won compounds back as you pull out again in order to reduce casualties. Much the same happened in Vietnam: take a hamlet by day, lose it at night when you go back to base. The allure of combat, and in some cases of officer career uplift, overrode experience of officers and units already in place.

It turned a successful strike against al-Qaida into a failed war of attrition that cost a quarter of a million lives and lasted 20 years. Similarly in Iraq in 2003, American forces took few casualties as armored divisions smashed into Baghdad while eliminating the entire Iraqi Army. An officer recalled 20 years later: "That's when the war actually began. I had friends on the initial push writing me (I was in Korea) and telling me that I'd missed the war. I didn't."[41] Bad tactics were not alleviated by a pervasive problem with local allies: massive financial corruption. Politically and ethically worse, corroding claims to higher moral legitimacy than the Taliban, was open sexual corruption of local mullahs, Afghan National Army generals, and Afghan National Police officers and generals.

Cruel sexual exploitation included routine rape of boys from poor families by armed Afghan allies. In valleys ostensibly anti-Taliban and loyal to the coalition, boys were dressed in makeup and girl's clothing and made to dance and sing for tribal elders, who then raped them. This centuries-old practice was so pervasive it had a name: *bacha bazi*, or "boy's play." I learned about that directly from young Afghan diplomats in Kabul in 2011. They said they were ashamed of it but that nothing could be done to stop it.[42] It was so commonplace that a U.S. adviser to the Afghan National Police once posted as a success story a boast that he got locals to agree to confine their sexual assaults of young men to captured Taliban.[43] The *New York Times* exposed the practice and NATO complicity in an investigation in 2015. It found "widespread sexual assault of boys by Afghan security force members" and that U.S. military were told not to intervene even "when their Afghan allies have abused boys on military bases." The United States was then recruiting rural militias to help hold territory against the Taliban. The moral decadence of turning a blind eye to child abuse followed the guns. U.S. soldiers were deeply troubled that "instead of weeding out pedophiles" the military was arming them, putting them in charge of village militias, and ignoring that they were vilely abusing children.[44]

It bewildered more caring American soldiers to be ordered to stand aside and let the abuse happen. Special Forces Captain Dan Quinn said: "The reason we were here is because we heard the terrible things the Taliban were doing to people, how they were taking away human rights." He beat up a militia commander he found with a young boy "chained to his bed as a sex slave." He was relieved of his command for doing so, then sent home from Afghanistan. Afterward, he resigned from the military.[45] Others who intervened or just reported abuses were punished for their dissent. They were disciplined and some were sacked when they broke from policy and tried to stop the rapes. The government in Kabul did nothing at all, the one in Washington very little more.

The practice did not go unpunished by the Taliban, followers of a different kind of sexually perverse, misogynist ideology. In 2018 a Kandahar police chief, General Abdul Raziq, was assassinated by a bodyguard who acted on Taliban orders. U.S. Army General Austin "Scott" Miller was nearly killed.[46] His public comment was that he had "lost a great friend." It was not admitted, though it was widely known, that Raziq was guilty of human rights abuses, including torture of prisoners. He was just too powerful an ally in the southern Taliban heartland to expose his blackheartedness and special wickedness.[47] Thus, *bacha bazi* and worse things continued under cover of an anti-Taliban war for modernization and universal human rights. In 2019 a child advocacy group reported that 165 boys were raped by the police and teachers in Logar Province. Afghanistan's National Intelligence Agency arrested the child advocates rather than the accused perpetrators.

In 2020, a 13-year-old boy was gang-raped to death in Kandahar by a police commander and six of his men.[48] And on it went, eroding support. And so the Taliban won the war.

Too many U.S. commanders were also unwilling to dissent from standard operating combat procedures. Pushing their troops into combat operations, disdaining civil administration and nation-building, they routinely turned a blind eye to corruption by their anti-Taliban allies. They focused their own attention and commands, and any visiting media, on active fighting and the body count of dead enemy. Attrition inflicted on the enemy by superior fire-power and technology was once again misidentified, as it had been 50 years earlier in Vietnam, as the way to win a counterinsurgency war. There was not a lot of documentation of this reality but officer witnesses saw it happen over and over. The battle culture of the U.S. military that lionizes combat was confused by the post-9/11 attrition wars. Learning happened on the ground, then it was forgotten as a fresh brigade commander went up the same valley to the same result: dead Taliban and dead or severely wounded Americans. And a lot of fresh animosity and more Taliban recruits determined to push the foreigners out of their valley and country. Any overall strategy broke down as policy and aggressive tactics outside the controlled cities varied, vale to vale. One officer recalled: "The war became a series of villagers making arrangements with local American commanders who rotated out every six months (USMC) and twelve months (U.S. Army)." The locals endured the battles new American commanders sought, then forged a renewed truce as the new leaders realized that "they were accomplishing nothing." The hope was always that the latest round of U.S. brigade commanders would possess more personal integrity than career ambition.[49]

It was discovered that sending female soldiers to talk to mothers worked better in many ways than assaulting Taliban in the valleys and on mountainsides. As long as they dressed in local clothes and wore makeup like local women: a mission exemption was made for wearing makeup off base, as long as it was removed immediately upon return. Just go around the men, assure worried mothers that the Americans and coalition did not want to kill their headstrong teenage sons out with the Taliban, and get them to talk their sons into laying down their arms and returning.[50] Then the lesson was forgotten yet again at HQs as experienced brigades rotated stateside and new commanding officers decided to forcefully push up the same valleys to kill Taliban.[51] The enemy responded in kind. Timed to each fighting season, attacks ramped up after the poppy harvest brought in cash to buy weapons in Pakistan's arms bazaars.[52] Money bought allegiance of older tribal leaders and of fighters, as senior Taliban commanders recrossed the border every year. The mighty would not admit military defeat for two decades. The weak could not achieve expulsion of the foreigners but accepted all recruits the occupation itself provided. A corrupt government and Afghan National Army collapsed as soon as U.S. air support ended. Taliban rushed into cities long denied them. In a final humiliation of superior technology but also political pride, the United States asked Taliban leaders to spare its embassy as it hurried to evacuate from yet another lost war. Helos on the rooftop in Saigon, redux.[53]

Wisdom and humility at the top in Washington would have helped in the post-9/11 wars. But there was mostly hubris when it all began in Afghanistan in 2001. There was also rage of an entire, aroused nation determined to harshly punish *someone* for the Twin Towers. First came a righteous assault on the source of the attack in rural Afghanistan and then, for far more mixed motives, an old enemy in Baghdad. Both wars degraded quickly. Massive military superiority encouraged battlefield overconfidence, while cultural arrogance led to overly ambitious efforts to forcibly implant modern Western values in premodern societies and antagonistic cultures. This deep-seated cultural arrogance about changing the destiny of faraway countries of which Americans knew little, principally a delusion about the political use of force by civilian leaders, in the end proved far worse than any military delusion.[54] It's what led to mission creep that became wholesale redefinition of the mission the military was tasked to carry out, for which it had little training or capacity to undertake.

Within two months the Taliban were soundly defeated militarily and asked for terms, offering to surrender in exchange merely for amnesty. U.S. Secretary of Defense Donald Rumsfeld haughtily announced in a news conference: "We don't negotiate surrenders."[55]

Twenty years of war later, all U.S. forces pulled out in defeat while asking the Taliban to stop shooting as they left and to provide protection at the Kabul airport. A far stronger Taliban and weaker anti-Taliban alliance had been tensing to resume a long civil war interrupted by outside powers. But tribal leaders and mullahs switched sides starting in secret from February 2020, then in 2021 with the same suddenness as they did in 2001 when the Northern Alliance had swept south under the wings of merciless American air power. With all the drones and Apaches and A10s departing, the Afghan National Army and the Afghan National Police collapsed as Taliban rolled unopposed into every provincial capital but one.[56] The reputation of too many anti-Taliban generals and officials for abuse of prisoners and sexual and financial corruption was a major factor in the quick collapse. The speed of the departure of their American ally and air support was another.

Bagram Airbase was emptied a month before the end, without informing the local Afghan commander. Taliban took the base on August 15, releasing 12,000 prisoners. Among them were 6,000 Taliban and several dozen al-Qaida. Then they retook Kabul amidst scenes of abject abandonment that reminded the world of forsaking Saigon in 1975. Only the Kabul air-port was open as tens of thousands rushed to get on the last aircraft out, some clinging to wings and wheels only to fall to their deaths as hubris flew home. It had taken 20 years of fighting to get back to the beginning, when the United States had refused to negotiate Taliban acceptance of a coalition and Northern Alliance victory. A senior U.S. adviser to the Joint Chiefs said about that bungled moment: "We were hugely overconfident in 2001. We thought the Taliban had gone away and weren't going to come back." He added honestly: "We also wanted revenge."[57] Few at his level found the courage to dissent in public. It wasn't just generals who failed. Politicians and top academics went along for most of the ride into strategic defeat and perhaps also into historical infamy.[58]

Another ally was deserted, after a quarter of a million lives lost and over a trillion dollars squandered. Another moral and reputational disaster incurred by the United States. An unwisely smug sponsor of the Taliban in neighboring Pakistan remained as an unstable power hosting hundreds of nuclear weapons. It now faced radical and unintended consequences from its policy of destabilizing its neighbor by supporting attritional war. Taliban were left ruling rubble fields and poppy fields, and perhaps looking forward to expanding into Pakistan. Maybe one day. But in the short run they had no experience in just keeping the lights on. As a winter of severe cold and famine approached, all foreign accounts and assets were frozen, and the outside world turned its back not just on the Taliban regime but the Afghan people. Taliban soon faced an insurgency of their own, targeting the Shi'a minority. On one side, a descent from pride to Predators and from hubris to humiliation. On the other, a climb from primitivism to primacy in a land reduced to ruin and chaos.

CHAPTER 7

TRUCES

On the ground, nobody thought at the beginning that the truce would be permanent. In Monaghan, one [IRA] Volunteer admitted to mixed feelings.... "Our lust to kill had not been satisfied."

All wars come to an end, if only from exhaustion.[1] To get back to peace belligerents often start with experimental halts: ceasefires or truces. A ceasefire returns combatants to apprehended hostility instead of active killing. Most often, it is only a brief respite from fighting that may yet get far worse. Culturally inspired truces are larger but no different. In 1914 elements of the Western armies paused fighting during the Christmas period, but it didn't happen again in the Great War. In 1968 the Tết lunar holiday ushered in the most widespread fighting to that date in the Vietnam War. Four years later, President Richard Nixon ordered what media dubbed the "Christmas Bombing" of Hanoi, the heaviest ever carried out. Ramadan is the "best month in Allah's eyes," a time for peaceful contemplation in Muslim practice. It often leads to calls for a halt to war, as also happens nearly every Christmas. In neither case do such calls evoke much response from modern states and armies.

Ramadan was conspicuous for intensified warfare from the start. Muhammad triumphed over a key Quraysh caravan at Badr in 624 and

Mecca fell six years later, both during Ramadan. Other key Ramadan battles, from Andalusia (711) to Al-Zallaqa (1086), marked the Muslim conquest of Iberia. The 1973 war between Israel and several Arab states is alternately called the "Ramadan War" or "Yom Kippur War," as religious traditions overlapped. More recently, Ramadan saw fighting among Muslims and with "infidels" in a crescent from West Africa across the Greater Middle East. Taliban refused to set, or broke, religious truces in Afghanistan. ISIS fighters in Syria and Iraq were radical beyond any possibility of cultural negotiations or expectation that they would honor an agreed ceasefire. Wherever such custom seems to prevail in bringing about a seasonal truce, below the surface are found more practical concerns and frontline interests. Yet it is also true that any truce engages us with enemies in more humane ways.

FRATERNIZATION WITH AN ENEMY WHO IS "just over there," within hollering or barter distance, is fairly common. If officers do not intervene or participate themselves, contact at a distance morphs into a local truce. That is what happened at Christmastime in 1914 along the upper reaches of the Western Front, as yet unhardened into the defense-in-depth system it would become. Smaller truces also occurred on sections of the Eastern Front. They were practical accommodations by soldiers in deadlocked positions, across from their once-and-future enemy. That is why Louis Barthas and his trench mates later tacitly agreed with Germans not to snipe or to fire on each other's work parties. Yet, spontaneous ceasefires also reflect little outbreaks of mutual respect and rectitude. They are a reach back to civilian habits and prewar humanitarian impulses. A local truce thus can be invoked by a need to render medical aid to unreachable wounded or lend dignity to the dead by burying them. That happened at Cold Harbor in Virginia in June 1864, when men in blue and gray stopped shooting briefly in order to gather in casualties before shooting started again. More rarely, a truce will arise from shared cultural sentimentality about a holiday season or mutual hope that the war will soon be over in any case, so why keep fighting? The truce at Christmas 1914, at the end of the beginning of a 52-month total war that would wreck Europe and begin the breakup of its overseas empires, arose from a mixture of all those motivations.

When cultural traditions encourage truces that mix with more pragmatic impulses and interests, the initiative is seldom taken at the top. Instead, the urge to cease firing percolates upward from the natural desire of troops to pause fighting, at least for a while. It says a great deal about who starts wars and who must fight them that the Christmas Truce of 1914 started among ordinary men who found themselves in the most extraordinary circumstances of their lives. Soldiers stopped shooting, laid down rifles, and some walked unarmed and unafraid to meet in no-man's-land. Perhaps 100,000 participated, or about 5 percent of all troops on the Western Front. Some men kept open and cheerful company, though not most or everywhere. There was no overarching truce. What happened was a series of local, disconnected fraternizations varying in duration and degree. In a few places, enemies walked out and shook hands. In other spots, they stopped shooting for a day or two but stayed in their own trenches. Some traded season's greetings and bits of food and small gifts. Others spoke about wives and families or lovers, of "Peace on Earth" and how the war must clearly end soon now that all the armies had stopped moving. Some sang carols at each other; others sang together. Most who could got royally drunk. Tens of thousands went beyond live-and-let-live practices that are seen in nearly every war, especially if officers are absent or decide to look the other way because they too are tired of fighting.

Truces were not confined to those who prayed to the Christian god. Atheists and agnostics took part, as did Jews in the French and German armies. Also animists and Muslims in African units and Hindus and Sikhs brought from India to shore up the Western Front.[2] It was bigger than any one religion or culture. It was at some level a moment of universal humanity breaking through the base inhumanity of war. It did not start from the top. Three weeks earlier, Pope Benedict XV called for a "Truce of God" over Christmas and was ignored or rebuffed, told by bloodied and warring states to mind his pews and his business. But governments were worried about the effect of the holiday on the armies, so they delivered trainloads of small comforts to their frontline troops.

British got tobacco and plum puddings. Germans feasted on sausages, schnapps, and drums of beer. French received soft cheeses, plucked geese, big sacks of chestnuts, and kegs of cheap red *pinard*. Wives and mothers sent their menfolk parcels of cakes or knitwear, so many that military transport was strained. A few ammunition trains were actually reassigned to haul millions of presents and huge amounts of mail to the front: morale mattered. It was naïveté about the duration and human cost of the war still to come and perhaps also gilded guilt. Shops in Paris, London, Berlin, and Vienna were decorated as if it were Christmas 1913, all sparkling with tinsel and toys. Shortages and sorrows had yet to bite hard for most civilians, as they would. Generals were all absent but worried. The commander of BEF II Corps in the hard-contested Ypres Salient told officers he feared a lack of "offensive spirit" might be brought on by winter weather and a looming holiday season. Attacks were ordered by rear HQs that merely piled on more soldier misery, suffering, and frustration.

It was as much about stalemate as it was about Christmas. On December 18, after yet another costly failed attack, in one small sector British and Germans had agreed to cease fire to allow each side to collect their dead.[3] This is not uncommon in war and can happen at any time of year. We do not know precisely where it started, partly because ceasefires began in different places and ways. Everywhere, it seems that it was the Germans who took the initiative. Other places slipped into ceasefires almost without meaning to, as seasonal songs were sung drunkenly and the revelry became infectious across no-man's-land. Once again, proximity mattered. In southern France the trenches were farther apart, so that men may have stopped shooting but they did not get out to mingle. At the Somme, opposing trenches were 80 to 100 yards distant on average: you could hear and sometimes see your enemy. BEF Private Frank Sumpter heard Germans singing "*Stille Nacht*" in the dark across the dead zone. Men in his brigade sang back. "One German took a chance and jumped up on top of the trench and shouted out 'Happy Christmas, Tommy!' No one fired a shot, which was marvelous, as before then you couldn't put your finger up without it being blown off. Of course, our boys said 'If he can do it, we can do it' . . . and with that we all jumped up and the Germans beckoned us forward to the barbed wire and we shook hands."[4] Similar scenes repeated in disconnected places and odd ways, although shared music and alcohol usually played key roles.

Sometimes, friendly insults were shouted, mostly in English or French. Lots of Germans worked in England or France before the war. They yelled that they drove a taxi in Manchester, waited on tables in Paris, or cut hair in Leeds or Marseilles. Some asked about the local football scores. As dusk fell a strange sight appeared on the German side of the trenches: hundreds of tiny fairy lights were twinkling atop the parapets, flickering into no-man's-land. Allied troops heard loud talk, drunken laughter, and husky male singing, then saw gray figures moving along the parapets. Thousands more fairy lights shimmered down miles of trench. It was hundreds of *Tannenbaum*, little Christmas trees illuminated with candles, shipped to the front to raise morale. At 8:30 p.m. a British officer telephoned his unit HQ: "Germans have illuminated their trenches, are singing songs and wishing us a Happy Xmas. Compliments are being exchanged but am nevertheless taking all military precautions."[5] Hand-painted signs appeared on top of some parapets, signaling "Merry Xmas" or "Season's Greetings." Some were ruder than that, boasting cheerful obscenities.

Along the Somme, a light snow descended on December 24 that made the torn, sinuous battlefield look like a Christmas card more than the grave of world peace that it was in fact. During the evening it was almost quiet on parts of the Western Front. Shelling stopped in many places, though not all. Fewer patrols went out and some snipers chose not to pull the trigger, though not all. Nearly 2,000,000 men went quiet, thinking of home and family or about dead and missing friends from a month before. If a marksman shot up one of the little trees, the Germans cheerfully lifted another one up top and soon the grinchy shooting stopped. Sparkling lights and cheerful chatter and singing broke down hostility across no-man's-land between the frontline trenches. Season's greetings were yelled back and forth in all the major languages of northern Europe.[6]

Christmas cheer dulled hatred of the moment while lubricating goodwill. Men drifted away into a respite from war on a river of beer, wine, whisky, and schnapps, and carols everyone knew such as *Adeste Fidelis*. One Scottish soldier wrote in his war diary that he had "met a German patrol and was given a glass of whisky and some cigars, and a message was sent back saying that if we didn't fire at them, they would not fire at us."[7] Germans climbed onto the parapets, arms down with hands open to show they were unarmed. "Fritzes" called over to "Tommies" and "Parlevuhs" to do the same, while some French hailed *les Boches*. Junior officers went into no-man's-land to arrange ceasefire terms. The men followed later, exchanging cigars and cigarettes, cheese and puddings and drinks. A few Tommies even agreed to be shaved by German barbers who had worked in prewar London or Birmingham. One private later wrote to his mother: "They firmly believe they are winning and that they will soon have the Russians beaten."[8]

Not everyone was peaceful at heart. Some toured the opposing trenches with an eye to coming back afterward in anger, to take out a machine gun whose position they now knew or to grenade a hated sniper whose loophole they located precisely in front of an area where comrades fell the week before.[9] Adolf Hitler, "Adi" to his trench mates, sulked the whole time, refusing to join in fraternization that disgusted him. The truce spread like a prairie fire, leaping over some sections but alighting and catching in others down the line. Among those who took part in widely scattered locales were Germans, Canadians, Australians, Irish, West Africans and South Asians (Muslims, Hindus, Sikhs), French, Belgians, and British. Also colonial units from Algeria and Congo and tropical islands sprinkled around the azure Caribbean.

The most elaborate ceasefire arrangements took place in the British sector along the Somme, where each side was at war in a country not their own, and perhaps feelings were less hardened toward Germans among the British than among the Belgians and French. Many of the latter thought that the British troops who fraternized were half-mad at best and treasonous at worst. Some British, especially men who survived the bloody Battle of the Aisne, also refused to consort.[10] British eager to arrange a ceasefire found Saxons far more likely to concur than Prussians, with whom lethal incidents occurred and local truces were much harder to arrange. One Saxon had made a pre-Christmas habit of climbing high inside a bombed-out brewery to call over to the British to ask how things were back in London. They shot at him many times, a British officer recalled. "One night I came out and called, 'Who the hell are you?' At once came back the answer, 'Ah, the officer. I expect I know you. I used to be head waiter at the Great Central

Hotel.'" Other British officers ran into the German prewar chef of the Trocadero, a high-society London nightclub they frequented often. Private Frederick Heath wrote home contemplatively that he heard Germans call, "'Come out, English soldier, come out here to us.'... We kept up a running conversation... all the while our hands ready on our rifles. Blood and peace, enmity and fraternity. War's most amazing paradox."[11] In a few places, no-man's-land briefly became everyman's land.

It is sometimes said that the truce took place only in the British sector but that is not true. French troops also took part, although the story was censored at high levels in France into the 21st century, while many French historians remained scornful. Recent research has confirmed many of the basic facts and stories. Filmmaker Christian Carion played a central role in the discovery. He was born in the Artois region, where "the war left a trail of cemeteries with well-tended lawns in the midst of fields. . . . Forty nations buried their sons in the earth of my homeland." The war was literally tangible to him, pervading his schoolwork and home environment. "Every autumn, my father and I collected artillery shells which had been brought to the surface by ploughing. We carried them in our arms and laid them down at the entrance to our fields. A *Renault 4* from the Prefecture came to load them up like potatoes and spirit them away." He lived directly on top of what had been no-man's-land. "None of the houses we inhabited were built before the 1920s and none of our furniture pre-dated that decade. Sometimes, one of these houses would subside as it was built over an old tunnel dug by soldiers. These incidents were treated as war damage and the family was granted government compensation." In the 1990s he researched the 1914 truce at the French Army archive at Château de Vincennes. The authorities did not want him there or any publicity about French participation in the 1914 ceasefire. To obtain access to official documents about the Christmas Truce he had to "justify the request on the pretext of working on the French attack of 17 December."

He found at Vincennes records of similar incidents about BEF involvement available in the Imperial War Museum archives. In 2005 he directed the feature film *Joyeux Noël*, a fictional account of the truce set at an intersection of German, British, and French trenches.[12] When he asked the

French Army to cooperate he was denied access to battlefield locations and resolutely told the Army could not be seen to be "involved in a film about rebels." *Rebelles* was the same word he had read in officer reports from 1914. The film was not well received by French historians, who thought it exaggerated the level of French participation. Thirteen years later, an archivist gave Carion records from *Deuxième Bureau*, France's military intelligence agency from 1871 to 1940. They showed that intelligence officers were sent by a deeply worried government to investigate after the fact. They left behind exquisite records. These included a handwritten note from German soldiers "in rudimentary French [that] warned . . . a colonel was due to visit their trench and they would have to open fire at about 2:00 p.m. So it would be a good idea to duck at about that time. However, it would definitely not prevent them from having a drink as planned at 5:00 p.m." The note was signed, "Your fond German comrades." Carion learned that a tenor from Bavaria had entertained French troops by singing arias into the silent night. He built the scene into his film.[13]

It was not universal. Down the majority of the Western Front shooting slackened but did not stop. Even the British suffered more than 100 dead over Christmas 1914. Most of the 2,000,000 men in the trenches simply stayed put, resting in quiet separation but not leaving the trenches or fraternizing. They shared an undeclared ceasefire but took it no further than that. However, in some areas it went much further. Perhaps something like overnight friendships formed, as letters changed hands and promises were made to visit when the war ended. Then they went back to their trenches to sleep it off, although a few drunken men woke early the next day on the other side. A thin dawn on December 25 saw renewal of cautious entreaties. As the ceasefires were resumed men eased out to meet once more in no-man's-land. Brutal reality hit them hard: daylight revealed corpses left unburied from fighting a week or month ago. Suddenly sobered men searched the bodies, looking for a pal from childhood or for a mate or a comrade. They could not stay festive. Christmas morning instead saw the overnight truces revived in order to bury the mingled dead. They started with their own but after a while nation hardly seemed to matter. French carried dead *Boches*, Germans dug shallow graves for mangled Tommies. All were united in the cold middle of a no-man's-land full of death, as one day we all must be united in mortality.

Shyly, as haltingly as first-time lovers on the morning after, with the dead removed young men quietly looked to restart the careful intimacies of the night before. Drinking recommenced. They exchanged *souvenirs*: the French word ultimately replaced "keepsake," with so many English speakers at war in France. Men gave each other whatever poor gifts a frontline soldier could give: a clay pipe, tobacco, buttons cut from a uniform, a belt buckle, or a cap. Generals were far behind the lines, at home with wives or in a château with a mistress. British GHQ hosted a party for officers in dress uniforms and women in ball gowns. On the other side, Kaiser Wilhelm II was dressed in a *Generalfeldmarschall* uniform he had not earned and wore stiffly, his chest glinting with unwon medals. All around were uniformed aristocrats: Junker officers dancing with bejeweled ladies. White-gloved waiters served the best foods.

Back in no-man's-land a few football games started, mostly "kickabouts" among the British. A few real balls mysteriously appeared but most were improvised from half-sandbags or ration tins packed with dirt. In some places, troops from opposing armies may have played "friendlies."[14] Games were childlike: helmets and caps for goal posts, no referees, no one kept score, like little kids playing street hockey. It helped that the mud was frozen and coated with fresh snow and that most players and fans were drunk. The pitch was the oddest in the history of sport, laid out on bits of flatness amidst shell craters, cleared of corpses but studded with unexploded shells and bordered by barbed wire on either side. Death, beer, and football. Never before. Never again. Except that the idea has so penetrated popular imagination that on the centennial in 2014 the British Army fielded a team against the German *Bundeswehr* in a commemorative rematch.

Orthodox Christmas was celebrated two weeks later, on January 6, 1915. That vitiated any largescale fraternization. Even so, in scattered places Orthodox Russian and Serbian troops responded positively to Catholic Austrian overtures made around December 25. Then the officer corps everywhere cracked down. No one was shot for fraternization, possibly because too many men had participated and executing even a few would draw unwanted attention to truces that were not officially approved or even acknowledged. Most units that took part were simply rotated out of the front line in their scheduled turn, sent on an expected leave or to rest and refit. HQs deemed a few units "contaminated" and reassigned them to other sectors of the front. Otherwise, no army took disciplinary action against fraternizers, despite some officers in private calling them "rebels" or even "mutineers," capital crimes in wartime. It was best to let the story lie: reprisals would be deeply unpopular inside the armies and on the home fronts. Although letters were intercepted and photographs and press coverage heavily censored, news of the ceasefires could not be contained for long. Neutral American newspapers were not yet subject to wartime censorship. The story also broke in Britain in early January when the *Daily Mirror* printed a photograph of over two dozen German and British soldiers standing together, unarmed and intermingled and clearly not hostile. Censorship was tighter in France, where Premier Raymond Poincaré recalled that his hometown had been annexed by Germany in 1871.[15] So, too, did others.

The truce of 1914 was not a missed opportunity to avoid all the horrors of the 20th century that followed, its wars and revolutions and genocides. One historian notes that at the time it occurred it was seen as interesting but unimportant, not an act of defiance but a truce "caused by rain, mud, curiosity, lack of personal animosity toward the enemy, and homesickness rather than by frustration and rebellion."[16] Yet it had moral meaning, notwithstanding. We do not need to elevate its import to find solace in its decency. Like most ceasefires, it had significance as a signpost of a desire to one day return to more normal relations, even if no one knew how to get back there as the war stalled briefly at the end of 1914. There was too much expectation on all sides that resuming fighting, committing more deeply to the war, would bring victory the next year. The ceasefires seem to us uniquely haunting and portentous only because we know the horrors that ensued later in the war, then after World War I and in good measure because of it. The truce did not hold because it was not official or widely approved. The nations were far too aroused by a million sons they together had already killed in 1914, sacrificing them on altars of national vanity. They did not say, as did Chief Joseph of the Nez Perce, "I shall fight no more, forever." So it started up again, the war to end war. It broke so much of the old world that a second and far worse world war would have to be fought to settle the immense issues that the first one left unresolved in 1918.

CHRISTMAS 1915 DID NOT SEE ANYTHING like the ceasefires of a year before. It was not just that the officer class made sure that it did not happen again. It was also that a second year of mass killing made most men jaded by death and war, yet also oddly accustomed to it. Disillusioned men like Louis Barthas found other ways to muddle through. There would be other ceasefires but for different reasons. Frontline officers still agreed to short truces to gather and bury the dead from either side. Such agreements could happen anytime after a fight left dead men in the open where corpse rats fed and flesh and morale alike decayed if nothing was done to retrieve bodies. It was sometimes about respect for the fallen. Most often, it was a practical response to the fact that the dead are a threat to the living. Recovery ceasefires were more pragmatic than prayerful, tied to the silence of the big guns and not to the holiday calendar. Mercy did play a role in ceasefires to allow medics to collect wounded, left behind after a failed attack and the inevitable counterattack.

After one German night raid later in the war, a British private relayed this typical account of post-1914 ceasefires in the trenches: "We shouted to the Allemands [Germans] to come and fetch their wounded. At first they seemed very dubious and would only show their helmets but we promised not to shoot." Cautiously, he wrote, a man "who wore the iron cross advanced boldly" right up to the British wire entanglements "and proceeded to assist a wounded man. Another followed, and amidst our cheers they carried him off." Before the German officer left he saluted and said: "Thank you, gentlemen, one and all. I thank you very much."[17] It is a tale of decency and basic decorum that speaks well to both sides. Small as it was, it still tells us nearly as much about humanity in war as does the Christmas Truce of 1914. The first year ceasefires were anomalous because they were triggered by a traditional holiday season. Even so, they had most of the usual marks of ceasefires in the trenches: agreement to bury the dead, followed by resumed hostilities. That is one reason they were hardly noticed at the time compared to the attention that they receive over a century later. People want to believe that there was something more powerful hidden deep inside the Great War that redeems all its suffering. Given the history of war in Europe, who may rightly blame them? More recently, the full-scale Russian invasion of Ukraine in 2022 recalled to everyone, or should, that peace in Europe is not an inevitable outcome of a shared culture or moral progress and enlightenment. That it is a thin reed whistling warnings of vainglorious ambition. And that we forget more than we remember or learn from history.

EASTER 1916 BROUGHT A DIFFERENT SEASONAL truce to the Southeast Front, where Habsburg troops faced Orthodox Russians. Friedrich Kohn was a medical officer with a Hungarian regiment in Galicia. In 1981 he recalled events in his sector around Easter in 1916, the same week British gunboats shelled central Dublin to put down an Irish nationalist rebellion. "The winter . . . was very severe and when I joined my regiment at the end of February the country was covered deep in snow. No military action was possible." When the thaw finally set in, "peace stopped." Artillery duels went on all day, often continuing overnight as well. It was the usual stuff of trench warfare, until the Easter holiday presented Kohn a great surprise. "About twenty Russians came out of their trenches, waving white flags, carrying no weapons, but baskets and bottles. One of them came quite near." A Habsburg soldier went out to meet the Russian, who asked "whether we would not agree to stop the war for a day or two and, in view of Easter, meet between the lines and have a meal together. We told him that first we would have to ask the military authorities whether such a meeting would be possible." Division HQ adamantly refused permission for a ceasefire, let alone close fraternization at the level of a meal in no-man's-land. But HQs were in the rear. This was about men within shouting distance. Who could hear laughter and song from the other side. Who shared similar thoughts about faraway homes. Who were sick of the war, of their officers, of the mud and lice.

At noon Russians "came out of their trenches and brought with them their military band, who came playing at full strength, and they brought baskets of food and bottles of wine and vodka, and we came out too and had a meal with them." Kohn recalled that during the meal everyone seemed to be embarrassed "but both sides were polite . . . and consumed the food and drinks we offered to each other. After a few hours we all went quietly back to our trenches." There was no prolonged ceasefire and no cessation of active hostilities. Men wearing different uniforms while fighting for historically hostile empires shared a meal, then went back to the work of killing one another. With one exception, born out of a personal coincidence: "I talked with a colonel who spoke perfect German and he told me that he had lived for several years in Vienna. When I asked him why he was always firing shrapnel at my first aid post he told me he knew exactly where it was. He promised to leave me alone and he would send a rocket if he had to leave. For the next fourteen days I was left unmolested. Then he sent me a rocket, telling me that his unit were leaving."[18] The next Russians into the line had no Viennese memories or sentiment for Kohn and the others in his regiment. Shelling of his aid post thus recommenced, as did a world war that widened and deepened until it ended both dynasties and empires these men killed and died for.

THE CARNAGE INFLICTED ON THE BEF on the first day of the Somme, July 1, 1916, was so huge that even some Germans were appalled by what they did. Whether compassion was extended to the British varied according to sector and the moral character of individuals. At the northern end, the attack made the least progress. Hundreds of wounded British were left lying in front of the German trenches, groaning in agony. Germans allowed British medics to collect the wounded the next day. At the village of Serre, however, snipers spent the day shooting wounded men lying in no-man's-land. It is unclear if this behavior was cruel or merciful, only that it stopped because of exceptional courage by two unnamed British stretcher-bearers. In the absence of any ceasefire agreement, they climbed atop the parapet and headed out to collect the wounded. As soon as they did, all sniping and shooting stopped. It stayed quiet until the bearers got back with their moaning burdens, then resumed. That suggests the German snipers were engaged in mercy killing and not ruthless murder. But perhaps not. Only they knew for sure.

Mercy was found scattered up and down the muddy Somme battlefield. Near the village of Gommencourt, Germans initiated a medical truce to allow the British to recover wounded. They raised a Red Cross banner above their parapet and waited as their medics went out first, followed quickly by British medics and then long queues of stretcher-bearers. At the village of Beaumont-Hamel everyone disobeyed standing orders against ceasefires to permit stretcher-bearers from each side to work unmolested. Again it was Germans who initiated the brief pause in fighting, raising a white flag high to signal their promise of protection from interference with medics and stretcher-bearers. They did not shoot even at men who took advantage to carry back Lewis guns and rifles dropped when the British attack wave was scythed down earlier by machine guns and rifle fire. The truce around the village resumed the next day as medical officers from either side, wearing bright Red Cross brassards, walked out to the middle of no-man's-land to set terms. Germans then carried British wounded who fell close to their first trench out to the middle, handing them over to British bearers.[19]

THE GREATEST CEASEFIRE OF ALL WAS the Armistice set for 11:00 a.m. on November 11, 1918. It did not arrive as a sudden veil of silence when the guns went "all quiet on the Western Front." There was fighting and killing right up to the ceasefire hour and beyond it. In the last week of the war an average of 2,300 men died daily on the crumbling *Westfront*. It was obvious to all that Germany had lost but how do you stop a war that killed 10 million men? You could not do it with little spontaneous truces. It would have to be negotiated from the top this time. It started on November 7, when a German delegation crossed French lines in three staff cars with horns and bugles blaring their progress through the lines. The fragile convoy was escorted to Compiegne Forest to meet *Maréchal* Ferdinand Foch, Supreme Allied Commander. German delegates were given 34 nonnegotiable demands, ranging from yielding territory and all major warships to requisition of 5,000 locomotives and 150,000 cars of rolling stock. Trains were to be taken even though Germany needed transport to stop spreading famine: the Allies said the food blockade would stay in place. Berlin had 72 hours to agree. Foch was begged for an immediate ceasefire but he denied it. He instead ordered all Allied generals to keep their "swords in the back" of the retreating enemy. British generals, perhaps wanting to reverse a stinging rout at Mons in 1914, attacked toward the town on the last morning of war. They lost 2,400 men to no greater purpose than martial vanity. French assaults led to 1,170 casualties. Americans lost 3,660 men attacking after midnight on November 10. German losses were 4,120. Total losses: 11,350. A raw statistic of real dead and wounded men. It is how most wars end: messily and bloodily.

On November 9, the day Kaiser Wilhelm abdicated, Foch repeated his general order to all Allied armies to keep pressuring a reeling enemy until Germans signed and the Armistice came into effect. German delegates finally signed at 5:10 a.m. on November 11. The last ceasefire of World War I was scheduled to start less than six hours later.[20] General John J. Pershing was commander of the American Expeditionary Force and thoroughly disgusted that Germans were being given any chance to negotiate. Self-consciously parroting Ulysses S. Grant at Vicksburg in 1863, he said that he wanted "unconditional surrender" by the enemy. From his HQ in Chaumont he informed all subordinates that an armistice would take effect at 11:00 a.m. Paris time. That was all. Nothing to clarify what they should do in the interim hours as the war ticked down. No caution was given against ambitious officers trying to seize a final chance for career glory by ordering attacks into towns or woods or marshland that troops could walk into peacefully in a few hours or in a day. And there was a real need for such orders.

Major General Charles Summerall ordered an attack across the Meuse at first light on what he knew would be the last morning of the war. Marines were shelled and machine-gunned, struggling on pontoons, then falling into chill river water. Over six hours 1,100 became casualties. A second attack stumbled into a foggy marsh and was met by concentrated artillery. With 16 minutes to go until the Armistice, a runner from Brigade HQ caught up to the attackers to deliver an urgent order. It was not a demand to officers on the spot to stop the useless killing. It read: "There will be absolutely no let-up until 11:00 a.m." As the moment crept closer, the opposing Germans ceased fire. They were astonished to see Americans still press their attack and were forced to start shooting once again. Over the last 11 hours before the 11:00 a.m. ceasefire, 320 Americans died and 3,240 were wounded. The last man to die was Private Henry Gunther, formally recorded a killed in action at 10:59 a.m. on November 11, a suspiciously tight to the ceasefire deadline official time.[21]

AN ALMOST CIVILIZED WAR WAS FOUGHT in North Africa from 1940 to 1943 between British and Commonwealth forces and Axis armies from Italy and Germany. Americans joined it in 1942. It was not at all the same as the merciless war of bestial savagery on the Eastern Front between the Red Army, the *Ostheer*, and Waffen-SS. There, Germans arrived not merely to take land but to exterminate. It was not at all like the brutal fight hastily trained Australians, Americans, British, Indians, and other Commonwealth troops waged against Japanese in Burma and across the South Pacific. That war was full of cultural misunderstandings smeared with racial assumptions and rising hatreds, fought almost without mercy on either side from the start. The war in North Africa was less soiled. It was waged atop a sand sea where armored divisions moved more like fleets than armies and it did not matter that vast territory was lost one week that could be recovered the next. After all, what navy cares about the waves it leaves behind? There was little fighting in towns or cities, which kept civilian casualties low. No one cared much about the politically indifferent and militarily harmless Arab and Berber caravans they passed. That was not the case on the Steppe or in China or Burma or the Philippines. When rules of the game were broken, as when Germans were beheaded by night raiders, everyone blamed the colonial troops: Moroccan Ghoums with the Free French forces or Mauri with the ANZACs.[22]

In the desert war in North Africa, opposing British and Germans sometimes fought to a clock, each side knocking off operations at the end of the shared "work day" around 5:00 p.m. On the whole, prisoners were treated well. When supply columns passed each other they did not engage. Medics and doctors were properly off limits and treated respectfully. That was all welcome on one level. On another, it concealed the ugliness of war that proceeded apace beneath the veneer of civilized form and manners. Regardless of civility, men were still blown apart by mines or burned alive inside "brewed up" tanks or shattered by artillery barrages or strafed and bombed by rival air forces. For men killed and wounded and traumatized in the same old brute ways, the desert war was not as tame or civilized as presented in distorting histories and films or in misguided popular memory.

When you elevate the enemy you uplift yourself. It is why the North African campaigns echoed romantically in postwar British memory, notably in films about the "Desert Fox," General Erwin Rommel. He was portrayed as the truly honorable enemy, a good German, a Knight Gallant deserving of the Round Table, able to ride against Lancelot, worthy of Tristan and Gawain and Galahad. His record was not like that of vile German generals who fought on the Eastern Front. Little was it known to the British public that other German generals held Rommel in contempt because he never fought in the East, the definitive theater they saw as the real war. We do not know what he might have done several circles deeper into the *Inferno* but we can anticipate it from what he actually did in 1940 in France. After his "Ghost Division" met ferocious resistance from Senegalese troops at the Château du Quesnoy and at Airaines, his troops murdered dozens of Black prisoners of war in a paroxysm of racist rage. He hid all that inside euphemisms in his diary and war dispatches.[23]

How much more comforting to instead recall a Knight's Tale about a British prisoner invited to have high tea with the gallant Rommel. Colonel George Lane fought in commando units and with the secret Special Operations Executive (SOE). On May 17–18, 1944, he twice crossed over to France in a motor torpedo boat on a reconnaissance mission near Ault preparing for the upcoming Normandy invasion. He was trying to discover if Rommel's beach defenses were using a new type of mine. A patrol caught Lane and another commando after they had dumped their cameras in the sea. They were told they would be handed off to the Gestapo to be shot but were instead interrogated by Wehrmacht officers. After a few days they were driven to a castle where Rommel gave them drinks and sandwiches and lectured about underhanded tactics in war. He told Lane that "gangster commandos" like him could be lawfully shot. It is impossible to imagine anything like tea with Rommel on the Eastern Front or in Burma.[24] That is why the romance of the Desert Fox holds, impervious to harsher truths about Rommel in France. Forgetting that his *Afrika Korps* forcibly took trucks from Italian allies so it could flee faster after defeat at El Alamein in late 1942, just before the first Americans arrived in theater at the other end of North Africa. It was hardly an honorable way to treat your major ally's infantry. But Rommel "played the game," as General Bernard Montgomery said. And it is only good form that matters if you want to believe that World War II was won, supposedly like wars of the more glorious past, "on the playing fields of Eton."[25]

The two SOE men were taken to a prison near Paris, where they heard other men being tortured or killed in their cells. They passed on to Spangenberg Castle, to be imprisoned with 300 other British officers. As the Allies advanced deeper into France, Lane escaped while he was being moved under guard. He hid in a roadside ditch, then climbed a tree. A German soldier followed him up the tree but turned out to be a deserter who was also waiting for the Allies to arrive. They headed for the local hospital, where a doctor agreed to treat the sick and wounded POWs that Lane went back for. Just a few years later, British films such as *The Desert Fox: The Story of Rommel* (1951) portrayed him as an anti-Nazi, gentleman soldier. That was despite the fact that his ascent up the ranks had much to do with being one of Hitler's favorites, dating to the campaign in Poland in 1939, and that his involvement with the *Valkyrie* plot to kill Hitler was at best tangential. He became the "Good German" in British postwar memory and popular culture, nevertheless.[26] It is a false image of moral valor well past its due date. But it persists.

MANY TIMES, MERCY TO AN ENEMY is not extended and a ceasefire is not agreed: the enemy is killed to the last holdout. That is most often a mark of the cruelty and heartlessness of the victor, or at the least, of his peaking battle lust and rage and desire for vengeance. On rare occasions, and in exceptional circumstances, withholding quarter may have been the right thing to do. Why should the Red Army have stopped killing the last Waffen-SS who fought to the last hour in ruined Berlin in May 1945? Many were non-Germans who had volunteered as true believers in a fascist New Order. They did vile things in Hitler's service, to towns and families of angry men fighting them house-to-house and street-to-street in Berlin.[27] Waffen-SS officers were mostly well-educated, privileged social insiders who longed for radical racial reconstruction of Europe. They had enthusiastically embraced the exterminationist goals and practices of Nazism. Others were merely crass opportunists who picked and then fought for the wrong side in a cataclysmic war and were left with no further place to retreat in 1945. They were denied the mercy they had denied to prisoners and civilians across Europe, paying with forfeit lives for the crimes they had committed. Was that wrong?

A similar calculus applied in Raqqa in Syria in 2017, where wildly murderous ISIS fighters made their last stand. They terrorized the city: burning people alive, crucifying or beheading, raping women inside forced marriages, selling young girls in sex slave markets. Then they fought until the whole city was rubble all around them, shooting from behind civilians presented as human shields while holding thousands more hostage. At the end, they asked for safe conduct to another part of Syria, saying they would surrender the ruined capital of their declared caliphate in exchange for the last few thousand civilian lives they controlled. Local elders wanted to accept the deal but American and top Syrian militia commanders refused. They decided it was not right or sound tactics to relocate such brutes to another place, where they would rape, torture, and kill more civilians and hostages. They had already done it with barbaric sadism across much of Iraq and Syria. A few local militia leaders and the Raqqa Civilian Council later agreed to a lesser deal that allowed only Syrian ISIS and their families to be bused out. No foreign ISIS fighters were included. American and coalition forces then systematically killed every holdout they could find.

IN 2020 TALIBAN WERE PLAYING THE long game while Americans wanted to get out of the war in Afghanistan. Caught in the middle were all anti-Taliban Afghans. It seemed incomprehensible to outsiders to learn that Afghan National Army (ANA) officers like Abdul Rashid Karwan and Taliban fighters were talking in Helmand Province. He had his throat slashed in 2015 by Taliban, who left him for dead. Yet, in 2020 he invited Taliban to lunch, extending an offer of safe passage. It happened on the fourth day of a week-long national ceasefire, arranged as a precondition to

U.S. diplomats and Taliban signing an accord that would permit U.S. withdrawal. The agreement was premised on a week of reduced violence to precede talks, hence the peace lunch.

Karwan was in an ANA outpost on the outskirts of Marja. In 2010 a U.S. offensive had destroyed many houses and buildings there. Taliban began to retake the area and town in 2015, when Karwan was caught and nearly killed. Fighting continued into 2020, pausing for the national ceasefire and talks 10 years after Americans had largely destroyed the area's infrastructure and killed a lot of young Taliban, with collateral damage to civilians. Karwan hoped the ceasefire would turn into real peace. So did his men. One of his soldiers shouted to a solitary insurgent perched on a motorcycle, his Kalashnikov slung over one shoulder. He promised traditional hospitality: "We'll bring a good chicken for you!" The man called back that he could not come to lunch, that if he met government soldiers it would mean trouble for him with his commander. Then he rode away. Other insurgents approached the ANA outpost from a nearby base, curious to talk. There was an unwritten agreement that a small stream was the ceasefire line, not to be crossed. Enemies stood a few yards apart for a few hours, mostly staring.

Lieutenant General Wali Mohammed Ahmadzai, the top ANA commander in Helmand, thought it was a turning point: "This war is just destroying everything. . . . We are tired, and the Taliban [are] tired."[28] But not tired enough. Taliban were winning by 2020, as the skedaddle agreement with the Trump administration signed in Qatar told everyone on all sides. A few hours of quiet was all that Karwan and other ANA soldiers got. Then gunfire rattled off the wall near one of his men. It was a turning point, after all: behind the scenes, tribal elders ostensibly allied with the ANA and police were starting to take Taliban money and getting ready to flip sides once the last American troops left. The foreigners had never really understood the Afghan people or the complex, horizontal loyalties of their traditional politics. They had fought a technological war to tactical and operational ends, without knowing how to connect battlefield success to any strategic goals. It did not help a failing cause that, like many Taliban also did, they had too often fought without mercy. That U.S. and ANA attack helicopters and drones and missiles killed so many civilians, or that kill squads and ginned-up special forces had in some cases made murder into a game.[29] It was all slow-motion disaster: moral, physical, political, strategic.

AFTER 1945 A PATTERN WAS SEEN wherein local ceasefires were supported by external intervention.[30] Examples include an early United Nations–sponsored truce between India and Pakistan in Kashmir in 1949. In more than 70 conflicts between 1945 and 2020, ceasefire observers or UN peacekeepers were interposed to try to keep the sides apart. Unforeseen was that this could remove incentives to arrive at permanent political solutions: in Cyprus and Bosnia war was apprehended by outsiders but always threatens to resume. In getting back to peace from active war it is essential to orchestrate a ceasefire before separating hostile troops. Only then can talks begin, leading to long-term settlement. Truces can lead to establishing a demilitarized zone or invitations to neutral observers or mediators or outside peacekeeping forces. Or they may be only pauses in war while enemies recover and rearm for the next round. This dichotomy means that quite often, diplomatic aspirations to broker a ceasefire moves too far from reality too fast. A fanciful example was a 2020 secular parallel to the *Treuga Dei* (the "Truce of God" applied to religious holidays in the Middle Ages in Europe), though much less effective: a pledge was made by a majority of UN members to uphold a "universal ceasefire."[31] It was passed in aid of a coordinated response, that never occurred, to the global COVID pandemic. Instead of peace, rampant disease was attended by economic contraction that exacerbated ongoing wars that continued in Syria, Sudan, Mali, Afghanistan, Ethiopia, and a dozen more places. Then a new war in Tigray was started by a Nobel Peace Prize winner, President Abiy Ahmed of Ethiopia. War is costly, yet sometimes belligerents see a truce as worse for their cause: Ukrainians in 2022 were not willing to consider anything beyond local ceasefires to facilitate medical or civilian evacuations, or prisoner swaps. Even so, since the vast majority of wars end short of decisive victory for either side, a truce eventually will be worth pursuing as the start of a path away from war and perhaps one day back to peace. We have few other choices. Eventually, peace is only made with one's enemy of the moment.

PART III

PROTECTED

CHAPTER 8

MEDICS

That was what Việtnam was like . . . foolishness, stupidity, courage, bravery, and . . . a kind of dazzling grace. And nowhere was that grace more clearly seen than in the medics.

— Ronald Glasser, *Broken Bodies, Shattered Minds* (2011)

Before the 17th century most wounded received little medical care beyond that provided by fellow soldiers, or women traveling with the baggage train or orders of nursing monks. Ming armies and the Ottoman Janissaries were notable exceptions: they built dedicated military hospitals. In India, a Greco-Arabic medical tradition called *unani* arrived a thousand years ago with Muslim migrations and invasions. It expanded widely under the Mughals. In Europe, the first military hospitals did not replace barebones monasteries and a few charitable hospices until several decades after the Thirty Years' War: *Les Invalides* in Paris (1676) and Chelsea in London (1682). The first military hospital in Imperial Russia opened in 1715, under Peter I. Wounded men were routinely left on the battlefield at that time, in local care or with none at all if their side lost. French armies pioneered modern military medicine during the many wars of Louis XIV. They were the first to utilize mobile field hospitals, during the Wars of the French Revolution, and "flying ambulances" (*ambulances volantes*), used to recover wounded while a battle still raged. France set up the first corps of modern medics, soldiers minimally trained in battlefield medicine (*infirmiers tenues de service*). Even so, everywhere into the 19th century treatment for wounds was backward: it often did more harm than good. If you survived camp disease and poultices, the amputation axe or knife and cauter, they put you out to beg. In numerous small wars still today, not all that much has changed.

THERE IS LITTLE THAT REDEEMS THE cruelty of war, but medics and nurses come closest by performing inspired acts of daily mercy. In 1841 six British physicians boarded a troopship bound for Hong Kong. They were heading into the First Opium War, part of an eventual 80 surgeons and assistants who went to China. As they arrived, Royal Navy gunships were bombarding coastal cities and reducing forts along the Pearl River. They found over 1,000 men suffering from high fever and dysentery in improvised wards and squalid hospitals. Rear Admiral Richard Parker arrived next. As a historian of the medical expedition put it, he had plans for a naval campaign but no higher moral purpose than sustaining "the balance sheets of opium runners."[1] Parker blockaded Canton in May 1841. A young lieutenant on HMS *Blenheim* wrote, "I am sorry to say that many . . . barbarous things disgraceful to our men" were done at Canton. Another lieutenant wrote, "There was a great deal of wanton cruelty on our side." Present were veterans of the grim Peninsular War in Spain, whose terrible brutalities were captured in memorably empathetic paintings by Francisco Goya. Even they said they never saw such butchery as carried out by British troops pursuing defeated Chinese in the cause of a monopoly drug trade.

More humane behavior came from the six doctors, who directed men to recover and care for wounded Chinese: "After the massacre at Ningpo [Ningbo] in March 1842, men were pulled alive from the piles of Chinese corpses and tended in British Army hospitals. Two months later at Chapu [Zhapu] Chinese prisoners were fed, had their wounds dressed, and then were given three dollars each before release on the simple promise that they would not fight again."[2] Several surgeons had reservations about the opium trade the Royal Navy served: it was wrecking a venerable civilization merely to keep ports open to private profit from opium imports. In

July 1842, things got much worse. British troops were followed by local brigands, taking turns sacking towns along the Yangtze. It was imperialism, barbarism, and anarchy all at once. The British paid a high price, or at least the troops did: fever took 25 percent of Royal Navy sailors and 50 percent of Redcoats in China. It did not matter to far-off opium merchants of the East India Company. Their profits were worth every life lost.

Not much was learned from China about contagion or barracks hygiene. Twelve years later Britain was again at war, with Russia in Crimea. There, only 3,000 men were killed by the guns out of 22,000 total British military dead. The rest succumbed to abysmal sanitation, dysentery, cholera, and truculent military and medical obduracy. In the midst of all that, things changed for the better as medical women went to the wars.[3] Women served in nursing corps starting with reforms by Louise de Marillac and Vincent de Paul in 17th-century France. They set up all-female religious societies that tended the sick and poor, giving all nursing a terminology rooted in these religious orders: *soeurs de charité de la miséricorde* (sisters of charity and mercy). In Crimea, French and British women nursed on one side and Russian women on the other. Women next served in large numbers in the American Civil War, then they went abroad with imperial armies in multiple Victorian "small wars" in Africa. The real breakthrough came everywhere during World War I. With mass conscription of males into multimillion-man armies, women were enlisted in uniform by all armies. Conditions forced them to pioneer blood transfusions, antiseptics for burn patients, and treatments for mental trauma and poison and blister gas wounds never seen before.[4] Women nurses shifted from images of saintly sacrifice to treating male trauma on a mass scale. Along the way they gained advanced professional skills, gratitude from badly wounded men, and eventually also begrudging social respect.

Hostility to women in military medical work was seen from the founding of the modern tradition by French *soeurs de charité* who were the first to go to Crimea, followed thereafter by Florence Nightingale. She was born into high social status and riches but came to see a wider world of misery and suffering when visited by Julia Ward Howe and her philanthropist husband in 1842. She is most famous for traveling to the Crimean War to nurse wounded soldiers, often over the objections of senior officers who thought women of her class in particular should not see the face of war, or naked and wounded and febrile and dying men. Conditions were awful: filthy wards, few supplies, and not much more medical knowledge than required for the usual amputations and compresses. Women nurses on the Russian side during the Crimean War faced far more desperate conditions, rates of epidemic disease, and mass casualties inflicted by better armed British and French troops. Private Russian efforts led to women volunteers entraining for the Crimean theater early in 1854. In November, the tsar's government sent 28 women down to the war zone, followed by hundreds more. There was resistance on both sides to women arriving to nurse. On both sides they went anyway, setting a crucial medical precedent for all future wars.

Nightingale is less well known for rejecting the germ theory of disease and modern preventions such as smallpox vaccination: she insisted that all sickness arose from miasma and poor sanitation, from putrid swamp air and dirty water. In fairness, she was not alone among medical practitioners of the time in holding on to the older theory. Less forgivable is that she objected to women nurses arriving in the Crimean peninsula without her say-so. She reacted with intense anger to a team of Irish Catholic nuns who traveled to the war without her permission: 15 Sisters of Mercy, who set up a nursing camp outside Balaclava in 1854. They provided care, comfort, and dignity to wounded and feverish men yet were were booed upon arrival at Portsmouth's dock when they returned to England. Worse, in Crimea they were left unsupported by an acutely hostile "angel of mercy" who set herself up as lady superintendent of nursing.[5] Yet, despite major character flaws of routine manipulation and credit-taking and rigid medical thinking, Nightingale did enormous good for women in military medicine and professional nursing.[6] Her legend was not entirely earned but it inspired many other women to become war nurses.

Five years later, large numbers of female nurses served in the American Civil War. At Shiloh they tended to 11,000 wounded Confederates. On the other side, they worked in hospitals filled to the brim with moaning and fevered Union men.[7] Mary Edwards Walker was born into a New York abolitionist family. She graduated medical school at 21, after 10 months training.

She was 29 when the Civil War broke out. She rushed to volunteer for the Medical Service but was denied an officer commission based solely on her gender. She chose to serve as an unpaid surgical assistant and later as a civilian contract surgeon. She was the first woman surgeon in U.S. military history, one of only seven women doctors attached to the Union Army.[8] For nearly two years, she performed battlefield surgery on casualties in field hospitals close to Union lines. She was at First Bull Run, Fredericksburg, Chickamauga, and Atlanta, and practiced in traditional Union Army hospitals in Washington, D.C. She made a habit of crossing Rebel lines to treat civilians and probably also to spy. She was captured in 1864 and held in a dismal POW camp for four months, until exchanged with two dozen male Union Army doctors for 17 Confederate surgeons.

As the war devolved into mass carnage, the old resistance to women in the medical corps started to break down out of military and medical necessity. It no longer seemed to matter that the "gentler sex" might be exposed to and also treat naked, howling, terribly wounded and tormented men. More women joined an always overwhelmed Medical Service or as nurses in rear hospitals or convalescence homes, bringing skill to treating wounds as well as compassion to the slowly dying. In November 1865, President Andrew Johnson approved a bill awarding Mary Walker the Medal of Honor, the first women so decorated. She was recommended for the award by General William T. Sherman. Along with 910 other Medals of Honor, hers was rescinded in 1917 when Congress set out new criteria and applied them retroactively. Walker refused to give hers back. It was restored posthumously in 1977.[9] After the war, she became prominent in advocating for women's rights. She was proudly arrested many times, including for illegally dressing in men's clothing in public: years of blood-wet gowns devolved into misogynist pettiness about petticoats.[10]

WE ASSOCIATE WARTIME NURSING WITH TREATING wounds. But much nursing instead involved dealing with epidemic diseases ranging from influenzas to smallpox. And "camp disease" (typhus), which pursued all armies back to camp along with unchecked infestations of lice. In Crimea, most Russian dead succumbed to endemic camp diseases and unsanitary conditions, not the enemy's guns. That was also true on the other side. In the American Civil War and Franco-Prussian War it happened yet again: disease killed more than the enemy did in sodden field works around Richmond and at the long siege of terribly overcrowded Metz. Influenza weakened all the armies in the trenches of World War I in 1918, but perhaps the *Kaiserheer* more than others. Imperial Japan lost more men to tropical diseases in the Pacific than it did to combat with Allied troops. Unchecked diseases continued to kill in wars of colonial suppression or liberation, from Africa to Latin America and Southeast Asia. In makeshift guerrilla stations and state hospitals, women nursed the sick through decades of civil war and cartel wars into the 21st century.

Typhoid was especially deadly. It killed nearly three times as many British soldiers on the Veldt during the Second Boer War than were taken down by snipers or Boer cavalry raids. It swelled up out of poor latrines and filthy water, made fetid by prolonged blockades of congested garrisons during the sieges at Ladysmith and Bloemfontein. Conditions at the Military Hospital in Natal were hardly a model but out in field hospitals it was much worse. One nurse wrote about a British Army mobile field hospital in South Africa in 1900, where clean water needed to avoid cross-contamination of patients was seldom if ever available: "There is no water for anything; the patients simply have their faces and hands washed in water that is quite green, got out of holes somewhere near the camp." It took a toll: "Body lice abound everywhere, there is no water to wash the bedpans, and the tins they drink out of are rinsed twice a day in this same dirty water." Despite the conditions, foreign women volunteers rallied to both sides. Some were seeking adventure; others wanted to serve as men did in support of what they saw as a higher cause. Some went to the Veldt to nurse or teach Boer children in concentration camps.[11]

Male nurses were there, too: Royal Army Medical Corps orderlies and St. John Ambulance volunteers. They were just as overworked and exposed to contagious disease as the women. But it was a new era. Newspapers were covering wars for empire as never before and eager to interview women nurses about hospital conditions. A royal commission looked into it, leading in 1902 to a permanent Imperial Military Nursing Service.[12] Still not enough: a world war loomed over the decade's horizon for which the British Army was unready at every level, including its medical services. No one else was ready, either. The U.S. Army Nurse Corps was a tiny service, created only in 1901. A Navy Nurse Corps followed in 1908. A *Service de Santé* was set up in France in 1903 atop an older and advanced medical system. It too was forced to expand many-fold in 1914.[13]

Religious nursing orders were preeminent and increasingly also international starting in the American Civil War and leading into World War I. Irish Sisters of Mercy founded a house in Pittsburgh, Pennsylvania, in 1843, working in regional hospitals while teaching nursing in an infant profession that in those days had few women. During the American Civil War a hundred Sisters of Mercy nursed soldiers from both sides. They were joined by 540 Catholic nuns from other orders who served as nurses everywhere from battlefields to rear hospitals to long-term hospices. Secular volunteers arrived after losing their sons or husbands, or they associated with benevolent societies and charities swamped by the agonies of protracted war.

A different order of Sisters of Mercy served the Russian Army in World War I, taking their order's name but not their confession from France. The Russo-Japanese War of 1904–1905 had shown that military medical services needed to be made permanent, that women volunteers no longer sufficed. With mass conscription of men planned from 1912, the Russian Army set up a rigorous medical course in St. Petersburg for educated middle- and upper-class women. Nursing was not a profession as yet to most women of means: more of a fancy or a volunteer pastime. Others were committed to it and determined.[14] It did not matter what your class or motive was once the guns of August bellowed in Poland and Galicia and millions marched to war. In all the tsar's domain in mid-1914 there were just 4,000 nurses. It was not even a fraction of the number that would be needed within only a few weeks.

Total war brought massive demand for surgeons, medics, and nurses. British women were traditionally barred from practicing as surgeons or studying medicine, except at the London School of Medicine for Women. However, during World War I the Endell Street Military Hospital was staffed exclusively by women doctors and nurses.[15] The acceptance of germ theory meant much greater emphasis on sanitation and prevention of infectious spread. Radiography also demanded higher skills, as did use of more advanced anesthetics. There were as yet no antibiotics but wounds at least were cleaned deeply and sterilized. Fever was monitored with a new invention from 1867: the first practical medical thermometer. Mass armies waging industrial war experienced many industrial-type accidents: crushing injuries from tractors and trucks, heavy artillery and odd tanks. Many women were traumatized by proxy as they dealt with mass woundings and the extreme violence that caused mutilations and physical and psychological trauma in the men they attended. Limbs were amputated in huge numbers after every battle, like an autumn's harvest. That's when longer-term nursing was needed.

Aircraft caused critical burns as they fell from the sky. Winters brought hundreds of thousands of cases of severe frostbite, while boredom and anxious youth produced the usual venereal diseases all year round. Stinking, foul-looking "trench foot" was revealed as a nurse peeled off a man's boots and sodden puttees. Yet none of that prepared any medical personnel, male or female, for poison and corrosive gases introduced to war beginning in April 1915: clouds of chlorine, bromine, lewisite, phosgene, and the infamous pea green, ground-hugging dichlorethylsulphide ("mustard gas"). Boys and men in wild, mortal panic had to be calmed as they thrashed and gasped to breathe, then stripped naked and the gas washed off using kerosene or gasoline. More arrived blinded or blistered, coughing and vomiting, stunned and terrified. Some drowned in effusions of lymph that collected in their airways, or had crisped flesh from a flamethrower attack and had to be bandaged like mummies. Long-term care followed, controlling wound infection and inflammation and overseeing physical and morale rehabilitation, all wrapped in suppurating physical suffering and deep psychological trauma.[16]

And yet, merciful women arrived from all over the world to serve as nurses or doctors with all the major armies. Australians and Canadians and others served in Voluntary Aid Detachments with the BEF.[17] Volunteers from the Caribbean and United States served in nursing orders and philanthropic hospitals. More came from neutral countries, nursing anyone who needed it under the auspices and symbol of the International Red Cross.[18] By the end of the war many thousands of women worked in casualty clearing stations quite close to the front, sometimes inside the range of the big guns of the next attack or counterattack. Nurses worked in rear area hospitals, inside hospital ships, on evacuation trains, and all across the home fronts in city hospitals and county clinics. More tended recovering veterans in convalescent homes. It became clear to everyone but intransigent misogynists that women doctors and nurses played a vital role in caring for injured soldiers and in both military and home-front morale. Women therefore became a more permanent fixture in modern wars. Only combat remained closed.

In World War II all major armies hosted professional nursing corps, largely though not exclusively female. Even so, once again there was a mad scramble to adjust to the vastly increased scale of a world war fought at maximum industrial commitment. This time more women who served overseas were already professionals in civilian nursing or were trained doctors and surgeons.[19] Military medicine overall was more sophisticated but still overwhelmed. At least nurses did not have to deal with killing gases as in World War I, except for rare cases. *Rikugun* used gas in China but not in the Pacific War, where Americans were capable of retaliation in kind. There was an accidental release of gas from Allied stocks in the port of Bari in Italy, when *Luftwaffe* bombers hit the Liberty ship *John Harvey*. The burning ship filled the lower harbor with poison clouds that rushing ambulances bravely drove into, not knowing it was gas. Medics and nurses were much more mobile in World War II, as were more motorized armies. They could not be certain where the front line was or if medical markings would be respected when they crossed it. They crossed it anyway, looking to recover wounded soldiers or to bring mercy to shattered civilians.

Nurses and doctors were once the only women allowed near a modern combat zone, at least from the more socially respectable classes; working-class women and peasants had always gone to the wars their men fought. But industrial war required a total national commitment, including by women at rising levels of engagement. They served in far larger numbers in World War II.[20] Nurses went to war on all sides in fights of dubious imperial purpose in French Indochina, Korea, Malaya, Kenya, Algeria, and Vietnam.[21] They served also in noncombatant jobs as clerical, logistical, radar, and vital communications workers. It was inevitable that women were allowed into combat as well, especially as Western armies shifted from male conscription to all-volunteer forces. Tens of thousands of American women marines and national guard served in Iraq and Afghanistan after 2001, firing at the enemy, taking fire, suffering trauma and grievous wounds as catastrophic and ruinous as male combatants.[22] In 2004 Tammy Duckworth's helicopter was hit by a rocket-propelled grenade. She lost both legs and part of one arm, becoming the first, but not the last, female double-amputee of the long post-9/11 wars.

Within 20 years women were accepted into all combat roles in most Western militaries. The shift was an advance for women's rights but also embedded more women in moral dilemmas raised by the wars they now joined as active combatants. Women are no longer as distant from choosing whether or not to pull the trigger as they were when going to the wars as "camp followers." They are beyond being just a mother buying war bonds to support her son's war. They are more directly ethically challenged than a Great War *munitionette* or World War II factory worker making bombs or bombers. There were female radar operators in danger in the Battle of Britain; a million young women in *Luftwaffe* antiaircraft crews; U.S. Army truck drivers and Allied shuttle pilots. Even so, Red Army deployment of women air and tank crews and combat infantry was a rare exception before the 21st century. Now there is a rising expectation in all modern militaries that women will fight.

Today, women still save lives in surgical, orderly, and nursing roles in modern militaries. But more than ever before, women also take part in war as life-taking combatants. They are engaged in all the foulness of modern war, not just in situations calling for mercy as a caregiver: they must also make hard choices that can lead to moral injury. In 2022 millions of women in Ukraine were shuttled outside the country in traditional roles as mothers with children and elderly parents. Nearly 60,000 others went straight to war in regular and territorial units. More joined and fought as irregular volunteers, although conscription was restricted to males age 18 to 60, who were forbidden to leave the country.[23] It remains to be seen whether women on the whole will behave differently than men in war. We know a lot about how women participated as life savers in past wars.[24] We are learning more about them as killers in contemporary and future wars.

———

IN THE U.S. ARMY DURING WORLD War II medics were hurriedly trained, often from scratch. They collected casualties under fire, stabilized wounded and sent them to the rear for more advanced treatment. Casualty clearing stations were the realm also of litter bearers, part of the first line of any medical aid. A soldier called out for a company aidman who went forward under fire to help him, accompanied by litter bearers with whom he worked closely. He might arrive to find the wound was not severe, that it should have been treated by the soldier from his own first aid kit. Or he never arrived. Then someone called for a second aidman to save the first. Most medics were popular and well respected. An enemy could use that to advantage. Snipers wounded rather than killed a man in order to lure out medics, who were shot knowing that other men were more likely to break cover to help. It was a trick used by snipers in nearly every army since rifles were invented. In Iraq and Afghanistan insurgents did the same but with potent IEDs, setting secondary bombs to kill medics who responded to the first large explosion. Allied bombers used this tactic on a grand scale during World War II, seeding German ruins with time-delayed bombs to kill first responders: rubble searchers and any medical personnel.

A U.S. Army aidman's main job was to reach a wounded man quickly and stabilize him: stop obvious bleeding, apply a splint or dressing and sulfa powder.[25] He administered morphine, ensuring the man did not get too much before he arrived or later from overeager buddies. That was a problem once the weather turned cold: slower circulation delayed absorption of the initial syrette dose, tempting soldiers responding to cries of pain to inject another one. Tourniquets were another matter, far too often tied too tightly or loosely, or hidden under a blanket so that they stayed on too long and doomed the limb.[26] An assistant surgeon in an advance aid station saw the wounded man next, preferably during the "golden hour" of most hope, before he arrived at the main battalion aid station to get plasma and triage. Or he might be hurried directly to a near rear surgery or field hospital or to a farther off surgical base. Technician 5th Class Alfred Wilson was an aidman during fighting along the Moselle. He moved among wounded lying in the open under German shelling until he, too, was hit by several fragments. He refused evacuation. Bleeding badly, he dragged himself along the ground to reach casualties. As he weakened from blood loss he told other men what to do. Then he died.[27] It was the kind of moral grace and routine courage under fire that made other men go to extraordinary lengths to protect medics. Wilson had counterparts in every army in that war, and in all armies in all modern wars.

Yet, not every medic later received the respect that was his due. The 320th Antiaircraft Barrage Balloon Battalion, an all-Black unit, landed on Omaha on D-Day. Corporal Waverly B. Woodson came under intense fire while he was still on the water, as so many did. He was bleeding from shrapnel in his thigh and buttocks after his landing craft hit a mine. Despite his wounds, he sprinted onto the wet sand and set up a medic station. He worked on wounded from his and other units for over 30 hours, amputating one man's foot to safe his life. Wounded could not be evacuated because landing craft were under orders not to do so while needed to bring in fresh assault waves. Men crawled or were dragged under what little natural cover there was, at the base of soft grass dunes. Woodson helped rescue four drowning British soldiers before he collapsed from blood loss, trauma, and exhaustion.[28] His reward, as with other Black soldiers, was to be passed over for a Medal of Honor for which he was nominated. A full U.S. Army investigation later concluded that the reason was straightforward racism. It was not until January 1997 that seven Black soldiers from World War II were belatedly awarded the Medal of Honor. Woodson's case was pending when he died in 2005, having spent decades working in the morgue at Walter Reed National Military Medical Center.[29]

Due to his faith, Private Desmond Doss refused to carry a weapon. Conscientious objection led to teasing and bullying and got him ostracized during basic training. He was on Guam and Leyte, serving with the medical detachment of the 307th Infantry Division. Unusually, his Medal of Honor citation is not for a single act of valor. It spans weeks of self-endangerment, starting with an ill-conceived assault on the 400-foot Maeda Escarpment, a high rock face nicknamed "Hacksaw Ridge." A counterattack with field guns, mortars, and machine guns drove the Americans reeling back. About 75 wounded men were left in the open, under fire. Doss did not hesitate. He remained with them, carrying men "one by one to the edge of the escarpment and there lowering them on a rope-supported litter down the face of a cliff to friendly hands."[30]

A week after that he went out 200 yards to bring in a wounded man under heavy Japanese rifle and mortar fire. Two days later, he crawled all alone to within eight yards of Japanese defending the mouth of a large cave. He worked under a shower of grenades as he treated four wounded men, then dragged each back to safety. Another day he stayed with exposed wounded during a night attack, while his company took cover. He was seriously hurt by a grenade, in both legs. He declined to call an aidman for five hours, fearing to expose another man to fire. While being carried on a litter during a tank assault he rolled off his stretcher to free it for a more critically wounded man. Then he was hit a second time.[31] He was one of 11 medics awarded the Medal of Honor, five in the European theater and six in the Pacific theater. Hundreds of other medics received silver or bronze stars; even more got purple hearts. It is hard to imagine more grace or compassion within the Vale of Tears that is combat than these acts of mercy and self-sacrifice.

In fighting just inland from the beaches of Normandy, a U.S. forward observer was shocked to see a German captain climb over one of the infamously impenetrable hedgerows and walk calmly toward the Americans. He seemed sure they would not fire on his white medic's coat with a bright red cross emblazoned on it. He handed over a note asking the American medical officers across the way to agree to a ceasefire to evacuate wounded and retrieve the dead. It was allowed; for two hours there was no shooting.[32] There were many examples of this type of medical truce, usually arranged at the urging of medical officers on one side and quickly agreed to by medical officers on the other, unless overruled by HQ.

Near Cologne in November 1944, Major Albert Berndt of the U.S. Army 28th Infantry Division was under orders not to seek a medical truce but decided that mercy trumped his orders. He strode to the German lines with a G.I. translator at his side and a white flag held aloft. A German *Leutnant* agreed to a medical ceasefire on his limited authority but warned Berndt that he could not speak for the more distant German artillery. It was a common enough exchange, reflecting battlefield realities. Berndt loaded wounded into three trucks and set out to an agreed site where he was told to gather his ambulances. German troops had already carried several American wounded there, covering them against the snow and cold with blankets and long greatcoats. They did so over objections of a bellicose Wehrmacht captain who looked ready to take Berndt and all American medics prisoner. U.S. artillery would not cooperate, either. It shelled the area as German and American medics worked together tending to wounded. Then they divided, each group of medics and wounded headed to their own lines.[33]

Medical ceasefires were most often arranged by outposts and forward aid stations closest to shifting combat lines after fighting subsided near where the wounded lay. Far more remarkable was pausing fighting for a medical truce. That is what happened at the "bridge too far" terminus of a failed offensive, Operation *Market-Garden* in the Netherlands in September 1944. This Allied sword thrust had aimed to "bounce the Rhine" all at once, crossing over to swiftly end the war. Germans and British engaged in intense combat at the last bridge at Arnhem, where commandos held one end and panzers held the other. The British perimeter progressively compressed under heavy weapons fire. Lieutenant Colonel John Frost and survivors of 2nd Parachute Battalion were driven under the bridge ramp by intense house flames and incoming mortars. Low on ammunition, scores of badly wounded were in cellars of nearby houses, in grave danger from multiple spreading fires.

Medical officers asked Frost for a truce to let them evacuate wounded. They intended to hand the worst cases to German care because the British were almost out of medical supplies. During a medical ceasefire lasting two hours, German medics and bearers evacuated 280 wounded commandos, even going into burning buildings to carry some out. It was not all above board: panzer infantry repositioned to better fighting positions closer to Frost's position. When fighting started up again it continued until the last paratroopers could no longer hold and Frost agreed to surrender. A German major told one British officer that their effort reminded him of fighting in Stalingrad.[34] Only on the *Ostfront* there were few comparable examples of combat halts in the interest of mercy.

THE 28TH INFANTRY HAD ATTACKED INTO the tangled woods of the *Hürtgenwald* early in November, two of its battalions taking high ground around a pair of villages. Jutting deeply into the enemy lines, the position was counterattacked from three sides by German infantry, panzers, and heavy artillery. Supply and evac routes ran along a narrow, rain-soaked forest trail. It was hard to reinforce or evacuate because shifting forward positions were under fire and taking casualties, while knocked-out trucks and tanks blocked the narrow road. Battalion surgeons Captains Paschal Linguiti and Michael De Marco used jeeps and tracked M29 Weasels to evac to a hillside cave, past which their ambulances could not go. When the dugout was targeted by German shelling all walking wounded were sent to the rear with medical escorts. Nonambulatory cases were laid on litters, many outside the small cave under blankets in falling snow. They held up little red crosses as Germans came to the cave several times, making sure no one was armed. Germans let more walking wounded leave unmolested. Incoming were also allowed to make their way to the cave aid station. One German commander offered to supply food and medicine but took the last working vehicle. Linguiti and De Marco stayed with their patients. Later, the Germans offered a medical truce to permit everyone to pull out casualties from the whole valley. Lightly wounded and any nonmedical personnel had to surrender but all U.S. Army medical staff and more seriously wounded were allowed to go.[35]

During an assault on the town of Schmidt two wounded G.I.s were snagged and exposed on barbed wire. Private Harold Sheffer waved a white cloth then stood up to be seen by the Germans, who stopped firing. An officer strode over to parlay and everyone took advantage of the pause to stand and stretch. Shortly after the two men were retrieved from the wire, shooting resumed.[36] Elsewhere in the woods a captured aidman was put to work helping wounded prisoners. Once they were stabilized, the Germans sent him with one of their medical orderlies to carry American wounded to a point between the lines. Mike Timko was wounded and knocked unconscious on December 2. When he woke up and realized that he could not move he called into the darkness, "Medic!" He was approached by two men who turned out to be Germans. One had studied in Chicago before the war. They patched Timko up, then carried him to his unit's forward aid station.[37]

Americans did much the same whenever the situation reversed. They treated German wounded under their control as if they were their own. In one case, a three-hour ceasefire was agreed to allow ambulances to remove 30 wounded men lying in pain and bloody *feldgrau*. Like the Germans at the cave dugout, it was American practice to exclude all nonmedical personnel and lightly wounded from these short battlefield amnesties. Armed men were banned from medical sites and, if found, were taken prisoner.[38] The U.S. Army Office of Medical History concluded from these and many similar occurrences that the Germans had practiced "continued adherence to the international laws and customs of war affecting wounded and those who cared for them on the battlefield."[39] There were always exceptions: individual violations by snipers, long-range fire on ambulances, and the almost standard Waffen-SS practice of ignoring any restraint of law, mercy, or custom. Then everything got worse in 1945, after catastrophic German defeat in the Ardennes.

To secure noncombatant immunity American medics wore distinctive red cross insignia, usually on their helmets and on armbands. Germans wore a type of white coverall. Under the laws of war medics were supposed to be unarmed at all times. To start, most Western Allied medics did refuse to carry weapons even for minimal self defense, relying only on the prewar rules and German decorum. Sometimes the law was strictly enforced by American and Allied medical officers, as in refusing any soldier permission to enter a forward aid station with his rifle or a combat knife and ordering all weapons stacked farther away. This practice did not always fit the topography. Sometimes a mortar or machine gun one or two companies over was set up too close to the aid station on a forested hillside, inviting counterfire. Or tanks pulled in to park in the same clearing as the ambulances, or artillery unknowingly broke a medical truce under fire orders from its HQ farther back.

Fighting grew more bitter across the German border in 1945 where small groups of fanatic bitter-enders made each town bridge or main street square a potential ambush site. Under worsening conditions of Wehrmacht disintegration and hangings of deserters and "defeatists," medical norms also broke down. Less professional *Volksstrum* and *Hitlerjugend* shooters mixed with Wehrmacht and Waffen-SS. Snipers targeted medics, aidmen, and stretcher bearers, identified from red-and-white medical insignia and helmet crosses. Shooting medics was so common that G.I. slang called their red-and-white markings "aiming stakes." Some aidmen began to carry side arms or grenades for protection. A few pulled out weapons to force Germans to carry wounded or protect them from an enemy clearly intent on finishing them off.[40] It was part of the collapse of older German civilization in the last days of Nazi defeat and vulgar nihilism. It should be recalled in that regard that in addition to German medical personal who served in the Wehrmacht, about seven percent of doctors joined the SS and participated in torture, murder, and genocide.[41] Yet, there were moments of mercy, too.

Elmer Richardson was a 25-year-old Iowan badly wounded in the Ardennes in an ambush on December 18, 1944. He was gut shot, a probable death sentence which he nearly made certain by avoiding capture for two days. In need of serious medical attention, he was taken to a Wehrmacht hospital set up in an abbey, where a doctor operated on him over the objections of other Germans. They thought he was too far gone to spend resources on, when so many of their own needed help. Ludwig Gruber did the surgery, taking hours to fix serious internal damage. Forced into uniform in 1940, Gruber served on the Eastern Front, patching, cutting, and sawing through years of sheer carnage. He gave his address to the young American, writing it out on a scrap of paper and asking that Elmer write to him after the war. He fought opposition from other doctors in order to keep a wounded enemy at the abbey and under rest and care for a week. A U.S. Army medical captain toured the hospital in the interim, under a flag of truce, and saw the care Richardson got. It was agreed that U.S. forces would not bomb or shell the abbey as long as Germans did not park any military vehicles there. Gruber and his truck driver patient wrote to each other a few years later. They had nothing in common beyond their meeting in the forest and their shared humanity. Their sons got in touch 70 years beyond the Ardennes battle, after the deaths of the fathers.[42]

GERMAN, JAPANESE, AND SOVIET ARMIES SHOT tens of thousands of their own men during World War II. Not only for desertion but because they did not recognize any psychological wounding, not even mental illness except for advanced cases of schizophrenia. They all called "cowardice" what is today more properly identified as traumatic stress. They shot boys and men rendered incapable of advancing to face the enemy because they were paralyzed with trauma from prior action. They executed those who could not even stand up out of a fetal crouch they had been forced into by fighting for causes not their own. It was utterly merciless.

By 1944, the U.S. Army and British and Commonwealth forces were more medically advanced when it came to trauma. Even so, their main interest remained getting casualties back into action as quickly as possible. PTSD was thus treated as temporary because it was thought to be emotional, not brain-based as we know today: a mapping to the brain area that regulates emotions caused by extreme fear of specific traumatic events and memories. Cases were labeled "exhaustion" to start. Of every 100 psychiatric cases in the U.S. Army in World War II, 90 were kept in theater, with many sent to do noncombat duty. Norbert Gubbels was made a rear area driver. Men were treated as close as possible to where they last saw combat, so that they could be returned to it faster. All but the most severely disturbed were kept at forward aid stations for 24 hours of rest, hot food, and quiet time. Worse-off cases were sent to the near rear for seven days in an "exhaustion center," but thence to a refresher training camp. The worst off went to a convalescent hospital in Britain for three weeks of mental evaluation.[43] PTSD as a combat injury was not fully recognized until the Vietnam War, and not as a brain wound until later. Most patients were diagnosed using nonphysical language such as "Acute Situation Reaction." They were rested for a while, then hurried back into the fight.[44]

MOST 20TH-CENTURY WARS LOOKED MORE OR less the same to medics: they did a kind of EMT medicine of bullet holes, puncture wounds, and quick triage. Ronald Glasser saw the worst of Vietnam as well as more recent wars in Iraq and Afghanistan. He recalled how 19-year-old medics behaved even late in the Vietnam War, a conflict most of them wanted no part of: "The continuing courage and self-denial of the medics was an extraordinary thing to witness. Even within an army being abandoned at the very edge of empire, the medics successfully struggled to keep their own alive."[45] In a weeklong battle for a position called on U.S. Army maps Hill 937 or in slang "Hamburger Hill," and on Vietnamese and People's Army of Vietnam maps Đồi A Bia, medics were severely tested. It started from the first minutes of combat. Over the next five hours every medic in the initial assault was hit: 15 wounded, 10 killed. More were brought in from two other companies. By nightfall every one of the replacement medics was also killed or wounded.[46]

Things changed a little for medics in the post-9/11 wars. Many physical wounds were different.[47] More massive explosive force from IEDs caused lost limbs rather than bullet punctures. In lieu of gut shots, eyes, heads, and brains were far more severely damaged. Instead of a ride from a forward aid station to a rear area surgical hospital by truck or jeep or helicopter, intercontinental evacuations were made to Germany or Britain or even the United States. The whole trip took less than a day. And yet, little had really changed amidst the blood and bandages. For medics, doctors, and nurses it still came down to skill and mercy. For wounded soldiers as well.

IT IS NOT ONLY UNIFORMED MEDICAL professionals who go to war. *Médecins Sans Frontières* (Doctors Without Borders) has treated tens of millions in war and natural disaster zones since 1971.[48] In 2014 the White Helmets civil defense organization was founded in response to war in Syria. It conducted urban search-and-rescue and treated civilian victims in almost impossibly violent conditions. It also documented, photographed, and provided testimony about war crimes, including chemical weapons attacks made by Syrian and Russian air forces.[49] It was targeted, and some of its people killed. As Russia invaded Ukraine in 2022, the government in besieged Kyiv put out a call to raise a foreign legion. Western veterans and less experienced volunteers headed to Ukraine to join the fight.[50] Moscow declared that foreign volunteers would not be accorded military status but treated instead as mercenaries, and thus subject to summary trial and execution as illegal fighters. Never mind that Putin's regime sent Wagner PMC, Chechnyan, and Syrian mercenaries into the war.[51] Moral consistency is not an imperial or propaganda virtue.

Some volunteers went to Ukraine for shallow personal reasons. One graduate student, who first tried to fight in Syria in 2019 but was turned away, said about leaving for Ukraine: "Everything here [Virginia] is just kind of empty and it doesn't seem like I'm doing anything important." But also numbered among the volunteers was "James," a retired medic who saw his first combat in Iraq in 2006, after replacing another U.S. medic who was killed by insurgents. He saw so much horror and death that back at peace for 10 years he remained traumatized, attending regular therapy sessions at a local veterans' hospital. As he watched Ukrainian civilians shelled mercilessly by Russian artillery and missiles, he could no longer stay at home. He left for Kyiv to try to help: "Combat has a cost, that's for sure; you think you can come back from war the same, but you can't. But I feel obligated. It's the innocent people being attacked, the kids. It's the kids, man. I just can't stand by."[52] Meanwhile, the brutality of the invaders even toward their own emerged as Ukrainians drove them back from early gains. Bodies were left behind or disposed in mobile crematoria, concealing from worried mothers the extent of the carnage in the Russian Army.

Starting in the 1990s, British national David Nott served as a volunteer surgeon in Afghanistan, Bosnia, Sierra Leone, Sudan, Chad, Liberia, Iraq, Libya, Gaza, Yemen, Syria, and Ukraine. What made him go? First, seeing the film *The Killing Fields* (1984) about the 1970s Khmer Rouge genocide in Cambodia, then watching news footage from Sarajevo. One image especially moved him: "There was this man on the television, looking desperately through the rubble for his daughter. Eventually he found her and took her to the hospital but there were no doctors there to help her. I thought, 'Right, I'm off.'" In 2019 Nott recalled his first experience in a combat zone: "As a young man, jumping off the aeroplane and running for cover then hopping into a bulletproof vehicle and being taken at high speed to the hospital was *Boy's Own* stuff, just how I wanted it to be. It was perfect."[53] It was an intriguing reaction. The *Boy's Own Paper* was published by the Religious Tract Society from 1879 to 1967. It sought to displace "Penny Dreadful" or "Penny Awful" stories with tales of muscular Christian adventure and illustrated sports and military derring-do tailored for young boys.

Nott arrived in Aleppo in August 2013, after 95 percent of the city's doctors had fled. Injured were moved only at night, ambulances running blacked out, without Red Crescent insignia. ISIS snipers were repainting a ruined cityscape red, indiscriminately shooting down civilians. Some were playing a targeting game. Instead of taking kill shots, one day they shot each victim in the groin, the next day in the thigh or the chest, and so on. One ISIS sniper specialized in shooting pregnant women. Nott had to treat a woman in advanced pregnancy to remove a bullet from the head of her dead, unborn child. Nevertheless, he went into the city with two other surgeons to treat ISIS wounded, including the brother of the fiendishly cruel Aleppo commander. Later he thought: "I had saved the life of someone who might go on to commit terrible crimes. Did that make me complicit, somehow? Perhaps it did. And yet, I still firmly believe that it was my duty to save his life."[54]

In 2014 Nott went to Gaza City when another round of fighting broke out between Hamas and Israel. As he prepped to operate on a perforated seven-year-old girl unconscious on a ventilator, the hospital security chief ran in to order everyone out immediately. He had been warned that the building was to be shelled within the next five minutes. Nott chose to stay with the immobile girl, as did "Mauro the anaesthetist." Back and forth Nott went among other people's wars. After a brief respite in London, he went back to the utter moral and physical collapse that was Syria, a combat zone for a dozen causes and proxy militias. ISIS knew him by then and 20 savage fighters approached to kidnap the last Westerner in ruined Aleppo. Free Syria militia kept them off. He realized that he was severely traumatized: he suffered a complete breakdown back in Britain. He was almost famous by then, his name in newspapers and on television and on the lips of politicians using his story to their own purposes. It might have been asked of him, in the words of the old nursery rhyme: "Nott, Nott, where have you been? Why, I've been to London to visit the Queen." He was speechless about Aleppo when asked about the city by Queen Elizabeth. She broke a dog biscuit in two and suggested that he feed her corgis. "There," he recalled the elderly Queen saying gently to him as he sat mute inside his trauma, "that's so much better than talking, isn't it?"[55]

CHAPTER 9

PRISONERS

This question [about torture of POWs] isn't about our enemies; it's about us.... Our enemies act without conscience. We must not.
—John McCain, Statement in the Senate (December 9, 2014)

When fighting on will gain no further advantage, offering to surrender may save one's own life or the lives of subordinates.[1] Accepting a surrender offer also saves lives of one's own troops, limiting violence and risk incurred trying to kill enemy holdouts. Surrender thus may or may not also involve mercy. Many who try to quit fighting are still killed, often with callous cruelty. Ancient Egyptians and Israelites would sometimes cut off ears or foreskins of captured prisoners. Across the Mediterranean, Sparta became synonymous with savagery. That garrisoned theocracy subdued its own conquered majority to serve a military elite one-seventh the size, enslaved prisoners of war, and raised its youth in brutality. For millennia, across much of the world death or life servitude was the price of losing at war. Charlemagne is still venerated in Europe despite ordering 4,000 unarmed Saxon prisoners slaughtered in 782. That was a war crime by any modern measure. In the 11th century, Byzantine Emperor Basil II had thousands of Bulgarian prisoners blinded, "ordering one in every hundred men to lose only one eye so that they could lead the rest of the mutilated army."[2] Byzantium was a power while Bulgars were not. State terrorism expressed that inequality. There was little mercy for inferiors.

Frederick II ("Barbarossa") blinded prisoners of war in northern Italy in the 12th century. As the dominant sovereign he could act with impunity, without fear of justice or retribution. Samurai took heads instead of prisoners, piling them at the feet of their *daimyo* after battle, a measure of how they should be rewarded for military service. Over most of history, if a man who surrendered was not put to death, slavery was the exacted price of sparing a life. Hence, the Yoruba wars fed prisoners of war into wide slave trades, as did many other conflicts. Prisoners of war might be tortured to death or ritually sacrificed. Many warrior cultures took body parts from the dead or from prisoners as war trophies: severed ears, noses, scalps, or teeth. A declaration of *bellum Romanum* (or *guerre mortelle*) meant that everyone in a resisting town could be put to the sword, including women and children. Often, in the midst of a swirling battle, among all the sword strokes and arrows or musket balls there might be no opportunity to cry for, or to offer, any kind of quarter. At times, prisoners escorted from the battlefield to the near rear while the fight continued remained a threat to escape and perhaps rejoin combat. That was the excuse given for English slaughter of French knights at Agincourt in 1415. There were many similar examples, and comparable excuses, in the baleful annals of war.

FROM THE OUTSET OF THE AMERICAN Civil War, southern guerrillas saw themselves as heirs to Minutemen of the Revolution of 1776. That meant resorting to the irregular tactics used against the British, likewise drawing on traditions of Louisiana backwoodsmen during the War of 1812 and on the Texas Rangers.[3] Guerrillas further dipped into their revolutionary heritage by roughly enforcing political and social conformity on dissenters, Unionists, and others living behind Confederate lines: submit or flee. As blockade squeezed the coasts and Union armies sliced the western Confederacy in half, by mid-1863 Rebel armies started to shed men who went home to form local guerrilla bands instead. In the war's last year, even that pattern broke down as soldiers turned outlaw and openly predatory.

One historian of the guerrilla war explains that men deserted outright or turned against the war and Confederate authorities in order to fight for themselves: "Many malcontents, army deserters, genuine outlaws, thieves and bullies, exploited the upheaval to loot, pillage, murder, and destroy."[4] The anarchy grew so bad that, in addition to Union reprisals, Confederate armies also retaliated with escalating violence against southern guerrillas and outlaw bands. The war overall became total in its political intentions: overthrow of the Confederacy and its social order rooted in an economy of enslaved labor.[5] Only its means stayed limited. Union generals aimed by the end not at reconciliation but retribution. They sought total moral, social, and political submission. It was that or lose the country. It is a feature of civil wars in general that as they become more bloody and intransigent, quarter is less frequently asked or received.

On the other side, from the start facing Black troops in Union blue enraged Whites wearing gray or butternut or in guerrilla bands. Blacks were deemed to live outside basic humanity, let alone any protection of law. Quarter was denied: they were murdered if taken prisoner, mutilated or scalped if already dead. On May 27, 1863, Captain André Cailloux of the Louisiana Native Guards, an all Free Black unit, was killed leading a charge against Confederate lines at Port Hudson. A ceasefire allowed both sides to retrieve their dead and wounded. But when Union bearers went out to collect Cailloux and his men Rebel sharpshooters kept shooting to prevent collection of any Black corpses. Port Hudson did not surrender for another 41 days, Cailloux's body decomposing in the high summer heat the whole time. When it was finally retrieved he was given a funeral in New Orleans attended by thousands of freed slaves in the city.[6] The episode was a milestone in symbolism of what the war meant to Black folk across a divided nation, beyond what it meant even to grieving White families who had also lost their men in Union service.

Confederate Secretary of War James Seddon declared in 1863 that Blacks serving in the Union Army would not be accorded rights as prisoners of war. Black wounded were often bayonetted or shot outright by Rebel troops, making the issue moot.[7] Worse was to come. On April 12, 1864, at Fort Pillow in Tennessee, Black prisoners had their eyes gouged out and were shot multiple times before their bodies were burned by men in Nathan Bedford Forrest's cruel command. A Union naval officer who saw the bodies wrote to Congress and to the *New York Times*, demanding retaliation in kind against Confederate prisoners: war breeds hate more surely than hate breeds war. The massacre at Fort Pillow and other murders of Black soldiers contrasted sharply with accepted surrenders and reasonable treatment of White prisoners.[8] At least before 1864, when General Grant ended the "parole" system of free release upon giving one's word not to take up arms again. The shift away from prisoner exchanges worsened matters sharply for captive men on each side. There were other exceptions: expectation of humane treatment did not extend to Unionists in the South or to Confederate guerrillas anywhere.[9] Dissenters deemed outlaw were shown little mercy. The war became harder as it grew longer.

IN MODERN CUSTOM AND MILITARY LAW, as well as morally and psychologically, an accepted surrender shifts the status of each party. They cease to be moral equals: prisoners become vulnerable wards of their captors. Taking prisoners incurs legal obligations and many practical difficulties. To start, one must escort them to the rear, which smaller units such as special forces or guerrillas may not be able to spare assets to do. Does that make a quicker killing morally acceptable? Or topography militates against mercy, as is often the case in trench warfare. Ernst Jünger disdained accepting or escorting prisoners back across no-man's-land, especially if he and his men were still under enemy fire. He regarded prisoners as "even more inconvenient when wounded." He recounted several instances when wounded or those trying to surrender in no-man's-land were shot down by him or his men, so the attack or patrol could press ahead.[10] Allied troops did the same. Deserters were a special case. So were unit surrenders. Next, one must guard and feed prisoners and care for wounded among them. That can put a real burden on captors, some of whom will be better positioned to cope than others. For guerrillas or resistance fighters or commandos moving behind enemy lines, it can be impossible to assume such obligations. A decision to kill becomes more a matter of tactics than ethics.

On patrol, with orders to take prisoners for interrogation back to your battalion HQ, an odd moral dynamic might occur. Success of a capture patrol means that to take some enemy alive you need to kill all the rest you come across, or they will shoot you in the back as you depart. You cannot leave enemy alive and behind as you awkwardly hump a disarmed and shackled prisoner across no-man's-land at night, or to a helo landing zone, or a Humvee waiting to race to the Green Zone in Baghdad or Mosul. That is different from the motivation to take trophy prisoners. Jünger, who loved war as much as or even more than he loved himself, saw taking captives as representing his total moral and psychological dominance over the enemy. Their fear and meekness swelled his sense of warrior achievement. Many other men had a different reaction to prisoners they took: anger and resentment at their enemy's newly protected status and the fact that for them the war was over. Rage and envy melded with combat fear could then overwhelm any compassion.

It mattered who your captor was and where you were taken. Whether you surrendered in Belgium or Serbia in 1914, or France or Ukraine in 1945, made a difference to your chance to survive. If you were Japanese and taken prisoner on a sunny Pacific island or in the interior of Burma you faced likely death. British forces took only 142 Japanese prisoners in the 1944–1945 Burma campaign, while killing 17,666.[11] Japanese ran amok repeatedly, killing prisoners and civilians at Nanjing in 1937 and Hong Kong and several other cities in 1941, and in Manilla in 1944. You were in deep trouble if you got in the way of the "Kill All" order issued by the *Rikugun* in China in 1940 and reiterated in 1944. It led to an unbridled rage that Chinese call *Sānguāng Zhèngcè* and Japanese later dubbed *Sankō Sakusen,* or the "Three Alls" order: "Burn All. Loot All. Kill All." If you were a Filipino guerrilla on the edge of final liberation in 1945, enraging the losing Japanese into sadism, you faced astonishing savagery that included mass immolations. Witnesses reported that before the Sicily landings in 1943 General George Patton issued a call that no prisoners should be taken. At least two soldiers later said that they acted on it, killing dozens. One man machine-gunned 37 hapless prisoners. He was convicted but pardoned and returned to active duty within a year.[12] Other commanders said much the same to their troops before the D-Day landings, worried that unblooded men did not yet hate Germans enough to fight at peak ability.[13] Or you may have met mercy far beyond the letter of any convention, depending on who was the individual man wearing the enemy's uniform at the moment you threw up your hands and threw yourself on his mercy. It came down to the character, and even the mood, of your captor at the moment of capitulation.

WIDESPREAD ABUSE OF PRISONERS IN WORLD War II occurred on the Eastern Front and in China and the Pacific. Allied armies were not exempt from harming Axis prisoners, although their crimes tended to be far less systematic. After the war, General Chris Vokes of the Canadian Army admitted: "There isn't a general or colonel on the Allied side that I know of who hasn't said, 'Well, this time we don't want any prisoners.'"[14] Unlike for ordinary soldiers, in the high command of the Canadian Army there was real professional admiration of German officers. Remarkably, that included 12th SS Panzer, a division that had murdered 156 Canadians in Normandy, as one historian of war crimes put it, "not in the 'heat of battle' but in planned, deliberate butchery."[15] HQs on both sides looked away and even at times tacitly agreed it was best not to take too many prisoners. Commanders often feared a weakened willingness to fight if a majority of troops truly came to see that it all could be stopped by their own surrender, or the enemy's. There developed an almost shared battlefield command culture of discouraging quarter if it was asked too easily, yet also not refusing quarter to the point of inspiring extra fighting because the enemy had lost all hope for mercy. Truly merciless fighting risked raising one's own casualties. There was also often just lack of command and control.

White-heat reactions by soldiers in direct contact could not be monitored. Rage rose as rumors of atrocity whipped across the ranks like heat from a prairie fire. All too often they were true. Then vengeance was taken not against the perpetrators, who had often moved on to another part of the fight, but the next man or unit wearing khaki or *feldgrau* or green or brown. It was worse once you were sure that you were losing, pushed back in defeat into your own country after lording it over other peoples for years. Japanese and Germans behaved with rising cruelty as they were driven out of their conquests back to wrecked homelands. And the war itself changed things. Its intensity and the scale of killing were unprecedented in all of human history. Too often, the enemy was indecent to your civilians who got in his way, and also got in your way. As the Red Army advanced it came across hundreds of atrocity sites formerly behind German lines. Then it arrived at the death camps in January 1945. Soldier rage took the form of rape and vengeance against German civilians, including gang rapes of many thousands of girls and women. Innocents were punished in place of the guilty, most of whom were far away wearing gray.

On the Eastern Front and in the Pacific War, hard calculations were made from the start in savage *guerres mortelle* without pity or relief. Soviet prisoners of the Wehrmacht and Allied prisoners of the *Rikugun* fared worse than most, both forces notorious for ill-treatment.[16] Western Allied troops and Germans also killed capriciously at times, and there were several small massacres in Normandy and the Ardennes. Japanese mass killings included Chinese in the Second Sino-Japanese War of 1937–1945, Asian partisans all across the occupied territories of the Japanese Empire, and Allied POWs. American and British and Commonwealth troops retaliated in kind, killing surrendering or captive Japanese as well as mutilating corpses and taking body part trophies.[17] It was all a vicious, mutual spiral into blinding hate and vengeance. Until it no longer mattered for too many men who they faced, on their knees and begging for mercy. Man, woman, or child, the quality of mercy was overstrained by too much war, falling on the helpless not as a gentle rain but in sheets of fire and barbarism.

The farther one was from the actual fighting, the less likely it was that cruelty ruled. There was kindness toward German and Italian POWs transshipped to Canada or the United States.[18] Many were allowed to work outside their POW encampments, coming to know local townsfolk and their employers well. In 2006, I interviewed a U-boat captain surfaced and captured by the Royal Navy in 1940. He worked in POW labor camps in Ontario and British Columbia, harvesting lumber. He so liked it that he emigrated to Canada in 1954, thence to the United States a decade later. In contrast, in the Deep South of the United States, Black soldiers guarding POW work details were served through kitchen windows while German prisoners were allowed to sit and eat inside.[19] An extreme example of this remarkable bigotry was burial of two POWs who died in a Texas camp in 1943. They were interred in the Fort Sam Houston National Cemetery in San Antonio under headstones engraved with an iron cross, with a black swastika at dead center. The inscription read: "He died far from his home for the Leader (*Führer*), people and fatherland." The headstones were not taken down until 2020.[20]

Reciprocal prisoner treatment by Germans and Western armies was far better than on the Eastern Front or the Pacific or in China. There were exchanges of medical personnel using protected trains and even mercy ships allowed to steam to neutral ports with lights on, certain of being unmolested.[21] There were local medical truces across North Africa, Italy, and France. Good treatment of German prisoners in the West is quite remarkable given that the Nazis kept 1.8 million French Army POWs as hostages and forced laborers in Germany from 1940 to 1945, joined by 600,000 Italians from 1943 to 1945. As in all other measures of callousness, it was not the same in the East. Neither side extended Geneva Convention protections even in theory. Each side massively abused prisoners of war as forced military labor. Each side employed brutal guards and executed prisoners. The Nazis were much worse, starving and freezing to death millions of Red Army men to rid the Wehrmacht of what it called "useless mouths." But descending from the eagle's point of view to harsh realities on the ground, a German suffered the same as a Russian when beaten or starved or shot.[22] A helpless, starving, and beaten man is just a man. He is not some abstract cause or nation.

Even when surrendering to 20th-century armies that did not make murder routine, it helped to offer labor in exchange for not being killed or beaten. The bargain was nonverbal, as with German or French or Russian prisoners in World War I who saw a bit of their trench broken by shelling or a successful attack and pitched in to buttress its caving sides. More commonly, prisoners stooped to carry stretchers bearing wounded fellow prisoners or their captors' wounded, either of which also got you moving in the right direction: away from the front line, to the enemy rear. They helped dress their captor's wounds or carried water or cooked or sewed.

In World War II everything was much worse. Killing prisoners as well as women and children was Nazi policy from the start. This provoked ferociously cruel responses from local partisans or Soviet troops once the tide turned.[23] *Rikugun* both spontaneously and systematically murdered tens of thousands of Western prisoners and hundreds of thousands of Asians: Chinese, Malay, Filipinos, and others. Soviet prisoners of Germans and Allied prisoners of the Japanese learned to appear useful beyond the tried-and-true ways of abject submission and manual labor. Some went further to avoid beatings, torture, or killing, giving up tactical intelligence, chancing harsh retribution if their side found out. In the case of many tens of thousands of Soviet prisoners, turning coat meant actively fighting in Wehrmacht or Waffen-SS divisions. Others were kept at the front as forced military laborers or *Hiwis*, prolonging life until the Red Army won and they could go home.[24] On Josef Stalin's order, many *Hiwis* were summarily executed as traitors after liberation in 1945.

JAPANESE MISTREATMENT OF CAPTURED ENEMY DATED to the First Sino-Japanese War (1894–1895), which saw brutal and frequent massacres of prisoners and civilians. Facing massive but internally divided and mismanaged Qing armies, Japan's generals did not lack confidence or ambition. After landing in Korea they marched north to seek a "decisive battle" on the Zhili plain of China. It was high aspiration, given the raggedy character of Japanese forces and a nonexistent logistics system. Food issues led troops to slaughter and eat oxen pulling supply and ammo carts. A desperate need for food pushed the Japanese toward Pyongyang, then on into China looking for storehouses. When hungry troops arrived in Pyongyang the Qing garrison withdrew to the Yalu. Now Japanese generals conscripted 150,000 local laborers, dressed for a winter campaign in bamboo hats with unit numbers painted on summer clothes. It was the beginning of a half-century to come of forced labor and abuse of civilians and prisoners.[25] Thousands froze to death. More ran away. Reprisals were harsh. In rage and exasperation, Japanese routinely massacred Chinese prisoners and conscripts. Lithographs depicted and celebrated the killings, including mass beheadings. The depravity echoed in celebratory ISIS and other radical jihadi murder videos recorded a century later in Iraq, Syria, and Afghanistan.

Japanese troops were bestial in Nanjing in 1937, with lesser massacres in Hong Kong and other cities. *Rikugun* troops practiced with bayonets on live prisoners or used them as target practice. Beatings were administrated daily in POW camps and on work details. Beheadings were not unusual. As the *Rikugun* was obviously losing the war in 1945, in Manila its troops butchered thousands of Filipinos with their knives and bayonets and burned alive thousands more. Orders for mass executions of partisans were written out and distributed in the city. One soldier recorded in his diary, which was introduced in evidence in postwar war crimes trials, "February 7, 1945: I personally stabbed and killed 10. . . . February 9: Burned 1,000 guerillas to death tonight. . . . February 13: At 16:00 all guerillas were burned to death."[26] Becoming a prisoner of the Japanese was always high risk. First, you had to survive the act of surrender: Japanese often killed individuals or groups of Australian, American, Filipino, and other Allied troops outright. If a surrender was arranged at the command level, as for British in Singapore or Filipinos and Americans at Bataan in 1942, chances were still quite high that guards would behead or bayonet or beat to death Allied POWs. It was often worse if prisoners were Asian: Filipinos, Malays, Indian, or Chinese. Japanese troops were even murderous toward Okinawans, more indifferent than invading Americans toward countryfolk who were not ethnic Japanese.[27]

Allied soldiers learned to respond in kind to tricks they decided were unfair or treacherous. They shot down many Japanese troops appearing to surrender, after encountering false surrenders that got men killed. On Guadalcanal, ruses included white flags that lured out Americans, then opening fire; feigning wounds and calling in English for a medic, then shooting or stabbing the corpsman who came to help; hiding grenades used to blow up stretcher bearers or nurses; killing doctors with their scalpels; booby-trapping severely wounded and corpses. Medical truces were few and far between as hatred and mistrust rose and also fear of tricks. It was not until late in the war, around mid-1945, that surrenders on Okinawa by large groups of Japanese troops were both offered and accepted. Allied revenge also got in the way of surrender. Cruel stories did not need to be true to lead to reprisal but they often were. Australians found their men gutted and then nailed to trees in New Guinea and took revenge when they got the chance.[28] Allied POWs at Rabaul were injected with pathogens and lethal poisons in crude experiments comparable to Josef Mengele's at Auschwitz and Shirō Ishii's at Unit-731. Shipwrecked nurses suffered, too: 65 Australian nurses were butchered right away while 32 were gang-raped, then shipped to Sumatra along with more captured nurses and other women. They were made to work as sex slaves (*ianfu*) in *Rikugun* rape camps.

Over 2,000 prisoners died at Sandakan Camp in Borneo. There were repetitions of the Bataan death march, some worse in proportion of the dead to survivors. After one tortuous, 160-mile death march only six British and Australian prisoners survived.[29] Thousands of Australian, British, and Indian Army prisoners were cruelly massacred. Some were eaten. Americans were also eaten ritually, not for food. As were Indian Army prisoners, with others used for routine target practice.[30] None of that cruelty helped Japanese efforts to induce Indian prisoners of war to sign up with the collaborationist Indian National Army, to fight the British in Burma and possibly invade India after that. By the end of the war, deaths of Allied prisoners of war in Japanese hands were seven times higher than under the Germans or Italians. From June 20 to August 15, 1945, the day of Japan's surrender, 33 American airmen were beheaded by Japanese officers in Fukuoka, Japan. There was an element in these executions of trying to emulate the two-stroke beheading methods they had read about in samurai histories and folk tales.[31]

And yet, isolated acts of respect for prisoners by Japanese also occurred. Mario Tonelli was a college football star at Notre Dame who played running back for one season for the Chicago Cardinals. On December 7, 1941, he was at Clark Field on Luzon, then fell back in retreat with the rest of General Douglas MacArthur's poorly generaled command. On April 9, 1942, Tonelli was among thousands of Americans and Filipinos taken prisoner at Bataan, thence forced on the Bataan death march. On the first day, his Notre Dame ring was taken at bayonet point by a guard. A *Rikugun* officer asked if one of his soldiers took something. Tonelli told him it was his football ring. The officer found it and gave it back, pressing it into Tonelli's hand and saying: "Hide it somewhere. You may not get it back next time.... I was educated in America.... I know a little about the famous Notre Dame football team.... I watched you beat USC in 1937."[32]

During over 1,200 days as a prisoner, Tonelli kept the ring in a soap dish that he buried beneath each prison barracks, to prevent discovery by Japanese guards or theft by another prisoner desperate to trade it for a little more rice. He was forced to dig graves for prisoners from Bataan and Corregidor at Camps O'Donnell and Cabanatuan. Then he spent many months in Davo Penal Colony, where only 805 men survived of 2,000 held there until 1944. He was loaded onto one of what later came to be called "Hellships," taking 62 days to move to Nagoya #7 Work Camp and a metalworks at Yokkaichi in Japan.[33] He saw B-29s overhead on the way to wreak vengeance on enemy cities. In August, a smaller American plane dropped a carton of cigarettes onto the work camp, with a message attached that said, "Hostilities have ceased. Will see you soon." The next day, drums full of fabulous food rations and medical supplies parachuted down. When his liberators arrived on foot, the former running back who clocked in prewar at 200 pounds weighed less than half that.[34]

Many Japanese soldiers and guards never regretted nor repented their sadism at Nanjing or en route from Bataan or in Manila. Nor what they did to those they called "comfort women" (*ianfu*) in rape camps. A few did. One spent the rest of his life trying to recover his integrity. Takeshi Nagase had been an interpreter for the brutal *Kempeitai*, the special state police who ran some prison and work camps. These included forced labor camps servicing construction of the 415-mile-long "Railway of Death" from Burma to Thailand. Over 100,000 Malay and Chinese and 16,000 POWs died building a jungle railroad that changed nothing about Japan's failing war effort. It is overgrown and collapsed today: barely 60 miles remain. After the war, Nagase was tasked to help locate 13,000 bodies for the Allied War Graves Commission, which he said "changed my whole life." He started to write and lecture about what he had done and seen. Wracked with profound personal guilt, he built memorials in Thailand, including a Buddhist temple erected close to the Tham Kham Bridge that was thrown across the Kwoi

Noi River, later misremembered on celluloid as the *Bridge on the River Kwai* (1957).[35]

Nagase was 21 years old when an interrogator in Kanchanaburi prison camp. He recalled the first time he entered Kanchanaburi: "It was surrounded by brazen vultures attracted by the stench of the corpses. I still shudder when I think of it." Also there was 22-year-old Eric Lomax, a Signals Corps engineer from Edinburgh. In 1943 he was caught with a hidden radio and escape map. Nagase whispered questions as Lomax was beaten near to death, then underwent water torture. He told Lomax he was sure to die. The Scot barely survived, as he "was beaten relentlessly." Decades later Lomax remembered the presiding officer's face, "full of latent and obvious violence." Above all, he despised Nagase, that "hateful little interpreter." For 50 years Lomax calcified hatred, carrying it inside like a stone baby that weighed him down: "I wished to drown [the interpreter], cage him and beat him."[36] Also decades later, Nagase recalled: "People who have been to hell do not forgive easily. And we were in hell. But I wanted to help him in some way. I searched my brain for the right English expression and as he was leaving the camp I said to him quietly, 'Keep your chin up.' I still remember his astonished face."[37]

In 1976 Nagase organized the first of a series of reunions of POWs and camp guards, an act of contrition for which he was much criticized in Japan, then still in generational denial of war crimes. Thai riot police stood stiffly as he held up a Thai flag, not a Rising Sun dating to the war. That act occasioned sharp criticism in Japan, to which he responded: "Do they know how many Thai people were slaughtered under that flag?" They surely did not, as such stories were widely repressed in Japan. Nagase once shocked British teenagers on an Imperial War Museum–sponsored trip to Japan by tearfully apologizing to them for the war and insisting that a nearby Japanese student also apologize. The confused boy brushed him off: "This is not a problem of our generation." The comment infuriated Nagase. He was helped by the reunions but remained haunted by the singular memory of a young Scot he came close to torturing to death: "I couldn't bear his pain. . . . He was crying 'Mother! Mother!' And I thought: what would she feel if she could see her son like this? I still dream about it." Nagase wrote to Lomax, disarming his

hatred with an "extraordinarily beautiful" letter asking for, but not antici-
pating, forgiveness and a chance at personal reconciliation.[38]

In 1993 Lomax wrote and agreed to attend a reunion. They met. Nagase
was so remorseful he could not even beg for forgiveness, which he did not
believe he deserved. Nor did he get it easily or quickly. Lomax had gone to
Thailand "not knowing what to expect and ended up comforting a shaking,
crying Nagase." He recalled: "I took his hand and said in Japanese, 'Good
morning, Mr. Nagase, how are you?' He was trembling and crying, and he
said over and over again: 'I am so sorry, so very sorry.' "[39] Nagase knew that
"he had hated me for fifty years and I wanted to ask him if he forgave me, but
I couldn't find a way. . . . So I said: 'Can we be friends?' and he said 'yes.' "[40]
On a later trip, Lomax visited the Yasukuni Shrine with Nagase, where he
was startled to see a monument to the *Kempeitai*. "It's like seeing a memorial to the Gestapo in a German cathedral." Inside was a steam locomotive
that ran on the Thai-Burma Railway but no recollection of the slave laborers
who died to build it. It was, he said aptly, "a monument to barbarism."[41]

Over time, Lomax forgave Nagase. They met repeatedly and became
friends in the sunset of their lives. Official memory wanted to isolate each
man from harder personal memories both their postwar societies preferred
be kept in the past, in the United Kingdom almost as much as in Japan. The
forgotten past of the war was treated at the official level as if it was a third and
foreign country neither man ever visited.[42] But their relationship trumped
politics. Restored humanity spanned the gap from past to present, each
man helping to heal the other: Nagase helped Lomax forgive while Lomax's
generosity of spirit salved Nagase's moral harm. Nagase spent 60 years
in human rights campaigning to make up for two years spent in the Thai
prison camp system, where he served the *Kempeitai* and Imperial Japanese
project and the Railway of Death. His humbling path to personal redemption disgusted Nationalists, whom it embarrassed if it did not quite shame.
But others were inspired. Tamura Keiko's work was to locate and help Allied
POWs in Japan. She said of Nagase: "The people who fought in the war
forgot their humanity, so it is a long battle to get them to see each other as
human beings again. That is what he does."[43]

Cruelty toward Allied prisoners was extreme and inexcusable. American as well as Australian, British and Commonwealth troops did nothing to compare by scale. Although there was more murder and mistreatment of helpless Japanese POWs than was meted out by Allied soldiers to Germans or Italians in the European Theater of Operations. Allied interrogators for the most part used humane means to interview Japanese military prisoners. On the other side, some Japanese prisoners succumbed to an official military and imperial culture that stoked shame and forbade surrender. Some organized POW rebellions, not to try to escape from Allied camps but to kill themselves.[44] Allied cruelty was not systematic, although many Japanese suffered gross abuse and indignities. Some were killed, as views hardened against compassion for hapless enemy on both sides. Hatred and racism born mainly of the war pulled men into sadism and barbarity, doing morally corrosive work: war breeds hate and cruelty more surely than hate leads to war. Bodily harm was inflicted on prisoners, moral harm on their abusers.

Demonizing enemies and lack of any cultural or psychological preparation to fight men of a different "race" was a two-way street. Allied troops came to see Japanese who would not quit as almost aliens. But many Japanese who surrendered to Allied forces over the last year of the war were equally shocked by the multiracial makeup of U.S. Army personnel or British and Commonwealth forces. Kojima Kiyofumi was a *Kaigun* (Imperial Japanese Navy) officer who surrendered in the Philippines in mid-1945. He was driven by jeep to a POW camp, where he expected to be seen as a curiosity: "A swarm of enemy soldiers came out to see us. . . . I guess they wanted to get a look at these funny-looking guys they'd caught." Instead, it was Kiyofumi who was surprised by what he saw there: "Blond, silver, black, brown, red hair. Blue, green, brown, black eyes. White, black, skin colors of every variety. I was stunned." It brought home to him for the first time what Japan had done: "I realized then that we'd fought against all the peoples of the world." At the same time, he was most taken with "what a funny country America is, all those different kinds of people fighting in the same uniform!"[45] Kiyofumi in later life became a leader of Soldiers Against War, an antimilitarist group active in Japan.

Allied reports on interrogations of Japanese prisoners of war demonstrated that they held a wide range of views, from fearful incomprehension to careful obfuscation about the Japanese cause. Only a few were actually nationalist or racial fanatics. When asked why Japan had a poor reputation, the most some admitted was that there were some "undesirable types" among soldiers.[46] One U.S. Marine Corps interpreter seemed to sense a deeper humanity as he communicated with men who sometimes killed themselves in front of him. Robert Sheeks was a marine language officer who converted from hate to compassion starting on Tarawa, where almost no Japanese surrendered. As he moved across the Pacific along with the war, he devised leaflets and approaches that lured hundreds of Japanese into surrender on Tinian and Saipan, the latter a place of massacre and nihilistic banzai despair and civilian suicides. He brought a touch of mercy to the war, always recognizing an essential humanity in suicidal, terrified, and indoctrinated men he interviewed. His decency saved many lives among Japanese who gave up instead of fighting to the last. And of G.I.s who did not have to dig out or burn out desperate, starving men inside burrows, caves, and holes.[47]

TERRIBLE ABUSES OF PRISONERS TOOK PLACE again in the Korean War, which stretched long past its stalemate date over issues of forced prisoner repatriation.[48] There were high-point moments as well. U.S. Army Chaplain Emil Kapaun showed an uncommon bravery while under attack by troops of the Chinese Volunteer Force (CVF), the People's Liberation Army fighting under a cover name. The attack took place near Unsan over two days, November 1–2, 1950. The American position was steadily compressed and close to being overrun. Kapaun showed himself to intense small arms fire, moving around exposed foxhole positions tending to wounded or dragging men from the open into a foxhole, or spading dirt in front of those he could not move to protect from bullets. His example encouraged others to come out to help. He had several chances to escape as the CVF assault broke down the perimeter but he chose to stay with the wounded. Sergeant Herbert Miller feigned death as a CVF soldier aimed his rifle straight at him from a few feet away. Kapaun strode over and pushed the rifleman away. "Why he never shot him . . . I'll never know." Kapaun picked

Miller up and carried him from danger. "Put me down. You can't carry me," Miller told the lightly built Kapaun, who replied: "If I put you down, they'll shoot you." He carried Miller like a knapsack, or gave a shoulder to support the wounded and hobbling man over three days' forced march, until they reached a Chinese POW camp.[49] Kapaun sneaked and foraged for food for the sick, whom he also bathed and cared for. He was caught by guards and punished many times, once forced to sit outside naked over a frigid winter night. He saved hundreds from beatings or suppurating wounds or murder. He died in the camp of pneumonia and dysentery on May 23, 1951.[50]

On the other side of that complex and multisided war, 14,342 Chinese POWs were unwilling to return to China after fighting in the third war of their horribly disrupted youths and lives: the Sino-Japanese War of 1937–1945, the renewed Chinese Civil War from 1946 to 1949, and a third war in Korea stretching into an unknown future. Many suffered from untreated PTSD, moral injury, or old wounds and illnesses from two earlier wars. Then they were forced to fight in Korea. Some volunteered but only under false pretenses, to get close to UN forces or South Korean lines so that they could defect. They were profoundly weary of war, in pain physically and psychologically exhausted, years removed from their families and any civilian life or comforts. Many were ideological opponents of the radical regime installed in Beijing: conscripted *Guomindang* soldiers who concealed their true loyalties from fellow prisoners, camp guards, and Communist Party indoctrinators.

Li Da'an was "beaten half to death" after surrendering to the Communists in 1948. Like all Nationalists, or "liberated soldiers" in Communist parlance, he was subjected to a full year of intense indoctrination and "thought reform." His captors did not want only his physical submission to their rules and regime. They demanded that his emotional and intellectual submission follow his physical surrender. It was a standard hard to meet, except by the very best dissemblers. Dissent was disguised. All lingering opposition to the Communists was hidden, or else prisoners faced more beatings and confinement. While still in a POW camp, before moving on to a full indoctrination site, Li broke. He asked his wife to bring poison so that he could commit suicide. After his release, he signed up to serve in the CVF fighting in Korea but his intention was always to defect to the UN side.[51]

Li Soon was driving a civilian truck when he was conscripted into the CVF. After making four trips to the Chosin Reservoir carrying military supplies, he decided to desert. He meandered to Shenyang but was unable to find work. He had to return to the CVF truck unit but always had one eye on escape. He recrossed the Yalu River on February 27, 1951, and defected three days later. He was not just a disgruntled truck driver who found himself conscripted into an army whose cause he opposed. While in a UN holding camp he became the founder and active leader of an anti-Communist prisoner group that clashed regularly with CVF prisoners who supported the Communist cause and war.

Lieutenant Liu Bingzhang's *Guomindang* unit surrendered in 1948. He spent two years in Communist POW camps, embittered about the lost war and new revolution: most of his family's land in Shandong had been confiscated. Forced to serve with the CVF in Korea, he deserted in late October 1950 while 60 miles from the Yalu. He walked several miles to give himself up to Republic of Korea (ROK) forces.[52] Li Soon, Liu Bingzhang, and many other former Nationalists waged open war with Communists in UN and ROK camps. Each side held ad hoc trials for treason, beat, tortured, and killed fellow Chinese. Consequently, U.S. prison guards began to segregate Chinese and North Korean POWs by Communist or anti-Communist leaning, not just by rank, gender, and nationality. With peace talks stalled in February 1952, the United Nations screened all prisoners to find anyone who wanted to refuse repatriation.[53] That aggravated the little civil wars inside the camps.

The first prisoner uprising had taken place in June 1951, with some camps taken over by POWs who refused to let UN personnel inside. Riots, assaults, murders, and kangaroo court executions took place in multiple camps. In February 1952, a battalion-scale assault on a POW site at Koje-do that was under Communist control failed to regain the camp. In May, the commander was taken hostage and held until the UN acceded to prisoner demands, including an end to repatriation screens. Similar divisions took place in camps holding North Korean prisoners, split between Communists and others. It was part of Chinese and North Korean infiltration tactics intended to affect the armistice talks. The U.S. Army took back Koje-do in

June in a three-hour battle.[54] Opposition to forced repatriation of these POWs hearkened to 1945 repatriation of Soviets who served as *Hiwis* or combatants with the Wehrmacht. That led to hundreds of suicides at places like Fort Dix and camps in Austria. Cold War politics made it impossible to forcibly return men to Communist custody in North Korea or China. Not after Stalin killed tens of thousands of repatriated Red Army soldiers after World War II, including some forced onto trains at gunpoint by American or British troops in the United States and across Western Europe.[55]

BEGINNING IN THE LATE 19TH CENTURY the British Empire was constantly at war in one or other of its overseas colonies. The methods used to suppress rebellion were often extreme. Newfound air power was used after 1918 against civilians in India, Afghanistan, Iraq, and Palestine, in campaigns where Arthur "Bomber" Harris learned his craft, later employing it to incinerate German cities. In 1945 the "liquidation of the British Empire" began, as Churchill phrased it, although he had once promised that he did not become prime minister only to preside over the empire's decline and dissolution. The empire, which he promised Parliament in November 1942 would last 1,000 years, crashed in just five when Jawaharlal Nehru announced on August 14, 1947, that at the next dawn "India will awake to life and freedom."[56] Only small bits were left after that. To retain them, the British turned once again to severe repressive methods in colonial conflicts. Ethnic Chinese "CTs" (communist terrorists) were suppressed by force in Malaya, while concentration camps reminiscent of the Second Boer War were used to detain 1.5 million Kikuyu to undercut the Mau Mau in Kenya. That led to thousands more civilian deaths, as it had in 1902 among the Boers in South Africa.[57]

Nonetheless, the British Army asserted at the beginning of the Iraq insurgency in 2003 that their counterinsurgency war doctrine had achieved a special level of legality and moral integrity. It said that British troops historically relied on minimal force, pursuing policies and tactics rooted in core liberal values. At best, this was a partial truth. At worst, callow self-deception about recent history. The main tactic in Aden, Cyprus, Kenya, Malaya, and Northern Ireland was naked force, as troops trained for war were deployed in colonial policing roles for which they were not trained. Tactics thus ranged from harsh "cordon and search" operations to forcible removals of entire populations, violent interrogation, free-fire zones, unauthorized "shoot-to-kill" practices, and harsh mistreatment of guerrillas who were deemed "gangsters, thugs, and bandits."[58]

The French did much the same in their terminal colonial wars in Indochina and Algeria. In both places, severity increased political opposition and encouraged more anti-French guerrillas to fight in units based outside the cities of Vietnam or in the Atlas Mountains and coastal cities of Algeria. Emmanuel Macron was the first French president born after the Algerian War of Independence. A half-century after the war ended he apologized for his country's wartime atrocities, for inducing torture and defenestration of human rights lawyer Ali Boumendjel during the Battle of Algiers.[59] Early in the Vietnam War it was U.S. policy to remove the population from Viêt Cong–dominated areas, housing peasants in towns the Saigon government controlled. Some Viêt Cong prisoners were kept in "tiger cages" by guards in the Army of the Republic of Vietnam, which gravely hurt the image of South Vietnam. On the other side, abuse of prisoners was endemic. The term "Hanoi Hilton" became a notorious byword for torture of American POWs. When those wars finally ended and British, French, and American troops went home, it was promised yet again that next time the Geneva rules would be fully respected.

Iraqis captured in Operation Desert Storm in 1991 were in fact mostly treated well, under rule-based policies probably made easier by a remarkably short war: just 100 hours. That changed after American rage was provoked by the terrorist attacks on the Twin Towers and other domestic targets. Treatment of some prisoners after 9/11 devolved into rendition black sites, Abu Ghraib abuses, waterboarding of high-value detainees followed by incarceration at Guantanamo seemingly without end, in a "forever war." Presidents George W. Bush and Barack Obama explicitly excluded al-Qaida from coverage by Geneva Convention rules. That may be seen as a defensible position given the genuine terrorist nature of that group. However, also excluding Taliban from military prisoner rights never was. Obduracy then pursued conflation. A refusal to distinguish between al-Qaida terrorists and

Taliban resistance, however repugnant was the latter's ideology, made it impossible to negotiate an end to war for 20 years. Meanwhile, al-Qaida and ISIS acted without mercy, beheading journalists and anyone who worked with the Americans.[60] It was a bleak record. Again it was promised that we would do better next round. The opportunity came when Russia invaded Ukraine for a second time, in 2022. Prisoners were sometimes exchanged but terrible things were done behind the lines by Russian troops, in zones of occupation where the only law was *lex talionis*. Brutal retaliation by some Ukrainians inexorably followed.

CHAPTER 10

CIVILIANS

We're running from the war. We'll return home when it quiets down, if anything is left.

—Viktoria Kriachun, refugee mother of three from Mariupol, Ukraine (2022)

Bellum Romanum did not end with the Roman Empire.[1] Today we distinguish between legitimate and illegitimate killings in the *jus in bello*, the laws of wartime behavior. In fact, those who are able to hurt us most badly receive more fair play, while those who cannot injure us in kind we obliterate. Laws of war were drafted by the powerful to favor themselves. The strong disdain them because they can, while the weak disregard them because they must. That means extremism at both ends with civilians trapped in the middle. The trend culminated in World War II when all sides used naval blockades to try to starve out the enemy, as well as air campaigns that targeted "enemy civilians." Occupation forces carried out "kill all" sweeps, "anti-bandit" campaigns, and exemplary massacres and executions. Partisans replied with ambushes and bombings, targeted assassinations, refusal to accept surrenders, and reprisal killing of suspected civilian informers. It is a well-worn pattern of war, where opposing forces are seldom balanced and asymmetry of capability leads to harsher measures.

More recently, Syrian aircraft dropped barrel bombs and chemical weapons on civilians who lacked air cover. Anti-regime militia responded with suiciders. Sri Lankan soldiers murdered Tamils, who turned to suicide bombers as everyone descended into depravity. *Genocidaires* in Rwanda killed 800,000 with clubs and machetes, so quickly self-defense was impossible: sometimes you cannot fight back in time as green-tarped lorries roll into town with killers onboard. Idi Amin filled Uganda's rivers with domestic enemies, choking reservoirs downstream with corpses, provoking Tanzanian intervention and his overthrow in 1979. He did not stand trial for his crimes; he lived out his natural life with stolen national wealth in Saudi Arabia. ISIS was not destroyed for years after it slaughtered Yazidi refugees on Mount Sinjar in 2014, enslaving or exterminating those it deemed "heretics." A junta in Myanmar faced few consequences for mass murder of Rohingya in 2017. Millions of Ukrainians fled arbitrary Russian shelling in 2022, as massed artillery destroyed eastern towns and villages at the leading edge of a tactic of creeping local advances. Civilians are always in someone's way.[2]

TARGETING PERSONS WHO WOULD TODAY BE classified as civilians for torture or killing was an established pattern in First Nations conflicts in the Americas. Precolonial wars were fought down to the village level between Iroquois and Algonquin in upper New York, Lower Canada, the Great Lakes, and St. Lawrence River valley.[3] During the Pequot War, 700 were killed in 1637 when White settlers burned a village at Missituck, then shot every man, woman, and child who tried to flee the flames. Some Mohegan and Narragansett warriors abandoned their alliance with the settlers in disgust. Others helped kill more of their Pequot enemies.[4] Settlers burned out Powhatan villages in Virginia in the mid-17th century. Wampanoag villages burned in New England and more tribal war scoured settlements from New York down to the Floridas. By the early 18th century a population advantage of 8:1 in English colonists over *Nouvelle-France* compelled the French to adopt the natural guerrilla tactics of First Nations allies, who knew how to fight under forest cover. The idea was to hold on, knowing the colonial wars were going to be decided not in forests in New England or the New York lake country but on battlefields in Europe and atop the seas. In addition, French troops and *Canadien,* Algonquin, and Métis allies were much better at guerrilla warfare. British fought but faltered with regiments of redcoats and colonial militia, then countered at midcentury with Rogers' Rangers, recruited in the backwoods of New Hampshire.

Cover and conceal. Use small-unit tactics. Live off the land. Learn marksmanship, not volley fire. Carry accurate hunting rifles, not military smoothbores designed for volleys. Never concentrate for a stand-up, line fight in the Frederickian manner of European armies of the day, while dressed in red or blue or white that made you an easy mark for ambush inside a forest clearing. Emphasize speed and mobility; make portage with silent birch canoes. Lie in wait to attack; withdraw to surprise-attack again. Recon, raid, and pursue. These were the methods of the Forest Nations and allied *Canadiens* who lived among them and often just like them. Also of Rodgers' Rangers. It meant civilians were as often as not targets whenever fighting began. Each side slugged it out with tromping regular troops but also raided deep into enemy territory, attacking villages and farms, killing civilians and scalping them, too. In 1759 Rodgers attacked the village of St. Francis on the St. Lawrence, killing 200 Abenaki, mainly women and children. Only seven of his men were killed but 49 died in a hard, fighting retreat against enraged warriors who were not in the village but nearby when the colonists crept in and murdered their wives and children. They used all their woodland and warrior skills to pursue and exact blood vengeance.

Then the French were gone, the British were gone, colonists became Americans and the forest wars were about who controlled the land, not beaver trapping and buckskin hunting grounds. War chiefs on one side faced U.S. Army generals on the other. Some, like General Andrew Pickens, were moderate and fair in their dealings with First Nations peoples.[5] Others, especially General Andrew Jackson, are remembered as exemplars of racist views and supremacist policies. He lobbied the governor of Tennessee in June 1812 to allow him to march state militia to Florida to fight the Creeks. He promised no mercy, to "carry fire and sword to the heart of the Creek Nation, and to learn these wretches in their own towns and villages what it is to massacre women and children."[6] Red Stick warriors of the Creek Nation *had* massacred white refugees huddled inside Fort Mims. Such atrocity stories about mutilated women and children enflamed the frontier. Settler land hunger that pressured the Creeks was the backdrop story. But that was no way to rally a virile young country to wage a race war. Massacre insisted on annihilation.

First Nations warriors did not hesitate to kill women and children, as doing so demonstrated you penetrated to the heartland of your enemy and had bested him there.[7] Whites showed from the start that they also would not hesitate to slaughter First Nations women and children. Creeks fell back to their Blackwater River towns. Jackson pursued and tragedy ensued: burned villages, dead innocents, raped women, massacred prisoners after battles Jackson had already won.[8] As often is the case, the brutality was justified with the rhetorical question: "Well, they started it, right?" It was the old query and the old lie in only moderately different guise, meant to hide one's own crimes behind a façade of the enemy's. Next it was the turn of Seminole, later of the Cherokee and Choctaw, as Jackson killed his way into the White House and onto the $20 bill. Displacement and "ethnic cleansing" from long-coveted lands was already an oft-told tale. A hundred retellings lay in the future, from the Great Lakes to the Rockies to the Pacific.

It was not all dishonor, betrayal, and atrocity. Some men of the advanced, armed power now migrating west from the eastern cities were honorable, although most wanted all First Nations gone from rich lands deemed God-given for White settlement or expansion of slavery. Already famous for a heroic military career, General James Miller was fondly admired in Nathanial Hawthorne's *The Scarlet Letter* (1850).[9] He had fought the Shawnee at Tippecanoe in 1811 and fought again in the Niagara peninsula campaign during the War of 1812. After, he worked in the Salem Custom House, where he was framed by Hawthorne as awkwardly out of place. Miller was the first governor of the Arkansas Territory, which stretched to the Texas Panhandle. He was reasonable as superintendent of Indian affairs, fair with Quapaw and Cherokee. He tried but failed to mediate a peace between two long-standing enemies, Osage and Cherokee. His efforts all went for naught when President Jackson in 1830 signed the policy that became infamous as "Indian Removal." Steamboats carried 80,000 dispossessed First Nations west, along with slaves. It was an unprecedented ethnic cleansing, meant to clear every last one from every acre east of the Mississippi.[10] As subjects but not citizens of the United States, First Nations were legally akin to slaves: outside the reach of law as their protector, yet under the full weight of law as their oppressor.

GUERRILLA PRACTICES AND HARSH MILITARY RESPONSES extended well past massacres of First Nation villages in American history. They also drew in White civilians in the Kansas-Missouri region when Free Soilers first fought "Border Ruffians" and other pro-slavers, starting in 1855. Then it got worse. It took time for Abraham Lincoln and his generals to realize that smashing the armies of the Confederate States of America (CSA) was not enough to bring Rebel states back into the Union. They needed to subjugate all defiant civilians as well. Lincoln brought tough-minded General John Pope east to shore up Federal forces as head of the newly formed and short-lived Army of Virginia. Pope ordered his troops to live off the land in Rebel areas, confiscate provisions from disloyal civilians, and carry out tough and indiscriminate reprisals against civilians for any guerrilla attacks. Measures ranged from exemplary burning of homes to summary execution and forcible deportations. Northern opinion reacted badly, so the measures were softened and Pope was replaced after also losing at Second Bull Run (August 28–30, 1862). In contrast, George B. McClellan would not make war on civilians. He hardly made war at all, in the view of his critics.[11]

Other generals were less reluctant. Ulysses S. Grant was already waging the kind of "hard war" in Tennessee and Mississippi that he later gifted to Lincoln in Virginia and the Deep South. For him the turning point was ferocious Confederate resistance at Shiloh (April 6–7, 1862). He saw that the enemy's volunteer morale was still so high that in addition to breaking armies, millions of civilians across the South must be forced to submit to Union authority. Only the most extreme means could achieve that: make a new kind of hard war across the whole spectrum of resistance, or lose the war and see the Union split. Grant's vision expanded until he came to see that sending armies deep behind Confederate lines to wreck everything of value to the enemy's war effort, from railways and economic infrastructure to civilian morale, was the way to win. Attrition of matériel and morale was the key, which winning battles would accelerate without being decisive in themselves.

Lincoln brought Grant and other western generals east because he, too, had evolved, from reluctant belligerent to ruthless wartime leader, who now believed that harder methods were necessary to victory. Lincoln signed and issued General Order No. 100, written by Professor Francis Lieber of Columbia College in New York and promulgated beginning on April 24, 1863. The "Lieber Code" ostensibly elevated humane conduct of war to lawful obligation, and limited excesses. It was really a response to Rebel guerrilla activity, which it sought to place outside all boundaries of civilization so that it could be dealt with by harsher means. It started boldly: "Military necessity does not admit of cruelty."[12] In the next article, it defined away "cruelty" as often necessary in the field, ranging from reprisals for outlawed acts to collective punishment and starvation of civilians: "War is not carried on by arms alone. It is lawful to starve the hostile belligerent, armed or unarmed, so that it leads to the speedier subjection of the enemy." Four articles later it allowed near absolution of crimes by Union soldiers. "The citizen or native of a hostile country is ... an enemy, as one of the constituents of the hostile state or nation, and as such is subjected to the hardships of the war."[13] That waiver anticipated one of the most malevolent of 20th-century wartime concepts: "enemy civilian." Lieber's code also endorsed the summary execution of deserters; hostage taking of civilians; collective punishments; and looting property, as long as plundering supported the just war to preserve the Union. Its strictures influenced lawyers meeting in Belgium in 1874 to expand the laws of war. They also influenced the Hague Conventions drafted in 1899 and 1907, on the eve of World War I.

A bloody Union defeat over the Seven Days Battles (June 25 to July 1, 1862), even bloodier victory at Shiloh, and an ever worsening of sharp war convinced Lincoln and most of his generals that winning the war required far harsher methods. They needed to suppress not just Rebel armies but the secessionist population, now deemed morally intransigent and politically beyond redemption except by force. Pope's express views in 1862 were mere prelude to what was coming in the campaigns of 1864–1865, and coming everywhere in the world after that. Lieber's code provided Union generals with a veneer of legal and moral cover for the hard measures they meant to take under the rubric of military necessity. It actually approved an elevated level of military reprisal against Rebel guerrillas and civilians, disguised as more civilized restraint. Its underlying logic was that modern states and civilizations had advanced beyond barbarism, even in war. Peace was the norm, war the exception: a retrograde phenomenon that could be tamed and cowed like a caged tiger. Then it accumulated all claim to justice and legitimacy to one side, arguing from righteous military necessity for extreme war against Rebel armies and guerrillas but also toward disloyal civilians.

Lieber proclaimed that severe harshness in war, far from being a necessary evil at very best, was actually a moral boon: "The more vigorously wars are pursued, the better it is for humanity. Sharp wars are brief."[14] Except that they are not. The allure of battle may have promised short wars but modern capacity for mobilization of whole societies nearly always delivered long ones.[15] It happened in Lieber's own day, under his gaze from 1861 to 1865. Social animosity changed to deep hatred as merciful restraint eroded, anguish and endurance alike increased with casualties, and deprivations encouraged depravities. In fact, Lieber's thesis was already disproven before Lincoln signed Order 100: a vicious fight beyond any rules in "Bloody Kansas" was in its seventh year. Guerrilla tactics and widely destructive cavalry raids were not what anyone expected before the war. They ranged from Kentucky and Missouri to New Mexico and out to the Colorado Territory. Requisition and reprisal against dissent and armed resistance was cruelly enforced. White women were seldom molested by passing Union troops but the armies of liberation did not resist raping freed slave women.[16] White men were protected only insofar as they were loyal to the Union. Military governors would have to judge. General William T. Sherman did so early on, taking hostages and reprisal-burning the large towns of Randolph, Tennessee, and Jackson,

Mississippi, in actions that predated and prepared his more famous march to Atlanta and across the South.[17]

Mercilessness always marked conflict in the western territories even before the start of the American Civil War: it both predated secession and lasted decades beyond Union victory. First Nations' resistance to armed White migration, then early counterinsurgency warfare by U.S. cavalry, was abundant. Lincoln proved capable of deploying severe methods against First Nations, too, though reluctantly for moral and prudential reasons and genuinely with "malice toward none." His grandfather had been killed by a Shawnee warrior in 1786 but that did not seem to influence the grandson's wartime views toward First Nations peoples. As a young man he served, rather than fought, in the Black Hawk War: he joked later, on the campaign trail, that the only blood he shed for his country was taken by mosquitoes. With his eye on the war in Virginia in 1862, he still had to protect a stream of settlers that never stopped heading west, as well as railway and telegraph projects threatened by Confederate guerrillas and First Nations warriors. He also faced a Confederate offer of alliance with the Cherokee Nation and several fresh "Indian Wars" in the Southwest, Colorado, and Minnesota. He approved formation of an all-warrior unit in the Union Army that fought in Kansas, only under strict instructions that it must only fight "other Indians." He well knew the public was not ready for "savages" wearing Union blue to kill White men, even if they wore Rebel gray or butternut.

A bloody rebellion broke out in Minnesota in 1862, marked by many acts of sadistic atrocity against civilians on both sides and out-of-control racial hatred. The Dakota War was a low point in Lincoln's presidency. General Pope had been sent back west in mid-1862 and promptly reduced the food supply available to all Sioux across Minnesota. He promised to "exterminate the Sioux. . . . They are to be treated as maniacs or wild beasts." Losing battles back east and short of troops, Lincoln and his cabinet discussed using paroled Confederates to fight "rebel" Sioux.[18] Hundreds were arrested and 300 Sioux warriors were condemned to hang. Some in Lincoln's cabinet strongly objected; others wanted it done. Minnesota's delegation in Congress threatened that clemency might provoke White mobs to far worse violence: vigilante groups were indeed forming. Their interest was to remove all Sioux and all Winnebago from the state, although no Winnebago were in the uprising.[19] Lincoln reviewed trial transcripts, discovering no real evidence against many of the condemned past the fact they were Sioux warriors. Sharp pressure was brought to bear to execute all captives anyway, including a Senate resolution rejecting any mercy by Lincoln.

Lincoln did not back down. Although preoccupied with terrible losses at Second Bull Run, enormous casualties at Antietam, and the issue of the Emancipation Proclamation with all that it entailed for Union politics and the war, he spent a month reviewing records and trial testimony from the Minnesota court. He settled on a Sioux faction irreconcilable to peace that committed rampage killings of White settlers, provoking retaliation murders of Dakota families. About 600 Whites had died and 100 Dakota, though more Sioux died later of hunger and disease. White dead were often mutilated; Dakota dead were scalped. Then surrender of the last Sioux fighters led to hundreds of prisoners and the hasty death sentences.

The last act of the Dakota War could have been worse. In the face of howling political opposition and public opinion, Lincoln granted clemency to 200 condemned Dakota, commuting their death sentences. He told the Senate that only two of the prisoners could be proven to be rapists. He made the key distinction that while many Sioux warriors fought in battles, they had not carried out massacres. He chose mercy but was still bound to order the largest execution in American history. In the hamlet of Mankato, 38 Mdewakanton Dakota he could not spare were hanged.[20] The next year, Lincoln proposed to reform the western clearance policy but little was or could be done with the Civil War underway. The executions took place between two invasions of the North by Confederate armies and with Union casualties rising exponentially. Piecemeal removal of First Nations therefore continued to the end of the war. It would accelerate after 1865, with Lincoln gone. Generals hardened by four years of war in the East against Rebel armies, guerrillas, and civilians went out to subdue the First Nations of the West, using the same means of scorched earth with which they beat the South.

From 1864 to 1865 it was not the battles of the American Civil War that decided the outcome, except insofar as they piled on death and misery to the deeper physical and moral attrition which was the basic means by which the war was won and lost. Even moderate Chief of Staff General Henry Halleck came around to hard war. He wrote to Sherman in December 1864, suggesting the example of Rome at Carthage: "Should you capture Charleston, I hope that by some accident the place may be destroyed, and if a little salt should be sown upon its site it may prevent the growth of future crops of nullification and secession."[21] It was a total war of destruction of railways and civilian infrastructure; food blockades; burning whole towns; cavalry raids deep into enemy territory; targeting civilians and especially the planter class right where they lived, ruining the plantations; burning food supplies of Confederate armies no matter how harsh the effect on civilians, whom Lincoln's government and Union law viewed as rebellious citizens but U.S. citizens all the same. There were Union guerrillas, too, wherever populations split apart between the Rebel and Union causes on local lines, confusing the great moral question that hung over a war reaching culmination.

The main instrument of victory had been found: an evermore capable and ruthless Union Army under leaders prepared to wage all-out war to final victory. Union gunboats carved the CSA in two. Union cavalry cut apart Missouri and Tennessee, then raided into Virginia and as far south as Alabama and Mississippi. It all culminated in Grant's grand strategy in 1864: five discrete invasions of the South, all at once. Inside the CSA something like a second civil war broke out between diehards and deserters, or just wild bands of hungry outlaws who preyed on everyone. The Deep South burned. The Shenandoah burned. Inflation soared and morale plunged. Naval blockade strangled a few final bits of trade. At last the Rebel cause collapsed into despair and defeat. Then into denial.

THE SAME MEN WHO BURNED PLANTATIONS and the Shenandoah to make Rebel civilians bend the knee did it all over again for another quarter-century, waging merciless campaigns against a much more vulnerable population, where they debased themselves in repeated massacres. They took the idea of hard war as good war west in "pacification" campaigns against still resistant First Nations. Carried out from 1865 to 1890 under successive command of the U.S. Army by Grant, Sherman, and General Philip Henry Sheridan, subduing the West echoed the themes, tactics, and mindset of 1864–1865: the way to undermine enemy resistance was to make his civilians feel what Sherman described in 1864 as "the hard hand of war."[22] Settlers encroached on First Nations land, killed the buffalo and burned villages, then demanded protection. The U.S. Congress discarded the old treaties, then veterans of the Union Army were sent out to deal with the turmoil and consequences. As in other 19th-century wars of empire, conquering armies pursuing the harshest methods followed settlers or the cross, the flag and the railways. Dust clouds raised up by wagon wheels foretold bloody confrontations to come. Ribbons of steel carried westward the cavalry's mounts and fodder, its mobile cannons and Gatling guns. An empire was on the march, swollen with ideas of manifest destiny, racial and cultural superiority, and obvious military prowess.

Sheridan and Sherman spoke about "exterminating" warriors but also women and children. It was not all about military domination. Hardened tactics played well back east as righteous vengeance for atrocities against Whites, regardless of who had struck first.[23] Sheridan was absolutely ruthless, commanding from 1867 to 1883 against Apache, Arapaho, Cheyenne, Comanche, Kiowa, the Great Sioux Nation, Ute, and others. Before heading out west to fight, in 1866 he promised "vindictive earnestness against the Sioux, even to their extermination, men, women, and children."[24] In summer, he chased warriors out on raiding parties, riding swift ponies. In winter, he attacked their fragile encampments to aggravate problems of insufficient food and shelter for their families. In 1873 he wrote to Sherman about these tactics: "I have to select that season when I can catch the fiends; and, if a village is attacked and women and children killed, the responsibility is not with the soldiers but with the people whose crimes necessitated the attack."[25]

After all, Sheridan rhetorically queried Sherman, was firing cannon into tepee nomadic villages anything different from what the Union Army did in the Civil War? "Did any one hesitate to attack a village or town occupied by the [Rebel] enemy because women or children were within its limits?

Did we cease to throw shells into Vicksburg or Atlanta because women and children were there?"[26] After 20 years of campaigning out west he softened a little, though he did not end ruthless suppression tactics. In rare contemplative mood, he mused about a defeated and abject enemy: "We took away their country and their means of support, broke up their mode of living, their habits of life, introduced disease and decay among them, and it was for this and against this they made war. Could any one expect less?" It was an honest question, only asked and answered too late to incur mercy from a ruthless warrior.

It was not always so clear to others who fought in the West. Some men who faced Southwest or prairie First Nations in battle developed deep respect not just for their warrior tenacity and fighting skills but for their free lifestyle and their humanity. George Armstrong Custer wrote home, long before he led men to their deaths at the Little Big Horn: "If I were an Indian, I often think I would greatly prefer to cast my lot among those of my people [who] adhered to the free open plains, rather than submit to the confined limits of a reservation, there to be the recipient of the blessed benefits of civilization, with its vices thrown in without stint or measure."[27] His Sioux enemies may have respected him as well. His body appears not to have been molested after Little Big Horn, whereas all his men were mutilated to disable them in the afterlife. Sherman also said gentle things far too late, coming to pity an enemy he was determined to destroy.[28] Even the overtly murderous Sheridan wrote pensively about First Nations defeat in his memoirs.[29] Meaning it or not.

Such expressions of respect served a dual purpose: admiration for the Great Plains warrior's tactics vindicated reciprocal tactics by the U.S. Cavalry, including attacking food supplies and civilians. At other times, it seemed genuinely romantic or sentimental, notably toward the end when the outcome was obvious and tragic by any scoring. Some U.S. Army officers thought that Great Plains and Southwest Nations had been corrupted into savagery by contact with savage Whites. A few considered their last stands of resistance to be truly noble. General George Crook told a West Point graduating class that while cadets might think Great Plains warriors were cruel

and treacherous, "so were our forefathers."[30] A number of Civil War veterans came to see that the whole West "had become a giant Andersonville
for Indian captives."[31] Or perhaps, given that Union troops and not Rebels
were in charge of all prisoners on the Great Plains, an Elmira.[32]

Professor Lieber shed his vaunted humanitarianism when it came to
dealing with another presumptuous resistance to the legitimate power of
the restored Union. In 1883 he called for physical extermination of the
Western Nations: "Extinction … the quicker the better."[33] Callow moral and
historical arrogance had not disappeared 150 years later. In 2021 a *Fox News*
television host harrumphed indignantly about claims to compensation or
revision of the historical narrative about how the West was lost: "This land
wasn't stolen. We won this land on the battlefield and we bought it, right?
We have the receipts."[34] Certainly all receipts that hunters submitted to the
U.S. government for slaughtering the buffalo on commission, in order to
starve out resisting First Nations families.

In summer, warriors on fleet ponies navigating the sea of grass were superior in mobility to U.S. Army cavalry, who did not know the terrain near
as well. In winter, their families were vulnerable to limited food supplies and
needed shelter from killing heat or cold. A key technique used to compel the
last warriors to submit was to starve their families and villages by protecting
rapacious buffalo hunters who slaughtered the herds. It was a food blockade
on land, starvation as national policy by any name. They could be starved
while exposed to a barren desert in the south, or to snow and ice on the
windswept northern plains. It hardly mattered if you did not see the children, women, and elders of First Nations as true civilians or with an equal
place in the Union.

Even if you did, Lieber's lethal code said that it was justified to starve
women and children to get to men still fighting. Theodore Roosevelt, who
had spent time slaughtering buffalo in the Dakota Country, wrote in 1886
with his usual artless bombast: "I don't go so far as to think that the only
good Indian is the dead Indian but I believe nine out of every ten are, and
I shouldn't like to inquire too closely into the case of the tenth."[35] Smug
racism in the distant East, starvation across the West, from the southern
deserts to the northern grassland. All the major powers would do it on an

immense scale in the two world wars, using scorched earth on land and ruthless interdiction and blockades at sea to cut food supplies, in sustained attempts to starve the other side's civilian population and thus compel military and political submission.[36]

Sheridan wiped out the southern herds to start, discouraging the Texas legislature from legally protecting the hoofed, migrating commissary of his enemy. Then he slaughtered the northern herds, protecting long-rifle hunters across Montana and other wild places. Decimation of the buffalo and Congress discarding an 1855 treaty is what sent Chief Joseph and desperate nontreaty Nez Perce (Nimíipuu) on an extraordinary fighting retreat. It stretched over 1,170 miles and 18 battles with pursuing U.S. cavalry. It ended with a last fight in the Bear Paw Mountains, just 40 miles shy of Redcoat protection across the Canadian border. Chief Joseph led the Wallowa band of Nez Perce in the surrender. White Bird led the Lamátta band, escaping after the last battle to reach Sitting Bull's camp in Canada. The 418 Wallowa Nez Perce who surrendered with Chief Joseph were entrained and sent under guard to Fort Leavenworth in Kansas, a place they had never seen before, had no connection to, and where they could hardly thrive. Another broken promise. Another broken people.

It was not the first time this was done. French troops had starved inland Algerian bands from 1830 to 1847, scorching grazing lands, slaughtering goat, sheep, and cattle herds. When survivors retreated into the desert they died there of exposure. Others were suffocated as French troops set fires and wafted thick smoke into sealed caves, a tactic they called *enfumades*.[37] Bounties were placed on Arab heads as the conquest became truly debased, in ways not forgiven or forgotten in occupied Algiers. German troops did much the same on the Kerch peninsula in 1941. They sealed in quarry caves with 3,000 civilians trapped inside, then piped in poison gas.[38] Not much in war is new. All the old evils just keep being reinvented.

In 1864 Dog Soldiers from an especially ferocious Warrior Society of the Cheyenne vowed to fight to the death. They drove pegs into the ground, lashed themselves in place, and fought to the last. The curtain that fell like a shroud on the tale of how the West was lost was not at all like that. It came to the Sioux at Wounded Knee Creek on December 29, 1890, in a reprise of the massacre of noncombatant First Nations at Sand Creek.[39] A raggedy column of Lakota women and children, with just a few warriors alongside, was moving under a flag of truce from Cheyenne River Sioux Reservation to the Pine Ridge Reservation. They were out looking for Chief Red Cloud (Maȟpíya Lúta), famed leader of an earlier lost rebellion. They were not going to talk about war. They wanted to consult him about the new religion of the Ghost Dance and to ask what to do about the missing buffalo. It was just 14 days after Chief Sitting Bull (Tȟatȟáŋka Íyotake) of the Hunkpapa Lakota was assassinated at Standing Rock Reservation.[40] The 7th Cavalry, Custer's outfit, intercepted the column and butchered almost 300, murdering them with rifles and Hotchkiss guns shooting down from a low hilltop. Bodies were found three miles away, suggesting long pursuit with intent to murder. Officers told investigators they had fired in self-defense at women who fired first. Eyewitnesses said soldiers had lured out small boys with promises of comfort, surrounded and killed them. There was little mercy in the saddlebags of the 7th Cavalry.[41] Yet, 20 men were awarded the Medal of Honor for their actions at Wounded Knee.

TR'S SHALLOW VIEW FROM THE WELL-LIGHTED social clubs of New York was not shared by all men who actually fought in the West. Captain William Clark served in the Great Plains Wars against Oglala and Cheyenne. He studied their cultures and histories and learned their sign language, at times helping to avoid fights. Like other officers, he could seem more critical of White settlers and eastern politicians than the battle behavior of the Sioux and Cheyenne he helped defeat. None of it stopped him or others from herding women and children onto scrub reservations or hunting down and killing their husbands and brothers. Clark was even complicit in the murder of the great war chief Crazy Horse (Tȟašúŋke Witkó).[42] Still, he spoke more decently about warriors who wanted to kill him than did comfortable New Yorkers such as Roosevelt, who helped destroy the food supply and livelihood of the Great Plains Sioux.

Lieutenant Charles Wood graduated from West Point but did not like it when he was commissioned as a junior officer in the U.S. Army. In 1877 he was in the wilderness near Sitka, Alaska, when he was called back to serve with the 21st Regiment heading out to confront the nontreaty Nez Perce Nation.[43] That was a term used for several Nez Perce groups who banded together to resist unilateral renunciation by Congress of their 1855 treaty, prelude to being forcibly removed from traditional lands to a reservation in Idaho. Wood worked as an aide-de-camp in the Regimental HQ, where he came to study and admire the nontreaty Nez Perce.[44] A local newspaper editorialized: "Their warfare since they entered Montana has been almost universally marked so far by the highest characteristics recognized by civilized nations."[45] Wood was present at the surrender and translated Chief Joseph's famous words.[46] He was deeply sympathetic, yet convinced the end of the Western Nations was inevitable, and justified by the interests of a higher civilization cutting across the continent while sowing oats and bibles in expropriated soil. He later came to reject all that. He regretted his past acts, provoked to radical renunciation of what he had done by the fatal collapse of European civilization into all-out war in 1914.

Captain John Bourke was a ferocious "Indian Fighter" and at one time also a hater. He saw a lot of action in the Southwest. Over time he learned to have respect for his foe. Instead, he arrived at contempt for Congress, which tore up valid treaties and financed black-hearted and protracted war. He might have added presidents who handed out Medals of Honor in bushels to men who murdered women and children. Bourke poured himself into First Nations languages and culture, moving off his early hatred toward cultural understanding. Afterward, he became a prominent anthropologist ("folklorist"). He understood that vice and virtue are not bound to "race" and that everyone's history is thus replete with repulsive practices and much savagery, including the country for which he had fought for years.[47] Guilt, loss, compassion. Scorn for all those back East who watched and cheered but never served. Admiration of warrior skill and ferocity right in front of him. Knowledge that no First Nation would survive much longer. Gnawing doubt that Western civilization was itself in a buffalo stampede approaching a steep bluff, below which waited a hidden deep-blood kettle.[48]

The pernicious idea that military necessity justified killing women and children in counterinsurgency campaigns in the Old West has not disappeared. A 2007 article published by the U.S. Army Center of Military History recounted a punitive raid into northern Mexico in 1873 that it said "successfully attacked [a] Kickapoo Indian village." It approved of a second raid on "a large Indian encampment" in the Red River territory that "burned the Indians' lodges and supplies and captured their herd of 1,424 ponies." It called that a winter logistical success for the U.S. Army, without noting that it was also a winter calamity for hundreds of women and children left without food, shelter, or transport. The subject of the appraisal, Henry Ware Lawton, was described as a "flawed giant and hero of four wars."[49] In one of those campaigns, he was present at the surrender of Geronimo (Goyaalé) in 1886. It made his name.

A decade later Lawton fought in the Philippines, bringing his 11-year-old son to the Pacific to see what war was like. TR's secretary of state, John Hay, called it a "splendid little war." It was, in fact, a vicious affair that went on for years after an initial U.S. naval victory. Nonetheless, Lawton's 21st-century admirer, who was clearly thinking about counterinsurgency wars in Iraq and Afghanistan, called the brutal campaign Lawton waged a century earlier "a laboratory for fighting insurgency."[50] This obtuse analysis concluded that Lawton had been "a proponent of enlightened colonial administration" who favored "a benevolent approach" to "native self-government," at least once American control was established by force.[51] One may only imagine what Lawton might have done with Apache helicopters and A10 gunships. Probably more or less what was actually done with that technology in counterinsurgency wars in the Greater Middle East a century later: fly over all local culture and tradition to kill insurgents but also too many civilians. And thereby lose long campaigns to convert "hearts and minds" to an imported cause of forcible cultural and regime change. That kind of tactical tunnel vision is exactly what morally discredited the Western counterinsurgency wars in Iraq and Afghanistan despite the callow nature of the enemy in both countries, turning them into operational and strategic defeats. No lessons learned. No doctrine altered. No history left unrepeated. We shall see it all again.

———————

THE PHILIPPINE-AMERICAN WAR (1899–1902) WAS SPLENDIDLY ruthless. It was characterized by widespread abuse of civilians, intended to undercut guerrillas by severing resistance fighters from logistics bases and family and village support. Draconian practices were imported from the "Indian Wars" fought after 1865. Others came from the Civil War. Still others dated to pre-Independence wars in the Great Lakes region, the ferociously violent settlement of Virginia, or the conquest and ethnic clearances of the Floridas. Filipinos rightly saw themselves as being at war with a foreign occupying power, but Americans claimed to face an illicit insurrection. Lieber's code thus provided legal cover to treat Filipino guerrillas as criminals instead of legitimate combatants. The war turned ugly as a result. Filipinos outnumbered Americans but were underequipped and outgunned. Some resorted to bows and knives against modern rifles, machine guns, and artillery. Most combat was by small units. Filipinos set up ambushes. Americans made retaliation sweeps, burned villages, and committed massacres and atrocities. All that lies mostly outside popular historical memory.

U.S. generals adopted brutal pacification methods that Filipinos recognized from their war against Spanish colonial occupation.[52] Suppression tactics looked to physical isolation of guerrilla fighters from noncombatants in "zones of protection" that forced villagers into dank, disease-ridden camps that ushered in large-scale civilian deaths. Half a world away, the British also used concentration camps to intern and isolate Boer women and children, who died in large numbers as a result. Besides internment camps, other familiar tactics included destruction of food crops and forced deportation or relocation.[53] Herding despondent and defeated First Nations onto scrub reservation lands almost seems like practice for what the U.S. Army carried out in the Philippines. General Jacob Smith provided a direct link: he was a trooper at Wounded Knee before he took command of U.S. ground forces in the Philippines.

Smith faced just as unequal an enemy in the Filipino resistance as he faced fighting the Sioux. He employed the same brutality he had participated in against the Lakota at Wounded Knee: "I want no prisoners, I wish you to kill and burn. The more you kill and burn the better it will please me. I want all persons killed who are capable of bearing arms (ten years of age and above)."[54] Smith was criticized in fierce anti-imperialist newspapers of the day. Instead of admonishment or prosecution for war crimes by the Army he was promoted twice, remaining in command in the Philippines until 1902. Others who suppressed First Nations of the American West brought scorched earth and targeting of civilians and food supplies to war on guerrilla resistance in the Philippines. Few were as reckless as Smith was in committing criminal intent to written orders, but most felt immune from consequences. Some killed with news camera bulbs flashing. Medals of Honor were again awarded by a distant government.

General Leonard Wood received one for fighting Geronimo and other Apache in the Southwest. He founded the Rough-Riders with Theodore Roosevelt. After TR happily killed a man in Cuba, Wood went to the Philippines where he killed far more, and women and children. As governor of Moro Province he introduced reforms such as the abolition of slavery. That angered slave-owning Moro. They attacked. Wood retaliated with burnings and massacres, using the same methods he first employed in the United States. However one judges the Moro *casus belli*, they surely did not deserve what was done to them in a different Battle of the Crater than the one most Americans know from their Civil War. Wood and Colonel J. W. Duncan were in command at Bud Dajo on March 7, 1906, a fight on the sloped sides of an extinct volcano on Jolo Island, a place of refuge for Moro hiding from the Spanish. The fighting opposed rifles, artillery, and gunships against Jolo Moro who were backed into the volcano crater armed with swords, machetes, and some improvised seashell grenades. It is better called a massacre than a battle. When it ended, only six Moro were left alive out of 900 men, women, and children.[55] U.S. troops posed for photos, standing over corpses in the crater as if they were on safari, a fairly common practice in most wars and armies ever since the invention of photography.[56] Roosevelt telegrammed his heartiest, manliest congratulations to Wood. Mark Twain was less impressed. He sharply criticized the U.S. Army, its on-the-spot commanders, and

Roosevelt's bellicose bluster. Certain facts and statistics Twain cited are now known to be inaccurate, but overall his passionate accusation survives as a righteous cry of outrage.[57]

WE USUALLY KNOW LESS ABOUT ORDINARY soldiers than the generals and politicians who send them out to fight. We know as much, and as little, about the Americans at the crater in the Philippines as we do about individual soldiers lost among uniformed millions of the two world wars. A few stand out, however. Right after graduation from a local *Gymnasium* at the age of 17, Karl-Heinz Rosch was conscripted into the *Luftwaffe*. He was hurriedly trained as a *Kanonier* (gunner) with a converted *Fallschirmjäger* (airborne) regiment, then deployed to the Netherlands to face arriving British and Commonwealth forces. German airborne had by then mostly converted to light infantry roles or joined panzer divisions strewn in front of the Western Allied advance to the Rhine in 1944 or the Red Army advance to the Vistula. Rosch's converted unit carried the "honorific" "Hermann Göring." But it should not be confused with the infamous Hermann Göring Division, which carried out extensive war crimes in Italy in 1943 and mercilessly suppressed the Warsaw Uprising in August 1944. Other *Luftwaffe* units were also named after its vain, corpulent leader.

Rosch was spared fighting on the feared *Ostfront*. His unit was billeted on a quiet family farm near the Dutch village of Goirle in Brabant. There, war reached out to touch him on October 6, 1944, just three days after his 18th birthday. Western armies were clawing back into the Netherlands following their setback in Operation Market-Garden in September. Upon hearing an approaching attack, Rosch's squad ran hard to crew the unit's artillery. As he ran, he saw two small boys playing outside the farmhouse. Ages four and five, they were oblivious to the approach of war. He raced over and scooped them up, tucking one lad under each arm. He then carried them to safety down the family's root cellar. Dashing back out to catch up with his vanished mates, Rosch was ripped apart by an incoming mortar. Killed instantly, he lay buried in the farmyard until 1948, when his remains were disinterred and reburied in the German military cemetery in Ysselsteyn, east of Eindhoven.

The family with whom he billeted remained silent about his saving of their two boys because they feared reprisals. In 2005 the story came out when the rescued boys, grown to adulthood, told it in public and thanked "the good German" who saved them from falling shells. A controversy erupted when a former town councilor proposed a statue of the dead 18-year-old, whom he called "a hero without glory." Herman van Rouwendaal responded to those who objected, "We will not be honoring the Wehrmacht but rather the humanity of a young German soldier." He hoped that a statue would advance reconciliation with contemporary Germans. He also wanted to counter what he saw as Dutch hypocrisy over a mixed wartime record that included deportation of Jews.[58] Collaboration had also extended to volunteering to fight for the Nazis in Waffen-SS 23rd Volunteer Panzer Grenadier Division (*Nederland*). There was also much brave resistance to the occupation and to the Nazis, including by some from Goirle who paid the ultimate price.

State funding for the statue was rejected and a public site was refused by the town council. However, private donations arrived and a half-sized statue of Rosch was cast. In 2008 this metal figure of the young German soldier was erected on private land, with the inscription: "In honour of all who do good in evil times."[59] He is cast as he last appeared in the final minute of a life thieved by Nazism, then by war. He is all gray, wearing a metallic Wehrmacht uniform topped by the notorious *Stahlhelm* (steel helmet). A small child is tucked under each teenage arm. You may search the Goirle town website but you will not find him there: no photo or directions are posted.

Why did Goirle town leaders choose not to honor a small act of decency in the midst of the horrific experience and memory of the Nazi occupation of the Netherlands? It could have acknowledged that some Germans, one dead boy in particular, had been kind and humane although certainly the Nazi occupation was brutal, vicious, and routinely murderous. The town council debated the issue. It concluded that erecting a statue of any German wearing a World War II uniform standing on Dutch soil was "too socially sensitive." After all, there was no memorial to commemorate five innocent Goirle men taken hostage by the Gestapo in 1942, lashed to posts, then executed in reprisal for a Dutch Resistance demolition attack on the railway to

Rotterdam. There was another real concern that in time proved prescient. The town was worried that a statue of any German soldier from World War II would be perverted into neo-Nazi propaganda. That the town would become a place of unclean fascist and White Supremacist pilgrimage. A search for Karl-Heinz Rosch indeed brings up links to neo-Nazi websites that glorify the SS and Wehrmacht, displaying vivid red-and-white Nazi banners.[60] A young man who acted with instinctive humanity in the last moments of his life has been indecorously adopted in death by indecent men nothing like him. His deed and memory are hijacked to perverse political purposes, adding moral insult to the mortal injury of a last moment in a life stolen at 18 summers.

CIVILIANS KEEP GETTING IN THE WAY in war. Most of those killed in World War II were noncombatants. There were new, brutal fights that rolled over civilian populations right after World War II: by the British in Malaya and Kenya, the French in Indochina, Dutch in Indonesia. The 1947 partition of India displaced over 10 million with massive "ethnic cleansing." More millions fled vicious civil wars in China and Korea. A million civilians died at French hands in Algeria, three million during 11 years of American war and bombing in Vietnam, Laos, and Cambodia. Mass killing marked a blood purge of the PKI (Communist Party) in Indonesia, the forgotten genocide of 1965. Starving civilians in secessionist Biafra came to symbolize the Nigerian Civil War by 1970. Refugees fled war or genocide in multiple failed states after that: Afghanistan, Congo, Iraq, Lebanon, Rwanda, Uganda, Sierra Leone, Sudan, and Syria. Arab villagers were gassed in Yemen by Egypt. Kurds were gassed in their home villages by Saddam Hussein. Iraqi Shi'a Arabs were hounded in drained southern marshland. Central America, Colombia, and Mexico were rent by narco wars that exceeded casualties in more recognized interstate conflicts. Ethnic and religious wars broke apart Yugoslavia, blighted Armenia and Azerbaijan, conscripted child soldiers into brutality in Chad, Liberia, Ethiopia, Myanmar, Sudan, and Congo.

U.S. missile strikes and bombs killed civilians in Iraq and Afghanistan over a 20-year period. Libya was bombed by NATO and devolved into an archipelago of warring tribes, with internal chaos driving some to such desperation they took to the sea in small boats. Saudis pummeled Houthi civilians in Yemen. Turks harried Kurds in refugee camps even as 600,000 civilians died during Syria's collapse and civil war. Russians dropped chemical weapons on towns that Bashar al-Assad could not retake with ground forces. Putin flattened Grozny in Chechnya in 1999 to secure his power with a popular war, marked by brutal *zachistka*, or "cleansing operations" aimed mainly at civilians. He attacked Georgia next, in 2008. It was Ukraine's turn starting in 2014, after it moved decisively toward Westernization, overthrowing a Putin protégé, applying for membership in the European Union, and embracing democracy. Instead it got a grinding war in Donbas, then all-out invasion in 2022. Indiscriminate shelling, bombing, and missile strikes sent millions of refugees streaming from Ukraine into foreign and refugee exile. Millions more were displaced internally. Tens of thousands were deported to Russia and held in "filtration camps," where they were screened for political views. Israelis never failed to retaliate if rockets flew in from Gaza or Lebanon. China keeps a million Uighurs in work camps. North Korea uses apprehended war psychosis to control its people. Myanmar brutalizes its Rohingya minority. All that disdain for the welfare of civilians makes a baleful record of "collateral damage," alongside premeditated murder and state terrorism. Yet, a full listing from the past 50 years alone might run for pages more. We struggle to inhabit a few islands of compassion and mercy in a storm sea of endless war and conflict.

Modern sensibility wants to believe that taking civilian hostages is uncivilized, something to be found only in history books about ancient conflicts. Yet, it remains today a way to assert dominance. In just the first weeks of war in Ukraine in 2022, Russian security services moved 45,000 unwilling Ukrainians to "filtration camps" across the Russian border, many from besieged, ruined Mariupol.[61] Threatening cities filled with civilians is a practice both ancient and modern, a way to exert political control and submission to armies waiting outside high medieval walls. It hardly matters if it is artillery firing into Paris in 1870 or Leningrad in 1942 or Aleppo in 2015 or Kharkiv in 2022. Over the past century, populations of hundreds of cities were held hostage to starvation as well as artillery and bombs. Every belligerent who could do it attacked civilians in World War II. After 1945 bombing became the primary means by which all great powers fought "asymmetrical wars" to coerce their enemies who had lesser air defenses and ground forces. Targeting of Ukrainian civilians by snipers, artillery, and missiles in Kyiv and Kharkiv and Mariupol showed that mercy is quickly set aside once force is chosen as an instrument of state policy. It was a reminder that was hardly needed, although it still shocked many. Yet, there was also grace amidst the ruins, as there almost always is. A former police commander in Mariupol offered to give himself as a hostage in exchange for safe passage of children out of the city. Vyacheslav Abroskin pleaded on Facebook: "Time is running out. . . . Instead of living children, I offer myself."[62]

PART IV

TECHNOLOGY

CHAPTER 11

STEEL

We shall take leave to be strong upon the seas, in the future as in the past; and there will be no thought of offense or provocation in that. Our ships are our natural bulwarks.

—Woodrow Wilson (1914)

At the conclusion of the Portsmouth Treaty that capped the Russo-Japanese War in 1905, *Scientific American* editors thought they had seen "the last great war to be waged between civilized powers."[1] Ten years later the odor of poison gas, first used in March 1915, still clotted viscous mud at the Ypres Salient. More than a million were already dead and the empires were only now going all-in for total war. Yet, an editorial in *Scientific American* that May blithely asserted: "One of the most assuring evidences of the fact that the world has been steadily advancing toward a higher civilization has been the development of a set of laws designed to soften, if not eradicate, the inhumanity of war."[2] It put all blame for torpedoing the passenger liner *Lusitania* two weeks earlier on the deficient character of Germans, not a shift to harder means by all major belligerents.[3] It called the sinking "cold-blooded" and cruelly planned, a condemnable byproduct of an illegal (because ineffective, and not "close") naval blockade. It was an argument from outdated naval law that ignored the Royal Navy's own illegal closure of the

Channel and North Sea, in preference to conducting a much more risky close blockade of German ports. It proclaimed that submarines were risible, "an utter farce ... outside the pale of legitimate warfare." With armchair editorial sanctimony, it finger-wagged at the *Kaiserliche Marine* but not at the just as ruthless Royal Navy. "There is such a thing as chivalry in war. It is even possible, if one has to fight, to fight like a gentleman."[4]

IN THE PEACEFUL DECADES IN EUROPE that followed the Crimean War, lawyers and reformers thought that even war might be made more rule-bound and humane. Among other initiatives, this led to codified rules of "cruiser warfare" in 1856 for surface ships on distance raids, supplemented in Hague Conventions of 1899 and 1907 and the Declaration of London in 1909. No mention was made of submarines because they were thought mere oddities, almost toys rather than real weapons of war. Nor aircraft carriers, which did not yet exist. War at sea was still thought to be about control of world sea lanes, with battleship versus battleship fleet actions deciding future wars via a reprise of Trafalgar.[5] Immense "castles of steel" were all that mattered: huge mobile artillery platforms whose sole purpose was to fight enemy battleships. Cruisers, light cruisers, fast attack or torpedo boats, torpedo boat destroyers (later, just destroyers), all evolved as escorts to protect the battleships. When the first all big-gun battleship, HMS *Dreadnought*, entered service with the Royal Navy in 1906 it made older battleships and smaller surface ships obsolete.[6] That included the German light cruiser SMS *Emden*.

Emden's hull was laid down in 1906, while its maiden voyage took place just five years before the start of World War I. Already it was antiquated. It was a coal-burning three-stacker with a crew of 361, displacing barely 3,600 tons. It was sleek but not fast at 25 knots flank speed and 12 knots cruising. That was no match for oil-fired turbines in all the newer, bigger warships. It had minimal 1.5-inch steel armor plating and 4.1-inch (10.5-cm) guns. In 1913 it was painted for peace, in parade all-white. Underarmored, undergunned and underpowered, *Emden* was sent to Asia to do minor colonial duty with the small East Asia Squadron. But you go to war whenever it starts with the ships you have available. Thus, when the July Crisis boomed into the guns of August, *Emden* and its captain and crew found themselves at war. They embarked on a tale out of time, a strange story of a man and moment memorable not for any lasting effects either had on naval war but for military and cultural oddity. Unforgettable also for all that was left behind, as in the Christmas Truce of that year. *Emden's* story speaks to how much war and the world suddenly changed in 1914. As a fading autumn of European triumphalism passed into a long winter of moral collapse and discontent, the world descended into savage murder on a scale so grand it shook religious faiths and any secular confidence in the foundation of modern civilization. Hamlet's outburst "What a piece of work is Man!"[7] thereafter held ironic resonance perhaps even Shakespeare did not intend. The passage from hope toward something closer to despair remains in the world today. No one is unaffected, even if unaware of pond circle consequences that lap our lives. At the least, we live without excuse for innocence about the cruelties of which humanity is capable and often also proud.

Emden's tale is from a twilight zone, a moment in that not-so-long-ago autumn when the old world still believed it could make war the old way, as if in a storybook or daydreams of small boys playing with model ships. War with decency, honor, mercy, wit. It started with cheers for bold deeds by an honorable enemy. It ended in the usual slaughter. The signs were there from the first days of the Great War on land, as armies collided with shocking violence that killed 1,000,000 before the year turned. Worse was to come: 1,200 miles of trenches,[8] artillery barrages, poison gas, machine guns, barbed wire, flamethrowers, food blockades, bombed cities, planned starvation, mass death. Nine million more deaths at least, with the best science on all sides devoted to improving methods of mass killing of the enemy. None of that was really new. But in 1914 the usual ingenuity and callousness of humanity at war had been forgotten after four decades of peace inside Europe, which kept its wars after 1870 far away, in places its peoples knew little and cared for not at all. Europeans lived out the last days of their Panglossian peace in cultural delusion that they were more moral and advanced than their ancestors, that history is progressive and tomorrow certainly will be better than yesterday. That is, of course, the worldview of children. As the rest of the century demonstrated.

Yet, far away in the China Sea for a brief moment the illusion held. It was personified by a naval officer who did his duty with a moral integrity unusual in any age. His name was Karl von Müller, undistinguished captain of SMS *Emden*, sent away from the main naval theater to do minor colonial duty for the *Kaiserliche Marine*. As of mid-1914 there was no hint of war. Officers of all the major navies in Asia dined together onboard or onshore, wary but civil. In mid-June the heavy cruiser flagship HMS *Minotaur* visited the German leasehold port of Qingdao and was entertained.[9] On June 20, Grand Admiral Maximilian Graf von Spee led his squadron on a cruise to the South Pacific, not knowing it would be for the last time. *Emden* stayed in port along with a few small auxiliaries, river gunboats, and skiffs. A week later, with a pistol, 19-year-old Gavrilo Princip changed world history in the sleepy Bosnian town of Sarajevo. At first, few anywhere altered their summer holiday plans. Müller was not so sure, as he read grim telegrams arriving from Berlin. On July 9 *Kaiserliche Marine* HQ advised that war was coming in Serbia and possibly elsewhere. On July 29 *Fregattenkapitän* Müller was ordered to find Spee. *Emden* readied to go to war. Every potential enemy warship of similar size and age was superior in guns, armor, speed, and steaming range. *Emden* was severely limited by reliance on coal. Even newer destroyers could overmatch this light cruiser.

As the last evening of peace and the daylight faded on July 31, *Emden* slipped away, its crew on double-duty or war watches. The next day, Müller learned by wireless that his country and his outdated little ship were at war, and with multiple enemies. Almost immediately, there was a close call: *Emden* passed through active wakes of an entire enemy squadron. The gentleman of war's first prize was taken on August 4 after his spotters made out smoke of a Russian armed merchant.[10] Misplacing irony over recent Russian history, it tried to run for safer Japanese waters. Müller fired blank warning shots, then 12 live rounds. High splashes encouraged the *Ryaezan* to stop. Müller politely removed its crew, then escorted his prize to Qingdao, where he hastily converted it to an auxiliary with guns taken off small river ships.[11] He recoaled and picked up the last of his crew from shore. Accompanied by a collier, he set out to "cry havoc" atop the waves. He believed his duty was to disrupt enemy shipping as long as *Emden* survived.

He just did not think that would be for long. All German warships in the Pacific were thousands of miles from home, in waters teeming with Allied patrols. They had no chance to return even to Qingdao. Yet, *Emden* would be uniquely alone after Müller steamed south to the Marianas to consult with Spee. The admiral and squadron headed to Chile, sending Müller back to the Indian Ocean to "wage cruiser war as best you can."[12]

Along the way, at his first officer's suggestion, Müller rigged a dummy fourth funnel out of canvas and wood so *Emden* appeared at a distance to be a four-stack cruiser. The ship was hastily repainted in standard gray, a job begun in Qingdao but completed haphazardly at sea. Müller had all ship's boats restenciled to say *Nagato Maru*, to sow confusion among *Emden*'s hunters if, or rather when, it was sunk. On September 9 lookouts spotted lights on the horizon. He fired two warning shots, then lamp-signaled in morse: "Stop your engines. Don't use wireless." It was a neutral, a Greek merchant carrying coal for the British. Müller offered the captain a German replacement contract and he happily agreed. The next day another steamer was stopped. *Indus* was on a Mumbai charter to pick up Indian cavalry and mounts for transport to France. Müller took any useful cargo, removed the crew, then opened the seacocks, sending *Indus* down to meet Davy Jones. One of *Emden*'s aft gunners was moved watching the *Indus* captain cry as his ship sank in a wild "howling intermingled with a crescendo of thundering noises."[13] Müller next sat silently outside Mumbai, a floating bit of Imperial Germany waiting for floating bits of the British Empire to come out, so he could sink them. The first ship stopped was loaded with cargo bound for neutral American ports. Müller was waging war according to cruiser rules. He determined these were neutral goods he could not touch. He transferred his prisoners, along with all his garbage, disabled the vessel's wireless, and let it depart.

And so it went, another day or week and more merchant ships stopped, their crews safely removed, the vessels sunk by flooding or gunfire or charges. Neutrals steamed off unhindered after cargo inspection. This was not the case in the highly contested Atlantic, where U-boats hunted indiscriminately and merchants broke the old rules by arming in defense or ramming. Müller kept two ships alongside, one as a collier, the other for prisoners. Twice, British crews among hundreds of men he let live and leave gave him three cheers as they hauled away on a neutral cargo ship, headed off to internment in a Dutch or other neutral port.[14] One rusty old bucket went down fast under *Emden's* gunfire to loud cheers from unpaid sailors, who really hated their ship and were happy to watch it sink. Then the game turned deadly, as it was bound to do.

Müller did not lust for blood. He was a capable rather than brilliant officer but always a reluctant killer. He was a good and decent man, doing his duty with as much grace and mercy as the circumstances of war permitted. He was always on the bridge, pacing back and forth, watching for tell-tale smoke over an azure horizon that might foretell another prize but eventually must signal *Emden's* doom. His worried crew rigged a wooden deck chair up top so that he could get some sleep. Müller paced, slept a little bit, and took all meals on deck. He was a deeply lonely man, burdened by command and knowing that luck must soon run out and that no skill of his could save *Emden* in the end.

But first, he decided to destroy the important Royal Navy oil storage facilities located at Madras. At night on September 22, *Emden* pulled into the outer harbor and turned on four searchlights, sweeping for the oil tanks. It fired 25 salvoes of 4.1-inch shells into the harbor, setting two of the six tanks on fire. *Emden* turned off its searchlights once docks were illuminated by the flames. For the first time since a Yangtze River patrol in 1911, before Müller was *Emden's* captain, its guns killed: a young naval cadet and four civilians died from errant hits. British opinion was stunned but impressed.[15] It had been 100 years since a British port was attacked by an enemy, let alone a daring and solitary small warship fighting thousands of miles from home. Winston Churchill, First Lord of the Admiralty in 1914, was determined to bring an end to *Emden*.

Müller returned to humane commerce-raiding, sinking or taking captive 13 more cargo ships after the raid on Madras, with no lives lost. He offloaded 600 prisoners to *St. Egbert*, sending them away to be interned, alive and well and cheering their enemy. He headed into another Allied port on October 28, raiding Penang off Malaya. There, he sank at anchor the outdated Russian Navy light cruiser *Zhemchug*. As Müller left the harbor,

Emden was fired upon by a French destroyer. He opened fire in the dark at what he thought was another French warship, which was actually a small, unarmed harbor patrol vessel. He stopped a passing British steamer outside the harbor to explain why he had not put his boats into the water to rescue crew from the *Zhemchug*: he had seen other boats headed in. He apologized for shooting at the harbor patrol boat by mistake.

Then the harsher realities of naval war *Emden* largely avoided until this moment split the dark with gun flashes and thunderous reports. An older French destroyer, *Mousquet,* headed into Penang as *Emden* pulled out sans its fake funnel, flying its double-eagle war flag now fully illuminated by Russian flames. *Mousquet* was outmatched but game. It ran the *tricolour* up its mast and fired a torpedo, before turning broadside to shoot its much smaller guns. Müller did not hesitate: "The third or fourth salvo struck the engine room. . . . After this, as the range closed, the *Emden* systematically demolished the destroyer, which showed no inclination to strike her colours."[16] It was a key, if technical, point of maritime law that would soon play a role in *Emden*'s terminal agony and destruction.

Müller steamed back to the shipping lanes to intercept empty troop transports returning from carrying Indian Army and ANZAC divisions to France. He thought they were unlikely to have warship escorts. Instead he would meet ANZAC Convoy #1 going the other way under escort by the battlecruiser HMAS *Australia*, the modern light cruiser HMAS *Sydney,* and the battlecruiser IJN *Ibuki*. They were just three ships out of 78 warships from four Allied navies that at some point hunted for *Emden*. A whole pack of hounds and drivers and skilled riders was closing in from several directions, on the scent of an especially clever fox. Also out on the hunt on this, *Emden*'s last day, were three Royal Navy cruisers and many more destroyers, an entire Japanese cruiser squadron, and various French and Russian warships seeking revenge.[17] Yet, the audacious Müller was not done tormenting the Allied navies and First Lord Churchill.

Müller steamed to Direction Island in the Cocos (Keeling) chain. The atoll serviced the only trans-Pacific oceanic cable linking Australia to India, thence the Middle East and Europe. *Emden* arrived on November 9, a coincidental yet portentous date in 20th-century German history: abdication of the kaiser in 1918, Hitler's failed Beer Hall Putsch in 1923, *Kristallnacht* in 1938, and the fall of the Berlin Wall in 1989 all took place on November 9. As *Emden* approached, its radio operator picked up a repeating broadcast from Direction Island's powerful wireless arial mast: "SOS Emden here . . . SOS Emden here." Müller did not know that ANZAC Convoy #1 was 52 nautical miles away, or that HMAS *Sydney* was racing to locate and sink him. He put a party of 50 men into two of his ship's boats with orders to go ashore and wreck the transmitter station and cut the vital sea cable.

Emden made a distraction beyond what Müller promised, Spee hoped, or Churchill feared. It had no chance of making it back to China, let alone to Germany. Its crew had a single future: continue raiding until found and forced to fight, when they would surely lose and most likely die. *Emden* was no longer white on its last day, as it appears still today in prewar photos and postcards, all boast and bunting. It was artlessly painted sea gray, streaked with rust, covered in black and greasy coal dust, its superstructure slick from thick smoke backflowing over its upper works and deck. On that deck were pigs, rabbits, ducks, geese and other live meat taken from captured merchants, casks of fish and beer, and crates of whiskey, sugar, and hard cheese, cigarettes and even toiletries. The landing party was ashore, politely wrecking the radio tower: the British asked the engineers to set their charges so that the falling tower would miss the tennis court. It was agreed.[18] They were still there, hacking into sea cables and smashing up wireless equipment, when *Emden*'s lookouts saw *Sydney*'s smoke. Then they counted four stacks, which meant it was an enemy cruiser. It was captained by George Glossop, a Royal Navy officer serving on the Australian ship to assist a new navy then in its infancy. Müller had no choice: he hauled anchor, abandoned the landing party, and ran. Too late.

Sydney had a two-knot speed advantage and longer-range guns, so Glossop turned away to increase distance, to keep *Emden* in his range but *Sydney* outside the reach of the light cruiser's smaller guns. Müller hence steamed all-out in pursuit, knowing he could neither outgun nor outrun this overmatching enemy warship maneuvering to destroy his own. Point-blank shooting and maybe a lucky hit or two was his only hope, then up close he could use *Emden*'s ship-killing torpedoes. He reported after the fight: "I had to attempt to inflict such damage on the enemy with [my] guns that he would be slowed down in speed significantly, before I could switch to a [more] promising torpedo attack."[19] When his rangefinders sited *Sydney* at 10,500 yards, Müller opened the match. It was 9:40 on a glorious, South Seas morning, light blue water and sky in all directions.

Müller's guns were quick and accurate, as Glossop later agreed. Its first salvoes bracketed *Sydney*, splashing on either side. Then *Emden* fired-for-effect. Three more salvoes of plunging fire smacked into the Australian cruiser, dropping armor-piercing high-explosive shells onto its upper superstructure and upper deck. *Emden*'s 4.1-inch shells weighed 38 pounds each and were no match for the enemy's armor protection. *Sydney* found the return range after 20 minutes of poor gunnery, then pounded back at *Emden* with salvoes from its eight 6-inch guns, firing 100-pound explosive shells that fell in high plunging arcs.[20] Chivalry was over. The war of gentlemen at sea was over. This was mortal combat.[21]

Over the next 95 minutes *Emden* fired over 1,500 shells in exchange for 670 coming the other way. It was not enough. Its hits barely penetrated *Sydney*, killed just four men and wounded eight. But a steel storm destroyed *Emden*'s radio, wrecked its steering gear, cut electric communication from the bridge to the guns and engine room, blasted men and animals and cargo overboard. The ship fell back on manual steering until it was reduced to handling with its engines alone. It never got within torpedo range. Its firing gear was all knocked out in any case. *Emden*'s funnels, masts, and most if its 10 gun mounts were smashed. One shell plunged into the aft magazine. Fire control came down to flooding to stop a raging blaze that threatened to explode the ship.

Dead and horribly burned and wounded men sprawled on *Emden*'s deck or were hurled or jumped overboard. Deep inside, desperate men struggled to breathe in blinding, choking smoke from burning coal and bitter cordite from the guns. Ventilation fans were smashed so that the air filled with barbeque smells of scorching animal and human flesh. One of the boilers ruptured. Scalded, hairless, faceless men ran screaming or fell, flesh steamed right off the bone. Such wounded were beyond help or hope, except perhaps the final hope of relief from their agony in a release by death. Still the shells whistled down, buckling and slicking *Emden*'s decks with oil, water, and blood.[22]

Listing hard, at 11:15 *Emden* ceased fire. Müller had guns still working but with a landing party still ashore and so many dead and wounded, no replacements for decimated fire parties or gun crews and no real hope to change the outcome. He later reported: "As I no longer had the capacity to damage the enemy, I then decided to put the ship, thoroughly shot to pieces and burning in many places, on the luff side of North Keeling Island in the breakers on the reef, to reduce it completely to a wreck in order not to make a useless sacrifice of the survivors."[23] He piloted his crippled ship at max speed to run aground on the coral ringing North Keeling Island, ramming it hard. It stopped, leaving the stern hanging clear. The gambit of making it obvious that *Emden* was no longer a threat to the enemy failed. *Sydney* did not stop shooting salvoes at a target that stopped shooting back. It sent dozens more 100-pound high-explosive shells whistling and thudding into silent *Emden*, a broken and hapless ship. Men dove into aquamarine that frothed over the reef, to swim ashore. They drowned or were cut apart by a jagged coral cliff as surf dragged them across the reef top. No more than 20 made it to the island. Meanwhile, Müller burned all his captain's logs and code books. Amidst screams and incoming high-explosive ordnance, no one thought to strike *Emden*'s war flag. Seeing no white flag raised on his enemy's mast, Glossop fired two more point-blank salvoes into the motionless and burning wreck. Then *Sydney* left to hunt down Müller's companion collier, the *Buresk*. Once spotted, it scuttled. Its crew moved to *Sydney* in lifeboats that were taken under tow.

Müller assembled his wounded in a cleared deck area in the forecastle, where two ship's doctors tended to them. Later, one doctor dove into the water to swim over the coral to aid wounded men on the island. But he hit his head on the reef and died. At 4:00 p.m. *Sydney* hove back into view. *Emden* was still flying its war flag so Glossop signaled a surrender demand in morse. He got no answer: *Emden*'s signal gear was ruined. Glossop took its silence to mean that "the captain would never surrender, and therefore, though very reluctantly, I again fired at her." He stopped only because a brave and desperate sailor scrambled up under heavy fire to haul down the war flag and raise a white flag in its place. HMAS *Sydney*, an Australian ship with seasoned British officers in charge, did not send aid to burned, wounded men sprawled on *Emden*'s deck, as Müller surely would have done. Glossop steamed away to see why the tower on Direction Island had stopped broadcasting. *Sydney* did not return for hours. Only then did ship's boats arrive to render medical aid and collect prisoners, many fairly demented by the day.[24] Müller was the last one off the wreck, in the long tradition of sea captains. Out of *Emden*'s 318 officers and crew 136 died during its only battle, or later succumbed to wounds or burns Sixty-five were wounded to varying degrees of severity. Some bodies could not be recovered. They were left on the wreck or onshore until the sloop HMS *Cadmus* was sent to Cocos to dispose of *Emden*'s dead. The search also recovered a confidential chest and safe and learned that the last quartet of *Emden*'s guns had been disabled: breech blocks and recoil pistons were removed and thrown overboard by the Germans after the ship hung up on the reef.[25]

Müller's landing party had long since absconded with *Ayesha*, a 97-ton British schooner. For two improbable months, it evaded searching Allied warships as it sailed around the southern tip of India. When it reached Yemen, the crew got out and walked across Arabia, avoiding British forces and Bedouin tribesmen to reach Istanbul in early 1915. An instant bestseller added to the *Emden* legend, in Germany and Britain alike. In the interim, surviving crew were moved to a POW camp on Malta. In October 1916, Müller alone was moved to a damp, gray camp in northern England, likely because the war had changed the world. Millions were dead. Millions more were amputees or traumatized or blind or burned faceless. Men died while on fire falling from the sky; died on the water in flaming oil slicks; suffocated in caved-in dugouts; holed by machine guns; sliced into by bayonet; and torn to pieces as "cannon meat" by the butchering artillery. It was all obscenity now. Müller's more decent and merciful war was over.

But not his story. In 1917 he led a tunnel escape by 21 officers. He was recaptured and thrown into solitary confinement. English damp aggravated his malaria. He seemed terminally ill and so was added to a prisoner exchange, handed over as a compassion case for palliative care by the neutral Dutch. Lying in hospital in the Netherlands he heard from a nurse that the kaiser had awarded him Imperial Germany's highest honor, the "Blue Max" (*Pour le Mérite*). In October 1918, he was entrained for Germany, sent home to die.

The next month the war ended. In the early 1920s he opposed the rising Nazis and won state election in Brunswick. But he died from lingering malaria in 1923: he was sickly to his last days and never recovered emotionally. His grief was laced with "survivor guilt" that is not uncommon among caring officers. His ship stayed stuck on the coral, surviving several salvage attempts before falling under protection of the Australian Historic Shipwrecks Act of 1976. What was left had by then slipped into the sea, where its steel bones lie today in meters of warm, blue water. *Sydney*'s mast and prow and one of *Emden*'s guns survive in Sydney Harbor, memorials to the Royal Australian Navy's first victory at sea. Also, to a moral paragon in the long history of war at sea.

Is that all it means? *Emden*'s story was not the great hinge that turned a critical naval battle or long campaign. It certainly did not decide the Great War at sea. That came down to food blockades by U-boats and Allied warships and convoys in the cold Atlantic. The war voyage of *Emden* did not decide much of anything past ending men's lives or ruining them. Nevertheless, it teases us with hints of what might have been because it reminds of what was left behind, perhaps forever. It also warns us that we, too, should wonder if we dwell in a twilight zone, a moral no-man's-land between ghosts of dead ideals from decades past and specters of the next great war's horrors yet to come. It was a lesser world when men like Müller were displaced, as they were, by the rising tides and logic of total industrial war. Far away from warm breezes in the South Pacific men were killing and dying already in 1914 not by hundreds, not by thousands, not even by tens or hundreds of thousands but in their millions. A brave new world lay just ahead of multimillion-man armies, waiver of the old laws of war at sea, a new kind of war in the air, rapid-fire artillery, poison gases, mass starvation, city bombing, industrial attrition, and multiple genocides. Müller's world of law, of almost quaint morality and good manners to be upheld even while at war, could not and did not survive. A terrible darkness instead descended like a shroud over the conduct of war. In Müller's homeland, the coming night would be blackest of all.

IT IS HARD TO SHOW MERCY to crew on a steel warship. The dilemma was made worse during the world wars because there was an unwritten rule in major navies forbidding captains surrendering their ships. That led to frequent ship-to-ship fights to the death as captain after captain refused to strike his ship's colors, while the other captain did not stop shooting at a floundering enemy until it surrendered. Individual navies had specific military cultures that emphasized fighting by the rules, or alternatively, encouraged captains to ignore the rules as they sought every possible advantage while in combat. Nevertheless, some ship's captains managed to locate mercy for a battered ship and crew, if only after they went into the water. As with Müller and Glossop, it seems to have come down to the good or indifferent character of captains in specific ship-to-ship actions.

Off the Chilean port of Coronel on November 1, 1914, the Royal Navy cruiser *Monmouth* was heavily damaged by fire from the German armored cruiser *Gneisenau,* steaming under *Kapitän zur See* Julius Maerker. As *Monmouth* retreated, its onboard fires illuminating it against the night, the German light cruiser *Nürnberg* also took it under fire. After many hits, *Monmouth* stopped return fire. *Nürnberg* turned a searchlight on *Monmouth*'s war ensign: a request to raise a white flag and give up the ship. There was no response. Then it turned. Perhaps *Monmouth* was planning to ram *Nürnberg* in desperation, with near hopeless courage. Maybe it was repositioning to bring its undamaged starboard guns to bear. Either way, *Nürnberg* resumed shooting until *Monmouth* sank with the loss of all 900 of its crew.[26] *Nürnberg*'s captain may have fired the last salvoes because he feared a *ruse de guerre* or misread the situation. He acted mercilessly, yet within agreed if narrow rules. Müller did the same, battering a French destroyer to bits at Penang because it kept fighting. Glossop did it with *Emden* hung on a coral reef, until it struck its war ensign and ran up a white flag. Ruthless actions at sea, every one. Yet, none of these acts was a war crime.

A month later, on December 8 off the Falklands, long odds caught up with *Emden*'s old squadron. Two British dreadnought battlecruisers sank four ships of the German East Asia Squadron which refused several demands to surrender.[27] One of the German cruisers that went down was *Gneisenau*. Captain Maerker had wanted to retire from the *Kaiserliche Marine* before the war, to raise bees. After the squadron left *Emden* in the Marianas, he kept a journal into which he vented his view that the war was senseless. Yet, he continued to serve and he, too, refused to surrender, then scuttled. Only 187 of his crew of 800 survived in near freezing water. He did not. One historian wrote of that decision: "The ship was led by a humane commander, not a bloodthirsty diehard. Yet, even this man did not surrender and his own life, and those of nearly 80% of his crew, were forfeit."[28] It was heroic self-sacrifice or bullheaded vanity. A different captain made a different decision at the River Platte in 1939, where Wilhelm Langsdorff scuttled the *Graf Spee*, named after Müller's commanding admiral, rather than battle it out with blockading British warships. Before he went back into port to kill himself after defying Hitler's direct order to engage, he said: "I will not allow us to get shot to pieces by superior forces. I prefer a thousand living young men to a thousand dead heroes."[29] Often, the merciful are revealed in victory. Sometimes, in defeat.

Other *Kriegsmarine* surface ships were captained by men who tried to fight the old way even in Hitler's war, while U-boats sank liners on sight and without warning starting on the first day.[30] One example happened in April 1940. The heavy cruiser *Admiral Hipper* and five escorting destroyers were carrying 1,700 mountain troops north when they met the Royal Navy destroyer *Glowworm*. They were on the way to a narrow neck of water at Trondheim, part of a much larger air, land, and sea surprise attack that struck six sites down the coast from Narvik to Oslo and also Jutland in Denmark. German warships ran into resistance from sleeping coastal batteries that never fired a shot until they were past but also fierce defense by older and outmatched Norwegian warships. As German ships suddenly appeared in the north, far outside the Baltic, Allied forces arrived almost at the same time. They were on a mission to lay sea mines and land troops to keep Norway out of German hands, denying transit of Swedish iron ore down the coast. That led to the first battle between capital warships since Jutland in 1916. Before that, the Admiralty received a report from *Glowworm* that it did not fully understand until after the war.

The 1,350-ton destroyer had detached from a four-ship screen of the battlecruiser *Renown* to search for a sailor who fell overboard during the night.

The report said it was engaging a superior enemy who should not have been there. Then all contact ended. Reports were also coming in about German capital ships exiting the Baltic Sea. Later, news arrived about multiple surprise air, land, and sea attacks in Denmark and Norway. The earlier signals about capital ship movements should have tipped off British intelligence. In the interim, *Glowworm* went silent without any explanation.[31] It was learned later that *Glowworm* chased two German destroyers, which disengaged because they were carrying mountain troops for the Trondheim invasion. They drew *Glowworm* onto the big guns of the *Admiral Hipper*, which displaced 14,000 tons with a battery of eight 8-inch guns. The mismatched pair fought a confused and close-quarters battle in ghastly visibility and swells. *Glowworm* was subsequently credited with ramming *Hipper* and supposedly crippling the much larger and more powerful ship. In fact, *Hipper* was damaged but not enough to stop its continuing to Trondheim. Badly crippled by heavy cruiser shells, *Glowworm* made smoke to escape but could not evade radar-guided guns piercing the fog.

Glowworm's captain, Lieutenant Commander Gerard Roope, tried to torpedo *Hipper* at intimate range but missed. He ordered ramming but struck only a glancing blow, possibly accidentally when his rudder jammed. The sideswipe knocked a German sailor overboard but otherwise caused nothing fatal. Except that *Glowworm*'s bow broke and its boilers had to be emergency-bled to prevent blowing the ship apart. Dozens of men went into the frigid water as Roope ordered his crew to abandon ship.[32] Watching all this was German Admiral Helmuth Heye. He positioned *Hipper* so that the strong current brought drifting survivors to him, then put his boats out to recover them from the ice cold and choppy Norwegian Sea. Roope helped his crewmen don life jackets and grab onto ropes Germans dropped down to them. When his turn came he was too weak to hold on and slipped under, lost at sea. Six rescued men were so badly burned they died later onboard *Admiral Hipper* but Heye's humanity saved 31. As exhausted men splayed on the deck of *Hipper*, "Germans congratulated the survivors on a good fight." Heye told them that their captain was "a very brave man." Later, he sent a message to the Admiralty via the International Red Cross suggesting that Roope deserved an award for highest valor.[33] The full tale of what happened to *Glowworm* remained unknown to the Admiralty until survivors returned from German POW camps in 1945. Roope was almost immediately awarded a posthumous Victoria Cross. Captain Heye later helped integrate West German naval forces into NATO.

CHAPTER 12

STEALTH

All attempts to rescue the crews of sunken ships will cease forthwith. This prohibition applies equally to the picking up of men in the water and putting them aboard a lifeboat, to the righting of capsized lifeboats and to the supply of food and water.[1]

—Admiral Karl Dönitz, *Laconia* Order, September 17, 1942

In 1914 Royal Navy Admiral William Henderson smugly predicted: "Even if a submarine should work by a miracle, it will never be used. No country in this world would ever use such a vicious and petty form of warfare!" The first article in the May 1915 issue of *Scientific American*, published just two weeks after the sinking of the passenger liner *Lusitania*, was an oddly mistimed paean to "superdreadnoughts" of the Royal Italian Navy. It predicted that country's superb engineers would lead creation of the "still greater battleship of the future."[2] It assumed universal agreement that all gentlemen made war on the surface of the sea, not from beneath it. Yet, over the next three years war stories in *Scientific American* about submarine sinkings, chases, and technology proved among the most popular.[3] As for poison gas, first used by the Germans at Ypres earlier that year, *Scientific American* concluded that such an abomination was akin to a duelist throwing vitriol in an opponent's face prior to cutting him apart with a rapier. "Bad form," as might be said in eating clubs of Princeton or Oxbridge or prewar dueling fraternities at Heidelberg. This naïve scientific optimism was soon mugged by the war's reality, leading the best scientists the world over to go to work on making new weapons for the belligerents.

FROM THE START IN 1914, SOME U-boat captains lusted for kills. They sank passenger liners and even illuminated hospital ships, and machine-gunned survivors and lifeboats in the water. In World War II, some captains from *Kaigun*, the *Kriegsmarine*, and Allied navies also committed this crime. War from under the sea seemed utterly merciless, cruel, and immoral as submarine war evolved. But there were exceptions. Not all Axis captains were without pity. Nor did Allied nations despise or fear U-boats when they first met the little boats off their coasts or at sea, not as they would come to do once the subs exploited weaknesses in surface fleets and merchant marines. As the 20th-century descended from limited war into total war, old rules and old ways were discarded by navies as moral anachronisms. The two world wars were redefined at sea and under the sea as all-out campaigns of truly merciless attrition and mutual blockades aiming for mass starvation. Yet, individual captains and crews persevered in upholding compassion. They fought with honor and exhibited courage in their allowance for mercy. They proved that, as vulnerable as the "iron coffins" were, one did not have to surrender decency to steel and stealth realities.

On September 22, 1914, *Kaiserliche Marine* submarine *U-9* stunned Allied navies when it sank three British armored light cruisers in just 90 minutes: HMS *Aboukir*, HMS *Hogue*, and HMS *Cressy*. Later that year, Austrian submarine *U-XII* shocked again as it hit the French flagship *Jean Bart* with a torpedo in the Strait of Ortranto, though without sinking the battleship. In 1915 *U-XII* hit a sea mine as it tried to sneak into Venice, killing all 17 crew. Italians salvaged the wreck, interring the bodies with all military honors.[4] Germany's U-boats pulled back from all "unrestricted submarine warfare" following the *Lusitania* crisis of 1915, abating conflict with the United States. But in January 1917, Berlin was desperate for another throw of the steel dice of war. It sent the U-boats back out with unrestricted target orders. This practice was also called "sink-on-sight." As such, it was adopted by the Royal Navy in World War II and also carried out ruthlessly by the U.S. Navy (USN) against Japanese shipping in the Pacific.

However, in Allied and American propaganda in 1917 outrage over the U-boats was all around, wrapped in hypocrisy and self-interest. After the war there was a carryover effort to punish U-boat crimes in court. It was downplayed that escorts had mercilessly hunted U-boats that could not readily surrender or were rammed early on by illegally armed merchants, as some captains tried to fight by cruiser rules. In 1936, a Naval Protocol was agreed by Nazi Germany and other naval powers which reaffirmed the rules of submarine warfare that had been laid down in the London Naval Agreement of 1930. Inside three years, it all came apart. During World War II, none of the major naval powers held back their submarine fleets from aggressive sink-on-sight tactics. Nor did they punish their own submarine captains for merciless and unlawful killing on the high seas. All the gloves were off. It was total war at sea.

On September 3, 1939, first day of another naval war between Allied navies and Germany, *U-30* torpedoed the passenger liner SS *Athenia,* bound for the United States with 1,418 onboard. It was a sign of things to come as all the navies quickly moved to "sink-on-sight." Targeting was unrestricted in the attrition or tonnage war waged in the Atlantic and later in starvation operations in the Pacific. As with other branches of military endeavor in an immense world war, submariners exhibited a range of ethical behaviors from murderous excess to deeply humane, honorable, professional conduct. One incident off the coast of West Africa encapsulated it all. In September 1942, *Korvettenkapitän* Werner Hartenstein took *U-156* to sea, heading for the Caribbean to hunt oil tankers. Six hundred miles off Liberia he torpedoed what he thought was a converted freighter. It was the 20,000-ton Cunard White Star Line RMS *Laconia,* armed and requisitioned as a troop ship. It carried 2,732 crew, women and children refugees, and Italian prisoners. It listed so badly as it sank half its lifeboats were put out of reach. Italians stayed locked in the cargo hold. Some who tried to break out were bayonetted by Polish guards. Later, others had their arms cut off with axes as they frantically tried to clamber into overloaded lifeboats.[5]

U-156 crowded 200 survivors onto its narrow deck, towing another 200 in four *Laconia* lifeboats.[6] Hartenstein signaled to Admiral Karl Dönitz, commander of all U-boats, and later of the whole German navy (as *Oberbefehlshaber der Marine*). Dönitz was a veteran of the U-boat war of 1914–1918, a former prisoner of war who would lose two sons in the "gray wolves" in the new war. Already by 1942 he was a thoroughly Nazified admiral: he would be the second and last *Führer* of Nazi Germany in May 1945, after Hitler killed himself. Hartenstein urgently asked Dönitz to arrange what he termed a "diplomatic neutralization of the scene of the sinking." He requested, in other words, that Dönitz negotiate an unprecedented cease-fire covering a tightly precise area of sea. He intended to travel on the surface even in daylight, with red cross markings to protect from Allied air or sea attack. He hoped available ships from Allied nations would steam all-out to rescue survivors.[7] He brought injured women and children inside *U-156* for medical treatment. Then he stayed on the surface for two days, with 200 survivors in lifeboats under slow tow and others able to barely stand on or cling to his deck. Three other U-boats came to help, taking survivors onto their narrow decks as well. Hartenstein openly broadcast the exact location of his fragile little convoy. He asked the British in Freetown and Vichy French in Dakar for help.

For two days an American B-24 Liberator made bombing and strafing runs at the exposed U-boats, either not seeing or not caring about vivid red cross flags draped across their decks. Maybe the aircrew did not see overfull boats towed behind *U-156* as they made strafing and bombing runs at low altitude? Many who survived the *Laconia* sinking drowned when *U-156* and the other U-boats were finally forced to dive. Dönitz lost all patience. On September 17, he issued to the whole U-boat fleet a "Triton Null Order." It became widely known as the *Laconia* Order after citation in his war crimes trial at Nuremberg.[8] It read: "All attempts to rescue the crews of sunken ships will cease forthwith. This prohibition applies equally to the picking up of men in the water and putting them aboard a lifeboat, to the righting of capsized lifeboats and to the supply of food and water." He instructed all U-boat captains that any rescue efforts "are a contradiction of the primary object of war, namely, the destruction of enemy ships and their crews." Dönitz closed: "Be harsh, having in mind that the enemy takes no regard of women and children in his attacks on German cities."[9] On the last point at least, he would be more right than wrong by mid-1943.

Geoffrey Greet was on RMS *Laconia*. He pulled drowning women and children, frantic Italian prisoners, and Polish guards into its too few and overloaded lifeboats. He watched hundreds of others float away, including "a young blonde girl with her hair floating around her on the sea and next to her was a woman with her hat on. Both were dead. It was macabre." At age 91 in 2011 he recalled: "No U-boat captain who would sit on the surface all that time and risk his own life is a bad man. . . . I didn't think much of him at first—after all, he had killed 2,000 of my fellow passengers. But by the end, I admired him."[10] Six months later *U-156* was sunk with loss of all officers and crew. During Dönitz's trial at Nuremberg it became obvious from testimony of Allied naval officers that they also had issued or followed policies as articulated in the *Laconia* Order. It had to be recognized at the trial that all sink-on-sight had violated surface rules written for cruisers in the 19th century, which could not be safely observed by submarines. They were too small to take on any survivors or give out precious provisions. Too vulnerable to ramming on the surface, if pausing to give warning before firing a deck gun or loosing a torpedo. Technology had changed the rules of the game for everyone. Except that on occasion, some captains showed there was a still a place for mercy in submarine warfare.

One submariner stood out in the *Regia Marina* (Royal Italian Navy). Captain Salvatore Bruno Todaro was a highly decorated submarine ace, so dedicated to fighting the right way it greatly annoyed Dönitz in particular. In June 1940, Todaro took charge as the new skipper of *Cappellini*, a Marcello-class submarine designed for Atlantic operations. He patrolled out of a new Italian naval base established at Bordeaux after the fall of France that June. On the night of October 16–17, he sank a Belgian steamer, the *Kobalo*. After it went down he circled, looking for anyone in the water. Over four days and nights he towed the 26 survivors he found on a raft behind *Cappellini*. Then the rope broke. At that point he had done his duty. He reasonably could have abandoned the detached raft, let it drift off, leaving 26 men to die. Maybe he could communicate their position and provide minimal supplies? Would anyone come to help in response to a message from an Axis submarine, or would they conclude that *Cappellini* was tracking the raft to use it as bait for a torpedo trap? Todaro saw that the raft was precarious and would not likely survive. He crowded everyone inside *Cappellini* and diverted, to deliver them to safe harbor in the Azores.

Then he did it again. On January 5, 1941, his lawful attack set the British armed merchant *Shakespeare* on fire. It raised a white flag, then quickly sank. Todaro searched for survivors and saved 22, taking a lifeboat under tow as he had six months earlier towed a raft. Again, he hit rough seas that must overturn the fragile craft he was towing. Once more, he took survivors inside his crowded submarine, delivering them safely to the Cape Verde Islands. Nine days later Todaro and *Cappellini* engaged the armed troopship *Eumaeus*. It fought hard, hitting his boat with multiple shells, killing one Italian sailor and wounding nine. He did not hesitate to put a torpedo into the ship as it called frantically for assistance. Knowing enemy warships were on the way he did not try to save *Eumaeus* survivors. Just as he anticipated, *Cappellini* was attacked by British aircraft en route to the Canary Islands. He was allowed a week to repair, then slipped away. Dönitz characteristically mocked Todaro as "Don Quixote of the sea," dressing him down for taking enemy crews into his boat and then diverting from a war patrol to deliver them to safe harbor. Todaro cuttingly rejoined: "A German commander doesn't have 2,000 years of civilization on his shoulders, as we do."[11] He transferred to La Galite naval base in Tunisia, where he was demoted to captain an armed fishing boat. Age 34, he was killed in December 1942, when his little coastal raider was strafed by an RAF Spitfire.[12]

Todaro left a lasting mark on his country's memory of naval war and on its postwar and modern maritime services. In 1955 the film *La grande Speranza* depicted a multinational Christmas inside the *Cappellini*, in which Todaro hosts rescued survivors of a ship he just sank. It helped reconcile Italy inside NATO and Europe. A series of Italian 212A *Todaro*-class submarines was launched in 2003, starting with the name boat *Salvatore Todaro*. His daughter was present at the commissioning. The ship's motto pays tribute to Todaro and the ideal of valorous honor: *Osare l'inosabile* ("Dare the Impossible").[13] In 2008 the *Todaro* became the first Italian submarine to visit the United States since World War II.[14] In 2018 the Italian Coast Guard explicitly cited Todaro's humane example. General Commander Giovanni Pettorino told hundreds of officers, who were then dealing with refugees fleeing war in North Africa, that they had a moral obligation to rescue people at sea. It did not matter that some in their government and public wanted no help to be given to floundering migrants. He paraphrased Todaro's famous retort to the heartless Dönitz and to all those who would operate on the seas without mercy: "We are sailors. Italian sailors with 2,000 years of civilization behind us. And that is what we do."[15]

Wilhelm Gustloff was a liner first converted to a troopship in order to transport the Condor Legion to fight for the Nationalist side in Spain in 1936. It served next as a holiday cruise ship for Nazi Party functionaries, a hospital ship, a floating barracks for U-boat trainees, then as an armed troop carrier for the Wehrmacht. In January 1945, several Western Allied and Soviet army groups, each 1,000,000 or more men in size, were pushing into Nazi Germany from east, west, and south. Cities were shaded by flickering shadows of "thousand-bomber raids" and left in smoking ruin as air fleets beyond prewar Nazi conception, let alone ability to build, flew unimpeded overhead. *Gustloff* joined a desperate effort to evacuate cut-off pockets along the Baltic coast and Courland, as unchecked submarine warfare came full circle from sinkings of *Lusitania* and *Athenia* by U-boats.[16] *Gustloff* now carried refugees, some 10,000 Germans fleeing westward by sea. About 1,000 were soldiers transshipping to Kiel. Others were Nazi Party members. The rest were civilians, including mothers with children. Some were one-time *Volksdeutsche* colonists running from homes or farms they stole in the failed *Lebensraum* annexations of 1939–1942. More normal refugees came from East Prussia or Pomerania, historic German lands falling under Red Army occupation. Those provinces were about to vanish into remade Poland after the war, part of the price of losing. It did not matter who: most of those who boarded *Gustloff* to escape from the East were going to die.

On January 30, 1945, overcrowded passengers were huddling from severe cold, only a few listening to Hitler's latest frenetic end-times broadcast. *Gustloff* steamed without escort then turned on its lights to avoid a collision with small minesweepers.[17] Around 9:00 p.m. it was hit by three torpedoes loosed by the Soviet submarine *S-13*. Only 1,252 out of 10,000 onboard could be rescued from icy waters that hovered close to minus 18° Celsius. It was the largest loss of life in the history of the seas, in wartime or in peace. It far exceeded lost lives on *Titanic, Lusitania,* or *Athenia*. The incident patterned U-boat precedents that torpedoed passenger liners in two world wars and the logistics devolution that converted all prewar liners into troopships. Converted liners thus were legitimate targets for sinking, meaning there was no war crime in *S-13* killing a ship repainted in the enemy's military gray. However, military history can be as much an argument about the present as a reconstruction of the past, or a recasting of the past in more favorable nationalist light. In 2008 the television network Zweites Deutsches Fernsehen (ZDF) broadcast *Die Gustloff*, two years after an openly revisionist TV film *Dresden*. Both depicted all Germans as innocent, even as the preeminent victims of Nazified officials and Allied barbarism.[18]

SURFACE SHIPS AND SUBMARINES OF ALL the belligerents brought both mercy and merciless war to the Pacific theater as well. On November 26, 1941, a damaged lifeboat carrying 62 seamen was spotted off Western Australia by an aircraft out looking for the missing cruiser HMAS *Sydney II*, successor ship to its Great War namesake. Hospital ship AHS *Centaur* was sent to lend all aid. It lowered food and medicine and was told at first by the rescued that they were Norwegians. They were actually crew from the German auxiliary cruiser *Kormoran*, a converted freighter sunk by *Sydney* a week earlier in a close engagement that saw both ships go down.[19] *Centaur* shifted nine onboard and took the wobbly lifeboat under tow but rough seas swamped it. *Centaur* distributed survivors into two of its own lifeboats and took them under tow. At the port of Carnarvon, they were joined by 100 *Kormoran* survivors collected by other ships. Australian Army guards also came aboard *Centaur*, an otherwise unarmed hospital ship.[20] It was a classically merciful episode in an increasingly hard war on and under all the oceans.

On May 14, 1943, *Centaur* was steaming off Moreton Island, Queensland, making a mercy run from Sydney to Port Moresby in New Guinea. It had red cross markings and was fully illuminated: clearly a hospital ship. It was torpedoed and went down fast, bow first. Two lifeboats floated away after breaking off. All the rest were lost. Dozens of survivors clung to the lifeboats and to barrels for 36 hours. They saw four ships passing and several aircraft but were not spotted in turn. Of 332 onboard *Centaur*, 64 were rescued when seen at last by an RAAF sub spotter, an Avro Anson. They were rescued by the destroyer USS *Mugford*.[21] It was not known who decided to torpedo a hospital ship but it had to be a boat sent out on war patrol by *Kaigun*. A formal protest was launched by the Western Allies with the government of Imperial Japan and with the International Committee of the Red Cross. Meanwhile, Australian hospital ships were told to run blacked-out and were hastily armed.

The government in Tokyo denied responsibility that December. Denial was repeated for decades after the war, although suspicion fell on three IJN submarines known to be in the area at the time. One was *I-177*, skippered by Captain Hajime Nakagawa. While in command of *I-37* the following year, he ordered survivors from three British merchants machine-gunned in the water. On trial at the War Crimes Tribunal[22] in Tokyo after the war, he presented the usual defense of following "superior orders," claiming this absolved him of guilt. That defense was done, and good riddance: he was convicted and sentenced to four years as a Class B war criminal. The controversy over who sank *Centaur* continued among historians until 1978. In a backhanded nod to rearward moral accountability, Rear Admiral Kaneyoshi Sakamoto effectively admitted that it was *I-177* and Nakagawa who sank *Centaur*. He gave no reason why.[23]

AN UNDERSIZED TANKER FLEET WAS MADE even more vulnerable by *Kaigun* refusal to use destroyers as convoy escorts. The admirals wanted destroyers kept with the main battle fleet for "the decisive battle" with the U.S. Navy they always counted on. They clung to the old doctrine long past realistic hope that they could fight such a battle or that it would change the inexorable outcome of a war of attrition they had never prepared to wage. Tankers steaming alone were prime targets for submarines and naval air attack. Losses were irreplaceable.[24] In 1945 what was left of the battle fleet was restricted to waters close to sources of fuel and under short air cover.

Desperate methods bespoke lack of logistics capability and strategic planning, such as carrying drum oil on battleships and using potato gasoline that competed with the dwindling home island food supply.[25] Japan built the third largest merchant marine before the war but lacked shipbuilding capacity to replace losses to prowling USN submarines, naval and land-based air patrols from the Philippines, and minefields laid in sea lanes around Japan by submarines and aircraft. Americans honestly called laying sea mines Operation *Starvation*. It was one element in a five-part USN program to eliminate all shipping around the home islands, to break with a food blockade Japan's will to continue fighting and, with supply interdiction, also its ability to do so. It was ruthless and effective. Well before the B-29s flew bombing missions out of the Marianas, submarines kneecapped Japan's war industry by interdicting key supplies, putting the U-boat record in the Atlantic to shame.[26]

The USN *Gato*-class submarine *Wahoo* made seven war patrols from October 1942 to October 1943. It achieved an unparalleled sinking record while also pioneering attack approach methods. All that made its buccaneer captain, Dudley Morton, a war hero ace. He was also a war criminal by any standard.[27] He thought nothing of slaughtering Japanese merchant mariners in the water or crews of even small fishing boats. On his fourth patrol to waters then still virgin to American submarines, the East China and Yellow seas, Morton took a crate of molotov cocktails with him to burn up sampans and other small civilian vessels.[28] Between March 19 and 25, 1943, *Wahoo* sank five small cargo ships in the Yellow Sea using new and more effective torpex torpedoes. Survivors had little time to live in such frigid waters but Morton was determined that not one would. He said it was to prevent reports of his presence.

On March 21, after sinking the freighter *Nitu Maru*, he surfaced and ordered the deck gun manned. He conned *Wahoo* to collide with a lifeboat, knocking it apart and throwing merchant mariners into lethally cold water. His 20mm deck gun shot them to pieces before they could freeze or drown. His crew was right there with their captain's refusal of mercy. They showed it on March 25 when *Wahoo* surfaced to use its gun to destroy another stalled freighter. As survivors flailed and drowned, freezing fingers unable to cling to broken wreckage, the last sound they heard was *Wahoo*'s crew taunting them from yards away in mock Japanese. Two days later, Morton rampaged down "Sampan Alley" taking out fishing boats and minor patrol craft with his deck gun: he was out of torpedoes. He sent divers across to search for documents, then had the wrecks burned with his uncrated molotov cocktails.[29] *Wahoo*'s turn came when it was depth charged by a Japanese floatplane on October 11, 1943.

In 1945 USN submarines started coming back from some war patrols with all or most torpedoes unfired. They reported that few or no worthy targets were left in Japanese home waters. They were told to go back, to destroy fishing sampans and trawlers if that was all they could find. Most fishing vessels were manned by Chinese or Korean crew. Even when Japanese crewed, they were hardly military targets. Some captains objected to such an inhumane order. Others gladly used deck guns mercilessly, as Morton had.[30] The naval war in the Pacific only seems more brutal than the war in the Atlantic or Caribbean, where ship-to-ship actions were also to the death and U-boats and convoy escorts showed little mercy after the first year or two. The Pacific saw more frequent and much larger surface battles than the Atlantic, where U-boats and convoys displaced the threat from commerce raiders and enemy fleets. Most fleet actions in the Pacific were decided by naval air power, as for the first time in the history of naval warfare opposing battle fleets never saw each other. At other times, packets of surface ships fought at close range and old ideals and each navy's honor boasts were sharply tested.

In a running fight off Samar in the Philippine Sea on October 25, 1944, three years into the Pacific war, U.S. destroyers and destroyer escorts designated "Taffy 3" fought a frantic rearguard action. Taffy-3 deliberately steered into the path of an onrushing *Kaigun* battlegroup in high-speed pursuit of six American "baby flattop" or escort carriers. They forced the superbattleship *Yamato* to turn from the path of a close torpedo spread but could not stop it. Then *Yamato*'s powerful escorts decimated Taffy-3, holing USN *Hoel* with heavy shells until it fishtailed, its forward turret firing as the stern plunged under water. Survivors clung to a floater net in the darkness, pulling in wounded, bobbing in spreading wakes of the passing enemy squadron. Japanese sailors lined ship railings in silence to watch the scene below, as four *Kaigun* battleships and eight cruisers passed so close that the men in the water and on the ships made eye contact. Admiral Matome Ukagi looked down from the bridge of *Yamato,* the greatest battleship ever built, elder sister ship to IJN *Musashi.* He gave no thought at all to mercy. He did not even consider detaching one of his smaller escorts or ships' boats to effect rescue. He thought only about the vanity of nations: "What do they think of the magnificent sight of our fleet?"[31] On April 7, 1945, *Yamato* was sunk by U.S. naval air power while on a Surface Special Attack Force (suicide) mission to Okinawa. It went down with the loss of 3,055 of its 3,332 officers and crew.[32]

Shallow nationalist and imperial pride led to increasingly futile death and cruelty in a war overmatched Japan was always going to lose, until it was unclear if there was any island of decency left in the Pacific. Desperate rearguard defense by American escorts overmatched by Japanese cruisers put more ships under water at Leyte Gulf, more men into roiling waters. Survivors from USN *Johnson* clung to ships' boats and makeshift rafts after abandoning ship. Tadashi Okuno was a sailor on a *Kaigun* destroyer passing by at speed. He recalled men floating or sinking "close enough to see their unkempt beards and the tattoos on their arms. One of our machine gunners impulsively pulled his trigger." Was this to be another war crime never to be reported by honorless officers or punished by a ship's captain or navy board or postwar tribunal? The angry sailor who pulled the trigger, starting to machine-gun men in the water whose deaths could not affect his ship or the outcome of the war, was stopped by an order in the dark. He "was checked by a loud voice from the bridge saying 'Don't shoot at escaping men! Stop shooting, stop!'" One sailor treading water and later rescued by a USN search ship reported that he saw an officer on the bridge of a passing destroyer salute the *Johnson* as it sank.[33] And so it goes in war, maritime mercy or high seas crime separated by a few dozen yards or a half-mile of salt sea. And the sudden impulses of either hatred or respect for helpless individuals.

In related but more distant fighting in Manila Bay, the Japanese surface fleet was sent into full-speed withdrawal while pursued by waves of USN carrier aircraft. The cruiser IJN *Nachi* was under repair in Manila when it was spotted by attack aircraft from USS *Lexington* with Task Force 38. They ruined it, blowing away its bow and stern with bombs and five torpedoes. *Nachi* lost 807 men killed, with 220 later rescued by destroyers *Kasumi* and *Akebono*. Then the planes circled back, strafing survivors thrashing in oily water. A target coordinator recorded the murders without shame, which says he also feared neither rebuke nor retribution: "Note by target coordinator: We circled down to 20 feet to make sure there were absolutely no survivors. Fifteen or twenty oily figures were served with .50 caliber just to make sure."[34]

It fit with Admiral William ("Bull") Halsey's admonition, erected on a billboard in Tulagi harbor, to "Kill Japs, Kill Japs, Kill more Japs!" Yet, such routine racism does not explain merciless crimes. From the start, Japanese were depicted by Americans in full racist language and imagery but they did much the same, calling Western troops dogs, frogs, insects, swine, reptiles, worms, and whales. It was the normal dehumanization used to break a taboo against killing and maiming, only expressed in racist-animal language by both sides. No one sits their soldiers down before they go to war and teaches them all the marvels of their enemy's history and culture. New hate born of the war led into overt racism, more than the reverse.[35] Mostly, strafing came down to the character or callousness of target pilots and their wingmen, to careful or wanton men at war. Captains and admirals then became responsible if they knew it happened and did nothing to discourage repetition, allowing war crimes to fly off the decks of their carriers or into a raft from barrels of a ship's Bofors 40mm.[36]

Already by the end of 1943, IJN submarine crews had adopted kill-all tactics that made sinking *Centaur* pale by comparison. Four IJN submarines are known to have committed merciless atrocities against hapless survivors, systematically machine-gunning men in the water, shooting up lifeboats, even pulling some men onboard to interrogate, prior to murder more cruel. These were not reckless acts by individual crews run amok. The order came from Admiral Mito Hisashi, commander of IJN 1st Submarine Squadron based at Truk. He told his boats and crews to go beyond even what Dönitz said to do in the *Laconia* Order prohibiting any sea rescue. Hisashi ordered the killings: "Do not stop with sinking of enemy ships and cargoes; at the same time carry out the complete destruction of the crews of the enemy ships. If possible seize part of the crew and endeavor to secure information."[37] Japan's war was descending into a cult of death. In 1945 two naval officers posted to Germany as liaisons were supposed to be delivered by U-boat to a Japanese submarine waiting in the Indian Ocean. They ended up in the Gulf of Mexico after the U-boat diverted and the German crew raised a white flag to surrender to a U.S. warship. All the Germans came out but the two Japanese naval officers stayed inside and poisoned themselves.[38] *Kaigun* leaders had other choices available than the ones they made, including how to fight and how to treat prisoners and shipwreck survivors. They chose to fight on to total desolation instead. And so purposeless slaughter continued all across Asia and millions were butchered. Cities disappeared under pillars of fire left by the B-29s. Skeletal men fought hand-to-hand to their last, in a pitiless war for the pride of Japan's officers, nation, and empire. All for vanity, the least original of all original sins.

AT THE START OF OFFENSIVE OPERATIONS by coalition forces in Iraq in 1991, USN helicopters observed white flags waved on top of two large oil rig platforms. Nine officers were aware of the white flags; only two raised concerns about carrying out an attack once they were seen. Helicopters and frigates fired for hours, then spent most of the night picking up dead and wounded and terrified Iraqis, pulling them from the water and securing a few life rafts. Five men were killed, 23 taken prisoner. A USN board investigated. It concluded that under naval law as then codified this attack was a fully justified shooting because "a unit must surrender to a unit." It said it was not clear to the Americans that was the case with white flags waved atop a stationary oil platform. The same narrow, self-excusing logic had been applied by the Royal Australian Navy when *Sydney* kept hammering *Emden*. The complication in 1991 was that Iraqis on the platform were soldiers, and land law said waving a white flag was the proper manifestation of an intent to surrender.[39]

So it goes when law enunciated as grand principle encounters complex situational and moral reality on a real battlefield. The conduct of war, even with the best intentions, is persistently an admixture of analysis and judgment about intricate situations. There is always a huge imbalance toward decisions that favor survival of assets and personnel on one's own side, which seems natural and inevitable. What remains is restraint on the margins, which is a matter of individual conscience more than legal limitations or concern over a future naval board review.

CHAPTER 13

WINGS

Unfortunately, bombs have no eyes. So, in accordance with America's humanitarian policies, the American Air Force, which does not wish to injure innocent people, now gives you warning to evacuate the cities named and save your lives.[1]

—Curtis LeMay, *Bombing Leaflet*, 1945

Dipping into mercy to offer quarter amidst the complexities of land war is hard enough, where the lives of men offering to surrender are spared far more often to discourage them from further fighting rather than from compassion or morality or law. Doing it at sea is more difficult. A sailor cannot ask for or accept personal quarter except during boarding actions, which hardly happen anymore outside piracy patrols, and there the rules are very different. Nor is there any place to retreat when beaten in a sea battle, except into a ship's boats or the ocean. Behaving with restraint looks to be almost impossible in aerial combat. War in the air hardly seems to allow for mercy as fighting reduces to machine versus machine, today using fire-and-forget missiles that dart miles beyond human control. Compared to infantry aiming a rifle, it is much harder to engage empathy for ant-like figures below who scurry over an orangish target grid. There may even be rough moral and psychological equations that lower empathy as distance or altitude increases from shooter to target. The gap from streaking jets to ground forces mixed up with civilians may be too great to seal, the impulse to fire too much bronco to bridle and tame. It is important to appreciate these sharp limitations. Especially as air war presents in popular media as almost antiseptic violence wherein machines only kill other machines, and the ground explosions are so massive that they obliterate all obscenity. Fantasy wraps vintage aircraft and the war they made in romanticized historical narratives. Media from TV news to movies to video games indulge an appetite for images of air war approaching technological fetishism. Yet, mercy is still possible. Humanity is in place on either side of the equation, waiting to be targeted and in every choice made to shoot a missile or fly over someone else's country to drop a high-explosive bomb.

We saw empathy in gentlemanly gestures early in World War I, in the first dogfights in history. That was before war in the air was a true extension of industrialized war overall, once sheer numbers of aircraft, attrition, and ruthless bombing patterns mattered more than air aces and romantic fables. Even so, mercy in the air also came from a World War II *Luftwaffe* pilot who chose not to shoot down a lumbering, wounded bomber in 1943. And from a *Kaigun* "Sea Eagle" who made more kills than any other Japanese pilot but would not shoot down a civilian plane whose windows he could see right into, recognizing women and children huddled in fear inside. We saw less of it in the skies above Vietnam. Airstrikes in Kosovo and Serbia in the 1990s were carried out by NATO with high precision, if not quite the surgical success that was claimed. Merciful policy and practice was seen in no-fly zones precisely enforced over Saddam Hussein's Iraq after 1991, before the 9/11 attacks enraged Americans into making drone and missile strikes across the Greater Middle East. Accuracy was the idea behind the "shock and awe" bombing of Baghdad in 2003 that looked only to kill Iraqi regime personnel, taking out infrastructure with limited collateral damage to civilians. Limited, but not none.[2] U.S. and NATO airstrikes in Afghanistan were often called off if high-value targets were too close to civilians. Mistakes were made but they *were* mistakes. That is a key point, distinguishing from air power making no effort to discriminate, as in Russian barrel bombs dropped on Aleppo in 2018 or cluster bombs on

Kharkiv and white phosphorus ordnance on Mariupol in 2022. Orders were given, bomb doors opened, cruise missiles flew, civilians died. Yet, it is just as clear that lack of ill intention by a distant USAF controller or F-18 pilot or French Rafale pilot gave no comfort to the family of a dead Iraqi or Afghan or Malian child.[3]

DURING THE GREAT WAR, 6,000 ROYAL Flying Corps (RFC) personnel were killed in combat while nearly 8,000 more died in training accidents.[4] Before that carnage took hold, before the lethality of the enemy's aircraft and airborne weapons robbed the new game of air combat of fun, it was not unknown for pilots to make elaborate and chivalric gestures of a kind they likely encountered in boys' adventure books. They might land beside a enemy they just shot down to lend an injured man aid or smiling greetings if he was okay. Or maybe offer him a cigarette. That was more possible at the beginning of war in the air because the fragile little fireflies they piloted could short-land on almost any grassy field or road. Back in their own dining halls and barracks, not pounded by guns or gas or shot through by snipers like woeful infantries they overflew, pilots would toast the fallen, host prisoners at drinks or supper, and think war was grand. Sentimentalism eroded over four years of soaring lethality but was not wrecked: other pilots would not let mercy go.

"Knights of the air" was always a curious metaphor, converting the most modern element of war into a feudal trope. "Pursuit plane" or "fighter" pilots were closer to real armored men of the medieval era than the idealized vision of chivalry they were said to stand for in newspapers, and which exists still in public imagination.[5] Real knights hacked and cleaved each other with great broadswords and axes, impaled with lances, smashed skulls with spiked maces, mowed down hapless infantry from horseback. A pilot's virtue also was killing, not honor that drew on courtly myths and church lies or novels and poetry of centuries past. Imagery of "knights of the air" was the work of governments, propagandists, and the newspapers (hardly distinguishable at times). Twisting in a mortal dogfight, a pilot sought every edge to help him kill his enemy. Some lamented that they only shot down a plane, lusting for a kill in the full sense if they saw a smoking enemy aircraft land. More often, shooting up another plane meant watching a foe burn alive as his wood-and-canvas contraption plunged to the ground in a red-and-black puffery of burning fuel, flesh, and aircraft, his screams wafting on the wind beneath your wings. Or you watched a man jump, knowing he would become a rumple of broken bones and jellied organs. Gazed as he flailed wildly, plummeting to meet an unforgiving inertial mass without a chute to slow or save him because it was considered bulky and awkward.

British ace James McCudden understood all that, writing in 1918: "One cannot afford to be sentimental when one has to do one's job of killing and going on killing." Nor was he. He carefully thought about his enemy only as a machine without any man inside. It was not an uncommon psychological trick by pilots to avoid realities of a fate that they all knew likely would be theirs, too. Nevertheless, every so often he would fly too close and see a scared human face looking at him out of a plane with black Iron Cross markings on its wings. It shook him to know he would kill a man and not a mere machine in a real war, not a game. German ace Julius Buckler had similar thoughts. He had already shot down 12 Allied planes as he watched a man jump and fall from a 13th burning aircraft: "I could endure everything again if I had to, but I would not want to experience my thirteenth victory a second time."[6] And still newspapers touted up kill scores in tables looking all the world like football results, with separate columns for pilot name, busted balloons, scout planes, and pursuit planes.[7]

The target of the air hero was to reach five "kills," which the French said made you an "ace." Then the aces competed to outdo each other in lethal, paired "jousts," sometimes by direct invitation, more often during group encounters where some pilots identified as aces via distinctive colored mark-up of their aircraft. Many dogfights were fatal but not all. German ace Ernst Udet in a Fokker and a British pilot in a Spad shared an odd experience in the air. Udet and his opponent flew in circles nine or ten times, trying to fix each other in their respective gunsights. Then the British pilot waved at Udet. "I don't know why, but all at once I felt very sympathetic to the man in the Spad. Without a thought, I waved back. This went on for five or six curves." As a German squadron appeared, the Spad chose the greater part of valor and skedaddled.[8] It was that flash of recognition of humanity again. All it ever takes is a sudden moment. Then you can never again forget that you are a killer of a man and not just a machine.

"Father of the German air force" Oswald Boelcke made all 40 of his leading scorer kills before the close of 1916, the year he died in a midair collision. Letters discovered a century later confirmed that Boelcke was trying to fight the old-fashioned way into 1916, a year filled with change and death. William Somervill and observer Geoffrey Formilli were on a recon flight from Lille when, looking out from his Fokker E IV fighter, Boelcke spotted their slow BE2c. He riddled their two-man aircraft, forcing it to crash land. In a field report written immediately afterward he described what happened after he landed beside the crippled enemy reconnaissance plane: "I went straight up to the Englishmen, shook hands with them and told them I was delighted to have brought them down alive." He stayed and "had a long talk with the pilot, who spoke German well. When he heard my name he said with a grin, 'We all know about you!'" He made sure that they were both taken by car to a hospital "where I visited the observer today and brought him some English papers and photos of his wrecked machine."[9] During the visit, Formilli wrote down a short letter addressed to his commanding officer and gave it to Boelcke. The unassuming ace agreed to fly across no-man's-land to drop the letter onto the airstrip from which the broken BE2c took off. Formilli wrote that both RFC men were alive, only lightly injured, adding that it was the famous Boelcke who shot them down. Their commander sent the letter on to Formilli's mother with a note about the odd, Don Quixote mail service: "The German machine very sportingly held on through heavy shell fire from us and the French and was chased by several of our machines and had to run a hot gauntlet on its errand but it escaped all right."[10]

Being a fighter pilot in World War I was arguably the least important of all specialist roles. It certainly was not decisive to the outcome of the naval war deploying mass starvation as a strategic weapon, or the ground war opposing tens of millions of men and whole empires of production. Perhaps that is why governments and weary publics hearkened to old cultural tropes of aristocratic honor: the idea of a selfless Arthurian knight, contesting for God and the right with tremendous skill, fairness, and forbearance. Leave aside that by 1918 air battles became industrial in scale, engaging flocks of squadrons. Not at all like one-on-one knightly jousts on winged steeds, in displays of dexterity and muted yet civilized violence.

Nevertheless, a few clung to the illusion to the end of the war and even long afterward. Three years before the Battle of Britain in 1940, veteran RFC pilot Cecil Lewis described air war as a game in which there is "a strong magnetic attraction between two men who are matched against one another. I have felt this magnetism engaging an enemy three miles above the earth. I have wheeled and circled, watched how he flew . . . each of us wary, keyed up to the last pitch of skill and endeavor." What about after Lewis shot the other man down and saw him plunge? "What a glorious and heroic death. What a brave man!" Lewis never left his school days' sensibility behind, mixing metaphors of Greek warriors, gladiators, and medieval knights-errant. He still indulged it just before the start of the greatest air war in history, which would kill many tens of thousands of aviators and rain ruin onto hundreds of cities, killing over 1,000,000 civilians. He still hoped: "If the world must fight to settle its differences, back to Hector and Achilles!"[11]

Air war expanded in scale and seriousness from 1916. Many of the best pilots died. Boelcke led all aces with 40 victories when he was killed at age 25. Richthofen, the leading "ace of aces," had 80 kills when he died at age 26. One out of every three RFC pilots died in combat. As the lethality of aerial combat grew, as machines were made faster and more powerful, veteran experience became the key factor in life-and-death encounters: the life expectancy of a rookie pilot dropped to just two weeks, and even veterans had no guarantee of survival. It was worse for badly overmatched air forces that simply could not keep up with aircraft production or new pilot training: the Russian, Austrian, and Italian air forces were shot to pieces. Meanwhile, late-arriving Americans were promised production by Congress to support all the Allied air forces well beyond their own. It never came close to meeting even American needs, gravely disappointing the British and French. As happened also on the ground with the American "beggar army" that was forced to borrow French artillery in 1918, a nascent air force borrowed most of its planes and equipment from the Allies, especially from France.

Massive air losses happened all over again in World War II, when aircrew took catastrophic casualties on a scale that dwarfed even the Great War. Already by 1943, the *Luftwaffe* was reduced to an ill-led shell of what it was in 1940, with almost no logistics capacity left and no long-range bombing capability. It had fighters for defense but little more, and they were increasingly outmatched on all fronts. There was hardly a fighter left over Germany's cities by the end days in 1945, strategically worthless *Wunderwaffen* jets notwithstanding. It happened to Japan in the Pacific and Southeast Asia as well. Out of 150 pilots who went to war with the naval air regiment of Saburō Sakai, the leading Japanese ace, three survived. No one called pilots "knights of the air" anymore. Allied bomber crews joined the journey into death: life expectancy on a B-17 was just 15 missions by 1943, but men were assigned 25 or more. That provoked Joseph Heller's famous ironic mockery that fear of being killed only confirmed that you were sane, and therefore you could not "section out" of the bomber war as someone diagnosed as crazy. "That's some catch, that Catch-22. . . . It's the best there is."[12]

BOMBING ENRAGED GERMANS, WHO FROM 1943 on were spurred by their gangster government to murder downed Allied aircrew.[13] My former neighbor, Karl Fasick, broke his leg after jumping out of a burning USAAF bomber as it plunged earthward in March 1945. He was arrested by the Gestapo and thereby, likely was saved: another member of his aircrew was beaten to death by incensed civilians after he parachuted into the town they had just bombed.[14] There were also occasions when Germans hid downed Allied crew at risk of dire consequences from Gestapo or Nazi Party thugs, or just aroused mob justice. Still, rage was the default for most. It was stoked by a flailing regime and expiring ideology that was unable to defend its skies, and thus needed to focus attention and blame on *Terrorflieger* (terror flyers) and *Luftgangster* (air gangsters).[15] In Japan, three men of the first American bombing of the war, the "Doolittle Raid" in 1942, were executed as terrorists. Thereafter, captured American aircrew were held separately from other POWs and regarded and treated differently. More captured aircrew were blamed for saturation bombing and starvation in 1945. Their murder was officially sanctioned by the Japanese government that year. Also in Laos in the 1970s, captured American aircrew were put to death.[16]

Given the intensity of bombing of German cities it is more than remarkable that on occasion mercy was still exhibited by *Luftwaffe* flyers. A few days before Christmas 1943, a strange encounter took place in the air war over Germany. A Bf-109 fighter flew escort, wing-tip to wing-tip, with a crippled B-17 "Flying Fortress" trying to limp back to its base in Cambridgeshire, England. It was coming back from a bomb run over the FW-190 fighter factory in Bremen. Charles Brown from West Virginia was the 21-year-old pilot of the four-engine heavy bomber, on his first combat mission. He had three badly damaged engines, a shredded rudder and nose cone, and internal damage to vital systems: oxygen, hydraulics, and electrical. His tail gunner was dead and several of his 10-man crew were wounded. There was a bullet fragment in his shoulder. The wounded men were in sharp pain because in the December cold and badly holed bomber, morphine syrettes were frozen.[17] As he looked out, Brown was startled to see a Bf-109 just a few feet off his wing-tip. Its pilot was a young Bavarian, Franz Stigler. He had multiple kills of Allied aircraft on his war record but grieved alone for a dead older brother, whose name was etched on the enemy's scorecard as a *Luftwaffe* night-fighter pilot killed by the RAF in 1940. "He's going to destroy us," Brown said to his copilot. Then one of those odd moments occurred: making eye contact with the enemy, Stigler decided not to pull the trigger.[18]

Stigler had been standing beside his fighter on a forward base watching the B-17 flying unusually low, almost as if it were looking to land. It briefly vanished from view behind a line of trees, then he spotted it rising, struggling and slow. He climbed into his fighter and rose in pursuit, moving directly behind the crippled bomber to make his attack run. He put his hand on the Bf-109's trigger guard, ready to fire machine guns or loose a rocket from an underwing gondola cannon kit. He was baffled that the tail gunner did not fire at him as he closed in, not knowing the man was dead. Stigler did not shoot. He drew so close he could see blood splattered on the tail gunner's white fleece flying jacket. He saw bits of fuselage were peeled off and that all guns seemed out of action. It was a helpless aircraft, waiting for him to claim as a trophy.

Stigler saw through holes in the fuselage that men inside were huddled over wounded comrades. In a flash of shared humanity, with full realization that there were indeed real men inside the machine, he chose mercy. He flew astride the cockpit and made direct eye contact, noting blood on the pilot's face and jacket. He remembered in that moment what his old-fashioned commander once told him: "You follow the rules of war. . . . You fight by rules to keep your humanity." He recalled another admonition: never shoot a man in a parachute after killing the machine. He thought these men who were coming back from bombing a German city were about as helpless as parachutists.[19] He would not kill them. That Franz Stigler was a good man was proven by these events. His story also illustrates that mercy and ethical behavior may be taught and encouraged by commanding officers. That leaders matter.

Stigler tried to get the B-17 to land and surrender so the crew could receive German medical attention. Then he tried to get it to divert to neutral Sweden, to the same end. He was not understood. Now he did something truly remarkable. Stigler nodded at the two confused Americans in the cockpit and motioned that they should follow as he flew in formation with the lumbering B-17, protecting it from ground fire.[20] There may have been confusion over whether this was a captured B-17 the *Luftwaffe* used for special forces ops and pilot training. Why else would a Bf-109 give close escort to an enemy bomber? It did not matter: anti-aircraft guns would not shoot with a German fighter so close to the target. Stigler flew all the way to the coast over open water of the North Sea. "He gave me a wave salute and then he left," Brown recalled 50 years later. As he peeled away, Stigler watched the B-17 continue over the sea at low altitude, unsure if the cripple would make it all the way to England. It did, landing at an alternative air base after the last neck of hours over frigid water flying nearly on fumes.

Brown's crew were told to keep quiet about what happened: best not to sow moral confusion about the enemy. Stigler wisely did the same with his *Luftwaffe* superiors. Both men returned to the air war, enduring its most intense phase. In 1990, Brown placed an advertisement in a combat pilot association newsletter, trying to locate the German pilot who spared him and his crew. Stigler saw it and wrote from his retirement home in Surrey, British

Columbia: "Dear Charles, All these years I wondered what happened to the B-17, did she make it or not?" They spoke by phone and arranged to meet in person in Florida. "He almost broke my ribs, he gave me a big bear hug," Brown recalled.[21] They grew close, going on fishing trips together. Brown later arranged for the extended families of his surviving crew to meet and thank Stigler in person. In 2008 the two reconciled enemies died within a few months of each other.[22]

ON THE EASTERN FRONT, BOMBING WAS tactical more than strategic but ethical dilemmas still clouded humane reactions. One woman bomber pilot in the famed Red Army Air Force (VVS) 588th Night Bomber Regiment, whom the Germans called "Night Witches" (*Nachthexen*), was troubled for decades afterward by what she did. Klavdia Deryabina was not allowed to talk about or report civilian deaths caused on bomb runs. It was forbidden as part of a Soviet culture of refusal to admit mistakes or crimes. A pilot or crew confessing error, let alone guilt or moral regret over killing Germans, could be shot by the NKVD. Superiors might be shot as well, arming them with a powerful self-interest to silence subordinates. Even so, Deryabina never forgot the German civilians she killed with her bombs. She spent the rest of her life suffering moral injury from things she had been compelled to do in her youth.

There were three all-women bomber regiments in the VVS. Early on they flew second-rate and third-rate aircraft, not being expected to accomplish much. By early 1943 their success earned the regiment the Guards honorific and they flew much better "Peshkas," or Petlyakov Pe-2 twin-engine tactical dive bombers. Deryabina's colleague in the renamed 46th Taman Guards Night Bomber Aviation Regiment, navigator Tatyana Sumarokova, flew over 700 bombing sorties. It's a staggering number that dwarfs the combat mission numbers worried about by John Yossarian, Joseph Heller's main character in *Catch-22*. She was denied the award "Hero of the Soviet Union" during and right after the war, but was named "Hero of the Russian Federation" in 1995. Catapulted to belated fame both inside and outside Russia, she ruminated on her experiences in interviews with foreign journalists. She admitted, but only after the Soviet Union had ended, that her conscience rested uneasily for decades. One mission in particular lingered in memory. Her air regiment had devastated an entire town in order to kill a single, high-ranking German officer. She lived afterward knowing that she had killed hundreds of civilians. Mournfully, she concluded: "In the Soviet years, nobody ever talked about these things. It is so personal, and everyone was suffering in their hearts."[23] She too suffered moral harm.

SABURŌ SAKAI OF THE *KAIGUN*'S NAVAL air arm is widely considered Japan's leading air ace of World War II: he claimed in his memoir to have made 64 kills, including two large bombers on the ground at Clark Field in the Philippines that he wrecked by strafing.[24] He first saw air combat in China against the *Guomindang*. He shot down his first American plane over Clark Field on December 8, 1941, within hours of the Pearl Harbor attack. He thereafter flew a Mitsubishi A6M2 Zero out of the major Japanese air and naval base at Rabaul, including on long-range missions to Guadalcanal. He flew out of Lae in New Guinea after that. He fought the British in Burma and against Dutch and Australians in the Dutch East Indies and Borneo, then against U.S. flyers across the Pacific. One day, sure that he would be killed, he persuaded two friends to perform aerobatics with him above a U.S. base in New Guinea.

He remembered: "We decided to do something as pilots: fly a great, beautiful flight to demonstrate our skills. . . . So when the rest of the flight turned for home [Hiroyoshi Nishizawa and Toshio Ōta, both air aces] joined me on my wing." They descended near the ground and did a loop three times over the airfield and hangers. The next day a P-40 dipped out of low cloud over his home base and dropped a note: "Yesterday you performed aerobatics . . . and it was really exciting. We applauded. Next time you come we'll be ready to dogfight. . . . We'll be waiting for you." After the war, he met some of the U.S. soldiers who were at Port Moresby "who saw our aerobatics that day. They told me they stopped firing their guns as we did our maneuver, and stopped to applaud us."[25] The stunt was youthfully exuberant, if fatalistic and more than faintly absurd. It captured Sakai's engaging and lively personality and helped make him famous among former foes after the war. He died amidst them during a U.S. Navy dinner where he was the honored guest. But his aerobatics above an enemy base was not the most notable thing he achieved as a Sea Eagle flying for his emperor and Imperial Japan, a man and a cause he came to loathe in his later years.[26]

Before escorting a bombing run to Java, Sakai was given orders to shoot down any aircraft he saw. He was high over the island, having already shot down an Allied fighter, when he saw a large, very slow plane: a civilian DC-4. He recalled: "As I flew closer I saw that it was full of passengers. Some were even having to stand. I thought that these might be important people fleeing, so I signaled to the pilot to follow me." He hoped to force the DC-4 to land so that important personages could be captured. However, "the pilot of the aircraft was courageous enough not to follow me so I came down and got much closer. Through one of the round windows I saw a blonde woman, a mother with a child about three years old." Under direct orders to shoot down anything not Japanese that he met in the air over Java, he could not do it. "I thought I shouldn't kill them." An instant of recognized humanity was the prompt for an act of mercy that bound him forever to the woman inside the plane. It often is, surprising even the merciful.

A solitary pilot knew the DC-4 was filled with women and children but that was not the only thought racing through his mind. The vast majority of Japanese military had little or no prewar contact with Westerners and were often baffled to learn just how multinational and multiracial the enemy was.[27] Sakai was different, having been schooled by an American couple well before the war. He recalled many decades later: "Mrs. Martin was good to me. And that woman in the airplane looked like Mrs. Martin." He flew ahead of the lumbering DC-4, signaling it to keep going. "The pilot saluted me [as did] the passengers." He openly disobeyed his superior's direct order. He dissented from the fellow Sea Eagles he flew with, and crowds of admirers in Japan eagerly following his score. He queried the moment and made a mindful decision. He chose mercy: "I didn't respect my orders that day but I still think I did the right thing. I was ordered to shoot down any aircraft, but I couldn't live with myself doing that. I believed that we should fight a war against soldiers, not civilians. So I decreased my record by one." And thereby, Sakai likely avoided causing moral harm to himself as well.

The moral and psychological chasm between a record of 64 and 65 kills was immense. He bridged it all alone in the cockpit of a Zero.[28]

———————

AS EARLY AS 2008, RAF AIR Chief Marshal Sir Jock Stirrup conceded that coalition information operations lagged behind the Taliban's online efforts.[29] That signaled a remarkable adaptation by the ideologically anti-modern Taliban to satellite phones, social media, radio and television, and viral online manipulations. It let their ideas penetrate political and social networks in vital areas not otherwise reachable from their rural bases. In Iraq and Syria, ISIS expanded operations into cyberspace in 2015, putting coalition forces there on the defensive with a downstream current of jihadi messaging. It gave what was only a local insurgency, albeit with global pretensions to a caliphate, a worldwide reach. It radicalized lonely teenagers online from Berlin to Bristol, from Michigan to Melbourne, and brought thousands of volunteers to fight for ISIS. Most cyber-arena military capability is highly classified. However, it is known that the Pentagon and other militaries developed new cyber tactics, munitions, and capabilities to respond to ISIS and the Taliban.

Already, the U.S. military had responded to cyber threat with lethal kinetic force. In 2011, Anwar al-Awlaki was killed by a drone strike in Yemen, meant to disrupt recruiting terrorists over the internet.[30] Junaid Hussain, identified as a terrorist hacker, was killed by an airstrike in 2015. Individual targeted killings may be justifiable. Even if they are, other countries are also able to carry them out, perhaps with lesser moral cause. That will have to be argued case-by-case as drones overfly borders and into once sovereign airspace, guided by satellites and *force majeure* but not necessarily higher moral reasoning. Precedent has been set: identify targets that are online threats, kill them with armed drones or precision air strikes or other methods of assassination. Cyber law and dialogue about targeting ethics are scrambling to catch up. They will likely chase forever, unable to overtake vaulting cyber or AI capacity.[31] Armed forces many years ago lost control of cyber and new media environments: every day across the internet and in shooting wars in Syria and Ukraine, anarchic groups and even individual hackers have waged private cyber war against large, nuclear armed or actively belligerent states.[32]

Western societies especially must contend with domestic pushback against targeted killings that use near-invulnerable air power. The politics of drone killings merge in quite unexpected ways with good doctrine and intentions to limit collateral civilian casualties. The *New York Times* reported on a "Talon Anvil" strike team run by a classified Special Operations unit, operating against ISIS in Syria from 2014 to 2019. It became so indiscriminate it "alarmed its partners in the military and CIA by killing people who had no role in the conflict: farmers trying to harvest, children in the street, families fleeing fighting, and villagers sheltering in buildings."[33] In Afghanistan, drones took out Taliban fighters riding on motorbikes or guarding crossroads, although mistakes were made. In the West, drones were seen as avoiding needless deaths, and thus as ethically superior to artillery or bombing and politically preferable to boots on the ground and messy infantry firefights. It was better to target "terrorists" and kill them one by one than saturation-bomb or attack with ground forces. That is not how Taliban and Afghan civilians saw the drones circling high overhead. To many Taliban, drone strikes were cowardly. When facing coalition troops, even though massively overmatched in firepower and equipment, the Taliban knew they were fighting a foe they could respect. Drones were different, unknown in prior combat experience. Taliban never saw the risk-free controllers of pilotless aircraft. Coalition forces saw that as the beauty of drone strikes. Afghans saw it as shameful.[34]

Fearful of large gatherings that seemed to bring the drones down, people stopped sending children to school, avoided local *jirgas* (dispute courts), and lived inside a broken community social life.[35] Drones imparted a profound psychological burden as they overflew vales and villages, circling ominously. Maybe a quick strike was on the way and more children were about to die? People screamed and ran, sometimes in frantic and futile circles. Probably many suffered traumatic stress afterward. No one was counting. It was an enormous disconnection between intended mercy and real-world effects. The idea was to limit civilian collateral damage but such high technology could not be cleanly launched into rural and mountain villages with full moral assurance. Mistakes were made. More and more noncombatants died. Large wedding parties were hit, wrongfully identified as insurgent gatherings around high-value terrorist targets.[36] In 2015 a long-distance missile strike destroyed a Doctors Without Borders hospital in Kunduz Province, killing 42. Drones flew, sometimes innocents died alongside the target or the wrong target was selected. In either case, hatred swelled on the ground for unseen controllers. Fresh recruits set out to seek vengeance.

While watching on live TV as Taliban moved into Kabul in August 2021, former U.S. Marine Ian Cameron recalled that in 2018 and 2019 his team of intelligence, artillery, and aviation specialists "deployed some of the world's most sophisticated technology against Taliban fighters who were primarily armed with rifles designed during World War II." For nine months, sitting in the control room, "we tracked and hunted . . . with multimillion-dollar, indefatigable Reaper and Predator drones. My shift [began] at 8 a.m. I killed men for the next eight hours." When he was done and back home, another civilian watching the Taliban in victory, he mused that they looked just like the 304 young men he had killed. Their fellow militants were taking over in spite of him. He felt biting doubt, recalling: "As the drones confirmed that it was a clean strike . . . the tension in the control room dissipated. But I remember feeling very differently after the strikes that did not go as smoothly . . . gradual tightening in my stomach as a post-strike review revealed that one of the bodies on the screen was too small to be an adult." It was in those instances, Cameron confessed, that "the video game stopped and the flesh-and-blood consequences of what we were doing hit me: a wave of sickness, regret and second-guessing." On his last day in the control room, the last time he would kill anyone on a live feed but at a great physical distance, "relief washed over me. Killing people remotely . . . was somebody else's job now. A great weight had been removed."[37] But not the moral harm it left behind. From his words, it was apparent that was a dead weight he still carried.

Cameron was not alone. Other drone operators carrying out Reaper missions, with all that entailed for their own psychological reactions, were classed as not engaged in combat and therefore not qualified for counseling or posttraumatic therapy. The program started out well-researched and careful about targeting decisions. However, at the end of 2016 the Obama administration loosened targeting rules as the fight against ISIS escalated in Iraq and Syria and the president looked to keep his political promises to pull ground forces out of unpopular wars. Instead of limiting long-distance strikes to "high-value targets," much lower ranking insurgents were hit by remote operators. In 2017 the Trump administration secretly loosened the rules even more, so that it was no longer the president or top generals making the strike calls based on extensive intelligence analysis. Special Operations officers much farther down the chain of command made the calls instead, acting as the "customer" to the lethal strike teams. The shift led to far more attacks and hence dead civilians, and to both PTSD and moral harm among Reaper operators who watched the hits and aftermath in 3D images on live high-definition monitors. Some started to refer to what they suffered as "soul fatigue."[38]

In Afghanistan it went on for two decades, even though policymakers knew that drone blowback was alienating Afghan allies, and that targeting or intelligence errors facilitated recruitment into Taliban ranks.[39] President Bill Clinton's as well as George W. Bush's counterterrorism director, Richard Clarke, came to understand that drone and other long-distance strikes created more "enemies for the United States that will last for generations." He warned, about 20 years too late, that many innocent people had been killed by a drone policy that he had supported and helped to implement: "All those innocent people that you kill have brothers and sisters and tribal relations. Many of them were not opposed to the United States prior to some one of their friends or relatives being killed. And then, sometimes, they cross over, not only to being opposed to the United States, but by being willing to pick up arms. So you may actually be creating terrorists [*sic*], rather than eliminating them."[40]

A year before President Obama left office, four veteran U.S. Air Force drone controllers wrote to caution that "the innocent civilians we were killing only fueled the feelings of hatred that ignited terrorism and groups like ISIS, while also serving as a fundamental recruitment tool." They added: "this administration and its predecessors have built a drone program that is one of the most devastating driving forces for terrorism and destabilization around the world."[41] In August 2021 Taliban guards protected Americans and others airlifted from Kabul Airport in the final hours of a military presence being abandoned in haste and humiliation. A final drone strike meant to protect the evacuees went awry, as so many had before during 20 years of war. It was first said to have taken out an ISIS-K suicide sedan heading to slaughter hundreds in the crowd trying to flee from the airport. That was not true. but the error took days to admit. Inside were ten civilians, including seven children. The driver had worked for 15 years for a U.S. nonprofit.[42] With no more troops on the ground but high-value targets still in the country, "over-the-horizon" strikes continue: in August 2022, al-Qaida leader Ayman al-Zawahiri was killed by a drone in downtown Kabul. We have entered a new period where conventional forces train to take on main forces of near-peer powers like Russia or China, leaving it to drones to carry out targeted killings against asymmetric foes. The allure of a clean kill is too great to stop flying over borders.

Air power kept the Taliban at bay and outside major cities for 20 years, at huge human and reputational costs. It did not even promise victory, except to a deluded public. In secret, for the whole duration of the war officials had fundamental doubts that their local allies could "ever become competent or shed their dependency on U.S. money and firepower."[43] The end began when the Trump administration signed a withdrawal agreement at Doha in February 2020.[44] A series of advance surrenders to Taliban leaders were negotiated in secret by Afghan generals and mullahs. These were implemented during the rapid collapse in 2021, as the Biden administration at last pulled all ground and air support from the Afghan National Army and the National Police. Military and financial corruption, along with toleration of sexual abuse and too many dead civilians, had undercut any final stand. Helicopters circled another U.S. Embassy halfway around the world. Desperate locals who feared retaliation for collaborating with U.S. forces flocked to leave yet another collapsing experiment. Far too many to accommodate. Another lost war. Another fiasco of cultural misunderstanding. One more failure of imagination and air power to win victory or to stave off defeat. Another legacy of failure and betrayal, to burden diplomacy and stain a national reputation. Then, with barely six months passed, Russia invaded Ukraine and Afghanistan was largely forgotten. That was welcomed by all those who preferred military failure not to dominate the TV news. However, it also meant that the standard process of asking what lessons were learned, including about the importance of mercy in counterinsurgency wars, has been aborted.

CHAPTER 14

CONCLUSIONS

It is easy for us all to imagine we are heroes when we are sitting in our kitchens, dreaming of distant suffering.

—M. T. Anderson, *Symphony for the City of the Dead* (2015)

Alongside cruelty and criminality, acts of merciful sensibility are found in war at the start and end more than in the middle.[1] The shift back to restraint is more profound than any conventions of white flags or handshake truces or diplomatic ceremony. It seems to be rooted in recall of prewar perceptions of shared humanity that stir natural feelings of mercy. This change is so powerful it will apply even to those who wanted to kill you the day before. That is another of the many things that make war the strangest of all behavioral arenas. It is crucial to escape from assumptions of innocence about war. We must ask if we are really always as decent as we say we are, or the enemy as loathsome. Crime and murder will be found on all sides in every war, although some armies surely behave more mercifully than others. Not everyone who fights in service to an unjust cause is unmitigated in ill intentions or will commit odious acts. Not everyone forced to serve tyrants, ideologies of faith or politics, or murderous regimes with abhorrent *casus belli* are as wicked as their leaders. We should expect to find some merciless soldiers from democracies and decent soldiers from tyrannies on the same battle-field. Merely proclaiming one's cause is just and honorable does not suffice. Honor is not enough. Valor is not enough. Law is not enough. Those whom we send to war also must be merciful.

War is about choice in the moral realm as much as in tactics and strategy. Pull the trigger or don't. Bind an enemy's wounds or abandon him to die. Punish reckless crimes or conceal them. War is not a treatise in abstractions of history or political science. It is not a theory cobbled from Thucydides or Sun Tzu or Machiavelli or even Clausewitz. It is not merely soulless force as prime mover. *Fortuna* and *virtú* intertwine as they always have and will. Character counts. Virtue and honor may be alternately inspired or discouraged by military codes and cultures. They cannot be guaranteed. They reveal themselves under fire, in trauma-inducing dilemmas where choices made may shock the chooser, leaving them suffering moral harm for a lifetime. War is not all faceless forces or tectonic plates moving history below a surface unengaged by flesh-and-blood people. There is no moral equivalent of war.[2] Nor a secret code that ensures that you preserve your honor and fight for the right. Nor absolution for civilians who stay at home but cheer a distant war as if following a sports team, excited by its vicarious thrill and violence. War is harder than that.

Individual characters of soldiers and a psychology of personal standards will most often trump military law, social mores, and moral philosophy. Trying to control combat behavior with strict legal codes is a worthy endeavor. But it seems to have a poor record of success. Combat is too fast, too beclouded by taut emotions always close to a snapping point and by the perennial moral fog of war. International and human rights legal expert Mark Osiel argues persuasively that a soldier or sailor or pilot, or now also a missile or drone operator, should be taught to center personal military identity in shared concepts of honor, even in old chivalric virtues and values. Doing so commences with self-control but also opens the psyche to "identity shaming." He cites an example from Vietnam where a soldier in a killing rage put the mouth of his rifle against the temple of a Vietnamese woman. An officer shocked the lad back to civilization not by shouting regulations out of the *Uniform Code of Military Justice* but by yelling, "Marines don't do that!" It jolted the boy back to decency.[3] If illegality of an act of killing or any wider atrocity is the expected floor of restraint, shame identity and merciful character might help us to raise the ceiling. Good officers matter a great deal in that endeavor. Accountability is everything.

Prior to the International Tribunal's rejection at Nuremberg of the ancient defense of *respondeat superior,* or "superior authority," soldiers were taught that their highest duty was to carry out orders with no questions asked. If you obeyed an illegal order you could always later assert *respondeat superior* as a defense, or at least in mitigation of any expected punishment. This idea was listed in the 1914 edition of the *British Manual of Military Law* and in the *U.S. Rules of Land Warfare.* After 1945, Tribunal judges rejected the claim made by German defendants, displacing it with an "absolute liability" doctrine.[4] That leaves the crux of the modern problem as an expectation of enforcement. Ideally, insistence on right conduct is located where combat meets behind-the-lines commanders and civilian political responsibility to apply the law. We must hope and ensure that our officer corps and civilian authorities enforce rather than evade accountability for war crimes by our soldiers, sent out to fight and kill in wars they did not start for complex causes they probably do not understand. It is an obligation of citizenship.

It is a truism that armed forces reveal the nature of societies that raise and supply them and send them off to fight. Callous regimes and arrogant political or religious ideologies are much more likely to unleash unpitying armed forces into war. But they are not alone in behaving without mercy. If you dragnet fish for conscripts to fill up divisions and corps, as in all the larger 20th-century wars, you will put into uniform more than a few violent, untamable young men. In any uniform, in every army. Give them a helmet and a gun and relentless chances to indulge their base nature, and you should expect crimes to be committed in your name. What you do next really matters, defining your society's reputation, revealing its true character. Do you hold your own to account, fess up to crimes, bring swift punishments down? Or do you deflect, defer, and deny?

Soldiers who enter combat face questions that those of us who do not go to war never face. Some are so hard to answer, so close to the bone of who we really are, as opposed to who we think we are or want to be, that we should ardently hope we never have to answer them. Yet, soldiers are not apart from us. We are complicit in their acts, no matter how much we may squirm or shift blame back onto them. We send soldiers to war, license their lethal force, ask them to do what we will not or we cannot. Most soldiers go to war only once, although some may go again by choice or coercion. The majority who experience combat find that once was more than enough. War burns up innocence and youth. It prematurely ages, breaking down minds as much as it breaks bodies. All those who make it back from war to peace with their conscience intact count themselves fortunate, knowing how many others suffered grievous moral injury. War weighs down its veterans and accuses all the rest of us who wish to condemn: "Thou dost stone my heart and makest me call what I intend to do a murder, which I thought a sacrifice."[5]

Mercy and cruelty intertwine in war. Acts of compassion may coexist with pitiless depravity within just a few yards. That is one of war's central paradoxes. Treachery and murder mark conflict, yet mercy and restraint also border moral no-man's-lands in every war. Amidst war's starkest cruelty, some will behave with pity even for their enemy. Even at risk to their own lives. They refuse wrongful orders. They do not pull the trigger against women and children or harm defenseless prisoners. There is never enough mercy in dark places of terrible violence. There is always some. We need more. One path to more humanity in war is to understand that mercy is not just an abstract ideal or solely a matter of personal character. It helps you win, especially in modern counterinsurgency wars.

Mercy can bring local allies over to your side or keep them there, whereas cruelty in power will drive them into armed camps of your enemy. Perhaps for generations. Mercy works toward final success far better than sheer indiscriminate violence or terrorizing civilians or denying quarter or mistreating prisoners. Act decently and you may still lose. Act indecently and you surely will. The choice before us all is whether or not to wage war like ancient Romans. We must not deny mercy, make the land a desert, and call that peace.[6] If we do, if we behave like some Western troops did in Iraq and Afghanistan and the Russian Army did at vastly more extreme levels of indiscriminate violence in Ukraine, we will lose future campaigns for "hearts and minds" that modern counterinsurgency reduces to, far more than than it does to tactics. If we abjure justice and compassion we will strand ourselves in parched deserts of future wars, far from the oasis of humanity that is mercy, lost in a sand sea of war's more usual moral aridity.

Since 1945 the world has moved down a road of threatening punishment after the fact for war crimes and atrocity, albeit hardly ever enforcing that internally or internationally. It may not be the best answer. Perhaps we should instill in all military training not only warrior values but an undisputed and shared sense of moral identity of the unit, tied into personal honor. Make being in Special Forces a calling to merciful service, not just a warrior ethos. Teach soldiers that mercy for a vulnerable enemy, as well as civilians, is as important to victory as knowing how to use advanced weapons. Officers must appreciate that if they do not take accountability for crimes as well as combat under their command, it will undermine the mission. It may actually lose the war. Teach that one's love of country will be best expressed as honorable compassion. Mercy is self-rewarding but also required to win counterinsurgency wars of the modern era. Soldiers are *not* instruments of surgical force, inserted and removed like a scalpel. They are armed arguments for your cause. Make your forces merciful arguments for and not against it. Or you will lose.

AUTHOR'S NOTE

They were going to look at war, the red animal war, the blood-swollen god.
—Stephen Crane, *The Red Badge of Courage* (1895)

Each new war we meet pushes older wars out of the mind's eye. Wars therefore must be re-created somehow or we will forget them, especially lost wars that are less easy to convert into heroic myth. Classicists are millennia removed from ancient Greece or Rome, or China in its Warring States period. Medievalists look back from centuries' distance at abandoned castles, disappeared duchies, and vanished honor codes and cultures. Military historians also explore war from afar. Even World War II is now stretching beyond living memory, and Korea and Vietnam are fast receding. It is no more disqualifying for a military historian not to have gone to war than it is for a classicist not to have walked the streets of Athens when it was a living empire or a medievalist not to have visited a plague house at the height of the Black Death. Even so, readers deserve to know if the historian whose judgments they are reading has seen war up close. Did he or she serve in the military? Although I was never a soldier, I have walked through and have worked in war zones. In passing through wars, I was never shot at, nor did I shoot at anyone. My experience is to have seen war from its edges, as if looking "through a glass darkly."[1]

I grew up in Canada during a long, quiet phase between its last war in Korea and its recent wars in Iraq and Afghanistan. Military aircraft on the way to Alaska, and thence Vietnam, overflew my house as a boy after refueling at a Canadian Air Force base. Their vapor trails and distant roar of engines, and listening to the body counts on the radio before running to school, was as close as I got. I tried to learn about war from a young age. I was taught by warriors (and I have since taught many warriors). Most of my schoolteachers were World War II or Korean War veterans but they would talk only obliquely about their wars to their students. My first real encounter with the issue of mercy in war came while a volunteer teacher in rural northern Nigeria, where I lived with a Biafran Army veteran housemate. He led the final defenders of the last airstrip in Biafra, as that surrounded and starving enclave was finally overrun in January 1970. One night he told me how, in the last days and last fight, he ordered a wounded enemy killed as he lay in the grass begging for mercy: "I said, give him one!" A pair of his conquerors, sergeants in the Nigerian Army, were posted to our boarding school by the military dictatorship. They handled all discipline, from weekly public whippings of boys to other brutal physical punishments derived from the military. My other contacts with the Nigerian Army came at roadblocks. I was twice arrested at gunpoint on trumped-up charges that did not stick. Another time, a Nigerian soldier threatened and smashed his rifle butt into the door of my car, clearing a path for a military convoy to pass. One market day, I watched a man accused of a minor theft stoned by a rural mob that had swelled almost out of nowhere. The hospitality as well as the hidden violence of Nigeria intrigued me, so I later wrote my master's thesis on ethnic conflict and the Biafran War.

I returned to Canada in 1980, after two years dwelling among people who are today plagued by runaway Boko Haram terrorism. On the way, I stopped in Belfast, where "The Troubles" were in full swing. Most buildings, notably the pubs, had all windows up to the second floor bricked over. That was to block any satchel bombs or hand grenades from being thrown in from street level. Red-haired and age 24, I looked Irish and local. Walking down a side street, a British Army patrol skittered and flitted around and past me in the blackbird-fashion of urban warfare tactics. They moved doorway to doorway, alert and searching, mortally afraid of snipers. That day, a 14-year-old boy was shot dead while writing graffiti on a stone wall, his paintbrush reportedly mistaken for a pistol. Two large IRA bombs went off, one in the neighborhood. They were only briefly on the BBC News: Peter Sellers had died in London. That was when I realized how distant most people these days prefer to stay from any conflict, even when their own country is involved.

I was a visiting scholar in Israel twice during the Second Intifada in 2001 and 2002. The streets of Jerusalem were tense and largely deserted of foreigners. We traveled to historical sites in the West Bank and walked in the Old City under armed guard. It was more strange than unnerving to wear ceramic body armor at the closed Gaza border crossing. You just stood where the Israeli Defense Force told you, outside any sniper's line of sight or fire. We were taken by a circuitous route to a hidden Border Police Force (*Mišmar Ha-Gvul*) base, to watch sniper training and snatch-and-grab re-creations. We practice-fired military weapons. One morning was deeply somber: a Hamas suicide bomber blew up himself and nearly two dozen teenagers at a disco in Tel Aviv. One speaker blamed the IDF, oddly saying the deaths were deserved because Israel allows women to serve. I worked in Honduras three times starting in 2009, leading groups of volunteers in a Global Water Brigade (the only brigade I ever served in). The drug wars were getting worse, so we were under constant armed protection. But I never felt directly threatened: you quickly realize that none of it is about you while walking or working inside someone else's war. Understanding is hard.

My longest exposure to war was five weeks spent in Kabul in 2011, training young diplomats at the Ministry of Foreign Affairs. Retired veterans of the Special Air Service and some other military contractors guarded our vehicles, which were checked for underside bombs each way. All windows were bulletproofed but not tinted: we could see mutilated survivors of severe war injuries begging in the streets and they could see us. At every stop widows in *chadaree* with small children, or mangled veterans, approached with outstretched hands. We were under strict orders not to open the windows, to prevent any Taliban throwing in a grenade. So we could do nothing to aid those pitiful beggars. I was a voyeur peering into the suffering of a war not my own. There were bolt holes and armored rooms in our closed compound, in case of Taliban assault. I kept a knife in the shower in case the building was attacked and I could not reach the steel safe room four floors down. I felt ridiculous. We were advised to stay off the rooftop because of snipers. I went up anyway, to watch and listen to the city. Attack and assault helicopters flew overhead in tight flocks, their lights blacked out, Special Operations Forces dangling legs out open doors like their fathers did over Vietnam. In war, *plus ça change, plus c'est la même chose*: the more things change, the more they stay the same.

We received live security feeds direct to our laptops, laying out real-time threat assessments and possible approaching Taliban. The choppers flew low and loud overhead all the time, heading out to a valley combat mission or back to Bagram Airbase. The night sky filled with choppers on August 6, after a Chinook went down with 38 killed, including 17 U.S. Navy Seals. I was supposed to meet a former student at Bagram base: he was in charge of perimeter security. But we could not manage it after the Seals were killed. Then he lost a 19-year-old in his unit while out on a war patrol. I did not see the colonel until he came to Boston nearly two years later, sick of war. We discussed another former student, full of life and enthusiasm before he was killed by an IED north of Baghdad in 2007. His father was an outspoken opponent of the Iraq War.

The inspiration for this book came from conversations with a master sergeant and former student who retired from the U.S. Army in 1998, after 20 years of service. Craig was often on covert insertion missions supporting CIA or other intelligence operations. He saw the worst of war in Bosnia during the "ethnic cleansing" that tore it apart. He went into Rwanda with an observe-and-advise team at the start of the genocide, where he saw hacked bodies in the streets and "stacked like firewood" in Amahoro Stadium in Kigali. He worked with isolated Peshmerga fighters of the Kurdish resistance to Saddam Hussein, whose regime used poison gas to kill many thousands of civilians at Halabja. He gave me a piece of shrapnel from a shell that vaporized one of his men: "We didn't even find a shoe." He told me about friends who never came back from Mogadishu and the six times he had killed enemy. One day he told me about an insertion by a four-man team in northern Iraq. It was not a combat story, just an encounter with local children in a small Kurdish village. Yet, it stayed with me more than any other.

Riding in civilian pickups, his team passed through a small village where laughing, running, shouting children swarmed the soft-skin vehicles and odd foreigners. They held out hands to clutch some chocolate or candy or a stick of gum, the type of rare treat they knew the Americans carried. The team stopped to toss candies out the truck windows, then started to pull away. That's when it all went wrong. Craig heard wild howling from behind. A powerfully built but severely mentally challenged boy, about 15 years old, was out-scampered by smaller and quicker children and had missed out on all the tossed candy. He was chasing the pickups, bellowing righteously over having been excluded. He jumped up onto the running board, reached through the window and grabbed Craig with both strong hands closing around his throat. The boy had no evident malintent. But he was big, real strong, and already heavily burdened by a life of daily exclusion from special things. Hollering mad, he was singularly focused on getting candy justice.

With his left hand on the steering wheel, unable to breathe or even gag for air, Craig struggled with his crossed-over right hand to loosen the boy's fierce grip, which he thought might crack his windpipe. He swerved the pickup suddenly, trying to toss the boy off the running board and door, hoping he might land uninjured on the hot sand. The kid hung on, tightening his hold around Craig's throat, yowling as the truck swayed wildly. Unable to loosen the boy's grasp with his free hand, Craig weakened. He thought he might pass out, crash, and roll the truck. Choking for air that just would not come, thinking that his life was in danger, he reached down to fumble out his sidearm. With one hand weakly clutching the steering wheel he lifted the gun, pointing it at intimate range at the wailing boy's temple. Death was all around in Iraq. What did one more death matter, really? And this was self-defense, right?

Why not just stop the truck and get his team members to pull the boy off? Perhaps that is what he should have done. That would be easy for me to write and you to think. Too easy, sitting back in our comfortable chairs at years remove, noting calm solutions and staking out soothingly abstract moral positions. Reality for soldiers in a combat zone is different, acting as they must under conditions of heightened fear and adrenaline rush, lethal threats and weapons all around. Whether or not the threat is immediate and real or only latent, choices made in a war zone are veiled in moral doubt and sudden mortal panic. Decisions must be reached too fast, inside a moral murk too easily pierced in civilian retrospective. There is no time to think. Survival instinct kicks in, masking clear cognition and merciful reasoning with primal fear and reflex. As it does in any animal struggling to breathe its next breath, thrashing against a cold, swift current that is pulling it down into forever nothingness.

I knew that Craig, a tough special forces veteran, six times had used his sidearm to kill. He told me that he regarded every shoot as justified, that he did not rethink or regret any one. His demeanor, need to confess, and obvious abiding moral harm said otherwise. But it was not my place to challenge his memory. However, this time I shrank from his tale, not wanting to hear how it turned out. I thought he was about to tell me his worst war story, about how he killed a 15-year-old kid over a candy bar. I braced to hear it. He looked straight at me and said quietly, "I chose not to pull the trigger." The powerful boy kept his death grip tight around Craig's throat. At last, his truckmate found some candy in a cargo pocket and reached it up and across the driver's seat, holding it out to the boy. He let go one hand to grasp the treat. Heaving for air and life, Craig braked. The boy jumped off and ran back to his village.[2]

The simple statement "I chose not to pull the trigger" is the most morally elegant thing I ever heard a soldier say. It led me back to other stories of unexpected mercy. To acts of restraint that were also acts of profound moral courage, refusing to do what the "red animal, the blood-swollen god" demanded. I wondered how anyone stood up against indecency, withstanding the pressures to conform to expectations that for most soldiers simply overwhelm private conscience. What made them do it? This book is not an answer to that question. It is, I hope, the start of a conversation.

Cathal J. Nolan
August 4, 2022

NOTES

Introduction

1. Wilfred Owen, *Poems* (London: Chatto & Windus, 1920).
2. In *Nicomachean Ethics,* Aristotle considered courage the cardinal virtue because it enables all the others.

Chapter 1

1. On this well-worn pattern and error in modern war, see Cathal J. Nolan, *The Allure of Battle: A History of How Wars Are Won and Lost* (New York: Oxford University Press, 2017).
2. "Battle for Kyiv Looms," *Washington Post*, March 20, 2022. Chornovol was a widow and mother of two, whose husband was killed fighting in Donbas in 2014.
3. Before World War II *respondeat superior*, or "superior authority," was still accepted as a defense by Western militaries. On the doctrine's rejection in modern laws of war, see Ilias Bantekas, "The Contemporary Law of Superior Responsibility," *American Journal of International Law* 93, no. 3 (July 1999): 573–595. The new standard is "manifest illegality," an order whose criminality is obvious on its face and must not be obeyed. Mark Osiel, *Obeying Orders: Atrocity, Military Discipline and the Law of War* (New Brunswick, NJ: Transaction, 1999), 13–90.
4. See below. On medical comparison of PTSD and "moral harm," see S. Maguen et al., "The Impact of Killing in War on Mental Health Symptoms and Functioning," *Journal of Traumatic Stress* 22 (2009): 435–443.
5. "I Have a Message for My Russian Friends," *The Atlantic*, March 17, 2022. The video was seen by millions. Several days later, Russian state TV attacked the message as an act of American imperialism.
6. Rupert Brooke, "Peace" (1914), *Poetry: Magazine of Verse*, April 1915.
7. Ernst Jünger, *Storm of Steel* (Garden City, NY: Doubleday, Doran, 1929), originally published as *In Stahlgewittern* (1920). It was republished seven times in his lifetime, in significantly varying editions. It was the signature book of the war.
8. Rupert Brooke, *The Dead* (1914).

9. Rupert Brooke, *The Soldier* (1914). See the puncturing biography by Nigel Jones, *Rupert Brooke: Life, Death and Myth* (London: Head of Zeus, 2014), 467–503.

10. Owen, preface to *Poems*. On the old lie, in *Dulce et Decorum Est* he wrote, "If in some smothering dreams, you too could pace behind the wagon that we flung him in... My friend, you would not tell with such high zest to children ardent for some desperate glory, the old lie: *dulce et decorum est pro patria mori.*" Quoting Horace: "It is sweet and right to die for your country."

11. Siegfried Sassoon, *War Poems* (New York: Dover Reprint, 2018). His famous "Soldier's Declaration" protest to *The Times* (July 31, 1916) is reprinted in most collections. Also at the website The Heritage of the Great War, http://greatwar.nl/sassoon/sassoondeclaration.html.

12. Robert Graves, *Goodbye to All That* (London: J. Cape, 1929).

13. Henri Barbusse, *Le feu* (Paris: Flammarion, 1916). This searing novel of war in the trenches won the Prix Goncourt. The motif survives in most French films about soldiers' experiences in World War I, such as *Capitaine Conan* (1997), *La Chambre des officiers* (2001), and *Un long dimanche de fiançailles* (2004).

14. H. G. Wells, *The War That Will End War* (New York: Duffield, 1914). President Woodrow Wilson used a variant when asking for a congressional declaration of war on Germany in 1917: "I promise you that this will be the final war, the war to end all wars." Address to a Joint Session of Congress, April 2, 1917. A naïve, optimistic 1933 review argued that World War I was indeed different from all prior wars that were lamented afterward, that it had in fact accomplished what Wells predicted. If only as a warning, see Louise Maunsell Field, "War Makes the Hero," *North American Review* 235, no. 4 (1933): 370–375.

15. Ernest Hemingway, *A Farewell to Arms* (New York: Scribner, 1929).

16. The medal went extinct along with Imperial Germany in 1918.

17. Hemingway, *A Farewell to Arms.*

18. Yet, breathless Hemingway worship is boundless. Even his absurd solo hunting of German U-boats off the coast of Cuba during World War II is taken seriously by too many. As is his preposterous behavior in France: "Hemingway accompanied [*sic*] American troops as they stormed to shore on Omaha Beach, though as a civilian correspondent he was not allowed to land himself." Thomas Putnam, "Hemingway on War and Its Aftermath," *National Archives* 38, no. 1 (Spring 2006). Actually, he got in the way of landing operations by managing to climb into a Higgins boat, part of the seventh wave at Omaha. That forced its driver to delay joining the assault in order to turn around to bring an inebriated fool playing at war back to the ship. His behavior in Paris, drunkenly pretending to soldier during the liberation, was utterly shameless at the time and in his later memorialization of it. Michael Taylor, "Liberating France Hemingway's Way: Following Author's 1944 Reclaiming of the Ritz Hotel," *SFGate*, August 22, 2004.

19. John Paul Sartre, *Iron in the Soul* (New York: Penguin, 2002).

20. Jünger, *Storm of Steel.* He recorded a different, less dramatic account of this March 1918 incident in his war diary, wherein he did not put a pistol to the man's head; he simply looked at the photo of a half-dozen children, and passed on. See Benjamin

Ziemann, *Violence and the German Soldier in the Great War: Killing, Dying, Surviving* (New York: Bloomsbury, 2017), 77–78.

21. Tim O'Brien, *The Things They Carried* (Boston: Houghton-Mifflin, 1990).

22. T. S. Elliot, *Gerontion* (1920).

23. Otto von Bismarck to the Reichstag: "The decision will come only from . . . the God of battles, when he lets fall from his hands the iron dice of destiny" (https://www.bartleby.com/348/1455.html).

24. Schiller's famous trilogy was finished in 1799. It comprises *Wallenstein's Camp* (*Wallensteins Lager*), *Piccolomini* (*Die Piccolomini*), and *Wallenstein's Death* (*Wallensteins Tod*).

25. Elisabeth Krimmer, *Representation of War in German Literature: From 1800 to the Present* (Cambridge: Cambridge University Press, 2010), 28.

26. Peter Wilson, *Europe's Tragedy: The Thirty Years War* (Cambridge, MA: Harvard University Press, 2011), 671–747.

27. Leo Tolstoy, *Sevastopol Sketches* (London: Penguin, 1985), originally published 1855; Leo Tolstoy, *War and Peace* (Oxford: Oxford University Press, 2010), originally published 1869.

28. Mark Nelson, *White Hat: The Military Career of Captain William Philo Clark* (Norman: University of Oklahoma Press, 2018).

29. See Danny Orbach, *The Plots against Hitler* (New York: Houghton Mifflin Harcourt, 2016).

30. "In war, truth is the first casualty" (Aeschylus, attributed). It is an oft repeated notion. For example, Samuel Johnson wrote in 1758, "Among the calamities of war be justly numbered the diminution of the love of truth."

31. William Shakespeare, *Life of King Henry V*, Act IV, Scene 1.

32. "US Has Bombed at Least Eight Wedding Parties Since 2001," *The Nation*, December 20, 2013. Saudis hit Houthi weddings in Yemen in 2015 and 2018. On another moral level, radical insurgents in Pakistan and Afghanistan deliberately attacked weddings with grenades or suicide vests. "Wedding Hit by Airstrike in Yemen," *New York Times*, April 23, 2018; "Explosion Rips through Kabul Wedding," CBS News, August 18, 2019; "Yemenis Seek Redress for U.S. Drone Strikes," *Washington Post*, January 27, 2021.

33. On PTSD see Chapter 8.

34. February 2020 email exchange, names withheld.

35. John Bates, a common soldier, to Henry V, in disguise, on the quiet eve of Agincourt in 1415. William Shakespeare, *Life of King Henry V*, Act IV, Scene 1.

36. The earliest rejection of the claim was in 1474 by a regional court in Breisach, for atrocities committed by Peter Von Hagenbach in service to the Duke of Burgundy. It resulted in Hagenbach's torture and beheading. Gregory S. Gordon, "The Trial of Peter Von Hagenbach: Reconciling History, Historiography, and International Criminal Law," SSRN, October 22, 2015, https://papers.ssrn.com/sol3/papers.cfm?abstract_id=2006370.

37. See the discussion of moral harm, below.

38. Stephen Crane, *The Red Badge of Courage* (1895; New York: Fleet, 1969).

39. Erich Maria Remarque, *All Quiet on the Western Front* (Boston: Little, Brown, 1929), originally published as *Im Westen nichts Neues* (No News from the West; 1929).
40. Jonathan Shay, *Achilles in Vietnam: Combat Trauma and the Undoing of Character* (New York: Scribner, 1994).
41. Maguen et al., "The Impact."
42. Karl Marlantes, *What It Is Like to Go to War* (New York: Grove, 2011); Douglas Pryor, "Moral Injury," Boston Graduate School of Psychoanalysis, May 15, 2015, https://bgsp.edu/; William Broyles, "Why Men Love War," *Esquire*, November 1984.

Chapter 2

1. Tzvi Abusch, "Development and Meaning of the Epic of Gilgamesh," *Journal of the American Oriental Society* 121, no. 4 (2001): 614–622; Alexander Ainian, "Heroes in Early Iron Age Greece and the Homeric Epics," in *Archaeology and the Homeric Epic*, ed. Susan Sherratt and John Bennet (Barnsley: Oxbow, 2017), 101–115.
2. The Ambrosian Hymn, or *Te Deum*, is a religious praise song dating to the fifth century CE. It was long associated with the ostensible piety of French kings but was converted at the court of Louis XIV into a state celebration.
3. C. I. Hamilton, "Naval Hagiography and the Victorian Hero," *Historical Journal* 23, no. 2 (1980): 381–398; Adrian Shubert, "Women Warriors and National Heroes," *Journal of World History* 23, no. 2 (2012): 279–313.
4. Homer, *The Iliad*, trans. Samuel Butler (London: Longman, 1898), Scroll 22, line 232.
5. In the *Iliad*, Achilles breaks the honor code when his desire for vengeance causes him to desecrate the body of his dead foe, the Trojan hero Hector.
6. Plutarch, *Lives* (Vancouver: Engage Books, 2020), 765–853.
7. Virgil, *The Aeneid* (New York: Penguin Classics, 2008), 47.
8. The classic account is Einhard, published along with Notker the Stammerer in David Ganz, ed., *Two Lives of Charlemagne* (London: Penguin, 2008). The best modern biography is by Mattias Becher, *Charlemagne* (New Haven, CT: Yale University Press, 2003).
9. Cyril Edwards, trans., *Nibelungenlied: The Lay of the Nibelungs* (Oxford: Oxford University Press, 2010).
10. Luo Guanzhong, *Romance of the Three Kingdoms* (New York: Penguin Classics, 2018), first published in the 14th century.
11. Thomas Mallory, *Le Morte d'Arthur* (New York: Oxford University Press, 1998), originally published 1485.
12. Congressional Medal of Honor Society, "Alvin C. York," https://www.cmohs.org/recipients/alvin-c-york.
13. *Sergeant York* (1941).
14. *Sands of Iwo Jima* (1949).
15. *To Hell and Back* (1955). Its title was taken from his autobiography, *To Hell and Back: The Audie Murphy Story* (New York: Henry Holt, 1949).

16. An uncritical paean in prose is David A. Smith, *Price of Valor: The Life of Audie Murphy* (Washington, DC: Regnery History, 2015).

17. "Accursed man." An outlaw. In Roman and Medieval Christian law, a banned person who could be justly killed by anyone, without a stain of murder.

18. Chris Kyle, *American Sniper: The Most Lethal Sniper in U.S. Military History* (New York: William Morrow, 2012).

19. *American Sniper* (2014).

20. Quoted in *Los Angeles Times*, February 3, 2013.

21. Ibid.

22. Ibid.

23. Kyle, *American Sniper, passim*.

24. Quoted in the Red Army memoir of Boris Gorbachevsky, *Through the Maelstrom: A Red Army Soldier's War on the Eastern Front, 1942–1945* (Lawrence: University Press of Kansas, 2008), 344.

25. David B. Edwards, *Caravan of Martyrs: Sacrifice and Suicide Bombing in Afghanistan* (Berkeley: University of California Press, 2017), 125–162; Mohammad Hafez, *Suicide Bombers in Iraq: The Strategy and Ideology of Martyrdom* (Washington, DC: USIP, 2007).

26. Nasra Hassan, "An Arsenal of Believers: Talking to the Human Bombs," *New Yorker*, November 12, 2001. Also see Bassam Banat, *Palestinian Suicide Martyrs* (Düsseldorf: VDM Verlag, 2011).

27. Joseph Heller, *Catch-22* (New York: Simon & Schuster, 1955).

28. "A Forgotten Hero Stopped the Mỹ Lai Massacre," *Los Angeles Times*, March 16, 2018.

29. Ibid.

30. The definitive new study is Howard Jones, *Mai Lai: Vietnam, 1968, and the Decent into Darkness* (New York: Oxford University Press, 2017), 312–346. In sharp contrast, some British mercenaries who contracted to Sri Lanka in the 1980s as helo pilots took part in gunship massacres of civilians. Phil Miller, *Keenie Meenie: The British Mercenaries Who Got Away with War Crimes* (London: Pluto Press, 2020), 189–214.

31. On the astonishing but also complicated range of public support for Calley that mixed with opposition to the war, see Jones, *Mai Lai*, 342–346.

32. "Trump Pardons Former Soldier Convicted of Murdering an Iraqi Prisoner," *Washington Post*, May 6, 1919; "Trump Clears Three Service Members in War Crimes Cases," *New York Times*, November 15, 2019.

33. "As Pandemic Rages, Sri Lanka's President Pardons a War Criminal," *New York Times*, March 28, 2020.

34. "UN Alleges War Crimes in Ethiopia's Tigray, Urges Eritrea Pullout," defensepost.com, March 5, 2021.

35. Jones, *Mai Lai*.

36. LeMay cut his bombing teeth over Germany before firebombing Japanese cities in 1945. Having incinerated Tokyo and some other cities, he relented and ordered leaflets dropped in advance of future bombing. Printed in Japanese, they read, "Unfortunately, bombs have no eyes. So, in accordance with America's humanitarian policies, the American Air Force, which does not wish to injure innocent people, now

gives you warning to evacuate the cities named and save your lives." It worked: many fled. Curtis Lemay, *Bombing Leaflet*, 1945. (See "Warning Leaflets," www.atomich eritage.org/key-documents/warning-leaflets and https://sciencemuseumofvirgi nia.blogspot.com/2011/01/lemay-bombing-leaflet.html.)

37. On November 29, 1864, the Third Colorado Cavalry under U.S. Army Colonel John Chivington attacked Cheyenne and Arapaho at Sand Creek in what was then the Colorado Territory. They massacred hundreds, including women and children. On November 27, 1868, Lieutenant Colonel George Armstrong Custer's 7th U.S. Cavalry attacked Chief Black Kettle's camp along the Washita River near Cheyenne, Oklahoma. Once again, women and children were slaughtered.

38. Like the white planter class in the Confederacy, the Five Nations were forced to emancipate Black slaves at the end of the Civil War. They refused to allow freed slaves traditional rights of tribal membership, an issue complicated legally and polit- ically by contested sovereignty concerning tribal treaty lands. Alaina E. Roberts, *I've Been Here All the While: Black Freedom on Native Land* (Philadelphia: University of Pennsylvania Press, 2021), 1–71.

39. Rates and kinds of atrocity varied island to island across an immense archipelago. Brian Linn, *The Philippine War, 1899–1902* (Lawrence: University Press of Kansas, 2000), 185–321. A much more personal account is Timothy Russell, "African American Soldiers in the Philippine-American War, 1899–1902," *Journal of African American History* 99, no. 3 (2014): 197–222.

40. Michael Morey, *Fagen: An African American Renegade in the Philippine-American War* (Madison: University of Wisconsin Press, 2019), 69–72.

41. Brett Reilly, "The True Origins of the term Việt Cong," https://thediplomat.com/ 2018/01.

42. Vũ Thanh Thủy, "The Vietnam War in the Eyes of a Vietnamese War Correspondent," in *Republic of Vietnam, 1955–1975*, ed. Tuong Vu and Sean Fear (Ithaca, NY: Cornell University Press, 2019), 127–137.

43. I remember hearing about the Huế killings on TV and radio at the time and reading about them in newspapers as a boy as I followed news about Tết.

44. Samuel Johnson, *Dictionary of the English Language* (1755).

45. Jeffrey Goldberg, "Trump: Americans Who Died in War Are 'Losers' and 'Suckers,'" *The Atlantic*, September 3, 2020.

46. *Inside Higher Ed,* January 20, 2021.

47. Goldberg, "Trump"; Philip Rucker and Carol Leonnig, *A Very Stable Genius* (New York: Penguin, 2017), 169–170; "Trump Calls for 'Patriotic Education,'" *New York Times*, September 18, 2020.

48. "Why should the Devil have all the best tunes?" Methodist saying (1773).

49. An evocative short essay against teaching vengeful hatred in the guise of worship and tradition is Shalom Auslander, "In This Time of War, I Propose We Give Up God," *New York Times*, April 17, 2022.

50. Micheál Ó. Siochrú, "Atrocity, Codes of Conduct and the Irish in the British Civil Wars 1641–1653," *Past & Present* 195 (May 2007): 55–86; John Barratt, *Sieges of the English Civil Wars* (Barnsley: Pen & Sword, 2009), Chapter 11.

51. On parallels and differences between the Irish and Indian independence movements, see the insightful Shereen Ilahi, *Imperial Violence and the Path to Independence: India, Ireland, and Crisis of Empire* (London: I. B. Tauris, 2016).
52. Tom Barry, *Guerrilla Days in Ireland* (Blackrock: Mercier Press reprint, 2011); Dan Breen, *My Fight for Irish Freedom* (Blackrock: Mercier Press reprint, 2011).

Chapter 3

1. Ecclesiastes 3:1 (paraphrase).
2. Maribel Fierro, "Decapitation of Christians and Muslims in the Medieval Iberian Peninsula," *Comparative Literature Studies* 45, no. 2 (2008): 145.
3. "They also serve who only stand and wait." John Milton, "When I Consider How My Light Is Spent" (1673). It was widely quoted in Britain during World War II to help shore up civilian morale among those with fighting men abroad.
4. David Bercuson, *Significant Incident: Canada's Army, the Airborne, and the Murder in Somalia* (Toronto: McClelland & Stewart, 1996).
5. John Price, "Racism, Canadian War Crimes, and the Korean War," *Asia-Pacific Journal* 10, no. 3 (January 15, 2012), article ID 3678. In 2011 a soldier alleged war crimes in Afghanistan but no proof emerged. "JTF2 Command 'Encouraged' War Crimes, Soldier Alleges," CBC News, January 18, 2011. When an Australian special forces scandal broke years later, Canadian authorities attributed the lack of comparable accusations to the handling of the Airborne Regiment scandal in Somalia. "Canadian Military Says 'No Concerns' Raised by Troops Working with Australians," *Global News*, November 24, 2020 https://globalnews.ca.
6. Max Hastings, "Wrath of the Centurions," *London Review of Books*, January 25, 2018.
7. Americans lost 52,173 aircrew in combat but another 25,844 in training accidents, over half in the United States. The United States lost 65,164 aircraft, of which 22,948 went down in combat zones (all causes). Another 21,583 aircraft were lost to accidents back home and 20,633 in accidents overseas. *United States Air Force Statistical Digest World War II*, December 1945, declassified 2011.
8. During production of *Das Boot*, Captain Heinrich Lehmann-Willenbrock of the actual *U-96* portrayed in the film, and one of Nazi Germany's top U-boat aces, and Hans-Joachim Krug, first officer on *U-219*, both served as consultants.
9. Jünger, *In Stahlgewittern*. He rejected Nazi overtures in spite of his virulent rejection of all liberal values and Weimar democracy. See Ziemann on his representativeness in *Violence and the German Soldier*, 63–91.
10. The raid was on the Gran Sasso (Operation *Oak*).
11. Glenn Infield, *Skorzeny: Hitler's Commando* (New York: Military Heritage Press, 1981); Asher Orkaby, "Forgotten Gas Attacks in Yemen Haunt Syria Crisis," *Bloomberg*, 2013, copy at http://www.tinyurl.com/y39wt8uq.
12. Orkaby, "Forgotten Gas Attacks."
13. David L. Robbins, *War of the Rats* (New York; Bantam, 1999), and see the feature film about Vasily Zaitsev at Stalingrad, *Enemy at the Gates* (2001).

14. "'Lady Death' of the Red Army: Lyudmila Pavlichenko," National WWII Museum, March 22, 2021, https://www.nationalww2museum.org/.

15. "Ukrainian Sniper Charcoal," *The Independent*, April 6, 2022; "Elite Russian Sniper Captured," *The Times* March 29, 2022.

16. Stephen Ambrose, *Band of Brothers* (New York: Simon & Schuster, 1992); *Band of Brothers* (HBO, 2001).

17. *Toledo Blade*, October 23, 2003.

18. Nick Turse, "Vietnam War Crimes You Never Heard Of," *History News Network*, n.d. Other examples in Hastings, "Wrath."

19. "'Kill Team' Images," *Spiegel International*, March 23, 2011; "US Army 'Kill Team' in Afghanistan," *Guardian*, March 20, 2011.

20. Ross Caputi et al., *The Sacking of Fallujah* (Amherst: University of Massachusetts Press, 2019) covers three sieges, from 2004 through 2016.

21. Interview, Afghanistan and Iraq wars veteran, July 25, 2021; "Ukrainian Children Used as 'Human Shields,'" *Guardian*, April 3, 2022.

22. Interview, Afghanistan and Iraq wars veteran, July 25, 2021.

23. "A Path to Healing 'Moral Injury,'" *New York Times*, December 9, 2017; S. Maguen et al., "The Impact of Killing in War on Mental Health"; K. D. Drescher et al., "Exploration of the Viability and Usefulness of the Construct of Moral Injury in War Veterans," *Traumatology* 17 (2011): 8–13.

24. Interview, U.S. Army Ranger, July 21, 2021.

25. Williamson Murray et al., "The Impact of Moral Injury on the Wellbeing of UK Military Veterans," *BMC Psychology* (2021), https://www.ncbi.nlm.nih.gov/pmc/articles/PMC8097892/<<<; Brandon Griffin et al., "Moral Injury: An Integrative Review," National Library of Medicine, n.d., https://pubmed.ncbi.nlm.nih.gov; Sonya B. Norman and Shira Maguen, "Moral Injury," U.S. Department of Veterans Affairs, n.d., https://www.ptsd.va.gov/.

26. Interview, Afghanistan veteran officer, July 25, 2021.

27. Interviews with two U.S. Army officers who each served multiple tours in Afghanistan, various dates. One was an intelligence officer on a command staff. The other led combat patrols in both Iraq and Afghanistan and served on a staff.

28. Notable was forced resignation in 2012, after a long-standing extramarital affair was made public, of retired four-star general and director of the Central Intelligence Agency David Petraeus. Although he was widely admired for what was called the "surge" strategy in Iraq, where limited success had more to do with the local "Sunni Awakening" than any military reinforcement, the scandal derailed his bid for the presidency.

29. Interview, Afghanistan veteran officer, July 25, 2021. I was provided the names of the commanders in question and the young Ranger who burned alive. I have withheld them. The logistics brigadier general subsequently worked in the private sector with the McCrystal Group, thereby converting incompetence and negligence in command into a lucrative lobbyist career after leaving the military.

30. Ibid.

31. Ibid.

32. *Report of the Independent Fort Hood Review Committee*, November 6, 2020, partly redacted by the U.S. Army.
33. Interview, U.S. Army officer (ret.), July 25, 2021. The American officer never knew the Iraqi brigadier general's first name. In the shared headquarters he was only refered to as "Saydee (Sir)," or "General Salah."
34. Ibid.
35. Ibid.
36. Ibid.
37. Ibid.
38. Ibid.
39. Ibid.
40. Interview with Iraq/Afghanistan veteran U.S. Army major often in the company of senior generals, July 21, 2021.
41. Ibid.
42. Various interviews, 2010, 2015, and 2020.
43. Interview, retired U.S. Army officer, July 21, 2021.
44. "MoD Has Settled 417 Iraq War Compensation Claims This Year," *Guardian*, November 6, 2021.
45. Hannah O'Grady and Joel Gunter, "SAS unit repeatedly killed Afghan detainees, BBC finds," BBC July 12, 2022. https://www.bbc.com/news/uk-62083196.
46. That soldier's lawsuit for defamation against several Australian news outlets was still underway at the time this was written in March 2022.
47. "Elite Australian Troops Unlawfully Killed 39 Afghans," CNN.com, November 19, 2020; "Australian Special Forces Suspected of 39 Murders," *Japantimes.com*, November 19, 2020.

Chapter 4

1. Joseph Conrad, *Heart of Darkness* (New York: Penguin, 2017).
2. A contrarian view is Gervase Phillips, "Who Shall Say That the Days of Cavalry Are Over?," *War in History* 18, no. 1 (2011): 5–32. On the late World War I revival of cavalry as key scouts and screeners, see Paddy Griffith, *Battle Tactics of the Western Front* (New Haven, CT: Yale University Press, 1994), 159–162.
3. Alfred Lord Tennyson, *The Charge of the Light Brigade* (1854).
4. Richard van Emden, *Meeting the Enemy: The Human Face of War* (London: Bloomsbury, 2013), 38–40.
5. Ibid., 45–46. A detailed account by a German officer of fighting after Mons is Walter Bloem, *The Advance from Mons* (London: Peter Davies, 1930).
6. Jünger, *Storm of Steel* (1920).
7. Fritz Kreisler, *Four Weeks in the Trenches: The War Story of a Violinist* (Boston and New York: Houghton Mifflin Company, 1915. Full text in English at https://net.lib.byu.edu/estu/wwi/memoir/Kreisler/Kreisler.htm.
8. Ibid.
9. Ibid.

10. Ibid.

11. Emden, *Meeting the Enemy*, 49–56.

12. Ibid., 185–186.

13. Charlotte M. Yonge, *A Book of Golden Deeds of All Times and All Lands* (London: Macmillan, 1871). Also see Susan Walton, *Imagining Soldiers and Fathers in the Mid-Victorian Era: Charlotte Yonge's Models of Manliness* (Farnham: Ashgate, 2010), 23–96. It conjured the notion that idealized male and martial virtues should also apply in family life, and in women's lives that were to be lived more vigorously.

14. D. M. Kelsey, ed., *Deeds of Daring by the American Soldier, North and South*, revised ed. (New York: Saalfield, 1903).

15. Bernard Giovanangeli, ed., *Portraits de soldats de la Grande Guerre* (Paris: Editions Bernard Giovanangeli, 2004).

16. Louis Barthas, *Le carnet des guerres de Louis Barthas—tonnelier, 1914–1918* (Paris: Le Editions Decouverte, 1978), especially 18th and 19th notebooks. Available in English as Edward Strauss, ed., *Poilu: The WWI Notebooks of Corporal Louis Barthas, Barrelmaker, 1914–1918* (New Haven, CT: Yale University Press, 2014).

17. This point is well argued by Jay Winter, "The Breaking Point: Surrender 1918," in *How Fighting Ends: A History of Surrender*, ed. Holger Afflerbach and Hew Strachan (Oxford: Oxford University Press, 2010), 299–309.

18. On his experiences at Verdun: Barthas, *Le carnet des guerres*, 161–208.

19. *Poilus* translates literally as "hairy ones." It was a colloquialism akin to "Tommy" or "Doughboy" or "G.I." or "grunt" or "*Landser*" or "*frontoviki*."

20. Strauss, *Poilu*, especially notebooks 10–16, pp. 186–336.

21. French strategy shifted from trying to breakthrough (*percée*) with blunt offensives to deliberate attrition (*grignotage*), or "nibbling away" at German strength and positions to take back the "sacred soil" of France in small bites. See Robert Ferrell, "What's in a Name? The Development of Strategies of Attrition on the Western Front, 1914 -1918," *Historian* 68 (2006): 722–746.

22. The term *verdeckter Militärstreik*, or "hidden army strike," was coined by Wilhelm Deist, senior historian at the Military History Research Office of the Federal Republic of Germany.

23. Strauss, *Poilu*, 7th notebook, pp. 116–119.

24. Ibid., 8th notebook, p. 137.

25. Ibid., 143–145.

26. Ibid., 11th notebook, p. 217.

27. Ibid., 12th notebook, p. 237.

28. Ibid., 244.

29. See also Giovanangeli, *Portraits de soldats*.

30. On the search for, and multiple deceits about, the "first hero" to fire his rifle in France, see Greta Fisher and Lauren Kuntzman, "Pride, Patriotism, and the Press: The Evolving True Story of the First American Shot of World War I," *Indiana Magazine of History* 115, no. 1 (2019): 42–56.

31. Medal of Honor citation for Daniel Daly: https://www.cmohs.org/recipients/daniel-j-daly-1.
32. Medal of Honor citation for Fred Stockham: https://www.cmohs.org/recipients/fred-w-stockham.
33. Cloying local hero stories about World War I were retold as late as the 1950s in the wake of both World War II and the Korean War, proving parochialism about wars distant in time and place never dies. See Margaret Ross, "Herman Davis: Forgotten Hero," *Arkansas Historical Quarterly* 14 (1955): 51–61.
34. "Barkley, John L.," medal citation at http://www.cmohs.org/recipient-detail/2502/barkley-john-l.php.
35. A combat moniker adopted after the Battle of Châteaux-Thierry, May 31, 1918. It was a smallish but key American fight within the much larger battle of Second Marne.
36. John L. Barkley, *Scarlet Fields: The Combat Memoir of a WWI Medal of Honor Hero* (Lawrence: University Press of Kansas, 2012), 181, originally published as *No Hard Feelings!* (1930).
37. Graves, *Goodbye to All That*.
38. Remarque, *All Quiet on the Western Front*.
39. Steven Trout, introduction in Barkley, *Scarlet Fields*, 3.
40. Barkley, *Scarlet Fields*, 183–184.
41. Ibid., 183–185.
42. Ibid., 186–192.

Chapter 5

1. The epigraph is from Randall Kaster, *When Hell Froze: The Story of Norbert Gubbels during World War II* (self-published, 2015), 1–26. Unreliable in some details and its larger conclusions, it is still a sweet and loving personal tribute, compressing 15 years of conversations between Kaster and Gubbels, his father-in-law.
2. Three full legions, and their families, were led by Publius Quinctilius Varus into a slaughter in the forest. Afterward, a second Roman army "in grief and anger, began to bury the bones of the three legions . . . while their wrath rose higher than ever against the foe." Tacitus, *Annals of Imperial Rome* (London: Penguin, 1996), 61–89. A study that presents fresh archaeological evidence but also breathlessly unsupported historical conclusions is Peter Wells, *The Battle That Stopped Rome* (New York: Norton, 2003).
3. Emperor Louis Napoleon was overthrown and the Third Republic founded in France. From inside the Hall of Mirrors in Versailles, Otto von Bismarck proclaimed the king of Prussia to be the kaiser of a Second German Reich.
4. Marc Bloch, *Strange Defeat* (New York: Oxford University Press, 1949), originally published as *L'Étrange Défaite* (1946); Ernst May, *Strange Victory: Hitler's Conquest of France* (New York: Hill & Wang, 2000); Karl-Heinz Frieser, *The Blitzkrieg Legend: The 1940 Campaign in the West* (Annapolis, MD: Naval Institute Press, 2005).
5. On the Americans in Operation *Market Garden*, see John C. McManus, *September Hope* (New York: Penguin, 2012). On the British, see Jonathan Fennell, *Fighting*

the People's War: British and Commonwealth Armies and the 2nd World War (Cambridge: Cambridge University Press, 2019), 551–560.

6. Robin Cross, *Operation Dragoon: The Allied Liberation of the South of France* (New York: Pegasus, 2019), 185–268; Anthony Tucker-Jones, *Operation Dragoon: Liberation of Southern France, 1944* (Barnsley: Pen & Sword, 2009).

7. Mark Zuehlke, *Terrible Victory: First Canadian Army and the Scheldt Estuary Campaign* (Vancouver: Douglas & McIntyre, 2007).

8. A compact but bitter *J'accuse* of American generals by a veteran of the forest battle is Robert Gaigan, "Failure of Leadership: The Huertgen and the Ardennes," *Bulge Bugle,* May 2004, 24.

9. Edward Miller, *A Dark and Bloody Ground: The Hürtgen Forest and the Roer River Dams, 1944–1945* (College Station: Texas A&M University Press, 1995), 93–153; Charles B. MacDonald, *The Battle of the Hürtgen Forest* (Philadelphia: University of Pennsylvania Press, 2003).

10. The real story is in Hugh M. Cole, *The Lorraine Campaign* (1949; Washington, DC: Center of Military History, 1993), 417–449.

11. On Patton's chivalric fantasies and explicitly Arthurian delusions, see Carmine Prioli, "King Arthur in Khaki: The Medievalism of General George S. Patton, Jr." *Studies in Popular Culture* 10, no. 1 (1987): 42–50. A more adulatory view is Jon Mikolashek and Paul Mikolashek, *Blood, Guts, and Grease: George S. Patton in WWI* (Lexington: University Press of Kentucky, 2019). Easily ranking among the worst war poems (or rather, rhyming verse) ever written is George S. Patton, "Absolute War and Peace, November 11, 1918," written while in France in 1918.

12. Canadian 1st Army, British Second Army, U.S. Ninth, First, Third, and Seventh Armies, and French First Army. The main objectives were industrial centers in the Ruhr and Saar regions. Berlin was still the ultimate target, though Eisenhower would later decide to stand aside as the Red Army moved to Berlin.

13. Lieutenant General Courtney H. Hodges, U.S. 1st Army, *War Diary* (1944).

14. Miller, *A Dark and Bloody Ground,* 93–153.

15. "Huertgen Forrest Aflame," *New York Times,* November 19, 1944.

16. "Hürtgen Forest Monument," *Arizona Republic,* October 22, 1995.

17. "1st Battalion, 22nd Infantry Monument to a Fallen German Soldier," https://1-22infantry.org/history4/lengfeld.htm.

18. "Hürtgen Forest Monument."

19. Ibid.

20. John C. Ausland, "Cruel and Now Forgotten, Like an Unmarked Grave," *International Herald Tribune,* April 29, 1993.

21. Photos and transcript at www.1-22infantry.org/history4/lengfeld.html.

22. "Medal of Honor Winner Tells of Four Day Battle in Huertgen Forrest," *New York Times,* May 21, 1945.

23. Graham A. Cosmas and Albert E. Cowdrey, "The Medical Department: Medical Service in the European Theater of Operations," U.S. Army Center of Military History, 1992, Chapter 11.

24. Official history of Company C, cited in Ben Hilton, "Bloody Hamich: Part 1," 16th Infantry Regiment Historical Society, March 23, 2018, https://www.16thinfantry.com/unit-history/bloody-hamich-part-1/.

25. Germans likely were dressed in *Eichenlaubmuster,* or oak leaf camouflage. Beach's men wore standard U.S. Army OD (olive drab) uniforms.

26. Gerald Astor, "Battle of the Hürtgen Forrest," *World War II,* November 2004: 18–20, 185–188.

27. Ibid.

28. "54 Wounded Saved in Rain of Shells: American Medics Brave Fire to Rescue Men Left in Huertgen Forest," *New York Times,* November 13, 1944.

29. Ibid.

30. I discuss the endgame and delusional allure of outmatched panzer armies in the second half of World War II in *Allure of Battle,* 442–489.

31. See Wilhelm Deist, "The Military Collapse of the German Empire," *War in History* 3, no. 2 (1996): 186–207.

32. On Ludendorff's colossal failure as an operational commander, see David Zabecki, *The German 1918 Offensives: A Case Study in the Operational Level of War* (New York: Routledge, 2006); Ian Passingham, *The German Offensives of 1918: Last Desperate Gamble* (Barnsley: Pen & Sword, 2006); Martin Kitchen, *The German Offensives of 1918* (Stroud: Tempus, 2001).

33. See Peter Caddick-Adams, *Snow and Steel: Battle of the Bulge, 1944–1945* (New York: Oxford University Press, 2014); John Eisenhower, *Bitter Woods: The Battle of the Bulge* (New York: Da Capo, 1995); Hugh Cole, *Ardennes: Battle of the Bulge* (Washington, DC: Center for Military History, 1995).

34. "Veteran Recalls WWII Battles," *Omaha World-Herald,* January 7, 2014.

35. Kaster, *When Hell Froze.*

36. On the character and treatment of tree burst wounds, see Headquarters Second Infantry Division, Office of the Surgeon, Medical Bulletin, December 1944, U.S. Army Medical Department, https://achh.army.mil/.

37. "Veteran Recalls World War II Battles."

38. Officially designated CCKW 6X6, the "deuce-and-a-half" was a cargo truck capable of hauling two and a half tons of supplies on-road or off-road, in all weather. The U.S. Army ordered over 800,000 built, in many variations from fire trucks to tankers and troop carriers. The model stayed in service into the 21st century.

39. Kaster, *When Hell Froze,* 48–66.

40. Germans attacked for the last time in Hungary in March 1945, their last offensive anywhere in World War II. It was even more futile than the Ardennes.

41. Both were anti-British, the first playing to IRA sentiments, as was the case during World War I. The second was a cheap thriller set in Azerbaijan in 1919.

42. Joseph Conrad, *The Heart of Darkness* (1899).

43. Multiple witnesses cited in "Veteran Recalls World War II Battles." Kaster says it was "a corporal named Blake" who argued for mercy and led the bearers. But he unreliably misidentifies Lieutenant Welch as "Lt. Wallace," says that it was Blake, not Sweet, who led the way to the arm, and that the rescue comprised three men when it appears to have had four. *When Hell Froze,* 142–143.

44. "Veteran Recalls World War II Battles."
45. Kaster, *When Hell Froze*, 135–152. This claim is not reported in media interviews with others who were there.
46. The terms "combat stress" and "battle fatigue" were World War II American variants for the dysfunctional symptoms of a condition called "soldier's heart" during the American Civil War, "shell shock" and "war neurosis" in World War I, and "post-traumatic stress disorder" or PTSD beginning in 1980, after the Vietnam War.
47. Kaster, *When Hell Froze*, 161–197.

Chapter 6

1. Siegfried Sassoon, "A Soldier's Declaration," written on June 15, 1917, and published in *London Times*, on July 31, 1917, which turned out to be the first day of Third Ypres, or Passchendaele, about which he also famously wrote.
2. Julie Elkner, "*Dedovshchina* and the Committee of Soldiers' Mothers under Gorbachev," *Journal of Power Institutions in Post-Soviet Societies* 1 (January 2004), https://doi.org/10.4000/pipss.243.
3. Masked Russian soldiers wearing green uniforms with no identifying insignia who moved into the secessionist Donbas region in 2014. Most were Special Operations Forces or units of Spetsnaz GRU military intelligence troops.
4. The ideological foundation behind the invasion was Alexsandr Dugin, *The Foundations of Geopolitics: The Geopolitical Future of Russia* (1997). See John Dunlop, "Aleksandr Dugin's Foundations of Geopolitics," in *Demokratizatsiya: The Journal of Post-Soviet Democratization. Institute for European, Russian and Eurasian Studies* (George Washington University). 12 (1): 41. ISSN 1074-6846. OCLC 222569720.
5. "Protester Storms a Live Broadcast," *New York Times*, March 14, 2022; "They're Lying to You," *Guardian*, March 15, 2022.
6. In April 2022, a new law restricted all private organizations, such as the Memorial Human Rights Group in Moscow, that tracked missing soldiers. The issue became acute in the wake of the sinking of the missile cruiser *Moskva*.
7. David Crowe, *Oskar Schindler* (New York: Basic Books, 2007).
8. John Rabe, *The Good Man of Nanking: The Diaries of John Rabe* (New York: Vintage, 2000).
9. Hua-ling Hu and Zhang Lian-hong, eds., *Undaunted Women of Nanking: The Wartime Diaries of Minnie Vautrin and Tsen Shui-fang* (Carbondale: Southern Illinois University Press, 2019).
10. "Abdol Hossein Sardari: An Iranian Hero of the Holocaust," U.S. Holocaust Memorial Museum, www.ushmm.org.
11. Fariborz Mokhtari, "Sardari, Abdol Hossein," in *Encyclopedia of Jews in the Islamic World* (Brill: online edition, 2010)..
12. *Glávnoje upravlénije lageréj,* or "chief administration of the camps." The Soviet forced labor camp system.
13. Alex Kershaw, *The Envoy* (New York: Da Capo, 2010); "Raoul Wallenberg," U.S. Holocaust Museum, https://www.ushmm.org. An overview is Lawrence Baron,

"The Holocaust and Human Decency," *Humboldt Journal of Social Relations* 13, no. 2 (1986): 237–251.

14. On the righteous, see https://www.yadvashem.org/righteous.html; on John Rabe Safety Zone and Memorial Hall, Nanjing University, see www.nju.edu.cn. Also see Emmy Werner, *A Conspiracy of Decency: Rescue of the Danish Jews during World War II* (New York: Basic Books, 2009).

15. https://www.yadvashem.org/righteous/stories/plagge.html; Michael Good, *The Search for Major Plagge: The Nazi Who Saved Jews* (New York: Fordham University Press, 2009).

16. "Some Russian Troops Are Surrendering or Sabotaging Vehicles Rather Than Fighting, a Pentagon Official Says," *New York Times*, March 1, 2022.

17. "Ukraine Offers Amnesty and Money to Russian Soldiers Who Lay Down Weapons," *National Post*, February 28, 2022.

18. "Bodies of Russian Soldiers Are Piling Up," CNN, March 24, 2022.

19. Richard Bessel, "The German Surrender of 1945," in Holger Afflerbach and Hew Strachan, editors, *How Fighting Ends: A History of Surrender* (Oxford: Oxford University Press, 2010): 395–406.

20. Jacques Mallet du Pan, "A l'exemple de Saturne, la révolution dévore ses enfants," in *Considérations sur la nature de la Révolution de France* (1793); Bastiaan Willems, *Violence in Defeat. The Wehrmacht on German Soil, 1944–1945*. Cambridge: Cambridge University Press, 2021: 244–258, 276–283.

21. Steven Welch, "Commemorating 'Heroes of a Special Kind': Deserter Monuments in Germany," *Journal of Contemporary History* 47, no. 2 (2012): 370–401.

22. See Omer Bartov, *Hitler's Army: Soldiers, Nazis, and War in the Third Reich* (Oxford: Oxford University Press, 1992).

23. This changed status applied to any territory annexed to Germany: Alsace-Lorraine, Austria, Danzig, Eupen-Malmedy, and the Sudetenland.

24. "Austria Unveils World War Two Deserters' Memorial," *BBC News*, October 24, 2014.

25. Ibid.

26. J. M. Diehl, *The Thanks of the Fatherland: German Veterans after the Second World War* (Chapel Hill: University of North Carolina Press, 1993).

27. A 2009 paper was published by the U.S. Army War College that laid out rising issues presented by the ubiquity of cameras in war zones, in cell phones carried by insurgents, or in phones and military equipment of American soldiers. Cori Dauber, "YouTube War," Strategic Studies Institute, November 2009.

28. "Ukraine Separatists Rewrite History of 1930s Famine," *New York Times*, April 29, 2015.

29. George Orwell, *1984* (London: Harcourt Brace, 1949).

30. The T-64 was a mainstay of Soviet armor from the mid-1960s. Redesigned and upgraded by the Red Army in 1985, it was supplemented by the cheaper T-72 and more advanced T-80. It was not used much in Afghanistan. Ukraine was the first war where the T-64 saw significant combat.

31. "It was a bright cold day in April, and the clocks were striking thirteen" (Orwell, *1984*, 1).

32. "Ukraine's Neglected and Battered Army Inspires Citizens to Pitch In," *New York Times*, September 22, 2014.

33. "We Didn't Kill Them," *Sydney Morning Herald*, January 31, 2015.

34. 1st Galician or 14th Waffen-Grenadier Division der SS.

35. Designated a "global terrorist group" by the United States in 2020. Use of White Supremacist mercenaries represents a much wider and ongoing trend to employ disownable soldiers-for-hire, as well as new patterns of chronic smaller wars waged without formal state engagement or under the laws of war.

36. The anti-Semitic German composer Richard Wagner was a favorite of Hitler and other leading Nazis. In deliberate contrast, Western special forces volunteers on the Ukrainian side called themselves the "Mozart Group."

37. "We Didn't Kill Them."

38. Photographs of unnamed Russian officer from his phone, and of Alexei Chaban in his tank, available in Reuters, "On Ukraine Battlefield, One Act of Mercy Becomes an Internet Meme," January 29, 2015, https://www.reuters.com/article/idIN113 976284820150129.

39. Ibid.

40. Interview, retired U.S. Army major, July 21, 2021. I was told the same thing in 2015 by two other active duty U.S. Army majors on leave in Boston.

41. Email exchange, March 22, 2022. Name withheld.

42. Conversations at the Ministry of Foreign Affairs, Kabul, August 2011.

43. Interview, retired U.S. Army major, July 21, 2021.

44. "U.S. Soldiers Told to Ignore Sexual Abuse of Boys by Afghan Allies," *New York Times*, September 20, 2015.

45. Ibid.

46. Miller was a four-star general in the U.S. Army, onetime Delta Force commander, and in charge of NATO's Resolute Support Mission from September 2018 to July 2021.

47. "Top Afghan Commander Raziq Killed in Kandahar Gun Attack," BBC News, October 19, 2018.

48. "An Afghan Boy's Rape and Death Prompt a Rare Response: Arrests," *New York Times*, October 9, 2020.

49. Interview, retired U.S. Army officer, July 21, 2021.

50. Interviews with two active duty U.S. Army majors on leave in Boston, March 2015. Nearly 200 female soldiers embedded in cultural support teams assigned to Special Operations Forces in Afghanistan from 2011 to 2014.

51. Interviews with various U.S. Army officers, 2020 and 2021.

52. "I flew o'er alpine valleys red with bright poppies, but not the fake kind that you wear to Remember. Opium blooms bought me more guns and jalopies each fighting season, open from May to November." Kali Altsoba, "Universal Soldier," in *Rikugun* (2019). ASIN: B0768JYTS9.

53. "U.S. Asks Taliban to Spare Its Embassy in Coming Fight for Kabul," *Washington Post*, August 13, 2021.

54. "How horrible, fantastic, incredible it is that we should be digging trenches and trying on gas-masks here because of a quarrel in a far away country between people

of whom we know nothing." Neville Chamberlain, on the day before the Munich Conference, on Czechoslovakia, September 28, 1938.

55. "Pentagon Briefing with Secretary Rumsfeld," *Washington Post*, November 19, 2001.

56. "Taliban Fighters Execute 22 Afghan Commandos as They Try to Surrender," CNN. com, July 13, 2021.

57. Carter Malkasian, senior adviser to General Joseph Dunford, Chairman of the Joint Chiefs of Staff under Presidents Obama and Trump, in "How America Lost Its Way in Afghanistan," *New York Times*, August 17, 2021. And see Carter Malkasian, *The American War in Afghanistan: A History* (New York: Oxford: Oxford University Press, 2021); Craig Whitlock, *The Afghanistan Papers: A Secret History of the War* (New York: Simon & Schuster, 2021).

58. "Officers with PhDs Advising War Effort," *Washington Post*, February 5, 2007. Officer intellectuals and academics were behind the "surge" in Iraq led by General Petraeus. They brought it to Afghanistan next, where it failed badly.

Chapter 7

1. The epigraph is from John Dorney, "Today in Irish History, The Truce, 11 July 1921," *The Irish Story*, July 11, 2011, https://www.theirishstory.com/2011/07/11/today-in-irish-history-%e2%80%93-july-11-1921-%e2%80%93-the-truce-2/#.Yp4p AXbMJPY.

2. Four million colonial soldiers, or *troupes indigènes*, from overseas empires fought in World War I, of whom 1.5 million were white (Australian, Canadian, New Zealander). About 1.5 million from India fought, and 2 million from Africa. Santanu Das, "Experiences of Colonial Troops," *British Library*, January 29, 2014; John Connor, *Someone Else's War: Fighting for the British Empire in World War I* (New York: I. B. Taurus, 2019). They were shamefully treated by the British after the war. In 2021 a Commonwealth War Graves Commission investigation showed that as many as 350,000 colonial troops were buried in shallow and unmarked graves or simply dumped in unkempt cemeteries.

3. Emma Hanna, "The Christmas Truce," December 3, 2014, blogs.ac.kent.uk.

4. Emden, *Meeting the Enemy*, 80.

5. Mike Dash, "Story of the WWI Christmas Truce," *SmithsonianMag.com*, December 23, 2011. The best overall account is Malcolm Brown and Shirley Seaton, *Christmas Truce* (London: Pan, 1984).

6. Marc Ferro et al., *Meetings in No Man's Land: Christmas 1914 and Fraternization in the Great War* (London: Constable & Robinson, 2007).

7. Ibid.

8. Emden, *Meeting the Enemy*, 82–83.

9. Ibid., 83–84.

10. Hanna, "Christmas Truce."

11. Dash, "Story of the WWI Christmas Truce."

12. It locates in one place many actual incidents from up and down the lines. Despite that and other weaknesses, it captures the spirit of the moment better than most

films. Cf. *Oh, What a Lovely War!* (1969). A vicious review of *Joyeux Noël* that almost wilfully misses the mark appeared in the *New York Times* on March 3, 2006.

13. Christian Carion, "How France Has Forgotten the Christmas Truce Soldiers," BBC News, December 25, 2014.

14. The veracity of accounts of football games between opposing sides is not helped by inclusion in Robert Graves's endlessly mocking *Goodbye to All That* (1929), which cannot be relied upon as a memoir but is a work of sharp fiction.

15. Carion, "How France Has Forgotten."

16. Terri Blom Crocker, *The Christmas Truce: Myth, Memory, and the First World War* (Lexington: University Press of Kentucky, 2015), 4.

17. Emden, *Meeting the Enemy*, 193–195. "Allemands" was Tommy slang for Germans, derived of course from French. More commonly, British soldiers called Germans "Huns."

18. Friedrich Kohn quoted in Emma Hanna, "An Easter Truce, 1916," www.gateways fww.org.uk/news/easter-truce-1916.

19. Emden, *Meeting the Enemy*, 195–197.

20. Joseph E. Persico, "Wasted Lives on Armistice Day," *Militarytimes.com*, January 12, 2018.

21. Ibid. Persico provides an excellent summary of committee hearings that descended into base political sparring as the Wilson administration faded.

22. Gerald Linderman, *The World within War: America's Combat Experience in World War II* (New York: Free Press, 1997), 90–98.

23. Martin S. Alexander, "French Surrender in 1940," in Afflerbach and Strachan, *How Fighting Ends*, 331–332.

24. George Lane obituary, *Daily Telegraph*, March 27, 2010.

25. "Waterloo was won on the playing fields of Eton" is a remark attributed to Wellington but likely apocryphal.

26. Petra Rau, *Our Nazis: Representations of Fascism in Contemporary Literature and Film* (Edinburgh: Edinburgh University Press, 2013), 129–131.

27. Martin Gutman, "Debunking the Myth of the Volunteers," *Contemporary European History* 22, no. 4 (2013): 585–607.

28. "A Glimpse of Peace in Afghanistan: With Fighting Paused, Soldiers Invite Taliban over for Chicken," *Washington Post*, February 26, 2020.

29. See below.

30. A stiff political science study that is nevertheless useful as a reference is Virginia Fortna, *Peacetime: Ceasefire Agreements and the Durability of Peace* (Princeton, NJ: Princeton University Press, 2004).

31. United Nations, "Now Is the Time for a Collective New Push for Peace and Reconciliation," March 23, 2020, https://www.un.org/en/globalceasefire.

Chapter 8

1. David McLean, "Surgeons of the Opium War: The Navy on the China Coast, 1840–42," *English Historical Review* (April 2006): 492.

2. Ibid., 493.

3. Ibid., 498–503.

4. An overview of nurses on the Western Front in World War I is Emily Mayhew, *Wounded* (New York: Oxford University Press, 2014), 82–103.

5. Evelyn Bolster, *Sisters of Mercy in the Crimean War* (Cork: Mercier, 1965)

6. Mark Bostridge, *Florence Nightingale: The Making of an Icon* (New York: Farrar, Straus and Giroux, 2008). A blistering study is F. B. Smith, *Florence Nightingale: Reputation and Power* (New York: Palgrave, 1982).

7. Barbara Maling, "American Nightingales: The Influence of Florence Nightingale on Southern Nurses during the American Civil War," in *One Hundred Years of Wartime Nursing Practices, 1854–1953*, ed. Jane Brooks and Christine E. Hallett (Manchester: Manchester University Press, 2015), 42–57; Jane Schultz, "Nurse as Icon: Florence Nightingale's Impact on Women in the American Civil War," in Lewis and Gleeson, *Civil War as Global Conflict*, 235–252. On Clara Barton and Civil War nursing, see Stephen B. Oates, *Woman of Valor: Clara Barton and the Civil War* (New York: Free Press, 1995).

8. John Greenwood and F. Clifton Barry, *Medics at War: Military Medicine from Colonial Times to the 21st Century* (Annapolis, MD: Naval Institute Press, 2005), 33–35

9. Medal of Honor citation for Mary Edwards Walker, Congressional Medal of Honor Society, https://www.cmohs.org/recipients/mary-e-walker; "Why the U.S. Revoked Hundreds of Medals of Honor," https://www.military.com/.

10. Mary Walker, *Hit: Essays on Women's Rights* (New York: American News Company, 1871).

11. Chris Schoeman, *Angels of Mercy: Foreign Women in the Anglo-Boer War* (New York: Random, 2013).

12. Charlotte Dale, "Traversing the Veldt with 'Tommy Atkins,'" in Brooks and Hallett, *One Hundred Years of Wartime Nursing*, 58–77.

13. A fine case study of national medical response to the immensity of World War I is Kirsty Harris, *More Than Bombs and Bandages: Australian Army Nurses at Work in World War I* (Newport, NSW: Big Sky Publishing, 2011).

14. Laurie S. Stoff, *Russia's Sisters of Mercy and the Great War: More Than Binding Men's Wounds* (Lawrence: University Press of Kansas, 2015), 15–18.

15. Wendy Moore, *No Man's Land* (New York: Basic Books, 2021).

16. Christine Hallett, "'This Fiendish Mode of Warfare': Nursing the Victims of Gas Poisoning," in Brooks and Hallett, *One Hundred Years of Wartime Nursing*, 81–100.

17. Christine Hallett, *Nurse Writers of the Great War* (Manchester: Manchester University Press, 2016), 187–210. An unvarnished account in short story form first published in 1916 was banned in Britain and the United States during the war. Ellen La Motte, *The Backwash of War* (Baltimore, MD: Johns Hopkins University Press, 2019).

18. Sarah Glassford, *Mobilizing Mercy: A History of the Canadian Red Cross* (Montreal: McGill-Queen's University Press, 2017), 81–128.

19. See Jan Bassett, *Guns and Brooches: Australian Army Nursing from the Boer War to the Gulf War* (Melbourne: Oxford University Press, 1992); Cynthia Toman,

An Officer and a Lady: Canadian Military Nursing and the Second World War (Vancouver: University of British Columbia Press, 2008).

20. See Elizabeth Norman, *We Band of Angels: The Untold Story of the American Women Trapped on Bataan* (New York: Random House, 2013).

21. On Korea, Vietnam, and after, see Mary Sarnecky, "Army Nurses in 'the Forgotten War,'" *American Journal of Nursing* 101, no. 11 (2001): 45–49; Kara Dixon Vuic, *Officer, Nurse, Woman: The Army Nurse Corps in the Vietnam War* (Baltimore, MD: Johns Hopkins University Press, 2010); Elizabeth Scannell-Desch and Mary Ellen Doherty, *Nurses in War: Voices from Iraq and Afghanistan* (New York: Springer, 2012). On medics in Vietnam, see Joe Parner, *SOG Medic: Stories from Vietnam and Over the Fence* (Newbury: Casemate, 2018); Elizabeth Norman, *Women at War: The Story of Fifty Military Nurses Who Served in Việtnam* (Philadelphia: University of Pennsylvania Press, 1990).

22. Kirsten Holmstedt, *Band of Sisters: American Women at War in Iraq* (Mechanicsburg, PA: Stackpole, 2008); Gayle Lemmon, *Ashley's War: The Untold Story of a Team of Women Soldiers on the Special Ops Battlefield* (New York: Harper, 2016).

23. "'We Are Not Afraid of Death': The Ukrainian Women Taking Up Arms against Russia," *Vice*, March 4, 2022.

24. A rare autobiographical novel by a Russian woman soldier is Tatiana L. Dubinskaya, *In the Trenches: A Russian Woman Soldier's Story of World War I* (Lincoln, NE: Potomac, 2020). She fought from 1916 to 1917, disguised as a man.

25. Sulfanilamide, an innovative disinfectant. It also came in tablet form.

26. Cosmas and Cowdrey, U.S. Army "Medical Department,"

27. https://www.cmohs.org/recipients/alfred-l-wilson; Cosmas and Cowdrey, U.S. Army "Medical Department." More on U.S. medics at WW2 US Medical Research Centre, https://www.med-dept.com/.

28. Linda Hervieux, *Forgotten: The Untold Story of D-Day's Black Heroes* (New York: Harper, 2015), 201–204, 212–214, 241–242, 251–254.

29. "He Saved Scores of Lives on D-Day," *Washington Post*, September 8, 2020. Also see the combat medic memoir of a Black veteran of World War II and Korea, Joseph Brown, *Black Soldier of Mercy* (Timberlake, NC: Righter, 2008).

30. Medal of Honor Society, "Desmond Thomas Doss," www.cmohs.org/recipients/desmond-t-doss.

31. Ibid.

32. Linderman, *The world Within War*, 105.

33. Ibid.; Cecil Currey, *Follow Me and Die: Destruction of an American Division in World War II* (New York: Stein & Day, 1984), 240–243.

34. "Arnhem Bridge," www.pegasusarchive.org.

35. Cosmas and Cowdrey, U.S. Army, "Medical Department."

36. Currey, *Follow Me and Die*, 95.

37. Mike Timko, "A German Medic Saved My Life," WWII Veterans' Memories, n.d., https://ww2veteransmemories.org/a-german-medic-saved-my-life/. See also Timko's obituary, at Parzynski Funeral Home, Tribute Archive, https://www.tribute archive.com/obituaries/19590438/Mike-Timko.

38. Cosmas and Cowdrey, U.S. Army "Medical Department."

39. Cosmas and Cowdrey, U.S. Army "Medical Department."

40. Linderman, *The World within War,* 134–135. During the Russian invasion of Ukraine in 2022 there were multiple confirmed reports of snipers shooting at medics and ambulances. See, for instance, *Sky News,* March 22, 2022.

41. Alessandra Colaianni, "A Long Shadow: Nazi Doctors, Moral Vulnerability and Contemporary Medical Culture," *Journal of Medical Ethics* 38, no. 7 (2012): 435–438.

42. "The Iowa Farm Boy Saved by an Enemy Doctor," *Des Moines Register,* September 30, 2015.

43. Cosmas and Cowdrey, U.S. Army "Medical Department."

44. Ronald Glasser, *Broken Bodies, Shattered Minds: A Medical Odyssey from Việtnam to Afghanistan* (Palisades, NY: History Publishing, 2011), 110. On PTSD and brain injuries, 113–172.

45. Ibid., 41.

46. Ibid., 65.

47. On wounds, see Mary Louise Roberts, *Sheer Misery: Soldiers in Battle in WWII* (Chicago: University of Chicago Press, 2021), Chapter 4.

48. https://www.doctorswithoutborders.org/who-we-are/history.

49. Officially called Syria Civil Defense: https://www.whitehelmets.org/en/.

50. International Defense Legion.

51. "Syrian Mercenaries Deploy to Russia en route to Ukrainian Battlefields," *New York Times,* March 31, 2022.

52. "'I Just Can't Stand By': American Veterans Join the Fight in Ukraine," *New York Times,* March 5, 2022.

53. "War Doctor David Nott: 'The Adrenaline Was Overpowering,'" *Guardian,* February 24, 2019.

54. David Nott, *War Doctor: Surgery on the Front Line* (London: Picador, 2019), 175–240.

55. Ibid., 303–348.

Chapter 9

1. A transcript of McCain's Senate statement is at https://www.usatoday.com/story/news/politics/2014/12/09/john-mccain-statement-cia-terror-report/20144015/.

2. Catherine Holmes, "Basil II the Bulgar-Slayer: Mutilation and Prisoners of War in the Middle Ages," in Afflerbach and Strachan, *How Fighting Ends,* 85–95.

3. Daniel E. Sutherland, "Guerrilla Warfare, Democracy, and the Fate of the Confederacy," *Journal of Southern History,* May 2002, 266–269.

4. Ibid., 284–289.

5. Francis Clarke, *War Stories: Suffering and Sacrifice in the Civil War North* (Chicago: University of Chicago Press, 2011); Drew Faust, *This Republic of Suffering: Death and the American Civil War* (New York: Vintage, 2008); Aaron Sheehan-Dean, "*Lex Talionis* in the U.S. Civil War: Retaliation and the Limits of Atrocity," in *Civil War as Global Conflict,* ed. Simon Lewis and David Gleeson (Columbia: University of South Carolina, 2014), 172–189.

6. Faust, *Republic of Suffering,* 50–51.

7. "Civil War Massacre Left Nearly 200 Black Soldiers Murdered," *Washington Post,* October 28, 2018. Also see Faust, *Republic of Suffering,* 44–48.

8. See Jonathan Steplyk, *Fighting Means Killing: Civil War Soldiers and the Nature of Combat* (Lawrence: University Press of Kansas, 2018), 189–225.

9. David Silkenat, *Raising the White Flag: How Surrender Defined the American Civil War* (Chapel Hill: University of North Carolina Press, 2019), 295.

10. Jünger, *War Diary,* quoted in Ziemann, *Violence and the German Soldier,* 75.

11. Charles Rollings, *Prisoners of War: Voices from Behind the Wire in the Second World War* (London: Ebury Press, 2008), 5–6.

12. An unusually honest and insightful discussion is James Weingartner, "Americans, Germans, and War Crimes: Converging Narratives from 'The Good War,'" *Journal of American History* 94, no. 4 (2008): 1164–1183.

13. Linderman, *The World within War,* 129–130.

14. Patrick Brode, *Casual Slaughters and Accidental Judgments: Canadian War Crimes Prosecutions, 1944–1948* (Toronto: University of Toronto Press, 1997), 105. Issuing a "no quarter" order denying even the possibility of combat mercy constitutes a war crime in modern international military law.

15. Ibid., 45.

16. A set of comparative essays is Kent Fedorowich and Bob Moore, eds., *Prisoners-of-War and Their Captors in World War II* (Oxford: Berg, 1996).

17. James Weingartner, "Trophies of War: U.S. Troops and the Mutilation of Japanese War Dead, 1941–1945," *Pacific Historical Review* 61, no. 1 (1992): 53–67.

18. Allan Koop, *Stark Decency: German Prisoners of War in a New England Village* (Hanover, NH: University of New England Press, 2000); Kevin Hall, "Befriended Enemy: German Prisoners of War in Michigan," *Michigan Historical Review* 41, no. 1 (2015): 57–79. Over 425,000 Axis POWs were held in U.S. camps, mostly Germans and Italians but also a few Japanese. In October 1944, 35,000 Axis prisoners were held in Canadian work camps, guarded by World War I veterans. Canadian War Museum, www.warmuseum.ca.

19. Ralph Young, *Dissent: The History of an American Idea* (New York: NYU Press, 2015), 394.

20. "Two Gravestones with Swastikas," CNN.com, December 25, 2020. Also see Antonio Thompson, "Winning the War behind the Lines: Axis POWs at Fort Benning," *Kentucky Historical Society* 105, no. 3 (2007): 417–460.

21. David Miller, *Mercy Ships: The Untold Story of Prisoner-of-War Exchanges in World War II* (New York: Bloomsbury, 2008).

22. A rare look at conditions for Axis POWs in Soviet captivity is Günter Bischof and Barbara Stelzl-Marx, "Lives behind Barbed Wire," in *Austrian Lives,* ed. Günter Bischof et al. (New Orleans, LA: University of New Orleans Press, 2012).

23. Linderman gets causation exactly backward, writing: "There followed a war that rapidly descended to the uttermost barbarity. Stung by partisan activity, the Germans adopted draconian countermeasures" (*The World within War,* 100).

24. *Hilfswillige* or *Hilfsfreiwillige,* military auxiliaries or "volunteer helpers" assigned to shrinking Wehrmacht and Waffen-SS combat units in desperate need of military laborers, cooks, and so on, so that all the Germans could fight instead.

25. The best single-volume history is Edward Drea, *Japan's Imperial Army: Its Rise and Fall, 1853–1945* (Lawrence: University Press of Kansas, 2009).

26. Ian Toll, *Twilight of the Gods: War in the Western Pacific, 1944–1945* (New York: W. W. Norton, 2020), 456.

27. A firsthand combat account is Eugene Sledge, *With the Old Breed at Peleliu and Okinawa.* [New York: H. Holt and Company, 1946] Novato: Presidio Press, 1981. Also see Ernie Pyle, *Last Chapter* (NOOK Book, 2015).

28. On savage fighting in New Guinea, see Edward J. Drea, *In the Service of the Emperor: Essays on the Imperial Japanese Army* (Lincoln: University of Nebraska Press, 1998), 103–104. Also see Morris Low, "Remembering the War in New Guinea: Japanese Perceptions of the Enemy," June 1, 2004, Australian War Memorial, http://ajrp.awm.gov.au/ajrp/remember.nsf/Web-Printer/46948CEA9 B54ADA6CA256A99001D9F0B /.

29. On Australian experience as prisoners of the Japanese see "Stolen Years: Australian Prisoner of War," https://anzacportal.dva.gov.au/resources/stolen-years-austral ian-prisoners-war.

30. Yuki Tanaka, *Hidden Horrors: Japanese War Crimes in World War II* (Boulder, CO: Westview Press, 1997); "Hidden Horrors," Alliance for Human Research Protection, December 10, 2014; "Japanese Ate Indian POWs, Used Them as Live Targets in World War II," *Times of India*, August 11, 2014.

31. Timothy Lang Francis, "'To Dispose of the Prisoners': The Japanese Executions of American Aircrew at Fukuoka, Japan, during 1945," *Pacific Historical Review* 66, no. 4 (1997): 469–501.

32. "Mario Tonelli: April 3, 1946 Death March," Today in History, April 3, 2018, www. todayinhistory.blog/tag/mario-tonelli.

33. See John Wyatt, *No Mercy from the Japanese: A Survivors Account of the Burma Railway and the Hellships 1942–1945* (Havertown, PA: Pen & Sword, 2009); Gregory Michno, *Death on the Hellships: Prisoners at Sea in the Pacific War* (Annapolis, MD: Naval Institute Press, 2001).

34. Obituary, Mario Tonelli, January 7, 2003, https://news.nd.edu/news/mario-g-motts-tonelli-1916–2003-ex-irish-star-survived-bataan/.

35. Based on the novel by Pierre Boulle, *Le Pont de la rivière Kwaï* (1952).

36. David McNeil, "Building Bridges over Hate," *Asia-Pacific Journal*, September 28, 2005, https://apjjf.org/-David-McNeill/1762/article.html.

37. Ibid.

38. Ibid.

39. Eric Lomax obituary, *New York Times*, October 10, 2012.

40. McNeil, "Building Bridges over Hate."

41. Eric Lomax, *The Railway Man: A POW's Searing Account of War, Brutality and Forgiveness* (New York: W. W. Norton, 2014); McNeil, "Building Bridges over Hate."

42. "The past is a foreign country: they do things differently there." Leslie P. Hartley, *The Go-Between* (1953).

43. Quoted in McNeil, "Building Bridges over Hate."

44. Compare the differing treatment of Allied prisoners in Gavan Daws, *Prisoners of the Japanese: POWs of World War II in the Pacific* (New York: William Morrow,

1994) with treatment of Japanese prisoners by the Allies in Ulrich Strauss, *Anguish of Surrender: Japanese POWs of World War II* (Seattle: University of Washington Press, 2005).

45. Haruko Taya Cook and Theodore Cook, *Japan at War: An Oral History* (New York: New Press, 1992), 378.

46. Allison Gilmore, "'We Have Been Reborn': Japanese Prisoners and the Allied Propaganda War in the Southwest Pacific," *Pacific Historical Review*, May 1995, 195–215; Law, "Remembering the War."

47. Gerald A. Meehl, *One Marine's War: A Combat Interpreter's Quest for Mercy in the Pacific* (Annapolis, MD: Naval Institute Press, 2011).

48. On British POWs in North Korean and Chinese custody, see Cyril Cunningham, *No Mercy, No Leniency: Communist Mistreatment of British Prisoners of War in Korea* (Barnsley: Pen & Sword, 2001).

49. "Chaplain Gets Medal of Honor 62 Years after Death," *AP News*, April 6, 2013; U.S. Army medal citation, www.army.mil/medalofhonor/kapaun/.

50. He was awarded a Medal of Honor posthumously in 2013. Eight years later, his body was discovered in an unmarked grave in Hawaii. See William Latham, *Cold Days in Hell: American POWs in Korea* (College Station: Texas A&M University Press, 2014), 74–77, 131–132, 142–143, 154–155.

51. David Cheng Chang, *The Hijacked War: The Story of Chinese POWs in the Korean War* (Stanford, CA: Stanford University Press, 2020), Chapters 2 and 3.

52. Ibid., 106–107.

53. Ibid., Chapters 5–7.

54. Cheryl Benard et al., *Battle behind the Wire: U.S. Prisoner and Detainee Operations from World War II to Iraq* (Santa Monica, CA: RAND, 2011), 17–32

55. Cathal J. Nolan, "Americans in the Gulag: Detention of U.S. Citizens by Russia and the Onset of the Cold War, 1944–1949," *Journal of Contemporary History* 25, no. 4 (1990): 523–545; Chang, *The Hijacked War,* Chapters 11–16. Chang correctly recenters the POW question in protracted negotiations. On U.S. politics and POWs, see Rosemary Foot, *A Substitute for Victory* (Ithaca, NY: Cornell University Press, 1990).

56. "Lost Empire," *Guardian*, September 2, 2019.

57. Caroline Elkins, *Imperial Reckoning: The Untold Story of Britain's Gulag in Kenya* (New York: Henry Holt, 2005). See also Caroline Elkins, *Legacy of Violence: A History of the British Empire* (New York: Random House, 2022).

58. The literature is now extensive. See David French, *The British Way in Counter-Insurgency, 1945–1967* (Oxford: Oxford University Press, 2012); Austin Long, *Soul of Armies: Counterinsurgency Doctrine and Military Culture in the US and UK* (Ithaca, NY: Cornell University Press, 2016), 152–169; Brian Drohan, *Brutality in an Age of Human Rights: Activism and Counterinsurgency at the End of British Empire* (Ithaca, NY: Cornell University Press, 2017).

59. "In Reconciliation Act, Macron Acknowledges Truth of Algerian Lawyer's Death," *Washington Post*, March 20, 2022.

60. "Afghan Interpreter for US Army Beheaded by Taliban," *CNN*, July 23, 2021.

Chapter 10

1. The epigraph is quoted from "Panic Grips Some Cities as Russia Tightens Cordon," *New York Times*, March 4, 2022.
2. On humanitarian intervention as policy and problem, see Philip Cunliffe, *Cosmopolitan Dystopia* (Manchester: Manchester University Press, 2020). Too Abstractly legalistic is Jai Galliott, ed., *Force Short of War in Modern Conflict: Jus ad Vim* (Edinburgh: Edinburgh University Press, 2019).
3. John Grenier, *The First Way of War, American War Making of the Frontier, 1607–1814* (New York: Cambridge University Press, 2005).
4. Alfred Cave, *The Pequot War* (Boston: University of Massachusetts Press, 1996).
5. See Rod Andrew, *The Life and Times of General Andrew Pickens: Revolutionary War Hero, American Founder* (Chapel Hill: University of North Carolina Press, 2017).
6. Quoted in Daniel S. Dupre, *Alabama's Frontiers and the Rise of the Old South* (Bloomington: Indiana University Press, 2018), 211.
7. Shannon French, *Code of the Warrior* (New York: Rowman & Littlefield, 2017), 164–169.
8. Thomas Kanon, "'A Slow, Laborious Slaughter': The Battle of Horseshoe Bend," *Tennessee Historical Quarterly* 58, no. 1 (Spring 1999): 2–15.
9. Nathanial Hawthorne, *The Scarlet Letter* (Cambridge: Cambridge University Press, 2010).
10. Claudio Saunt, *Unworthy Republic: The Dispossession of Native Americans and the Road to Indian Territory* (New York: W. W. Norton, 2020).
11. T. Hunt Tooley, "'All the People Are Now Guerillas': The Warfare of Sherman, Sheridan, and Lincoln, and the Brutality of the Twentieth Century," *Independent Review* 11, no. 3 (2007): 357–358.
12. Article 16. Text online at Yale Law School: Avalon Project, https://avalon.law.yale.edu/. And see Burrus Carnahan, "Lincoln, Lieber, and the Laws of War: The Origins and Limits of the Principle of Military Necessity," *American Journal of International Law* 92, no. 2 (April 1998): 213–231.
13. Articles 17 and 21.
14. Article 29.
15. I make the argument at length in *Allure of Battle*.
16. Thavolia Glymph, *The Women's Fight: The Civil War's Battles for Home, Freedom, and Nation* (Chapel Hill: University of North Carolina Press, 2020).
17. Tooley goes much too far by claiming it is "quite comparable" to rank Sherman's war in the Deep South against the secessionist planter class and his application of collective guilt to Hitler's genocidal scheme for *Lebensraum* and vaguely to "Stalin's ideas on the subject" ("'All the People,'" 360–365). Of course, it is not.
18. David A. Nichols, "The Other Civil War: Lincoln and the Indians," *Minnesota History* 44, no. 1 (Spring 1974): 1–15.
19. Ibid.
20. Ibid. In detail, see Scott W. Berg, *38 Nooses: Lincoln, Little Crow, and the Beginning of the Frontier's End* (New York: Pantheon, 2012).

21. Lance Janda, "Shutting the Gates of Mercy: The American Origins of Total War, 1860–1880," *Journal of Military History* 59 (January 1995): 7–26.Halleck quoted at 18.

22. A superb, concise argument tracing the tactics of the American Civil War through to the western suppression campaigns of 1865–1880 is Janda, "Shutting the Gates of Mercy." Sherman quoted at 15. An older account that touches this theme is Robert Utley, *Frontier Regulars: The United States Army and the Indian, 1866–1891* (New York: Macmillan, 1984).

23. Utley, *Frontier Regulars*.

24. Quoted in Janda, "Shutting the Gates of Mercy," 22.

25. Ibid., 21.

26. Ibid.

27. Quoted in Thomas C. Leonard, "White and the Army Blue: Empathy and Anger in the American West," *American Quarterly* 26, no. 2 (1974): 180, https://www.jstor.org/stable/2712234. Original in George A. Custer, *My Life on the Plains* (Norman: University of Oklahoma Press, 1962), 19–22.

28. Robert G. Athearn, *William Tecumseh Sherman and the Settlement of the West* (Norman: University of Oklahoma Press, 1956), 674–67, 82–83, 99–101.

29. Philip Sheridan, *Personal Memoirs* (New York: Webster, 1888), 88–89.

30. Quoted in Leonard, "White and Blue," 181.

31. Ibid.

32. Called "Hellmira" by Rebel inmates, this barracks prison in Elmira, New York, was built to hold 4,000 prisoners. It swelled in mid-1864 to over 12,000. Of those, nearly 3,000 died over the winter months, mostly from starvation and exposure to harsh winter weather. Michael Horigan, *Death Camp of the North: The Elmira Civil War Prison Camp* (Mechanicsburg, PA: Stackpole, 2002).

33. Quoted in Leonard, "White and Blue," 177.

34. Jesse Waters, *The Five*, Fox, July 5, 2021.

35. On TR's views, see Thomas G. Dyer, *Theodore Roosevelt and the Idea of Race* (Baton Rouge: Louisiana State University Press, 1980), 69–88.

36. The Western Allies continued their food blockade of Germany six months after the Armistice was signed on November 11, 1918.

37. John Lynn, *Another Kind of War: The Nature and History of Terrorism* (New Haven, CT: Yale University Press, 2019), 59–61.

38. Catherine Merridale, *Ivan's War: Life and Death in the Red Army, 1939–1945* (New York: Henry Holt, 2006), 147–150.

39. Robert Scott, *Blood at Sand Creek* (Caldwell, ID: Caxton Printers, 1994).

40. The order came from the U.S. Indian agent at Fort Yates who feared the Ghost Dance meant Sioux were about to go to war. They were not. Jerome Greene, *American Carnage: Wounded Knee, 1890* (Norman: University of Oklahoma Press, 2014); Peter Cozzens, *The Earth Is Weeping: The Epic Story of the Indian Wars for the American West* (New York: Knopf, 2016), 447–466. Dated but pathbreaking at the time is Dee Brown, *Bury My Heart at Wounded Knee: An Indian History of the American West* (New York: Henry Holt, 1970).

41. Testimony by Lakota and 7th Cavalry in David Grua, "In Memory of the Chief Big Foot Massacre," *Western Historical Quarterly* 46, no. 1 (Spring 2015): 31–51.

42. Nelson, *White Hat.*
43. A term used to refer to several war bands of Nez Perce who fought the U.S. Army in the Nez Perce War from June to October 1877.
44. "Lieutenant C. E. S. Wood," U.S. Forestry Service, www.fs.usda.gov/.
45. Quoted in Jerome Greene et al., *Nez Perce Summer, 1877: The US Army and the Nee-Me-Poo Crisis* (Helena: Montana Historical Society Press, 2000).
46. Ibid., 309–312. 484–485n. The scene is re-created in the film *I Shall Fight No More, Forever* (1975).
47. Leonard, "White and Blue," 183–184.
48. Great Plains Nations often hunted communally by stampeding buffalo herds into ambushes, trapping them with fire or atop frozen lakes or in deep snow. One method was called *pis'kun* by the Blackfoot, which may be translated as "deep-blood kettle." There were hundreds of kill sites, or "buffalo jumps." Head-Smashed-In Buffalo Jump in Alberta is a UNESCO world heritage site.
49. Steven Ossad, "Henry Ware Lawton: Flawed Giant and Hero of Four Wars," *Army History* 69 (Winter 2007): 4–25. The flaws referenced in the subtitle are not moral indifference or war crimes but his drunkenness and tactical errors.
50. Ibid., 19.
51. Ibid., 21.
52. Peter G. Gowing, "Moros and Indians: Commonalities of Purpose, Policy and Practice in American Government of Two Hostile Subject Peoples." *Philippine Quarterly of Culture and Society* 8, no. 2/3 (1980): 125–49. http://www.jstor.org/stable/29791679.
53. An overview is Cathal J. Nolan, "The Philippine-American War, 1899–1902," in *Life, Liberty and the Pursuit of Happiness: A History of the American Experiment* (Arlington, VA: Bill of Rights Institute, 2018). https://billofrightsinstitute.org/essays/the-philippine-american-war.
54. Quoted in Tooley, " 'All the People,' " 370.
55. Andrew Bacevich, "What Happened at Bud Dajo? A Forgotten Massacre," *Boston Globe*, March 12, 2006; Ronald Edgerton, *American Datu: John J. Pershing and Counterinsurgency Warfare in the Muslim Philippines, 1899–1913* (Lexington: University Press of Kentucky, 2020), 168–178.
56. "US soldiers pose with the bodies of Moro insurgents, Philippines, 1906," https://rarehistoricalphotos.com/moro-insurgents-1906/.
57. Samuel Clemens, "Comments on the Moro Massacre" (March 12, 1906). Reprinted in *Mark Twain's Weapons of Satire: Anti-imperialist Writings on the Philippine-American War*, ed. Jim Zwick (New York: Syracuse University Press, 1992), 170–173.
58. "Dutch Honor a *Wehrmacht* Soldier," *Die Welt*, October 17, 2008.
59. Ibid.
60. A rare website not polluted by neo-Nazi leanings or links is Brabant Remembers, "De Goede Duitser," https://www.brabantremembers.com/strijd-1944/de-goede-duitser-geen-sprookje/.
61. "Civilians Abducted," BBC.com, March 25, 2022.
62. "Abroskin to the occupants," *Front News Ukraine*, March 25, 2022, https://frontnews.eu/en/news/details/24317.

Chapter 11

1. Editorial, *Scientific American,* December 16, 1905, 474.
2. "War, Humanized and De-humanized." *Scientific American,* May 22, 1915, 468.
3. *Lusitania* sank on May 7, 1915. The editorial was published on May 22.
4. "War, Humanized and De-humanized."
5. J. A. English, "The Trafalgar Syndrome," *Naval War College Review* 32, no. 3 (1979): 60–77.
6. An overview is Robert K. Massie, *Castles of Steel: Britain, Germany, and the Winning of the Great War at Sea* (New York: Random House, 2003).
7. *Hamlet,* Act 2, scene 2, l. 303.
8. The count combines the Western Front, Eastern Front, Italian Front, and other trench systems from the Caucuses to Arabia, Palestine, and Syria.
9. Dan van der Vat, *Gentlemen of War* (New York: Morrow, 1983), 21, published in Britain as *The Last Corsair* (London: Hodder & Stoughton, 1983). A concise version of the *Emden* story is Max Hastings, *Warriors: Portraits from the Battlefield* (New York: Vintage, 2005), 111–133.
10. Before the invention of radar and sonar, the only way to spot a ship in the distance was by its smoke in the day and its lights at night.
11. In December 1914, renamed SMS *Cormoran II*, it steamed into Guam and thus into American internment.
12. Der Vat, *Gentlemen of War,* 41–42. On the German dilemma, see Peter Overlack, "Force of Circumstance: Graf Spee's Options for the East Asian Cruiser Squadron in 1914," *Journal of Military History* 60, no. 4 (1996): 657–682.
13. Friederich Lochau, *On the Raging Seas: Memoirs of an Ordinary Seaman during World War I* (Wandsbeck: Reach Publishers, 2012).
14. Der Vat, *Gentlemen of War,* 42–60.
15. Ibid., 61–68.
16. Ibid., 91–92.
17. Ibid., 98, 119. Also see Lionel Fanthorpe, "The Cruise of the *Emden*," in *Warships and Sea Battles of World War I*, Bernard Fitzsimmons, ed. (London: Phoebus, 1973), 33–43.
18. Photograph of the downed mast and other aspects of the engagement at www.navy.gov.au/hmas-sydney-i.
19. Der Vat, *Gentlemen of War,* 106–108.
20. *Syndey* also had a single 13-pounder and 4 X 3 pounder guns.
21. A short but decidedly Australian view is Tom Frame, *No Pleasure Cruise: The Story of the Royal Australian Navy* (London: Allen & Unwin, 2005), 103–115, *passim.* Also see the documentary collection "Action between HMAS Sydney and SMS Emden," Australian War Memorial, https://www.awm.gov.au/collection/E85317. The most complete work is Wes Olsen, *The Last Cruise of a German Raider—The Destruction of SMS Emden* (Birkenhead: Seaforth Publishing, 2018).
22. A graphic description by *Sydney*'s chaplain, who went onboard *Emden* as it hung on the reef after the battle, is "Vivian Little diary," November 9–14, 1914, State Library of New South Wales, www.acms.sl.nsw.gov.au/_transcript.

23. Quoted in der Vat, *Gentlemen of War*, 111.

24. See Dr. Leonard Darby of the *Sydney*'s letter about treating *Emden* wounded, written that day: "Report of Surgeon L. Darby, R.A.N.," State Library of New South Wales, www.acms.sl.nsw.gov.au. Also see David Stevens et al., "Treatment of Casualties from the Sydney-Emden Action," in *The Face of Naval Battle: The Human Experience of Modern War at Sea*, ed. John Reeve and David Stevens (London: Allen & Unwin, 2004).

25. One of two recovered guns was displayed in Britain during the war. It was later lost, studied to see why *Emden* had achieved such rapid fire, and then perhaps cut up for scrap. The other was taken to Australia and put on permanent display in Hyde Park in Sydney. Two more full guns and two additional barrels were recovered in 1918. Wes Olsen, "The Emden Guns," Naval Historical Society of Australia, https://www.navy history.org.au/the-emden-guns/.

26. On Graf von Spee in the South Atlantic and the Battle of Coronel, see Geoffrey Bennett, *Naval Battles of the First World War* (London: Penguin, 1968), 71–122; Massie, *Castles of Steel*, 225–254.

27. Bennett, *Naval Battles*, 71–122.

28. Holder Afflerbach, "Going Down with Flying Colours?," in Afflerbach and Strachan, *How Fighting Ends*, 201–202.

29. Ibid., 203. On a much grander scale, Langsdorff's defiance of Hitler was paralleled on land when General Wilhelm von Paulus surrendered at Stalingrad.

30. See the sinking of SS *Athenia* by U-30, below.

31. Evan Mawdsley, *War for the Seas: A Maritime History of World War II* (New Haven, CT: Yale University Press, 2019), 35–36, www.hmsglowworm.org.uk.

32. Ibid. An account of the sea fight is Henrik Lunde, *Hitler's Preemptive War: The Battle for Norway, 1940* (Newbury: Casemate, 2010), 102–108.

33. http://www.vconline.org.uk/gerard-b-roope-vc/4588090140.

Chapter 12

1. *Laconia* Order, September 17, 1942. Quoted in David Bercuson and Holger Herwig, *Long Night of the Tankers: Hitler's War Against Caribbean Oil* (Calgary: University of Calgary Press, 2014): 237

2. "Renewing of Italy's Navy," *Scientific American*, May 22, 1915, 468ff.

3. Daniel Schlenoff, "Centennial of a Calamity," *Scientific American* 311, no. 1 (July 2014): 92–95.

4. Nicolle-Melanie Goll, "Our Weddigen," in *1914: Austria-Hungary, the Origins, and the First Year of World War I*, ed. Günter Bischof et al. (New Orleans, LA: University of New Orleans Press, 2014), 220–221.

5. "The Laconia Incident," September 12, 2017, www.warhistoryonline.com.

6. Bercuson and Holger, *Long Night of the Tankers*.

7. David Bercuson and Holger Herwig, *Long Night of the Tankers: Hitler's War against Caribbean Oil* (Calgary: University of Calgary Press, 2014), 237.

8. Transcript of Donitz's testimony defending the *Laconia* Order available in English as "Nuremberg Trial Proceedings Vol.13 (May 9, 1946), Avalon Project, Yale Law School, https://avalon.law.yale.edu/imt/05-09-46.asp.

9. Quoted in ibid. Also see Konrad Graczyk, "'Laconia Order' and the Responsibility of Admiral Dönitz before the Nuremberg Military Tribunal," *Scientific Journal of the Military University of Land Forces* 184, no. 2 (2017): 5–41; and James P. Duffy, *The Sinking of the Laconia and the U-boat War : Disaster in the Mid-Atlantic* (Lincoln: University of Nebraska Press, 2013).

10. Alan Bleasdale, Review of BBC docudrama *The Sinking of the Laconia*, January 2, 2011, *The Guardian*.

11. S. Bernacconi, *Da testimone—Uomini, fatti e memorie fra la cronaca e la storia* (Ferrara: SATE, 1984), 30. I am grateful to Dr. Stefano Marcuzzi for the reference and its translation.

12. Leonce Peillard, *La Battaglia dell'Atlantico* (Milan: Mondadori, 1976). I thank Dr. Stefano Marcuzzi for this reference and its translation.

13. www.marina.difesa.it/EN/thefleet/submarines/Pagine/todaro_en.aspx.

14. *Proceedings*, U.S. Naval Institute, September 2008, 92, www.usni.org.

15. "Italian Coast Guard Says It Has Moral Obligation to Save Those at Sea," *The Shift*, July 21, 2018.

16. On panic and flight from Königsberg see Willems, *Violence in Defeat*, 188–242.

17. "75 Years On, Little Known about the *Wilhelm Gustloff* Sinking," *Deutsche Welle*, January 30, 2020; Howard D. Grier, *Hitler, Donitz, and the Baltic Sea* (Annapolis, MD: Naval Institute Press, 2013), 167–214.

18. Discussion of the film *Die Gustloff* in Bill Niven, "The Good Captain and the Bad Captain," *German Politics & Society* 26, no. 4 (2008): 82–98.

19. *Sydney* lost all 645 crew, the most grievous loss in Australian naval history. "HMAS *Sydney II* and the *Kormoran*," Australian War Memorial.

20. Christopher Milligan, *Australian Hospital Ship* Centaur: *The Myth of Immunity* (Brisbane: Nairana Publications, 1993).

21. Ibid.

22. International Military Tribunal for the Far East.

23. Kaneyoshi Sakamoto, *History of Submarine Warfare* (Tokyo: 1979).

24. Mawdsley, *War for the Seas*, 350–369.

25. I discuss this more fully in *Allure of Battle*, 511–523, 536–547.

26. This was recognized in the official history, Air Force Historical Support Division, *U.S. Army Air Forces in World War II*, www.afhistory.af.mil.

27. Toll misses this point in *Twilight of the Gods*, 316–322, 325–330.

28. Ibid., 318.

29. Ibid., 319–321.

30. The spirit of the submarine campaign is captured in the 1951 operations history by Vice Admiral Charles Lockwood, commander of USN Submarine Force Pacific Fleet. See Charles Lockwood, *Sink 'Em All* (New York: Dutton, 1951).

31. Toll, *Twilight of the Gods*: 282–283.

32. "H-044-3: 'Operation Heaven Number One' (*Ten-ichi-go*): The Death of *Yamato*," Naval History and Heritage Command, https://www.history.navy.mil.

33. Toll, *Twilight of the Gods*: 286–287.

34. Quoted in Eric Lacroix and Linton Wells, *Japanese Cruisers of the Pacific War* (Annapolis, MD: Naval Institute Press, 1997), 356.

35. I discuss race, hate, and war at more length in *Allure of Battle,* 547–551. A much different view is John Dower, *War without Mercy: Race and Power in the Pacific War* (Princeton, NJ: Princeton University Press, 1987).

36. The U.S. Department of Defense mentions none of this in its for-the-public on-line summary of submarine warfare in World War II. Instead, it says that American submarines "also played humanitarian and special operations roles in the campaign against Japan." Article 2114035, www.defense.gov.

37. Mawdsley, *War for the Seas,* 364.

38. Linderman, *The World within War,* 151.

39. Horace Robertson, "The Obligation to Accept Surrender," *Naval War College Review* 46, no. 2 (1993): 103–105.

Chapter 13

1. "Warning Leaflets," www.atomicheritage.org/key-documents/warning-leaflets.

2. In 2003 the United States wanted to wage a "light footprint" ground war in Iraq. It tasked the USAF to minimize civilian or collateral casualties in planning and targeting decisions. Then the war went long. David Stubbs, "Operation Iraqi Freedom Air Campaign, 19 March–2 May 2003," *War in History* (August 2021): 727–748.

3. On a French strike that hit a wedding in Mali, see "A Wedding, an Airstrike, and Outrage at the French Military," *New York Times,* March 30, 2021.

4. Linda Robertson, *The Dream of Civilized Warfare: WWI Flying Aces and the American Imagination* (Minneapolis: University of Minnesota Press, 2003), 106.

5. Avalon Hill made a board game in 1987 called Knights of the Air. World War I video games about the air war include *Wings of War, Dawn Patrol, Ace of Aces, Aces High,* and *Richthofen's War.* Movies about the air war include *The Dawn Patrol* (1930) *The Blue Max* (1966), *Aces High* (1976), and *Flyboys* (2006).

6. Emden, *Meeting the Enemy,* 209–213. Buckler's memoir was published in English as *Malaula! The Battle Cry of Jasta 17* (London: Grubb Street, 2007).

7. "Balloon buster" was a Great War term for scout plane or fighter pilots early in war who excelled at shooting down observation balloons and dirigibles.

8. Peter Fritzsche, *A Nation of Flyers: German Aviation and Popular Imagination* (Cambridge, MA: Harvard University Press, 1992), 88.

9. Oswald Boelcke, *An Aviator's Field Book,* Project Gutenberg, 2021, https://www.gutenberg.org/ebooks/30011.

10. "Gentlemen of the Skies," *Daily Mail,* September 7, 2012.

11. Cecil Lewis, *Sagittarius Rising* (London: Peter Davies, 1936), 45–46.

12. Heller, *Catch-22,* Chapter 5..

13. Kevin Hall, "Luftgangster Over Germany: Lynching of American Airmen in the Shadow of the Air War," *Historische Sozialforschung* 43, no. 2 (2018): 277–312.

14. Interview, Karl Fasick, USAAF 8th Air Force, September 1996. He was liberated from a military hospital in the Netherlands by the advancing Canadian Army.

15. The most complete study is Kevin Hall, *Terror Flyers: The Lynching of American Airmen in Nazi Germany* (Bloomington; Indiana University Press, 2021).

16. Timothy Lang Francis, " 'To Dispose of the Prisoners': The Japanese Executions of American Aircrew at Fukuoka, Japan, during 1945," *Pacific Historical Review* 66, no. 4 (1997): 469–501. 480.

17. Adam Markos, *A Higher Call: An Incredible True Story of Combat and Chivalry in the War-Torn Skies of World War II* (New York: Penguin, 2012).

18. "Two Enemies Discover a 'Higher Call' in Battle," CNN, March 9, 2013.

19. Ibid.

20. Markos, *Higher Call.*

21. Stigler obituary and Brown interview, CTV News, May 11, 2008.

22. Ibid.

23. Robyn Dixon, "This woman flew Soviet combat missions in WWII," *Washington Post,* May 8, 2020.

24. Saburō Sakai, *Samurai!* (Boston: E. P. Dutton, 1957). He wrote a second autobiography published in Japanese, which I do not read: Saburō Sakai, *Kûsen kiroku* (Tokyo: Kôdansha, 1992).

25. "Interview with Saburō Sakai," www.microsoft.com/games/combatfs2. The interview for Microsoft was for the video game Combat Flight Simulator 2: World War II Pacific Theater, which used him as a model Japanese fighter pilot.

26. Sakai said about Emperor Hirohito in 1994, "Whose name was on the battle orders? Over three million died fighting for the emperor, but when the war was over he pretended it was not his responsibility. What kind of man does that?" Obituary, *New York Times,* October 8, 2000.

27. Law, "Japanese Perceptions of the Enemy."

28. Ibid. Also, interview in Cook, *Japan at War: An Oral History.*

29. Jock Stirrup, "Afghanistan: A Journey, Not a Destination," Royal United Services Institute, December 2008, www.govnet.co.uk/publications.

30. Al-Awlaki was an American citizen. Still, the Department of Justice decided that his killing by a drone strike was lawful. "Memo Justifying Drone Killing of American Al Qaeda Leader Is Released," *Los Angeles Times,* June 23, 2014.

31. Michael N. Schmitt, "Taming the Lawless Void: Tracking the Evolution of International Law Rules for Cyberspace," *Texas National Security Review* (Summer 2020).

32. John Arquilla, *Bitskrieg: The New Challenge of Cyberwarfare* (Medford, MA: Polity Press, 2021), Chapter 3; "Volunteer Hackers Converge on Ukraine Conflict with No One in Charge," *New York Times,* March 5, 2022.

33. "Civilian Deaths Mounted as Secret Unit Pounded ISIS," *New York Times,* December 12, 2021.

34. Edwards, *Caravan of Martyrs,* 148–149.

35. Ibid., 149–151.

36. "US Has Bombed at Least Eight Wedding Parties since 2001," *The Nation,* December 20, 2013; "Explosion Rips through Kabul Wedding," CBS News/AP, August 18, 2019.

37. Ian Cameron, "I Killed Taliban Fighters from an Air-Conditioned Room," *Washington Post*, August 22, 2021.

38. " The Casualties at the Other End of the Remote-Controlled Kill," *New York Times*, April 15, 2022.

39. "Recent Drone Strikes Strain U.S. Ties with Afghanistan and Pakistan," *New York Times*, November 29, 2013.

40. "Former Counterterrorism Czar Richard Clarke: U.S. Drone Program Under Obama 'Got Out of Hand,'" transcript, *Democracy Now*, June 2, 2014. https://www.democ racynow.org/2014/6/2/former_counterterrorism_czar_richard_clarke_us.

41. Vegas Tenold, "The Untold Casualties of the Drone War," *Rolling Stone*, February 18, 2016.

42. "Military Analysis Raises Questions about Deadly Drone Strike in Kabul," *New York Times*, September 5, 2021.

43. "Afghan Security Forces' Wholesale Collapse Was Years in the Making," *Washington Post*, August 16, 2021.

44. "Afghanistan's Military Collapse: Illicit Deals and Mass Desertions," *Washington Post*, August 15, 2021.

Chapter 14

1. The epigraph is from M. T. Anderson, *Symphony for the City of the Dead: Dmitri Shostakovich and the Siege of Leningrad* (Somerville, MA: Candlewick Press, 2015).

2. William James, "The Moral Equivalent of War" (1906), www.uky.edu.

3. Mark Osiel, *Obeying Orders: Atrocity, Military Discipline and the Law of War* (New Brunswick: Transaction, 1999): 22–23, 173–186, 233–246.

4. Annemieke van Verseveld, "Superior Orders," in *Oxford Bibliographies*. https://www.oxfordbibliographies.com/view/document/obo-9780199796953/obo-9780199796953-0133.xml.

5. *Othello*, Act 5, Scene 2, ll. 63–65.

6. Tacitus, quoting Calgacus, enemy of Rome: "They make a desert and call it peace." *The Agricola and The Germania* (London: Penguin, 2010), 30/4.

Author's Note

1. Corinthians 13:12.

2. Conversation with Master Sergeant (Ret.) (name withheld), Boston, 2009.

INDEX

For the benefit of digital users, indexed terms that span two pages (e.g., 52–53) may, on occasion, appear on only one of those pages.

Abenaki, 188

Abu Ghraib, 184

Admiral Hipper, 226–28

Afghanistan, 25–27, 47–51, 54–57, 100–1, 114–19, 138–40, 153, 207, 256–61. *See also* Taliban

Agincourt, 166

AHS *Centaur,* 236–38

air war, 7, 22–23, 34–35, 38, 44, 153, 182–83, 244–61, 279n.8

al-Awadi, Jassim, 53–54

Algeria, 184, 199, 207

Algonquin, 187–88

allure of battle, 11–12, 48–49, 114, 192–93. *See also* attrition

al-Qaida, 114, 184–85

ambulances, 4, 89–90, 143–44

American Civil War, 121, 146–47, 148–49, 166–68, 190–96

American Expeditionary Force. *See* US Army

Amin, Idi, 187

ANZACs, 135, 218

Apache, 196

Arapaho, 196

Ardennes, 79–80, 83, 91–99, 158

Aristotle, 273n.2

Armée Française. See French Army

Armistice (1918) 80, 133–35

artificial intelligence (AI) 5, 256, 257

artillery, 62–78, 92–93, 155–56, 158, 187

attrition, 14–17, 62–78, 114, 116, 190–209, 231

Australia, 56–57, 174–75, 219–20

Australian Defence Forces, 56–57, 174–75

bacha bazi, 114–16

Barbarossa, Frederick, 165–66

Barbusse, Henri, 14, 274n.13

Barkley, John Lewis, 74–78, 80

Barthas, Louis, 69–74, 121, 130

Basil II, 165–66

Bataan death march, 174, 175–77

Beach, John, 88–89

Belgium, 66, 90–91. *See also* Ardennes

bellum Romanum, 166, 186

Berndt, Albert, 155–56

Biafra. *See* Nigerian Civil War

Biden, Joe, 260–61

Bismarck, Otto von, 19, 79–80, 275n.24, 283n.3

Blackfoot, 299n.48

Blackhawk War, 193

blockade, 34–35, 37, 67–68, 133–34, 148, 166–67, 194–95, 198–99, 213–14, 298n.36

Boelcke, Oswald, 248

Boer War, Second, 148–49, 203

Bosnia, 162–63

Bourke, John, 200
Britain, 183. *See also* British Army;
    Commonwealth Forces; Royal
    Flying Corps; Royal Navy
British Army, 56–57, 62–63, 66–67, 69–
    70, 79–80, 83, 106, 121–30, 132–33,
    144–45, 169–70, 183–84
British Expeditionary Force. *See*
    British Army
Brooke, Rupert, 13–14, 17, 20
Brown, Charles, 251–53
Buckler, Julius, 247
Bulge, Battle of. *See* Ardennes
Bundeswehr, 128
Bush, George W. 184, 259
bushidō, 3

Cailloux, André, 167
Cambodia, 162–63
Cameron, Ian, 258–59
Campbell, Angus, 57
Canada, 43–44, 81, 170, 187–88, 199
Canadian Army, 43–44, 81, 170, 279n.6
Capellini, 233–35
Carion, Christian, 126–27
cavalry, 62–63
ceasefires 5, 63–65, 66–69, 89, 120–40.
    See also Christmas Truce; medics;
    Ramadan; Têt
Chaban, Alexi, 110–14
Chamberlain, Neville, 288–89n.54
Charlemagne, 30, 165–66
chauvinism, 3
Chechnya, 23
Cherokee, 38–39, 189–90, 193, 278n.38
Cheyenne, 20–21, 196, 199–200
Chief Joseph, 129–30, 199
child soldiers, 207
China, 102, 143–45, 169–70, 207. *See
    also* Chinese Civil War;, Chinese
    Volunteer Force; Guomindang;
    Korean War; Nanjing Massacre;
    Opium War; Sino-Japanese Wars
Chinese Civil War, 181–83
Chinese Volunteer Force, 180–83

chivalry, 3, 213–14
Christmas Truce (1914) 72, 120, 121–
    30, 214–15
Churchill, Winston, 183, 218, 219
civilians, 4–5, 21–22, 25–26, 34–37, 38–
    39, 138, 170–71, 186–209, 244–45
Clare, Percy, 69–70
Clark, William, 20–21, 200
Clarke, Richard, 259
Clausewitz, Carl von, 263
Clinton, Bill, 259
Comanche, 196
combat, 6, 15–18, 25, 26–27, 87–99, 265
Commonwealth forces 171, 178, 179,
    205, 289n.2. *See also* ANZAC;
    Australian Army; British Army;
    Canadian Army; Indian Army
Congo, 61, 94–95, 207
Conrad, Joseph, 61, 94–95
conscience, 2, 5, 17, 18–19, 100
Coronel, Battle of 225
counterinsurgency warfare (COIN)
    47–51, 54–57, 186–205, 265–66.
    See also Afghanistan; American
    Civil War; Boer War; British Army;
    Dakota War; First Nations; Great
    Plains Wars; Iraq; Kenya; Lieber
    Code; moral harm; Philippine-
    American War; Syria; Việtnam War
courage, 1–2, 6, 273n.2
Creek War, 188–89
Crimea, 62, 101, 145–46, 147–48, 214.
    See also Ukraine
cruelty, 1–2, 3, 5, 11–12, 17–18
cruiser warfare, 214–24, 225
culture, 6, 19–20, 117, 120–31, 166
cyberspace, 5, 256, 257

Dakota War, 193–94
Daly, Daniel, 74–78
Declaration of London (1909) 214
Deltgen, René, 94–95
Deryabina, Klavdia, 253
desertion, 6, 68–69, 100–2, 104–8, 137,
    159, 160, 168, 191

dissent, 100–19, 167–68, 225–26. *See also* desertion; moral protest

Doctors Beyond Borders. See *Médecins Sans Frontières*

Donbas. *See* Ukraine; Vladimir Putin

Dönitz, Karl, 229, 231–33

Doss, Desmond, 154–55

Driant, Émile, 70

drones, 5, 108–9, 256–61

Duckworth, Tammy, 151–52

Eastern Front, 80–81, 90, 97, 106, 121, 156–57, 172, 253–54

Egypt, 136–37, 207

Eisenhower, Dwight, 81–82, 90–91, 284n.11

El Alamein, Battle of 136–37

Ethiopia, 37, 140

Falaise, 80–81

Fasick, Karl, 250–51

Finland, 82–83

First Nations, 20–21, 187–90, 193–94, 196–200, 203–4. *See also* Abenaki; Algonquin; Apache; Arapaho; Blackfoot; Cherokee; Cheyenne; counterinsurgency; Creek War; Dakota War; Great Plains Wars; Kickapoo; Kiowa; Iroquois; Nez Perce; Pequot War; Powhatan; Sioux; Trail of Tears; Ute; Wampanoag

Formilli, Geoffrey, 248

Forrest, Nathan Bedford, 167–68

Fort Pillow massacre, 167–68

France, 70, 73–74, 80–81, 283n.3. *See also* Free French; French Army; trench warfare

Franco-Prussian War, 147–48

Free French, 80–81, 135

French Army, 70–74, 79–80, 126–28, 172, 282n.22

Friedrich II, 19–20, 188

Frost, John, 156–57

Gaza, 34, 163

Gees, Hubert, 85–77

generals, 12–13, 71–72, 81–82, 86, 90–91, 118, 135, 188–205

Geneva Conventions, 184

Germany, 16, 20, 73–74, 79–80, 90–92, 283n.3. *See also* Kaiserliche Marine; Kriegsmarine; Nazis; Nuremberg Trials; U-boats; Wehrmacht; World War I; World War II

German Army, 62–78, 79–99, 282n.23. *See also* Bundeswehr; Kaiserheer; trench warfare; Wehrmacht; World War I; World War II

Gestapo, 100–1, 102, 105, 137, 178, 206–7, 250–51

Glaser, Ronald, 160

Glossop, George, 220–24, 225

Goebbels, Joseph, 45, 94–95

Göring, Hermann, 205

Graf Spee, 225–26

Grant, Ulysses S. 134, 167–68, 190–91, 194, 195–96

Graves, Robert, 14, 75, 290n.14

Great Plains Wars, 20–21, 38–39, 196–99, 278n.37

Great War, 1–2, 61. *See also* SMS *Emden*; trench warfare; World War I

Greet, Geoffrey, 233

Gruber, Ludwig, 159–60

Guadalcanal, 174–75, 254

Gubbels, Norbert, 92–99

guerre mortelle, 166, 171

Guomindang, 181–83, 254

Habsburg Army, 63–65, 131–32

Hague Convention (1899) 66–67, 191, 214

Hague Convention (1907) 191, 214

Halleck, Henry, 194

Halsey, William, 240

hard war, 190–200. See also American Civil War, Lieber Code

Hartenstein, Werner, 231–33

Heller, Joseph, 34–35, 250, 253–54

Hemingway, Ernest, 16, 17, 20, 274n.19

Heye, Helmuth, 227–28
Hilfswillige, 172–73, 182–83, 294n.24
Hirohito, 304n.26
Hisashi, Mito, 240–41
Hitler, Adolf, 20–21, 45–46, 79–80, 90–
    99, 125, 137, 225–26, 232, 235–36
Hitler Youth, 105, 159
Hitlerjugend. See Hitler Youth
HMAS *Australia*, 218
HMAS *Sydney*, 218–24
HMS *Dreadnought*, 214
HMS *Glowworm*, 226–28
HMS *Monmouth*, 225
HMS *Renown*, 226–27
Hodges, Courtney, 82–83
honor codes, 1–2, 3, 18–19, 33, 62–
    63, 276n.5
hospital ships, 230, 235, 236–38. See also
    AHS Centaur
Hürtgen Forest, 3–4, 81–90, 157–58
Hürtgenwald. See Hürtgen Forest
Hussein, Saddam, 51–52, 207, 245–46

ianfu, 174–75, 176–77
IEDs, 50, 51, 108–9, 161
IJN *Yamato*, 239–40
illegal orders, 2–3, 21–22. *See also* laws of
    war; superior orders
India, 207, 219–20, 223
Indian Army, 175, 219
Indonesia, 207
infantry, 35–36, 38, 47–51, 54–57, 62–63,
    65–66, 74–75, 87–88, 93, 136–37,
    152–53, 157–58, 205, 244–45, 246–
    47, 257, *See also* counterinsurgency;
    trench warfare
Iraq, 30–33, 47, 51–54, 100–1, 108–9,
    114, 120–21, 153, 169, 184, 207,
    242, 245–46, 256, 257
Iroquois, 187–88
ISIS, 53–54, 120–21, 138, 163, 173–74,
    184–85, 187, 256, 257, 258–60
island-hopping, 81–82
Israel, 163–64
Italian Army, 135–37, 172

Italian Navy. *See* Regia Marina
Italy, 81

Jackson, Andrew, 188–89. *See also* Creek
    War; Trail of Tears
Japan. See *Kaigun*; *Rikugun*; *Sino-*
    Japanese Wars
Japanese Army. *See Rikugun*
Japanese Navy. *See Kaigun*
jihad, 3, 173–74. *See also* al Qaida; ISIS;
    suicide bombers; Taliban
Johnson, Floyd, 89–90
Jones, James, 11–12
Jünger, Ernst, 15–18, 45, 63, 75, 168, 169,
    279n.10
Just War theory, 3, 7, 24–25

Kaigun, 179, 230, 237–42
Kaiserheer, 16, 62–63, 66–67, 79–80,
    121–30, 147–48
Kaiserliche Marine, 4–5, 213–14, 225–
    26, 230–31. *See also* SMS *Emden*;
    U-boats
Kapaun, Emil, 180–81, 296n.50
Kempeitai, 176–78
Kenya, 151–52, 183–84, 223
Kickapoo, 202
killers, 15–17, 25, 28, 30–34, 42–57, 74–78
Kill Team, 46–47
Kiowa, 196
Kiyofumi, Kojima, 179
Korea, 42, 173–74, 180–83, 207
Korean War, 42, 180–83, 207
Kosovo, 245–46
Kreisler, Fritz, 63–65
Kriegsmarine, 225–28, 230. *See also*
    Graf Spee; Hipper; Karl Dönitz;
    Laconia Order; U-boats; Wilhelm
    Langsdorff
Kurds, 207
Kyle, Chris, 30–34

Laconia Order, 231–33
Lane, George, 136–37
Langsdorff, Wilhelm, 225–26, 301n.29

Lauter, Felix, 89–90
laws of war, 1–2, 21–22, 23, 66–67, 86,
     168, 184, 186, 191–93, 213–14,
     230–31, 256, 257, 262–64, 294n.14,
     See also illegal orders; Lieber Code;
     superior orders; war crimes
Lawton, Henry Ware, 202–3
Lebanon, 207
Lee, Robert E. 3–4
LeMay, Curtis, 38, 244, 277–78n.36
Lengfeld, Friedrich, 83–87
Lewis, Cecil, 249
Leyte Gulf, Battle of, 240
Libya, 207–8
Li Da'an, 181, 182
Lieber Code, 191–93, 203
Lieber, Francis, 191–93
Lincoln, Abraham, 190–93
Li Soon, 182
Liu Bingzhang, 182
logistics, 81, 190, 196–99, 202–3, 235
Lomax, Eric, 176–78
London Naval Agreement (1930) 230–31
Louis XIV, 17, 79–80, 276n.2
Louis XV, 19–20, 79–80
Ludendorff, Erich von, 90 91
Luftwaffe. See air war
Lusitania crisis. See SS *Lusitania*

Machiavelli, Niccolò, 79–80, 263
Maerker, Julius, 225–26
Mali, 245–46
McClellan, George B. 190
McCudden, James, 246–47
Médecins Sans Frontières, 161–62, 257–58
medical truces. *See* ceasefires; medics
medics, 2–3, 4, 11–12, 66–67, 84–
     85, 143–64
memorials, 73–74, 86–87, 105, 107–8
military history, 3–4, 18–19, 28, 39–40,
     126–27, 235
Miller, Herbert, 180–81
Miller, James, 189–90
Miller, Scott, 115–16, 288n.46
Montgomery, Bernard Law, 136–37

moral fog of war, 3, 24
moral harm, 5–6, 11–12, 23–24, 25, 26–
     28, 47–49, 98–99, 253–54, 255–56,
     258–59, 263. *See also* superior orders
moral protest, 6, 101. *See also* dissent
Morton, Dudley, 238–39
Müller, Karl von, 4–5, 214–24, 225
Murphy, Audie, 30–31
Myanmar, 187
Mỹ Lai, 35–37, 38–39, 46–47

Nagase, Takeshi, 176–78
Nakagawa, Hajime, 236–37
Nanjing massacre, 102, 169–70, 173–
     74, 176–77
Napoleon, 17, 20, 30, 94–95
nationalism, 3, 20, 73–74
NATO, 39, 90–91, 114, 227–28, 234–35,
     245–46, 265–66
Naval Protocol (1936) 230–31
naval war. *See* war at sea
Nazis, 16, 20–21, 80–81, 91–92, 98–99,
     100–1, 102, 103–4, 105, 137–38, 159,
     172, 205–7, 230–31, 250–51. *See also*
     Gestapo; Joseph Goebbels; Adolf
     Hitler; Hitler Youth; SS; Waffen-SS
Netherlands, 205–7
New Guinea, 174–75, 236–37, 254
Nez Perce, 129–30, 199, 200
Nigerian Civil War, 207
Nightingale, Florence, 145–46
Nixon, Richard, 120
no-man's-land, 3–4, 17, 62–78. See also
     trench warfare; truces;
     World War I
North Africa campaigns, 80–81, 135–37
Norway, 226
Nott, David, 162–64
Nuremburg Trials, 24, 231–33, 264

Obama, Barrack, 172, 184–85, 259–60
O'Brien, Tim, 17
officers, 17, 43–44, 47–51, 54–57, 72–73,
     114–19, 128–29, 170, 214–24,
     252, 263–64

Okinawa, 174–75
Operation *Desert Storm*, 184–85.
Operation *Greif*, 94
Operation *Market Garden*, 80–81, 156–57, 205
Operation *Overlord*. *See* Normandy
Operation *Starvation*, 231, 237–38
Operation *Wacht am Rhein*, 91
Opium War, 144–45
Orwell, George, 109–10
Osiel, Mark, 263–64
Ostfront. *See* Eastern Front
Ostheer. *See* Wehrmacht
Owen, Wilfred, 1–2, 14, 274n.10

Patton, George, 81–82, 169–70, 284n.11
Paulus, Wilhelm von, 301n.29
Peninsular War, 143–44
People's Liberation Army, 180–83
Pequot War, 187–88
Petraeus, David, 280n.29, 289n.58
Philippine-American War, 38–39, 202–5
Philippines, 38–39, 169–70, 174, 202–5, 237–38, 254
Plagge, Karl, 103–4
Poland, 235
Pope, John, 190, 191, 193–94
Powhatan, 188
Prien, Günther, 45
prisoners of war, 28, 75–78, 98–99, 165 85
propaganda, 6, 12–13, 28, 39, 42, 45, 113–14, 230–31. *See also* Joseph Goebbels; George Orwell; Vladimir Putin
PTSD, 23–24, 26–28, 33, 51, 160, 258–59, 286n.46. *See also* moral harm
Putin, Vladimir, 11–12, 101–2, 109–10, 161–62. *See also* Crimea; Ukraine

quarter, 1–2, 166–67, 244–45, 265–66, 294n.14
Queen Elizabeth II, 163–64
Quinn, Dan, 115

Rabe, John, 102, 103

Railway of Death, 176–78
Ramadan, 120–21
Raziq, Abdul, 115–16
reason, 2, 23–24, 61
Red Army, 80–81, 82–83, 91–92, 97, 103, 106–7, 111–12, 113–14, 137–38, 172, 182–83, 235
Red Army Air Force (VVS), 44, 253–54
Red Crescent, 163
Red Cross, 227–28, 236–37
refugees, 4–5, 11–12, 97–98, 102, 104, 187–89, 207–8, 235
Regia Marina, 229–30, 233–35. *See also* Salvatore Todaro
Remarque, Erich Maria, 15–16, 26–27, 75
respondeat superior. *See* superior orders
Richardson, Elmer, 159–60
Richthofen, Manfred von, 44, 75, 249
Rikugun, 102, 147–48, 169–70, 171
RMS *Laconia*, 231–33. *See* Laconia Order
robots, 5
Roger's Rangers, 187–88
Roman Army, 79–80, 194–95, 283n.2
Rommel, Erwin, 135–37
Roope, Gerard, 227–28
Roosevelt, Franklin, 90
Roosevelt, Theodore, 38–39, 203, 204–5
Rosch, Karl-Heinz, 108, 205–7
Royal Australian Navy, 218–24
Royal Flying Corps, 246
Royal Italian Navy. *See Regia Marina*
Royal Navy, 143–44, 213–24, 226–28, 230–31. *See also* HMS *Glowworm*; SMS *Emden*; U-boats
Ruggles, John, 83
Rumsfeld, Donald, 117
Russia, 11–12, 25–27, 47, 63–65, 101, 104–6, 109–14
Russian Army, 11–12, 25–27, 47, 63–65, 101, 104–6, 110–14, 131–32, 148–49, 184–85. *See also* Red Army
Russo-Japanese War, 149, 213–14
Rwanda, 187, 207

Saipan, 180

Sakai, Saburō, 4–5, 250, 254–56
Salah, BG, 51–53
samurai, 22, 26, 42, 165–66
Sardari, Abdol Hossein, 102–3
Sassoon, Siegfried, 14, 100–1
Schiller, Friedrich, 19–20
Schindler, Oscar, 102
Schroder, Heinrich, 95–97
Schwarzenegger, Arnold, 12, 26–27
Sedan, 79–80
Seddon, James, 167–68
Serbia, 63, 65–66, 169–70, 216, 245–46
Shakespeare, William, 1–2, 21–22, 24,
    30, 214–15
shared humanity, 1–3, 6, 73–74
Sheeks, Robert, 180
Sheridan, Philip, 195–99
Sherman, William T. 147, 192–
    93, 194–99
Siegfried Line. See Westwall
Sino-Japanese War, First (1895)
    42, 173–74
Sino-Japanese War, Second (1937-1945)
    102, 169–70, 171
Sioux, 20–21, 193–94, 196, 199–
    200, 203–4
Skorzeny, Otto, 45–46, 94
Smith, Jacob, 203–4. See also
    Wounded Knee
SMS Emden, 214–24, 225
SMS Gneisenau, 225
SMS Nürnberg, 225
snipers, 30–34, 46, 75–76, 84–85, 101–
    2, 163
soldiers, 3, 15–17, 21–22, 23–27, 43, 62–
    78, 114–19, 121–30
Somme, 66, 72–73, 123, 124, 132–33
Soviet Union. See Red Army; Russia
Special Air Services, 56–57
special forces, 56–57, 139–40, 168, 266
Spee, Maximillian Graf von, 216–17, 220
Sri Lanka, 37, 187
SS Athenia, 231, 235–36
SS Lusitania, 229–31, 235
SS (Schutzstaffel) 102, 103–4, 206–7
Stalin, Josef, 172–73, 182–83

Stigler, Franz, 251–53
Stirrup, Jock, 256
Stockton, Fred, 74–75
Student, Kurt, 45–46
submarines, 7, 45, 229–43. See also
    U-boats
Sudan, 207
suicide, 23–24
suicide bombers, 6, 33–34, 37, 186, 187
suicide tactics, 239–40
Sumarokova, Tatyana, 253–54
Sun Tsu, 263
superior orders, 12, 24, 27–28, 34–35,
    237, 264, 273n.3, 275n.37. See also
    laws of war; Nuremberg Trials
surrender, 62–63, 79–80, 88–89, 93, 167–
    68. See also prisoners of war
Syria, 23, 108–9, 120–21, 138, 161–62,
    163, 186, 207, 245–46, 256, 257

Taliban, 47–51, 54–57, 115–16, 120–21,
    138–40, 184–85, 256–61. See also
    Afghanistan; counterinsurgency
Tarawa, 180
Tennyson, Alfred, 20, 62
Têt, 39, 120, 278n.43
Thirty Years' War, 19–20, 79–80, 143–44
Thompson, Hugh, 35–37
Thucydides, 263
Three Alls order, 169–70
Tiger Force, 46–47
Timko, Mike, 157–58
Tinian, 180
Todaro, Salvatore, 4–5, 233–35
Tolkien, J. R. R. 66
Tolstoy, Leo, 20
Tonelli, Mario, 175–76
Trail of Tears, 38–39, 189–90, 278n.38
trench warfare, 3–4, 61–78, 214–24. See
    also no-man's-land
Tresckow, Henning von, 21–22
Triton Null Order. See Laconia Order
truces. See ceasefires
Trump, Donald, 36–37, 39, 258–
    59, 260–61
Tsen Shui-fang, 102

Twain, Mark, 204–5

U-boats, 4–5, 7, 45, 213–14, 229–33,
     279n.9. *See also* Karl Dönitz;
     Laconia Order
Udet, Ernst, 247–48
Uganda, 187, 207
Ukagi, Matome, 234–35
Ukraine, 4, 11–12, 23, 25–26, 36–37, 46,
     104–6, 108–14, 130–31, 161–62,
     187, 245–46, 260–61
Ukrainian Army, 11–12, 47, 110–14, 152–
     53, 184–85
Uniform Code of Military
     Justice, 263–64
Union of Committees of Soldiers'
     Mothers, 101
United Nations, 37, 42, 140, 181–83
US Army, 26–27, 46–56, 74–78, 79–99,
     152–60, 249
US Navy, 7, 45, 230–31, 238–43
USN *Wahoo*, 238–39
Ute, 196

Vautrin, Minnie, 102
Verdun, 14, 70–71, 72–73
Vietnam War, 25–26, 30, 46, 47, 49–50,
     100–1, 160–61, 184, 245–46,
     278n.43. *See also* Mỹ Lai; Tết
     Offensive
Vokes, Chris, 170
Voltaire, 42, 79 80
Võ Nguyên Giáp, 3–4
VVS. *See* Red Army Air Force

Wadani, Richard, 105–8
Waffen-SS, 105, 107–8, 111–12, 137–38,
     158, 172–73, 206, 294n.24
Wagner PMC, 111–12, 161–62, 288n.35
Walker, Mary, 146–47
Wallenberg, Raoul, 102–3
Wampanoag, 188
war, 2, 21–25

horrors of, 21–23, 66–67, 113–
     14, 149–50
as moral realm, 2–3, 23–24
See also air war; civilians; cruelty;
     laws of war; moral harm; officers;
     soldiers; trench warfare; war at sea;
     war crimes
war at sea, 22, 213–28, 229–43
war crimes, 3, 5, 21–22, 23–24, 25–26,
     36–37, 46–57, 106, 230–31, 236–
     43, 250–51, 264, 266
war heroes, 3–4, 29–41
war stories, 12–13
warriors, 3–4
Wehrmacht, 12, 79–99, 100–1, 103–4,
     105, 106–8, 113–14, 157–58, 172,
     205–7, 294n.24
Welch, Morgan, 96, 97
Wells, H. G. 17, 274n.14
Western Front. *See* Christmas Truce;
     trench warfare; World War I
Westheer. See Wehrmacht
West Wall. *See* Westwall
Westwall, 81–83
White Helmets, 161–62
White Rose, 100–1
Wilhelm Gustloff, 235–36
Wilson, Alfred, 153–54
Wilson, Woodrow, 213, 274n.14
Winnebago. *See* Dakota War
women, 3, 4, 11–12, 116–17, 138, 143–
     44, 145–53, 174–75, 253–54. *See
     also* civilians; medics; *ianfu*
Wood, Charles, 200
Wood, Leonard, 204–5
Woodson, Waverly, 154
World War I, 3–4, 13–17, 25–26, 62–78,
     80, 121–38, 213–24, 246. *See also*
     air war; Christmas Truce; trench
     warfare; truces
World War II, 11–12, 46, 79–99, 135–36.
     See also air war; Ardennes; Britain;
     Courland; Eastern Front; Falaise;

Finland; France; Hürtgen Forest;
Kaigun; Normandy; North Africa;
Rikugun; Second Sino-Japanese War
Wounded Knee, 199–200, 203–4

Yad Vashem, 103, 104

Yasukuni Shrine, 178
Yemen, 45–46, 162–63, 207,
  223, 275n.34
York, Alvin, 30–31, 74
Ypres, Battles of, 66–67, 122–23, 229–30,
  286n.1